Money and Security

TROOPS, MONETARY POLICY, AND WEST GERMANY'S RELATIONS
WITH THE UNITED STATES AND BRITAIN, 1950–1971

This study examines the connections between the transatlantic security system and the international monetary system during the Cold War. The question of who would bear the enormous cost of British and American troops stationed in West Germany became a contentious issue that burdened relations between the Federal Republic and its major allies from the 1950s to the 1970s. Washington and London saw this cost as a major reason for the decline of their currencies and therefore called on Germany to underwrite or "offset" these expenses; and Germany reluctantly agreed to trade money for security. By investigating the linkage between monetary and military policy this book demonstrates the crucial importance of domestic politics for the formulation of foreign policy and illuminates transatlantic history during the Cold War from a new angle.

Hubert Zimmermann is Assistant Professor for International Politics at the Ruhr-University in Bochum, Germany. He has written several articles on German, American, and British foreign and economic policy, and he has received research grants from the GHI in Washington, D.C., and the European University Institute in Florence.

T0371195

PUBLICATIONS OF THE GERMAN
HISTORICAL INSTITUTE, WASHINGTON, D.C.

Edited by Detlef Junker
with the assistance of Daniel S. Mattern

The German Historical Institute is a center for advanced study and research whose purpose is to provide a permanent basis for scholarly cooperation among historians from the Federal Republic of Germany and the United States. The Institute conducts, promotes, and supports research into both American and German political, social, economic, and cultural history, into transatlantic migration, especially in the nineteenth and twentieth centuries, and into the history of international relations, with special emphasis on the roles played by the United States and Germany.

Recent books in the series

Sibylle Quack, editor, *Between Sorrow and Strength: Women Refugees of the Nazi Period*

Mitchell G. Ash and Alfons Söllner, editors, *Forced Migration and Scientific Change: Emigré German-Speaking Scientists and Scholars after 1933*

Manfred Berg and Geoffrey Cocks, editors, *Medicine and Modernity: Public Health and Medical Care in Nineteenth- and Twentieth-Century Germany*

Stig Förster and Jörg Nagler, editors, *On the Road to Total War: The American Civil War and the German Wars of Unification, 1861–1871*

Norbert Finzsch and Robert Jütte, editors, *Institutions of Confinement: Hospitals, Asylums, and Prisons in Western Europe and North America, 1500–1950*

David E. Barclay and Elisabeth Glaser-Schmidt, editors, *Transatlantic Images and Perceptions: Germany and America since 1776*

Norbert Finzsch and Dietmar Schirmer, editors, *Identity and Intolerance: Nationalism, Racism, and Xenophobia in Germany and the United States*

Manfred F. Boemeke, Gerald D. Feldman, and Elisabeth Glaser, editors, *The Treaty of Versailles: A Reassessment After 75 Years*

Susan Strasser, Charles McGovern, and Matthias Judt, editors, *Getting and Spending: European and American Consumer Societies in the Twentieth Century*

Manfred F. Boemeke, Roger Chickering, and Stig Förster, editors, *Anticipating Total War: The German and American Experiences, 1871–1914*

Roger Chickering and Stig Förster, editors, *Great War, Total War: Combat and Mobilization on the Western Front, 1914–1918*

Gerd Althoff, Johannes Fried, and Patrick J. Geary, editors, *Medieval Concepts of the Past: Ritual, Memory, Historiography*

Manfred Berg and Martin H. Geyer, editors, *Two Cultures of Rights: The Quest for Inclusion and Participation in Modern America and Germany*

Elizabeth Glaser and Hermann Wellenreuther, editors, *Bridging the Atlantic: The Question of American Exceptionalism in Transatlantic Perspective*

Jürgen Heideking and James A. Henretta, editors, *Republicanism and Liberalism in America and the German States, 1750–1850*

Money and Security

TROOPS, MONETARY POLICY, AND WEST GERMANY'S RELATIONS
WITH THE UNITED STATES AND BRITAIN, 1950–1971

HUBERT ZIMMERMANN

Ruhr-Universität
Bochum, Germany

GERMAN HISTORICAL INSTITUTE
Washington, D.C.
and

CAMBRIDGE
UNIVERSITY PRESS

CAMBRIDGE UNIVERSITY PRESS
Cambridge, New York, Melbourne, Madrid, Cape Town,
Singapore, São Paulo, Delhi, Tokyo, Mexico City

Cambridge University Press
The Edinburgh Building, Cambridge CB2 8RU, UK

Published in the United States of America by Cambridge University Press, New York

www.cambridge.org
Information on this title: www.cambridge.org/9780521399180

First published 2002
First paperback edition 2011

A catalogue record for this publication is available from the British Library

Library of Congress Cataloguing in Publication data
Zimmermann, Hubert.
Money and security : troops, monetary policy, and West Germany's relations
with the United States and Britain, 1950–1971 / Hubert Zimmermann.
p.   cm.
Includes bibliographical references and index.
ISBN 0-521-78204-X
1. Germany – Military relations – United States.   2. United States – Military relations –
Germany.   3. Germany – Military relations – Great Britain.   4. Great Britain – Military
relations – Germany.   5. Germany – Armed Forces – Appropriations and expenditures.
6. United States – Armed Forces – Appropriations and expenditures.   7. Great Britain –
Armed Forces – Appropriations and expenditures.   1. Title.
UA710 .Z567   2001
337.43–dc21   00-069892

ISBN 978-0-521-78204-3 Hardback
ISBN 978-0-521-39918-0 Paperback

Contents

Abbreviations

AA	Auswärtiges Amt
AAPD	Akten zur Auswärtigen Politik der Bundesrepublik Deutschland
amemb	American Embassy
APUZG	*Aus Politik und Zeitgeschichte*
BA	Bundesarchiv, Koblenz
BAOR	British Army on the Rhine
BBA	Bundesbank-Archiv
BEA	Bureau of European Affairs (DOS)
BGBL	*Bundesgesetzblatt*
BIS	Bank of International Settlements
BMF	Bundesfinanzministerium
BMVg	Bundesverteidigungsministerium
BMWi	Bundeswirtschaftsministerium
BPI	*Bulletin Presse- und Informationsamt der Bundesregierung*
CAB	PRO, Cabinet Papers
CDU	Christlich Demokratische Union
CEA	Council of Economic Advisers
CM	Cabinet Meeting
Cmnd	HMSO, Command Paper
CSU	Christlich Soziale Union
CY	Calendar Year
DAFR	*Documents on American Foreign Relations*
DDF	Documents Diplomatiques Françaises
DDRS	Declassified Documents Reference System
DEFE	PRO, Defence Ministry Files
DF	Decimal Files, NA

| DOD | Department of Defense |
| DOS | Department of State |

EC	European Community
EDC	European Defense Community
EEC	European Economic Community
EFTA	European Free Trade Area
EPU	European Payments Union

FAZ	*Frankfurter Allgemeine Zeitung*
FDP	Free Democratic Party
FIG	Franco-Italian-German Trilateral Agreement
FMOD	German Federal Ministry of Defense
FO	British Foreign Office
FRUS	Foreign Relations of the United States
FTA	Free Trade Area
FY	Fiscal Year

GAB	General Agreements to Borrow
GATT	General Agreement on Tariffs and Trade
GPO	U.S. Government Printing Office

| HMSO | Her Majesty's Stationery Office |

| IFZ | Institut für Zeitgeschichte, Munich |
| IMF | International Monetary Fund |

| JCS | Joint Chiefs of Staff |
| JFKL | John F. Kennedy Library, Boston |

| KCA | Keesing's Contemporary Archives |

| LBJL | Lyndon Baines Johnson Library, Austin |
| LES | Ludwig Erhard Stiftung, Bonn |

MAAG	Military Assistance Advisory Group (U.S.)
MAC(G)	Mutual Aid Committee – Germany (U.K.)
MB	Ministerbüro
MBFR	Mutual Balanced Force Reductions
MC	Military Committee
MGFA I–IV	*Militärgeschichtliches Forschungsamt, Freiburg, ed., Anfänge westdeutscher Sicherheitspolitik, vols. I–IV*
MLF	Multilateral Force

| NA | National Archives, Suitland, Maryland |
| NHP | Nuclear History Program |

NPT	Nonproliferation Treaty
NSA	National Security Archive, Gelman Library, George Washington University, Washington, D.C.
NSAM	National Security Action Memorandum
NSC	National Security Council
NSF	National Security Files
NYT	*New York Times*
OECD	Organization for Economic Cooperation and Development
OEEC	Organization for European Economic Cooperation
OHI	Oral History Interview
PA–AA	Politisches Archiv des Auswärtigen Amts, Bonn
POF	President's Office Files (JFKL, LBJL)
PP	Public Papers of the Presidents of the U.S.
PPP	Pre-Presidential Papers (JFKL)
PREM	PRO, Files of the Prime Minister's Office
PRO	Public Record Office, London
PSSD	*Public Statements of the Secretaries of Defense*
RAF	Royal Air Force (U.K.)
RAND	Research and Development Corporation (U.S.)
RG	Record Group (NA)
SACEUR	Supreme Allied Commander Europe
SDR	Special Drawing Rights
SF	Subject Files, NA
SecState	U.S. Secretary of State
SPD	Sozialdemokratische Partei Deutschlands
T	PRO, Treasury Files
TAF	Tactical Air Force
TIAS	U.S. Treaties and Other International Agreements
USAREUR	U.S. Army Europe
VDB	*Verhandlungen des Deutschen Bundestags, Protokolle*
VfZ	*Vierteljahreshefte für Zeitgeschichte*
VPSF	Vice Presidential Security File (LBJL)
WEU	Western European Union
ZBR	Zentralbankrat (Board of the Bundesbank)

Preface

On January 1, 1999, the common European currency, called the euro, was launched. The first steps toward this epochal project, which challenges the very idea of the nation-state as no other measure in the history of European integration has, lay in the 1960s and 1970s, when the post-1945 dollar-based monetary system broke down amid convulsive currency speculation. It has become very clear since January 1999 that the success of the euro will depend not only on its economic soundness but also on issues of international politics and security. This study identifies and analyzes the manifold links between money and security in the era of the Cold War, underscoring the intricate relationship between geopolitics and the world economy. There is no reason to believe that this close link will be any less salient in international relations in the twenty-first century.

Writing this book has been an enjoyable experience much of the time. This is largely because most of it was written at the European University Institute in Florence, a place where the pursuit of academic excellence and Tuscan life-style create a unique environment for advanced research. To the staff of the EUI and the many friends I met there, I am deeply indebted, as I am to the German Academic Exchange Council (DAAD), which financed two years of my stay in Florence. In addition, this book would have been impossible without the help of the German Historical Institute (GHI) in Washington, D.C., especially its former director, Detlef Junker, and its current acting director, Christof Mauch. The GHI awarded me a six-month grant for archival work, and it generously supported the publication of this book. Special thanks go to the senior editor of the GHI, Daniel S. Mattern, and the GHI copy editor, Annette M. Marciel, for their work on the language, style, and flow of the manuscript. Finally, I greatly benefited from the advice and comments of

Richard T. Griffiths (University of Leiden), Wolfgang Krieger (University of Marburg), Alan S. Milward (EUI), and Marc Trachtenberg (UCLA). This book is dedicated to my parents.

Bochum, September 2000   Hubert Zimmermann

Introduction

On a cloudy, late summer day in Berlin, at a time when the research for this book was already well under way, its subject was officially declared history. After almost fifty years of uninterrupted presence, American, British, and French soldiers left their garrisons in the formerly divided city on September 8, 1994. A solemn ceremony at the Brandenburg Gate, featuring German Chancellor Helmut Kohl, French President François Mitterrand, British Prime Minister John Major, and U.S. Secretary of State Warren Christopher, concluded one of the last chapters of the Cold War. The highly symbolic event had many less spectacular precursors. After the epochal year 1989 similar ceremonies were held in many German cities as Allied troops moved out of the bases that had been maintained since the end of World War II. Rousing farewell speeches emphasized the bravery of the troops, the success they had with their mission of safeguarding the freedom of (West) Germany, and the magnanimity of the countries that had sent them. The return of the soldiers to their home countries signaled the end of an era.

Yet, despite the fact that the Cold War is generally declared over, NATO troops are still present in many places in Germany. Their continuing presence suggests that the significance of these troops always stretched beyond the obvious, that is, the protection of West Germany against the threat from the East. The large-scale Allied stationing of troops in Germany was among the most conspicuous and peculiar phenomena of the Cold War period in Europe. Such a long peacetime presence of foreign troops in an Allied country is without precedent. The British and American troops, on whom this study concentrates, were a major factor in the political relations between these countries and the Federal

1

Republic of Germany (FRG), in the military balance between East and West, and in the construction of a stable peace in postwar Western Europe. Less well known is the fact that these troops also held great importance for the international monetary relations of the Western world. It is this surprising fact that lies at the heart of the two fundamental themes of this book: the connection between monetary and security policies in transatlantic relations during the Cold War and the way in which this money–security link informed and shaped American, British, and German foreign policy.

The empirical foundation of this study is provided by a multidimensional analysis of an issue that bedeviled Bonn's relations with the stationing countries from the 1950s until well into the 1970s: Who should carry the foreign exchange costs caused by the troops' enormous need for German currency? Like tourists, Allied troops had to convert their own currencies into the local currency to pay for goods and services. The sheer number of soldiers and the costly nature of their task made this foreign exchange cost a major factor in international economic relations. The history of the so-called offset- or support-cost negotiations, in which the United States and the United Kingdom tried to recover their foreign exchange losses from the government in Bonn, is marked by some of the most acrimonious exchanges between the Federal Republic and its allies of the past fifty years.[1] What seems at first sight to be an almost ceaseless bickering about often minor sums of money was in reality an expression of fundamental political and economic conflict. At stake was not only money and military security but also the political position of the Federal Republic vis-à-vis its allies. The United States and Great Britain saw in the negotiations an important means of employing German resources for the defense of the West, a core objective of their postwar policy. What drove the conflict to an even higher level was that both also came to regard troop costs as a cause of the monetary crises that plagued the Western world during the 1950s and 1960s. This interpretation was plainly rejected by the Federal Republic. Owing to these multiple implications, the troop-cost negotiations became a fundamental issue in the international political economy of transatlantic relations during the Cold War.

1 "Support-cost payments" were direct, budgetary payments made by the West German government toward the cost of maintaining allied troops on its territory. "Offset payments" were indirect measures that were meant to offset the stationing country's loss of foreign exchange. For example, West Germany would place orders for weapons in that country or would invest in its capital markets. "Occupation costs" were West German contributions toward covering the expenses of the occupation forces from 1946 to 1955. The term *troop costs* covers all West German payments for the support of allied troops.

This study pursues three interrelated objectives: (1) to provide a history of the troop-cost negotiations and to link those negotiations to the economic and political relations among Germany, the United Kingdom, and the United States; (2) to show how economic, particularly monetary, factors in German–American and German–British relations influenced political–military relations and vice versa, as well as to address the question of what exactly was the connection between the developments in the international monetary system and Allied troop maintenance in Germany; and (3) to highlight trends in American, British, and, in particular, West German foreign policy regarding the role of economic diplomacy during the Cold War. Special attention will be given to tensions arising from the simultaneous integration of Germany into European institutions, into the Atlantic Alliance, and into the international monetary system.

Reconstructing the history of offset- and support-cost negotiations is necessary because of the scarcity of archive-based historical research in this field and the gaps in the few existing published works. However, I have not concentrated on the technicalities and the day-to-day conduct of these negotiations. Neither is it my intention to speculate on how a fair arrangement might have been made. Estimating the value of the troops is a political, not a financial matter; their overall cost is almost impossible to quantify.[2] It is therefore crucial to place the negotiations within the context of numerous related issues, such as the debates about troop levels, international monetary relations, armaments trade, military strategy, "European" questions, and domestic political and economic factors. All these issues were present in the negotiations. They provide an ideal starting point for taking a fresh look at many questions of international history during the Cold War.

The claim that security and economic issues are closely linked in international relations is certainly not new. During a Congressional hearing on the future of U.S. troop maintenance in Europe in 1971, for example, Martin Hillenbrand, assistant secretary of state for European affairs, remarked that the deployment of U.S. troops had been conducive to a "climate of receptivity toward American economic activity in Europe. I

---

2 In times of crisis, e.g., during the Berlin crisis of 1958–61, the troops were naturally regarded as more "valuable" than in times of détente. These fluctuations render it hardly surprising that NATO never found a formula for institutionalizing the distribution of the costs. Attempts by political scientists to calculate fair burden sharing miss this point completely. See, e.g., Mancur Olson and Richard Zeckhauser, "An Economic Theory of Alliances," *Review of Economics and Statistics* 48 (1966): 266–79; Jacques van Ypersele de Strihou, "Sharing the Defense Burden Among Western Allies," *Review of Economics and Statistics* 49 (1967): 527–36.

don't like to imply that our troops in effect are hostage to European good behavior in the economic area, but obviously it would be foolish to deny at a psychological level that there is a certain relationship here."[3] Such statements have been repeated in elaborated form in a great number of very diverse scholarly works on the economic and political relations between European countries and the United States, particularly in connection with monetary affairs.[4] The links between political–military and economic–monetary factors have sparked increased interest by many political scientists dealing with international relations or international political economy since the 1970s.[5] However, empirical studies that thoroughly and systematically analyze how these links were formed, how they worked, and what exactly their consequences were, especially studies that take a historical perspective and are based on extensive archival research, are almost nonexistent.[6] This book aims to be a first step toward closing that gap. Broadly speaking, the goal is to reintegrate monetary history into the historiography of the Cold War, which typically is dominated by security issues.

The main problem in the international monetary system from the 1950s to the 1970s was the increasing pressure on the currencies of the United Kingdom and the United States, culminating in the breakdown of the postwar monetary system in the early 1970s. Simultaneously, the Federal Republic became one of the strongest monetary powers in the world. Despite the strength of its currency, however, its monetary policy was restrained in many ways by its commitment to the Western alliance. The reality of foreign troop presence in Germany was an important factor in this respect. As the strength of the deutschmark (DM) symbolized the re-emergence of Germany as a major player in world politics, the monetary problems of the United States and Great Britain came to be widely interpreted as portents of decline. Washington and London were unwilling to abandon the central role that their currencies played in the world

---

3 U.S. Congress, House of Representatives, Committee on Armed Services: Special Subcommittee on NATO Commitments, 92d cong., 2d sess., Oct. 1971–Mar. 1972, 12574.
4 See, e.g., David Calleo and Benjamin Rowland, *America and the World Political Economy: Atlantic Dreams and National Realities* (Bloomington, Ind., 1974); Susan Strange, *International Economic Relations of the Western World, 1959–1971* (Oxford, 1976), 270–5; the articles by Frank Costigliola and William S. Borden, in Thomas G. Paterson, ed., *Kennedy's Quest for Victory: American Foreign Policy, 1961–1963* (Oxford, 1989), 24–85; Diane B. Kunz, *Butter and Guns: America's Cold War Economic Diplomacy* (New York, 1997).
5 For an assessment of recent work in this field, see Michael Mastanduno, "Economics and Security in Statecraft and Scholarship," *International Organization* 4 (1998): 825–54.
6 Susan Strange, "Political Economy and International Relations," in Alan Booth and Steve Smith, eds., *International Relations Theory Today* (University Park, Pa., 1995), 154–74.

economy. The ultimate measure of the success of their effort was the balance of payments, which records all payments of a given country to foreign countries and determines the strength of its own currency. Military expenditures abroad, of which troop stationing was a major component, were a conspicuous negative factor in the British and the American balances of payments during this era. Evidently, overseas military expenditures were not the only or even the main cause of the monetary disequilibria of the 1960s and 1970s, but they were an easy and popular target for governments struggling with balance-of-payments deficits. The simplest solution would have been to redeploy the troops to the home country. The catch in such a move was that the American and British troops in Europe had acquired an enormous political and military importance within the framework of Cold War politics. Thus, the United States and Britain saw themselves confronted with the dilemma of having to assign more relative value either to their central economic goal of strengthening the balance of payments or to vital security considerations. How this choice was resolved is a major theme of this study.

An issue that embodies such important political and economic issues also illuminates structural changes in West Germany's position in the international system from 1950 to 1971. The "German Question," understood as the problem of how a re-emerging, powerful West Germany would fit into the European structure of power, is a fundamental problem that informs most research on German foreign policy.[7] It lay (and still lies) at the heart of many political issues in postwar Europe. It was often argued that the danger of a German hegemonic position in Central Europe would arise only if and when reunification actually took place. In reality the problem never disappeared from the minds of West European and American politicians after the war. How does the troop-cost issue figure within this broad context? The significance of Anglo–American troop stationing was twofold: control of the Soviet Union and control of Germany, that is, "double containment."[8] This double control function was tacitly but widely acknowledged, and changes in troop levels inevitably affected its credibility. Could the United States and Great Britain risk unleashing

---

7 Dirk Verheyen, *The German Question: A Cultural, Historical, and Geopolitical Exploration* (Boulder, Colo., 1991), 2–3, highlights four principal dimensions of the German question: (1) German identity, (2) the reunification issue, (3) Germany's place in the international environment, and (4) German political and economic power in a narrower regional context.
8 This interpretive framework is lucidly outlined in Wolfram F. Hanrieder, *Germany, America, Europe: Forty Years of German Foreign Policy* (New Haven, Conn., 1989). See also Norbert Wiggershaus, "The Other 'German Question': The Foundation of the Atlantic Pact and the Problem of Security Against Germany," in Ennio di Nolfo, ed., *The Atlantic Pact 40 Years Later: A Historical Appraisal* (Berlin, 1991), 111–26.

the haunting specter of an uncontrolled Germany so shortly after the demise of Nazism just to save an admittedly large sum of money?

Even more important to this research is the extent to which the German Question became an economic one after 1955, when the Federal Republic was politically and militarily bound to the Western camp. Twice in the twentieth century, Germany used impressive economic gains to launch assertive, ultimately militarily aggressive foreign policies. The most significant development in the Federal Republic during and after its integration into the Western alliance system was its spectacular economic success in the 1950s and 1960s. This provoked concern that the Federal Republic might use its economic weight to pursue irresponsible policies. In its relations with its Western allies Germany – or the German question – therefore figured not only in the debates about nuclear participation but also increasingly in an economic context. This is a historical process that can be followed to the present, when the looming economic hegemony of Germany is a major issue in European policy.

Surprisingly, the role of economic diplomacy has only recently attracted increased attention in accounts of postwar West German foreign policy. The traditional concentration on "classical" attributes of foreign policy (military and alliance politics) has led historians and political scientists to neglect the more subtle instruments of foreign economic policy.[9] And yet it is economic diplomacy that has been and still is the most important and effective instrument of German foreign policy.[10] This is particularly conspicuous in the field of monetary policy. During the 1950s the DM became one of the strongest currencies in the world. It would indeed be curious if this spectacular development had not had a deep influence on issues of foreign policy. Many of the arguments dealt with in this book reappear in one form or another in contemporary discussions of the – real or imagined – consequences of Germany's economic power. It is impossible to understand past and present German foreign policy without attempting to trace the impact of economic power; within this framework, the troop-cost conflict offers extremely instructive examples. The same is true for American and British policies.

While researching these issues it became clear to me that the significance of the results goes well beyond the confines of the topic and relates

---

9 Hans-Jürgen Schröder, "Wirtschaftliche Aspekte deutscher Aussenpolitik in der Adenauer-Ära," in Franz Knipping and Klaus Jürgen Müller, eds., *Aus der Ohnmacht zur Bündnismacht: Das Machtproblem in der Bundesrepublik 1945–60* (Paderborn, 1995), 121–38.

10 For a concise argument along these lines, see Gottfried Niedhart, "Deutsche Aussenpolitik: Vom Teilstaat mit begrenzter Souveränität zum postmodernen Nationalstaat," *APUZG* 2 (1997): 15–23.

to a whole series of academic debates that deal with the way foreign policy is formulated and executed. First, the troop-cost conflict shows how modern states interact in alliances characterized by a pattern of simultaneous competition and cooperation. Second, the conflicts analyzed in this study are an instructive demonstration of the way domestic politics influence the formulation of foreign policy. Despite the often arcane nature of the negotiations, domestic considerations weighed heavily in all decisions and on all sides, and I illuminate this domestic background wherever possible. Third, the troop-cost conflict contributed to the debate on the relative nature of American hegemony and on British economic and military decline after 1945. All these issues were considered when I wrote this book, and although I could not pursue them in any systematic way, I hope that the results of my research will be helpful to scholars working on those questions.

LITERATURE AND SOURCES

Although Allied troop maintenance in Germany was one of the most conspicuous manifestations of the postwar military–political settlement in Europe, it has not been studied extensively. Most scholarly work on this subject situates it within the framework of general strategic and political questions.[11] A tentative consensus has been reached in this respect, which explains the long-term presence of the troops in Europe as a necessary complement to nuclear weapons and argues that the value of their presence depends on nuclear strategy. However, strategy explains only a small part of the continuity of Allied troop maintenance in West Germany. Political factors were far more important. These also have been extensively researched, and the concept of double containment is a useful framework for explaining how the American Seventh Army and the British Army on the Rhine (BAOR) became such essential parts of the

---

11 Most influential is John Lewis Gaddis, *Strategies of Containment: A Critical Appraisal of Postwar American National Security Policy* (New York, 1982). See also David N. Schwartz, *NATO's Nuclear Dilemmas* (Washington, D.C., 1983); Jane E. Stromseth, *The Origins of Flexible Response: NATO's Debate over Strategy in the 1960s* (New York, 1988); John S. Duffield, *Power Rules: The Evolution of NATO's Conventional Force Posture* (Stanford, Calif., 1996). For an assessment of the strategic debate in the Alliance, see Marc Trachtenberg, *History and Strategy* (Princeton, N.J., 1991). For details of troop location, structure, and for changes over the years, see Simon Duke, ed., *U.S. Military Forces and Installations in Europe* (Oxford, 1989); Simon Duke and Wolfgang Krieger, eds., *U.S. Military Forces in Europe* (Boulder, Colo., 1993); Lee Gordon, "The Half-Forgotten Army: A Survey of British Forces in Germany," *The Economist*, Nov. 28, 1970; Dieter Mahncke, ed., *Amerikaner in Deutschland: Grundlagen und Bedingungen der transatlantischen Sicherheit* (Bonn, 1991); Daniel J. Nelson, *A History of U.S. Military Forces in Germany* (Boulder, Colo., 1987).

Western security structure that emerged during the 1950s. However, remarkably little research has been done on the troop-cost problem and its impact on political-strategic questions as well as on the economic relations of the countries involved. Historical research based on archival sources is especially rare.[12] This is surprising given that the history of Allied troop maintenance is marked by an uninterrupted series of conflicts over this issue. Disagreements about financial questions were much more frequent in the Western alliance than strategic or political divergences. When the latter arose, they were often closely linked with the cost issue.

The period up to 1968 is extensively documented by both published primary sources and archival material. Biographies, journals, and newspapers were a necessary complement in my research to understand the crucial domestic context of many issues. Even so, primary sources are the foundation on which my research rests. Some of them are available in edited form. For U.S. policy, the Foreign Relations of the United States (FRUS) edition and the microfiche collection of newly declassified documents, the Declassified Documents Reference System, were the most useful. These editions provide good documentation of major issues but unavoidably lack detailed material on the subject. Material in American archives filled in the gaps in the record. I carried out research at the John

---

12 In the Anglo–German context, see Wolfram Kaiser, "Money, Money, Money," in Gustav Schmidt, ed., *Zwischen Bündnissicherung und privilegierter Partnerschaft* (Bochum, 1995), 1–31; Harald Rosenbach, "Die Schattenseiten der 'Stillen Allianz': Der deutsch-britische Devisenausgleich, 1958–1967," *Vierteljahrschrift für Sozial- und Wirtschaftsgeschichte* 2 (1998): 196–231. A few paragraphs based on archival evidence can be found in Olaf Mager, *Die Stationierung der britischen Rheinarmee: Grossbritanniens EVG-Alternative* (Baden–Baden, 1990); Werner Abelshauser, *Wirtschaft und Rüstung in den Fünfziger Jahren*, vol. 4 of *MGFA* (Munich, 1996); Daniel Hoffmann, *Truppenstationierung in der Bundesrepublik Deutschland: Die Vertragsverhandlungen mit den Westmächten* (Munich, 1997).

The history of German–American offset payments was the subject of a number of early political science studies: Elke Thiel's *Dollar-Dominanz, Lastenteilung und Amerikanische Truppenpräsenz in Europa* (Baden–Baden, 1979) extensively discusses the economic background but suffers from the complete absence of archival material; in *Troop-Stationing in Germany: Value and Cost* (Santa Monica, Calif., 1968) Horst Mendershausen provides a brief but well-informed analysis; and Gregory F. Treverton's *The Dollar Drain and American Forces in Germany: Managing the Political Economics of Alliance* (Athens, Ohio, 1978) is based on interviews with participants in the events and on privileged access to government documents, and is particularly strong on the 1966–7 crisis. The use of archival material is confined to David P. Wightman, "Money and Security: Financing American Troops in Germany and the Trilateral Negotiations 1966/67," *Rivista di Storia Economica* 1 (1988): 26–77; he adopted a similar approach to the one I take here; in *Kernwaffen und die Glaubwürdigkeit der Allianz: Die NATO-Krise von 1966/67* (Baden–Baden, 1994) Helga Haftendorn places the issue within the broader context of the strategic discussions in NATO during the mid-1960s; and Harald Rosenbach's "Der Preis der Freiheit: Die deutsch-amerikanischen Verhandlungen über den Devisenausgleich 1960–1967," *VfZ* 4 (1998): 709–46, concentrates on Ludwig Erhard's visit to Washington, D.C., in 1966.

F. Kennedy Library in Boston, Massachusetts, at the Lyndon Baines Johnson Library in Austin, Texas, and at the National Archives in Washington, D.C. I also consulted important smaller collections, such as the George C. McGhee papers at Georgetown University and the National Security Archive.

Extensive published documentation is lacking in the case of the United Kingdom. The Public Record Office, however, provides an immense amount of compelling and comprehensive material for all questions related to troop costs and monetary policy. The material is concentrated in the files of the Prime Minister's Office, the cabinet, the Foreign Office, the Treasury, and the Ministry of Defence. These files were consulted and evaluated for the years up to and including 1967. Unfortunately, documentation on British policy after 1967 was not available at the time of publication, and the analysis of the British position during these years thus remains preliminary.

Published sources on the German side are limited. The recently initiated publication of German diplomatic documents covers the years 1963–70.[13] Archives with relevant material are spread all over Germany. The Political Archives of the German Foreign Office (Politisches Archiv des Auswärtigen Amtes) in Berlin holds material on the details of negotiations, although many high-level documents are still classified. The sources in the German Federal Archives (Bundesarchiv) in Koblenz fill in some of the gaps. Highly rewarding are the papers of politicians involved in the negotiations (Herbert Blankenhorn, Heinrich von Brentano, Franz Etzel, Fritz Schäffer, and Karl Theodor Freiherr von und zu Guttenberg), as are the files of the Federal Chancellery (B136). The central files of the Finance and Economics Ministries (B126/B107) also were very helpful. Regarding sources on German monetary policy, some documentation in the archives of the German Federal Bank (Bundesbank) in Frankfurt am Main was useful. Smaller collections, such as the Defense Ministry sources, which have been declassified for the Nuclear History Project, the Ludwig Erhard Foundation in Bonn, and the Institute for Contemporary History in Munich, were also consulted. Very important, particularly for the crucial year 1966, is the military diary of former Defense Minister Kai-Uwe von Hassel. The files of the Defense Ministry in the German Federal Military Archives (Bundesarchiv–Militärarchiv) in Freiburg, however, were less useful for the period of this research, owing in large measure to the lamentable state of declassification.

13 See Institut für Zeitgeschichte, on behalf of the Auswärtiges Amt, ed., *Akten zur Auswärtigen Politik der Bundesrepublik Deutschland 1963–1970* (Munich, 1994–2001).

The statistical material presented particular difficulties. Relevant official statistics are scarcely available and often unreliable. The influence of troop maintenance on the balance of payments, for example, is a question that depends very much on interpretation. Balance-of-payments statistics are subject to numerous revisions by governments, and the accounting method varies from country to country. Additionally, they were often manipulated for political reasons. Reservations regarding the reliability of the statistical material cited are mentioned whenever necessary.

1

On Whose Shoulders? German Rearmament and the Cold War Burden

GERMAN REARMAMENT AND ALLIED TROOP MAINTENANCE IN GERMANY

When in May 1955 the Paris Accords came into effect, the long and tortuous process of forming an integrated Western security system was finally concluded after more than five years of negotiations. The major stumbling block had been the politically sensitive question of whether and how the former enemy, Germany, was to be integrated into this structure. The result of the multinational effort was spectacular. It encompassed not only the rules for rearming West Germany but also the establishment of Bonn's sovereignty and its inclusion in NATO only ten years after the end of World War II. A reaffirmation of the continuity of large-scale NATO troop presence on German soil was a further core element of the settlement. American, British, French, Canadian, Dutch, Belgian, and Danish troops changed their status from occupiers to protectors.

The diplomatic events leading up to the Paris Accords, their political and military causes, and their implications have been the subject of much historical research.[1] Much less is known about the economic foundations

---

1 With references to the vast literature, the four volumes of the Militärgeschichtliche Forschungsamt, ed., *Anfänge Westdeutscher Sicherheitspolitik (MGFA I–IV)* (Munich, 1982–96) provide a meticulous account of the issue. Recent collections containing many excellent articles on German rearmament and related issues include Fred Heller and John Gillingham, eds., *NATO: The Founding of the Alliance and the Integration of Europe* (Basingstoke, U.K., 1992); Klaus A. Maier and Norbert Wiggershaus, eds., *Das Nordatlantische Bündnis 1949–1956* (Munich, 1993); Jeffry M. Diefendorf, Axel Frohn, and Hermann-Josef Rupieper, eds., *American Policy and the Reconstruction of West Germany, 1945–55* (New York, 1993). See also Thomas A. Schwartz, *America's Germany: John J. McCloy and the Federal Republic of Germany* (Cambridge, Mass., 1991); Hermann-Josef Rupieper, *Der besetzte Verbündete: Die amerikanische Deutschlandpolitik 1949–1955* (Opladen, 1991); David Clay Large, *Germans to the Front: West German Rearmament in the Adenauer Era* (Chapel Hill, N.C., 1996). The construction of the transatlantic security system is analyzed in Marc Trachtenberg, *A Constructed Peace: The Making of the European Settlement, 1945–63* (Princeton, N.J., 1999). The following paragraphs are based on this literature.

of these events,[2] which are crucial to understanding the results: The formation of the Atlantic security system was inevitably shaped by fundamental economic factors in postwar transatlantic relations (and vice versa). Paying special attention to these economic factors, I briefly review the origins of the two elements that, in addition to the American nuclear guarantee, were pivotal for the Atlantic security system as it emerged in 1954–5: Western troop maintenance in Germany and West German rearmament. The link between these two elements is particularly emphasized.

The process leading up to the Paris Accords can be interpreted as an enormous multinational sharing of the burden initiated by the United States and the United Kingdom as a reaction to the emerging global conflict during the late 1940s. A series of diplomatic confrontations had led to a rapid disintegration of the wartime coalition between Roosevelt, Churchill, and Stalin, resulting in a struggle that was to dominate world politics for the next fifty years: the Cold War.[3] Its decisive battlefield was Europe. As tensions rose, most Western politicians agreed that a further expansion of the Soviet sphere of influence into Europe had to be countered by all means. "Containment" of Communist expansion worldwide, but above all in Europe, became the central tenet of Western security policies. This strategy, successful in the end, had one great disadvantage: Military security came with a high price tag. Would economic prosperity, the other, probably even more important objective of Western societies, survive another war economy, especially after the recent dislocations provoked by World War II?

The Americans and the British soon agreed that a meaningful containment policy in Europe was impossible without the use of European resources. This meant, in particular, that the economic potential of Germany, now divided into four zones of occupation, had to be employed in the increasingly costly pursuit of the Cold War and that the West German population had to be brought into the common effort. Certainly, the contributions that France, the United Kingdom, and the United States extracted from their respective zones (occupation payments, reparations, the use of German technical know-how, and so forth) amounted to formidable sums. However, they were by no means enough to cover the expenses required for the defense of German territory and of the

2 Cf. Werner Abelshauser, "Wirtschaft und Rüstung," in *MGFA IV* (Munich, 1996), 1–186.
3 For some time now, the issue of the origins of the Cold War has been one of the most hotly debated subjects in the study of contemporary history. For a recent reappraisal of this debate, see John L. Gaddis, *We Now Know: Rethinking Cold War History* (Oxford, 1997).

European Cold War border. These forced contributions were exceedingly unpopular in West Germany and therefore quite counterproductive in the effort to win the population over to the Western side. In the long run the Germans would align themselves wholeheartedly with the West only if they were given some measure of political equality. Thus, containment and the establishment of a sovereign German state on the territory of the American, British, and French zones of occupation became closely linked.

Military authorities in the United States and Britain had arrived at the conclusion soon after the war that a direct and voluntary contribution by means of a German army was the only solution to the security problem in Europe. What made military sense was far from politically acceptable, however, and those plans remained strictly secret. Then, in June 1950, North Korean troops, backed overtly by China and covertly by the Soviet Union, crossed the demarcation line in divided Korea. They were stopped only by a massive intervention of U.S. forces. The outbreak of the Korean War and the lessons drawn from it created the necessary political preconditions for an attempt to turn military plans into reality because it was easy to imagine a parallel scenario in divided Germany. Western military power was seen as completely insufficient to stop a similar attack in Europe, especially after the Soviet Union had demonstrated that it had the atomic bomb. The countries adhering to NATO, founded in 1949 but still very much an empty shell, embarked on a massive rearmament program.

The government of the United States in particular undertook a significant expansion of its commitment in Europe.[4] It came to see the various economic aid schemes, such as the Marshall Plan, as insufficient to achieve stability in Europe and allow Europeans to defend themselves. Economic aid was replaced by large-scale military aid.[5] In addition, the deployment of large conventional forces in Europe seemed imperative to deter communist aggression. The American government was certain that as long as the economic, political, and military circumstances of the European democracies remained fundamentally unstable the only way to defend Europe from possible attack was the large-scale deployment of American and British forces. The Europeans were urgently requesting precisely that. It was no easy task for the U.S. government to convince the American public of the necessity for a massive reinforcement of the small

4 Duffield, *Power Rules*, 28–74.
5 Robert A. Pollard, *Economic Security and the Origins of the Cold War, 1945–50* (New York, 1985), 241.

remaining U.S. force in Europe. The commitment was approved by Congress in 1951, only after bitter debate.[6] The level of acrimony showed that an extended U.S. troop engagement in Europe was widely perceived as a major shift in American foreign policy. For the first time American forces were deployed on a permanent basis in Europe during peacetime. In all probability Congress gave its consent only because the government gave credible assurances that the measure would be temporary and the financial burden on the United States would last only for a transitional period, until the Europeans had rebuilt their own forces. Nobody at that time thought that the presence of U.S. troops would outlast even the existence of the Soviet Union. Undoubtedly, the government itself did not expect a perpetual stay, as Dwight D. Eisenhower later recalled: "After all, when we deployed our six divisions to NATO, the deployment was never intended to be permanent and we informed congress that this was a temporary measure, particularly related to the buildup of West German forces."[7]

Clearly, the Americans were not at all eager to shoulder the burden of Europe's conventional defense by themselves. Already in 1949–50 the cost of economic aid and military commitments weighed heavily on the American budget – without any reasonable prospect of an imminent reduction.[8] Apprehension that the United States alone would have to settle the Cold War bill in Europe was not unjustified. Britain and France were increasingly engaged in the defense of their crumbling colonial empires, and other NATO countries lacked the necessary resources. The only country that had the potential significantly to relieve the United States of its burden by means of conventional troops and financial support was still-occupied West Germany. A European force, capable of replacing the large U.S. presence, seemed impossible without the use of German manpower. Thus, the idea of rearming Germany became closely linked to the U.S. troop commitment. The rationales behind the re-creation of a German army were no longer limited to the military arguments of the generals or to the political argument of aligning the Germans with the West. Now they were founded on powerful economic necessities, too.

6 On the "Great Debate" over a prolonged massive U.S. military presence in Europe, see Phil Williams, *The Senate and U.S. Troops in Europe* (New York, 1985); Ted Carpenter, "U.S. NATO Policy at Crossroads: The 'Great Debate' of 1950–51," *International History Review* 8 (1986): 389–414; Bruno Thoss, "The Presence of American Troops in Germany, 1949–56," in Diefendorf, Frohn, and Rupieper, eds., *American Policy*, 411–32.
7 Memorandum of discussion at the 390th NSC meeting, Dec. 11, 1958, in FRUS 1958–60, VII, 367.
8 Melvyn P. Leffler, *A Preponderance of Power: National Security, the Truman Administration, and the Cold War* (Stanford, Calif., 1992), 304–11; Pollard, *Economic Security*, 222–42.

It was this "burden-sharing" component that was the driving element behind tenacious American (and British) pressure for rapid German rearmament. However, the practical implementation of this project proved extremely difficult.

Already in September 1950 U.S. Secretary of State Dean Acheson confronted the NATO partners with the American intention to permit and pursue the partial reconstruction of Germany's military potential in order to use it in the defense of the West. His first proposal was a "package deal" explicitly linking the feasibility of U.S. troop commitments to West German rearmament.[9] Due to their still fresh wartime memories, European opposition to the plan was even stronger than anticipated. The reconstruction of a German military and the inherent restoration of German sovereignty were difficult to swallow so soon after the war. French resistance in particular was almost insurmountable. However, the danger of American disengagement or a stop to its military and financial support, in addition to the Soviet threat, convinced French leaders that they would have to accept some level of German rearmament. But how to sell that to the French people? In an attempt to contain the German military potential with a control scheme, the French government in 1950 launched the so-called Pleven Plan for an integrated European army that would prevent the reconstruction of independent German forces. After some hesitation the Americans and the British agreed to participate in talks about this proposal. Four years of intensive, protracted negotiations and diplomatic arm-twisting on the subject of the so-called EDC (European Defense Community) followed.[10] In August 1954, however, the French parliament voted down the project. The plans for Germany's integration into Western defense organizations had failed.

Despite the negative vote, American, British, and French politicians continued with vigorous efforts to find a new scheme that would make German rearmament acceptable to the French public. Finally, in October 1954 France agreed to West Germany's accession to NATO and to the revived Western European Union (WEU), founded in 1948 by Britain, France, and the Benelux countries. Numerous control mechanisms, such as Germany's renunciation of the production of atomic, biological, and chemical (ABC) weapons, were included in the treaties. The central

---

9 Dean Acheson, *Present at the Creation: My Years in the State Department* (London, 1970), 437–40; see also Marc Trachtenberg and Christopher Gehrz, "America, Europe, and German Rearmament," *Journal of European Integration History* 6 (2000): 9–36.
10 On the EDC, apart from *MGFA I–IV*, see Gero von Gersdorff, *Adenauer's Aussenpolitik gegenüber den Siegermächten 1954* (Düsseldorf, 1994).

elements in this framework of "containing" West Germany were doubt-less the American and British pledges to keep their forces in Germany. Those two powers thereby manifestly demonstrated that, in contrast to the interwar period, they intended to remain directly involved in Euro-pean affairs.[11] This had an ironic result: The political framework of German rearmament required of the United States and the United Kingdom a costly commitment, instead of relieving them of a burden, which had been a central objective of both the Americans and the British in pushing the whole process.

The Paris Accords of 1954, which codified these events, also meant the end of the occupation period for West Germany, which regained most of its sovereignty. Thus, the foundations for a German contribution to Western defense were in place. The question now changed from "if" to "how." This important question had remained unresolved, and various political and economic obstacles hampered the rapid creation of a German army. The quarrel between West Germany and its NATO partners about the exact form of the Federal Republic's contribution to the Cold War effort began. If Germany could not immediately supply its own forces, what else would it provide? How much of the burden of common defense would it have to shoulder? This lasting controversy over burden sharing became one of the most important issues of NATO policy. The troop-cost question was the main area of contention.

In summary, the urgency with which the United States and the United Kingdom had pushed forward the debate about a German defense con-tribution in 1950–4 resulted not only from the need to tie Germany to the Western camp or from military exigencies, as the otherwise useful concept of "double containment" implies. The pressing burden of defense expenditure and the perceived necessity to maintain and pay large con-ventional armies abroad made the utilization of German resources indis-pensable if there were to be any hope of ever reducing this cost to the United States and United Kingdom and simultaneously maintaining a credible defense posture in Europe.[12] The political circumstances of German rearmament, however, required the prolonged presence of American and British forces as a controlling factor against the reawaken-ing of adventurous German policies. These contradictory objectives and

---

11 American, British, and Canadian assurances to maintain their troops in Europe are reprinted in FRUS 1952–54, V/2, 1351.
12 See also Matthias Peter, "Britain, the Cold War, and the Economics of German Rearmament, 1949–51," in Anne Deighton, ed., *Britain and the First Cold War* (London, 1990), 273–90.

the unresolved problem regarding the form of Germany's contribution are the structural background to the conflicts analyzed in this book.

THE END OF THE OCCUPATION REGIME AND
THE FINANCING OF ALLIED TROOPS

Until now, the defense burden in Europe during the Cold War has been referred to only in the abstract. What was the exact size of the effort, especially for the three powers that bore the major part of the cost: the United States, the United Kingdom, and Germany?

In the Paris Accords, Germany agreed to contribute twelve divisions to common defense, to be formed by 1959. Cost estimates for the buildup of this army reached DM 50–80 billion, with a projected yearly allocation of DM 9 billion, that is, about 30 percent of the annual West German budgets in the late 1950s. Initially, the funds for rearmament were expected to equal what Germany paid toward the expenses of the occupation forces. Those were formidable sums. According to German sources, between 1948 and 1956 West Germany paid about $11 billion to the occupation powers. In the early 1950s occupation costs and related expenditures absorbed about 15 percent of Germany's net social product and in some years as much as 35 percent (!) of all expenses in the federal budget.[13] As long as Germany was occupied, the occupation powers were free, in principle, to demand whatever funds they needed for the maintenance of their troops. The end of the occupation period in 1955 implied the termination of these occupation payments.[14] The payments had covered nearly all of the DM expenditures for allied troops on German soil and were Germany's major contribution to the Cold War prior to joining NATO. When in 1954 the Americans and British pledged the continued presence of their troops in Germany they were faced at the same time with the prospect of having to finance them all by themselves.

13 For these figures, see "Leistungen der Bundesrepublik Deutschland für die ausländischen Streitkräfte," *BPI 1961*, 221–4; Lutz Köllner, "Die Entwicklung bundesdeutscher Militärausgaben in Vergangenheit und Zukunft," *APUZG* 22 (1984): 29; Werner Abelshauser, "The Causes and Consequences of the 1956 West German Rearmament Crisis," in Heller and Gillingham, eds., *NATO*, 314; Lutz Köllner and Hans-Erich Volkmann, "Finanzwissenschaftliche, finanzwirtschaftliche und finanzpolitische Aspekte eines deutschen Beitrags zur EVG," in *MGFA II*, 748; Gerd Hardach, *Der Marshallplan* (Munich, 1994), 238.
14 This refers only to occupation payments in the Western zones. Berlin remained occupied territory until the 1990s, and the Federal Republic paid the expenses of allied troops stationed in the city.

In 1955 the United States maintained an army of 261,000 men in Germany, about 10 percent of total U.S. military personnel.[15] In the Western European Union (WEU) treaty the United Kingdom committed itself to keeping in Germany four divisions and the Second Tactical Air Force, comprising 105,000 men. These represented about 15 percent of all British troops under arms. For both countries the cost of these commitments was only a portion of the resources employed for the defense of Europe, which included the cost of nuclear weapons, material supply, logistical support, and so forth. Thus, the commitment of their governments to the defense of German territory created a heavy burden on American and British taxpayers, and, what proved to be the much more contentious issue, it also meant heavy strains on the balance of payments of both countries.

It is very important to distinguish between the troop costs that fell on government budgets and the share of this budgetary cost that came about through foreign exchange, that is, in German marks. The budgetary cost, according to NATO rules, was to be assumed by the country that maintained the forces, wherever they were stationed. In fact it was only marginally different for troops abroad than at home. It might have been even higher in the home countries, due to various allowances granted to allied forces in Germany by the Status of Forces agreements and to the lower cost of living in Germany at that time.[16] The only way to get rid of the budgetary cost was to disband the troops. To get help for the American and British budgets therefore was only a secondary matter in the troop-cost negotiations; the foreign exchange cost was the core issue.[17]

---

15 Mendershausen, *Troop-Stationing*, 52. For allied troop levels between 1955 and 1971, see Table 3, Appendix 1.

16 These agreements regulated the conditions for the presence of foreign troops in the Federal Republic and granted allowances, such as free use of buildings and territory, reduced telecommunication tariffs, tax exemptions, duty free gasoline, and German assumption of damages caused by the troops. See Truppenvertragskonferenz, Dec. 7, 1959, BA, B126/34103, BFM, Dept. IIE. For a summary of the agreements, see KCA 1952, 12226–7; KCA 1960, 17849. For their history, see Hoffmann, *Truppenstationierung*.

17 Precise figures as to the budgetary cost of the American and British European commitments are difficult to find. Usually they were not specified in military budgets, contrary to the foreign exchange cost. In November 1959 the U.S. budget director estimated the cost of the American NATO commitment, including backup, aid, and so forth, at $4 billion, of which $1.2 billion were converted into local currencies. See 424th NSC meeting, Nov. 12, 1959, in FRUS 1958–60, VII, 512. A 1970 estimate put the annual cost of U.S. forces in Europe at between $7 and 9.5 billion, of which $1.9 billion went across the exchanges. Roughly one-third of the cost was spent on operations (payroll, supply, transport, maintenance) and the rest for equipment, construction, administration, and training. See Edward R. Fried, "The Financial Cost of Alliance," in John Newhouse, ed., *U.S. Troops in Europe: Issues, Costs, and Choices* (Washington, D.C., 1971), 106–7, 129–30. The British published estimates on the budgetary cost only in the 1960s. In 1966 the budgetary

This economic consideration was one of the major reasons for both the United States and Britain to plan for only a temporary presence, that is, until European forces were available in sufficient numbers. Their hopes were quickly shattered. The most important reason – from a long-term perspective – was that their troops acquired an eminent political importance that far overshadowed their military significance. The American forces became a crucial element of postwar European policy, for they guaranteed control by the United States of German rearmament and economic reconstruction. This was of central importance to all European countries that had been at war with Germany. For Germany, however, the U.S. troops were an essential element of NATO's security guarantee. When the United States in 1956 first hinted that it was considering redeployment, the reaction in European capitals made one thing abundantly clear: American hopes for a short stay in Europe were proving too optimistic.[18] The United States had to shoulder the cost of its commitment for the time being. In the mid-1950s this did not seem to be too much of a problem for the Americans. The situation was wholly different in the British case, and the British government had been keenly aware of this throughout the rearmament debate.

The lack of a firm British commitment to provide troops for a European army was a major factor in the failure of the European Defense Community (EDC) in 1954.[19] Hesitations over a formal commitment of troops were due more to financial considerations than to a principled unwillingness to commit forces to continental defense. Foreign Secretary Anthony Eden stated in a 1954 telegram to his American counterpart, Secretary of State John Foster Dulles:

Once the EDC is in force and the Germans are bearing their full share of defense expenditure we must face the certainty that after what may not be a very long period we shall cease to receive any German contribution towards the costs of maintaining our forces in Germany. . . . At present levels this would mean that we should have to finance an extra 80 million pounds in foreign exchange. This would present us with very great difficulties.[20]

---

cost was estimated at $437.2 million. Of this sum, $249.2 million consisted of expenditures in marks (DM). See KCA 1966, 21266.

18 For this episode, and for a more extensive discussion of the political and strategic importance of U.S. troops, see Chapter 7 in this book.

19 The most recent monographs on this subject are Saki Dockrill, *Britain's Policy for West German Rearmament, 1950–1955* (New York, 1991); Hans-Heinrich Jansen, *Grossbritannien, das Scheitern der EVG und der NATO Beitritt der BRD* (Bochum, 1992); Mager, *Stationierung*.

20 Eden to Dulles, Mar. 6, 1954, PRO T 312/53, Tel. 874.

During the EDC debate apprehension that the Federal Republic would soon spend all its defense funds on its own forces, leaving the United Kingdom to foot the bill for its troops on the continent, was a major preoccupation of the British cabinet.[21] The tenor of the discussion was that the United Kingdom could not take on any additional economic burden, especially on its balance of payments. Whether this could be avoided by troop reductions, U.S. aid, further German payments, or administrative savings would remain an open question as long as the result of the EDC negotiations was unclear. When it became obvious that a British troop commitment was essential to create a meaningful European security structure, the problem went unresolved.

In the end the serious doubts about the financial feasibility of a troop commitment in Europe were swept aside. The political and economic benefits of a British commitment seemed to outweigh the financial sacrifices. First, Britain, like the United States, was interested in getting the Germans to share the cost of the Cold War, especially considering that the British economy was growing at a much slower pace than that of Germany. Many British politicians attributed this to the fact that the German economy was unburdened by military expenditures. If a British commitment was necessary to overcome the impasse in the German rearmament question because France, in particular, insisted on such a pledge, Britain would have to grasp the nettle. Second, a British troop commitment helped to keep the U.S. troops in Europe. This was a major objective of British foreign policy, particularly after Dulles had threatened an "agonizing reappraisal" of U.S. policy toward Europe in case the EDC project foundered. In addition, the Americans made their interest in a British commitment quite clear to Her Majesty's government. Last, the troops could be useful in influencing continental politics, given the abstinence of Britain from the new supranational institutions in Europe, such as the European Coal and Steel Community (ECSC). This last point is the most ambiguous because Britain never managed to achieve a clear idea of the political role its troops should play on the continent, as we shall see later in this book.

Faced with the choice between those political benefits and the financial burden, the British government finally accepted the formal troop commitment. It was embodied in the WEU treaty, and the wording clearly reflects British ambiguity. The United Kingdom pledged to

---

21 See, e.g., the following cabinet memoranda: PRO CAB 129, C(52)36, Feb. 13, 1952; C(52)106, Apr. 4, 1952; C(52)141, May 3, 1952; C(52)162, May 14, 1952; C(52)185, June 9, 1952; C(53)112, Mar. 23, 1953.

continue to maintain on the mainland of Europe, including Germany, the effective strength of the United Kingdom forces which are now assigned to the Supreme Allied Commander, Europe, that is to say four divisions and the Second Tactical Air Force. . . . She undertakes not to withdraw these forces against the majority of the High Contracting Parties who should take their decision in the knowledge of the views of the Supreme Allied Commander, Europe. This undertaking shall not, however, bind her in the event of an acute overseas emergency. If the maintenance of the UK forces on the mainland of Europe throws at any time too great a strain on the external finances of the United Kingdom, she will . . . invite the North Atlantic Council to review the financial conditions on which the UK forces are maintained.[22]

When this declaration was made it was hailed as a great success for British diplomacy. It was the major element in the British effort to save the Western security structure after the failure of the EDC. However, the inconvenience this pledge would cause for Britain in the years to come probably contributed greatly to its later reluctance to participate in other supranational institutions in Europe.

In 1955–6 the British government was concerned less about the long-term effect of its decision and more about the immediate financial impact. The surprisingly quick resolution of the German rearmament problem had created the unwanted situation whereby German payments would soon cease, British troops would become tied to European defense through international agreement, and yet West German troops, which might replace them, were still on the drawing board.

Certain delays in German rearmament had been foreseen by the stationing countries; they therefore insisted on including a clause in the NATO Finance Convention, signed in Paris, that guaranteed an extension of occupation payments for one year (until mid-1956) to cover the period until West German rearmament gained momentum. This extended scheme obligated Germany to pay a total of $762 million in monthly allocations on a sliding scale.[23] The NATO Finance Convention reserved for the allies the right to negotiate a further extension. The Germans, however, understood May 1956 to mark the end of payments for foreign troops – wrongly, as it turned out. It soon became clear that the German military buildup would proceed much more slowly than expected. A reduction of the Anglo-American contingents at this early stage of the Cold War was unthinkable, and Washington and London realized that the

---

22 Protocol no. II on Forces of WEU, Art VI, Oct. 23, 1954, in HMSO, Cmnd. 9498, Treaty Series, 1955.
23 NATO Finance Convention (amended), in FRUS 1952–54, V/2, 1342–3.

desired burden-sharing result of German rearmament was still a long way off. Paradoxically, the Federal Republic in 1955–6 had almost no defense expenditures. In this situation the extension of German financial contributions toward the cost of these forces in Germany seemed a natural and justified request. The stationing countries were faced with fierce domestic criticism about the high cost of their military commitments. To justify the politically necessary extension of troop maintenance this financial burden had to be kept within certain limits, or better, be completely neutralized. If a German army was not established quickly enough, the Federal Republic would continue to pay rather than have a free ride on the Western defense structure.

But one of Germany's major objectives during the EDC debate was to get rid of the occupation costs. Numerous quarrels between Bonn and the occupying powers arose from this issue.[24] The termination of occupation and the establishment of the Paris Accords made further payments – in whatever form – unacceptable to the German government. Widespread public protest against the dismantling of German industries and the confiscation of goods and facilities by the victorious powers after World War II were still political issues. Memories of the humiliating reparations scheme of the Versailles Treaty after World War I added to the negative symbolic value of occupation costs in German public opinion. A continuation of payments for foreign troops after 1955 seemed particularly unjustified because other NATO members with foreign troops on their soil paid no such contributions.

In December 1955, participating for the first time officially at the annual NATO Council meeting, the German delegation was confronted with an unpleasant surprise. Because of the slow pace of German rearmament and the impact of troops on their balance of payments, Britain, France, and the United States demanded the continuation of payments beyond May 1956.[25] The German ministers rejected the requests, and the meeting soon degenerated into an exchange of mutual recriminations. The British minutes recorded that the German finance minister "Dr. [Fritz] Schäffer (who was beginning to get heated) had to say that such a request was quite unacceptable to the Federal Republic. There was no

24 The issue is largely neglected by historical research. See Christoph Henzler, *Fritz Schäffer 1945–67: Eine biographische Studie* (Munich, 1994), and Hubert Zimmermann, "Besatzungskosten, Stationierungskosten, Devisenausgleich: Der Konflikt um die Kosten des Kalten Krieges," in Detlef Junker, ed., *The United States and Germany in the Era of the Cold War, 1945–1990*, 2 vols. (forthcoming).

25 Record of a meeting between Schäffer and allied defense ministers, Dec. 16, 1956, in FRUS 1955–57, IV, 44–9; BA, B126/51520.

legal basis for it, and it was open discrimination."[26] Back home, Schäffer embarrassed the Allies with public announcements that their demands were not in accordance with the NATO treaty and that he would strictly oppose any further payments. The first open argument on the troop-cost issue had begun. It became largely an Anglo-German conflict. The United States, although faced with a much higher financial cost, still profited from the overwhelming strength of its trade and regarded the dollar losses caused by its troops with relative equanimity, as long as the overall balance of payments was under control. It was difficult to imagine that the era of the postwar dollar gap in Europe was already over and would soon give way to a period of dollar glut, fed in great part by American military expenditures in Europe.

BRITISH TROOPS IN EUROPE AND THE BALANCE OF PAYMENTS

The British reacted more strongly than the Americans to Schäffer's refusal even to discuss the issue of troop costs. The German finance minister's intractability touched a sore point in British postwar economic policy, namely, the stability of its currency. All through the postwar decades Britain went to great lengths to safeguard and strengthen the traditional role of sterling as an international reserve currency. This became a primary, if not the most important objective of British foreign economic policy after the war. Many volumes have been written on the wisdom or folly of this policy, all trying to find an answer to the questions of whether sterling policy was a decisive factor in Britain's relative economic decline and what the actual reasons were for the failure to stabilize the British currency.[27] Here I concentrate on the link between British security and sterling policies, and I try to separate myth from reality in the preoccupation of British politicians with the cost of their troops in Europe.

A review of British foreign policy, prepared in 1956 by officials from the Treasury, the Foreign Office, and the Ministry of Defence, stated, after listing Britain's fundamental foreign policy objectives:

26 Record of ministers' meeting in Paris, Dec. 16, 1955, PRO CAB 134/1048, MAC(G)(55).
27 The following list is necessarily selective. Additional works on the subject will be referred to throughout: B. W. E. Alford, *British Economic Performance, 1945–75* (London, 1993); Alec Cairncross and Barry Eichengreen, eds., *Sterling in Decline: The Devaluations of 1931, 1949, and 1967* (Oxford, 1983); Alec Cairncross, *The British Economy Since 1945* (Oxford, 1992); Alec Cairncross, *Managing the British Economy in the 1960s: A Treasury Perspective* (Oxford, 1996); J. C. R. Dow, *The Management of the British Economy, 1945–1960* (Cambridge, 1970); Alan S. Milward, *The European Rescue of the Nation-State* (London, 1992), 347–95; Sidney Pollard, *The Wasting of British Economy: British Economic Policy 1945 to the Present* (London, 1982); Susan Strange, *Sterling and British Policy: A Political Study of an International Currency in Decline* (London, 1971).

There are many areas or aspects of policy in which a failure could make it more difficult for us to attain these aims. But there is one, success in which is a matter of life or death to us as a country. This is the maintenance of the international value of sterling. . . . Success in this is the greatest single contribution we can make to the maintenance of our position in world affairs and to the success of the policies which the free world is seeking to pursue.[28]

The quotation illustrates the curious mix of sentimental commitment, political motivation, and economic reasoning that was characteristic of British postwar monetary policy. During the heyday of the British Empire the international role of sterling had been one of the mainstays of British influence in the world. Until the mid-1950s about 50 percent of all international transactions were still conducted in sterling, and Britain managed the reserves of the numerous countries that formed the so-called Sterling Area.[29] At least as a monetary power, nobody yet equaled Great Britain, apart from the United States.

The financial consequences of World War II, however, had seriously undermined this position. Britain emerged from the war as the most indebted country in the world. Naturally, this provoked grave doubts as to its financial stability and the strength of its currency. Since the conference of Bretton Woods in 1944, where the United States and Britain had worked out a blueprint for the postwar international monetary system, London had struggled to stop the erosion of its monetary power. The expected co-management of international monetary relations together with the Americans proved to be beyond the strength of Britain's economy. It had been envisaged in Bretton Woods that the pound would be made convertible against all major currencies, particularly the dollar, as soon as possible after the war. Indeed, free convertibility was an indispensable attribute of reserve currencies. The first disastrous attempt to re-establish the unrestricted convertibility of the pound in 1947, however, ended in a rush to convert sterling into dollars, which resulted in the merciless plundering of Britain's currency reserves. Even the 1949 devaluation against the dollar did not re-establish confidence in the British currency. The move toward free convertibility had to be postponed for an indefinite period. In the meantime, the chronically weak British currency was shielded against trouble by American help and by the

---

28 "The Future of the U.K. in World Affairs," June 1, 1956, CAB 134/1315, PR(56)3; reprinted in David Goldsworthy, ed., *The Conservative Government and the End of Empire, 1951–57*, pt. 1 (London, 1994), 62–3.

29 Harold James, *International Monetary Cooperation Since Bretton Woods* (Washington, D.C., 1996), 90. The countries of the Colonial Empire and many former colonies, such as Australia, India, Ireland, New Zealand, South Africa, and so forth, all belonged to the Sterling Area.

European Payments Union.[30] Britain's financial policies in the 1950s were designed to escape this dependence on other nations and to allow movement toward free convertibility.

These objectives were repeatedly undermined by recurring balance-of-payments problems and frequent waves of currency speculation that impeded the accumulation of a sufficient level of reserves to back the pound. Another devaluation as a way out of this situation was out of the question. The government also repeatedly considered and rejected a flexible exchange rate for the pound in the early 1950s.[31] During the mid-1950s, however, the British government gradually became more strongly committed to the exchange rate of $2.80 per pound. It was to defend this rate until 1967, despite the increasingly higher cost of doing so. British politicians employed a wide range of arguments in support of this policy: the influence of the London City, which profited from the reserve currency status of sterling; political considerations with regard to the United States and the Sterling Area countries, which were both against devaluation; fear of adverse economic effects at home; and reasons of prestige and the idea that the reserve role of sterling was central to maintaining the international influence of Britain. This last point particularly made successive prime ministers and chancellors of the exchequer fervent defenders of the sterling's exchange rate. The task compelled the government to take a series of restrictive economic measures in the domestic economy and to make constant efforts to trim its external commitments in order to restore confidence in the currency. None of these policies was a decisive success. Sterling remained fundamentally weak.

In a debate lasting to the present, dozens of explanations for this predicament have been extended, such as the backwardness of the British economy and its organizations, the policy of stop-and-go cycles (alternate stimulation and restriction of the economy by the government) to cope with payment deficits, expansive government policies at home and abroad,

---

30 The EPU was an intra-European financial clearing mechanism designed to facilitate trade by means of multilateralizing the settlement of balance-of-payments imbalances. Every month, bilateral balances between the member countries were set off against each other to establish each country's overall position toward the EPU. When a country's position was negative, it was required to correct it through a mixture of debts and hard currency payments. This was advantageous for countries that tended to run huge deficits with other EPU countries. In the absence of the EPU, deficits would be settled entirely with dollars or gold. More recently, the EPU has seen increased interest as a subject of research: Jacob J. Kaplan and Günther Schleiminger, *The European Payments Union: Financial Diplomacy in the 1950s* (Oxford, 1989); Barry Eichengreen, *Reconstructing Europe's Trade and Payments: The European Payments Union* (Manchester, U.K., 1993); Monika Dickhaus, *Die Bundesbank im Westeuropäischen Wiederaufbau 1948–58* (Munich, 1996).
31 Alan S. Milward, "The Origins of the Fixed-Rate Dollar System," in Jaime Reis, ed., *International Monetary Systems in Historical Perspective* (London, 1995), 135–51.

speculation, etc. An additional culprit was particularly prominent in the government and the press: military commitments abroad, specifically in Europe.[32] The 1954 WEU pledge had greatly enhanced Britain's prestige on the continent and served several important political and military objectives, but it appeared to endanger the attainment of a sound and stable monetary position for the pound. Already in 1952 the chancellor of the exchequer, Rab Butler, had stated "that, in the interest of sterling stability, he would not be able to take on substantial foreign exchange losses caused by the commitment in Germany."[33] After the termination of occupation payments the Bank of England was forced to purchase DM on the London exchange market for use by its Rhine Army.[34] According to the British government, this impeded the United Kingdom's ability to amass reserves and forced it to counter the negative effects by making payments within the framework of the European Payments Union (EPU).[35] The Federal Republic appeared to benefit greatly from Allied troop maintenance, boasting an impressive balance-of-payments surplus and an ever stronger currency. Therefore, the argument went, German support-cost payments were a just means to recoup the foreign exchange that Britain lost through aiding European security. It seemed to be a simple trade-off: a stable currency or the stationing of troops in Europe. Formulated differently: Britain faced a choice between the political merits of troop maintenance in Europe and the interest in sterling stability. It turned out that the British government preferred to incur the odium of prolonged and acrimonious negotiations with the Germans rather than take on the cost for the sake of vague political benefits. And yet: Did these perceived alternatives – troops in Europe or sterling stability – correspond to reality? Was the British troop commitment in Europe really an important factor in the pound's weakness?

32 Malcolm Chalmers, *Paying for Defence: Military Spending and British Decline* (London, 1985).
33 Defence and Economic Policy; cabinet memorandum by Mr. Butler, Oct. 3, 1952, CAB 129/55, C(52)320, reprinted in Goldsworthy, ed., *Conservative Government*, 35.
34 The British and French acquired the deutschmarks needed for their troops on the free market. Each month the Americans presented dollar checks at the Bundesbank to acquire marks at an agreed-on exchange rate of DM 4.20. When the dollar came under pressure in the late 1950s the Bundesbank protested this method (if the market price of dollars was only one pfennig lower than the agreed-on price – most of the time it was even less – the Bundesbank would lose $150,000 a month). In the context of the offset negotiations of 1961 the Bundesbank and the United States reached a compromise. Henceforth, the price for troop dollars was fixed anew at the beginning of each month. For documentation on these issues, see NA, RG 59, DF 1960–63, 862a.13.
35 Committee on Services Cost in Germany, CG(56)4, financial secretary memorandum to the Treasury, May 25, 1956, PRO CAB 134/1209.

The figures seem to support the government's interpretation. From 1955 onward the British EPU position, which recorded the British payments balance with the rest of Europe, was negative, showing an accumulated deficit of $1.137 billion between 1955 and 1959.[36] The local foreign exchange cost of British troops in Germany during the same period amounted to about $708 million. Reserves in the second half of the 1950s were between $2.120 billion and $3.231 billion.[37] Thus, at first sight there seems to be a strong impact of troop cost in Europe on the overall payments position.

However, such a straightforward comparison of one factor in the account with an overall payments measure (such as troop cost with EPU deficit) is a very ambiguous indicator. A redeployment of large parts or the whole of the Rhine Army, including equipment, would have had an effect in other areas of the German-British payments statistics. A contraction of domestic demand in Germany might have freed resources for exports, and the opposite effect might have occurred in Britain, thus augmenting German gains from the trade imbalance. In addition, the cost of redeployment would have put a heavy one-time burden on the British balance of payments. Another point is that the United Kingdom realized substantial foreign exchange earnings from foreign troops on its own soil, namely, Americans and Canadians. Their expense amounted to an annual average of about $200 million, which easily matched the British cost in Germany.[38] A British redeployment from the continent was likely to provoke a movement of these troops as reinforcements for allied troops in Germany. For all these reasons consensus was never achieved within the British government regarding the extent to which the balance of payments would benefit from withdrawals; the wide range of estimates is not surprising, given the many variables that would have to have been taken into account.[39] Moreover, it seems that the British estimated the foreign exchange need of their troops rather generously. The Germans repeatedly complained that a British soldier seemed to need considerably more DM than his French or American counterpart to fulfill his task. Thus, the precise impact of the troops on the external balances seems considerably lower than the mere figures of the foreign exchange cost indicate. And,

36 EPU, *Final Report 1951–1958* (OEEC/Paris 1959), 36.
37 For these figures, see Appendix 1, Table 4.
38 Balance of payments, 1946–56, Cmnd. 9871, HMSO 1956, 44; balance of payments, 1956–59, Cmnd. 861, HMSO 1959, 18.
39 For an example of the difficulties of such an estimate, see report by officials: local defense costs in Germany, Jan. 8, 1958, PRO CAB 129/91.

Table 1.1. *Current balance, reserves, and liabilities in the United Kingdom*
(in millions of dollars)

	UK current balance	UK reserves (gold + foreign exchange)	UK total liabilities	Liabilities owed to the Sterling Area
1953	+526	2,518	11,211	7,834
1954	+638	2,762	11,701	8,187
1955	−221	2,120	11,326	8,061
1956	+652	2,133	11,463	8,008
1957	+678	2,273	10,970	7,302
1958	+977	3,069	11,133	7,053

Sources: United Kingdom, Balance of Payments, 1946–56 (2), Cmnd.122, HMSO, April 1957; United Kingdom, Balance of Payments, 1956–9, Cmnd. 861, HMSO, October 1959. British balance-of-payments statistics were subject to numerous, considerable revisions. Because the argument is about the contemporary perception, I chose corresponding statistics.

as we shall see, a big part of this cost was covered by German payments – yet the pound still remained weak.

The real significance of troop cost can be assessed only if it is placed within the larger context of the British monetary problem. It is striking that the official British balance of payments looked rather positive until the mid-1960s. This did not prevent frequent rushes of speculation that denoted a fundamental lack of confidence in sterling on the markets. One major reason for the uncertainty about the position of sterling was the calamitous gap between British reserves and liabilities, the latter always being four times the size of the former.

These huge liabilities are linked to the role of sterling as a reserve currency for the Sterling Area. Most of the claims against Britain resulted from the war and were held by Sterling Area countries, as Table 1.1 shows. Thus, the commitment to the Sterling Area countries or the almost identical British Commonwealth was directly linked to the commitment to preserving the value of sterling. Devaluation would have been a blow for most Sterling Area countries and their reserves. It would have been a disaster not only for British prestige but probably also for its trade because a larger share of British trade was still conducted within the Commonwealth than with Europe. This link caused the ups and downs of Britain's relations to its former dominions to be far more important to the confidence of the market in sterling than the cost of the BAOR. It also explains why Britain chose the troop-cost issue to tackle its currency problem rather than pursuing a policy that might have embarrassed its traditional partners.

Of all these partners, the Americans were crucial because of Britain's ultimate dependence on their financial support. Throughout the postwar period Britain had to earn substantial sums to pay back loans from the United States and international organizations, such as the International Monetary Fund (IMF), the Export-Import Bank, and the EPU. Those loans amounted to about $168 million per year in the mid-1950s, growing precipitously after the Suez crisis, with its disastrous effect on Britain's external balance. Since the great July 1946 loan, which saved the country from its desperate postwar financial situation, Britain had been unable to end its dependence on American money. This dependence was partly necessity, but it also expressed a political choice. The close identification of British sterling policy with the pursuit of harmonious relations with members of the Commonwealth and the United States made it very likely that, in the case that British monetary policy necessitated choices that touched on the interests of foreign countries, Britain would rather accept conflicts with the continental Europe of the Six than with the United States or the Commonwealth. And because taking restrictive measures in the domestic economy to strengthen the external balance was not an easy choice either, troop costs became a preferred target, regardless of their actual responsibility.

The 1954 commitment to station troops on the European continent had been made in a unique situation that conferred a series of political advantages on the United Kingdom. Thereafter, however, British politicians did not have a consistent strategy with which to capitalize on this commitment. Instead, it was resented as a liability. This sentiment increased and decreased in conjunction with the sterling situation, although the cost of the troops in Europe was not a major cause of British monetary difficulties, contrary to the argumentation of the British government. Its absence would not have altered the basic components of the British monetary position and its monetary policy. Nevertheless, Britain continued to pick quarrels with its European partners regarding this issue instead of addressing the deeper causes of its balance-of-payments problem. Troop reductions in Europe and support-cost demands were popular subjects; they seemed to demonstrate activity, but ultimately they were just window dressing. Their fundamental cause was a deep ambiguity toward the political role of the troops in Europe that derived from an indecisiveness in Britain's whole approach toward Europe. Thus, support-cost and troop-level questions became issues of highly symbolic and political value, and expressions of basic lines of British policy in this period.

FOREIGN TROOPS AND THE GERMAN BALANCE OF PAYMENTS

From 1954 on, the German balance of payments was in recurrent surplus. This was due mainly to a large surplus in Germany's trade balance. An often neglected but almost equally important factor was the increasing foreign exchange receipts from foreign troops, notably the Americans. These receipts had a huge influence on the German balance of payments, particularly after the termination of occupation payments. At the end of 1959, when the increasing deficit of the American balance of payments focused attention on the reasons for the German surplus, the Bundesbank (West German central bank) prepared a report that investigated in detail the influence of foreign troops on Germany's external balance.

Between 1950 and 1959 Germany acquired nearly 16.5 billion marks ($3.926 billion) in foreign exchange from foreign troops on German soil, despite the occupation and support costs paid to the stationing countries during this period.[40] Sixty percent of these receipts accrued in the period 1957–9. This reflected a decline of German payments, particularly of those to the United States. Dollar exchanges by American troops alone represented 87 percent of the total. The BAOR, which continued to receive payments, exchanged sterling in the amount of 1.3 billion marks ($309 million). Compared with the accumulated trade surplus of Germany over the period ($5.095 billion), the importance of these receipts for the German external financial position becomes very obvious. The German balance of payments during the period 1950–9 had an overall surplus of about DM 40 billion ($9.524 billion). Theoretically, this amount would have been almost halved were it not for the presence of foreign troops in Germany. The Bundesbank also compared these foreign exchange receipts with the reserves in gold and foreign exchange the Federal Republic accumulated between 1950 and 1959 (DM 21.8 billion; $5.190

---

40 Memorandum on the impact of foreign exchange accruals from foreign troops on the balance of payments and on currency reserves, Dec. 4, 1959, BBA, B330, vol. 10161. American sources put the figure for dollar exchanges, rising steeply after 1956, at DM 15,392.7 million ($3.665 billion) between 1945 and 1960; this corresponds roughly to the Bundesbank figure. See Dewey A. Browder, "The GI and the *Wirtschaftswunder*," *Journal of European Economic History* 22 (1993): 610.

billion). The report concluded that "a considerable part of the augmentation of German monetary reserves can be attributed to the stationing of foreign troops in the Federal Republic."[41]

As in the case of comparing British troop costs to overall balance-of-payments statistics, certain reservations have to be expressed in the German case before establishing too simple an interpretation of the monetary impact. It is impossible to calculate the exact extent of the commitment of German economic resources for services to foreign troops.[42] How did these claims impede the German ability to employ these resources elsewhere, for example in export-oriented industries? Many costs are not reflected in foreign exchange calculations, for example the use of huge areas for military training purposes, housing, and other facilities. Where would the German workforce, whose services made up the biggest part of the troops' foreign exchange cost, have been employed?[43] In this context one might recall that during the late 1950s and 1960s serious labor shortages existed in Germany. Immigrant foreign workers solved the problem; money transfers to their home countries, however, became a major negative factor in the German balance of payments. Complicated side effects like these prevented any agreement between stationing and host countries on the exact extent of the foreign exchange cost of the troops. Usually, however, the Federal Republic accepted the figure presented by its allies. Despite these reservations, it is beyond doubt that foreign, especially American, troop maintenance played a considerable role in the accumulation of German balance-of-payments surpluses. It provided Germany, which had suffered from a critical dollar shortage until the early 1950s, with sufficient liquidity for debt repayments and vital imports, particularly from the United States, without impeding domestic investment. Thus, a phenomenon exclusively related to West Germany's role in the Cold War became an important factor in transforming it into one of the strongest monetary powers in the world. This clear monetary gain would, however, rapidly become a political liability.

---

41 Memorandum, Dec. 4, 1959, BBA, B330, vol. 10161. These figures are related only to the impact of the troops on the German reserve position. Research on the overall economic consequences of foreign troop stationing in Germany is still at a preliminary stage. It is clear, however, that the impact was considerable on both the microeconomic and macroeconomic levels. For example, U.S. forces were counted among Germany's largest employers during the 1950s. For many cities and regions, foreign garrisons remain an important economic factor to this day. See Browder, "GI and the *Wirtschaftswunder*," 601–12.

42 Mendershausen, *Troop-Stationing*, 85; Fried, "Financial Cost," 127–9.

43 About half of the foreign exchange cost was caused by civilian labor. Other services and exchange by soldiers accounted for the rest. See Committee on Services Cost in Germany, CG(56), June 6, 1956, PRO CAB 134/1209.

During 1955, a year in which sterling was under consistent speculative pressure leading to a considerable year-end deficit, the BAOR made provisions for the impending cessation of occupation payments. Considerable savings could be achieved because British troops in Europe under the occupation regime had lived "on a more generous scale than elsewhere because the German government has footed the bill."[44] However, these cuts did not weaken the determination of the British government to have the remaining cost covered by Germany. The British urged the United States to join in an official request for an extension of occupation payments, now called support costs.[45] This proved to be more difficult than expected. The Americans adopted a very cautious attitude based on a clear perception of the political difficulties that new requests would cause for the German government. A certain unease at the prospect that the United States would have to settle the bill in the end by providing further aid to Germany may also have played a role. However, the growing impression that the Federal Republic was not very eager to contribute to its own rearmament led to American acquiescence to British demands. The NATO meeting in December 1955 seemed a convenient moment for the request, but, as we have seen, the action proved abortive. The Germans, represented by the hard-nosed Schäffer, refused to concede to the Allies any legal right to further support payments.

After this inconclusive meeting official requests were formulated by the Three Powers despite West Germany's openly voiced opposition to negotiations. The British aide-mémoire flatly rejected Schäffer's argument that Article IV/4 of the NATO Finance Convention excluded any further cash payments.[46] Pointing out the low level of the German defense effort, it warned of rising domestic pressure in Britain toward reductions in the BAOR should Germany continue to resist payments. The aide-mémoire did nothing to alter the Federal Republic's stance. The Germans rejected the contention that they spent less on defense than all the others and argued that nobody requested payments from other countries with

---

44 Treasury memorandum, July 25, 1955, PRO T 225/424; Committee on Services Cost in Germany memorandum, May 1956, CAB 134/1209.

45 For an extensive account of the support-cost negotiations of 1955–6, see an account of the negotiations leading up to the agreements on support for the forces in the year 1956–7. Hoyer Millar to Lloyd, Aug. 3, 1956, PRO CAB 134/129.

46 U.K. aide-mémoire to German government, Jan. 26, 1956, PA-AA, MB 301/62. Art. IV/4 of the NATO Finance Convention contained a declaration of intent by Germany that, after the end of the occupation period, it would be ready to talk with the stationing countries about further support.

NATO troops on their soil.[47] Mutual irritation mounted considerably during the first months of 1956 as both sides used the press to increase the pressure. The matter became an issue of broad public debate in Britain and West Germany.[48]

Parliaments, newspapers, and private citizens in both countries urged their respective governments to stand firm. The Germans felt that they already shouldered a heavy burden in the Cold War because of the stark fact that their country was divided. The attention of the British concentrated more on the spectacular economic revival of Germany. Strong mutual disdain persisted behind the thin curtain of reconciliation. The support-cost problem did nothing to allay this. In analyzing the support-cost negotiations, one must take into account the psychological situation of the United Kingdom as a victor in the war now having to beg for financial assistance from its former enemy, to whom the British forces also provided military protection. This gave the support-cost question a particularly hostile twist that should not be underestimated. The extensive documentation on the support-cost negotiations shows this sentiment clearly. It formed the background of British frustration with the issue, expressed in the form of recriminations against Germany's resistance to paying for its own security. "The British people, who after all won the war, cannot accept that the Germans are treating the U.K. like dirt, while they have things their own way. They will not agree to keeping British soldiers in Germany, if the Germans do not play the game," Harold Macmillan, then chancellor of the exchequer, said to Dulles. He somewhat prophetically added: "It may take a little longer for the U.S., but ultimately the U.S. may feel that way, too!"[49]

For the moment the major worry of the U.S. government was that the public quarrel might give rise to British procrastination in other policy areas: "When their reserves decline, they become very sensitive about various policies. Their financial difficulties affect all of their policies and contribute to their position on such matters as the Common Market."[50] The Americans agreed with the British argument that the Germans were having a free ride on the Western defense machinery. They therefore decided to assume a tougher stance and agreed to a common presentation by the three allied ambassadors at the Auswärtiges Amt (West

47 Finance Ministry memorandum on stationing costs, June 21, 1956, BA, B126/34100.
48 Blankenhorn to Adenauer on conversation with Steel, Feb. 20, 1956, BA, Blankenhorn papers, 60; Kirkpatrick to Adenauer, Apr. 13, 1956, ibid., 61/1; *FAZ*, Feb. 7, 1956.
49 Memorandum of conversation, Dec. 11, 1956, in FRUS 1955–57, IV, 127.
50 Telegram from the North Atlantic Council meeting, Dec. 17, 1955, in FRUS 1955–57, XXVI, 62.

German Foreign Office), with U.S. Ambassador James B. Conant taking the lead. He bluntly accused the Germans of leaving it to others to pay for their defense and demanded the immediate resumption of support-cost negotiations.[51] Still, the German position, represented by Schäffer, did not change. Then Dulles, French Premier Guy Mollet, and British Prime Minister Anthony Eden wrote simultaneously to German Chancellor Konrad Adenauer expressing their concern about the Federal Republic's position.[52] At this point it became obvious to the German government that the situation might get out of hand. Schäffer came under increasing attack from his colleagues for his stubborn policy, and Adenauer told him to stop any further public comment on the issue. He and Foreign Minister Heinrich von Brentano came to the conclusion that concessions were unavoidable.[53] Consequently, the Finance Ministry was "relieved" of its responsibility for the question and the Foreign Ministry took over. Schäffer did not yield; he even threatened to resign. But in the decisive cabinet meeting Adenauer argued that in the interest of harmonious relations with Germany's most important allies, troop-cost payments were unavoidable. Despite Schäffer's opposition, the cabinet decided to honor the requests.[54]

At the end of April, Brentano went to London and offered an $83 million cash payment for 1956–7 and an advance payment of $107 million for arms purchases. He informed the British government that the Federal Republic preferred to continue the talks bilaterally to avoid another staging of the three Allied ambassadors at the Auswärtiges Amt.[55] The British, exasperated by the slow progress of the talks, agreed. Force-fully, they made the Germans aware of the political importance of the subject. The German minutes noted: "Warning by the chancellor of the exchequer that we are heading toward a catastrophe – break-up of NATO, pull-back of British troops – if an acceptable solution is not found rapidly. Very heavy strains on Anglo-German relations due to this problem. . . .

51 An Account . . . , Aug. 3, 1956, PRO CAB 134/129; Finance Ministry on representation made by allied ambassadors, Mar. 2, 1956, BA, B126/34100.
52 Mollet to Adenauer, Apr. 26, 1956; Dulles to Adenauer, Apr. 26, 1956; and minutes of cabinet meeting, Apr. 25, 1956; all in BA, B136/3131.
53 Brentano to Adenauer, Mar. 1956, reprinted in Arnulf Baring, ed., *Sehr verehrter Herr Bundes-kanzler! Heinrich von Brentano im Briefwechsel mit Konrad Adenauer 1949–1964* (Hamburg, 1974), 188; Erhard–Adenauer correspondence, Erhard to Adenauer, Feb. 29, 1956, LES; Adenauer to Schäffer, Mar. 2, 1956, BA, B136/3131; Brentano to Adenauer, Apr. 13, 1956, BA, Brentano papers, 156/5; Brentano to Adenauer, Apr. 20, 1956, ibid., 156/6.
54 Schäffer to Herwarth, Feb. 9, 1956, BA, B102/51520; excerpt of minutes of cabinet meeting, June 6, 1956, BA, B126/34100.
55 Adenauer to Macmillan, Apr. 26, 1956, PRO T 234/30.

When the support-cost question is resolved, we could count upon a real intensification of economic and political relations between both countries."[56]

During the course of the talks it became clear to the British that demanding a sum larger than that of the year before was unrealistic because of the results of Germany's parallel negotiations with the United States, France, and other countries. The Americans, with their much larger force, had accepted an amount of $155 million.[57] Even this had been approved by the German cabinet only after very strong pressure by the U.S. government and against the continued resistance of Schäffer, who denounced this as "eternalizing of the occupation statute."[58] Finally, Britain settled for a $95 million (or £34 million) cash payment and a secret declaration of intent by the German government to buy British arms in the amount of $524 million during the following nine months.[59] In 1957 Germany paid a grand total of $357 million (or DM 1.5 billion) to the stationing countries. Their original requests had amounted to $571 million; payments for the previous year had totaled $762 million.

The agreement was criticized in both the British and German parliaments. British parliamentarians complained that the payments fell far short of previous payments and of the actual cost of the troops. Several speakers demanded a withdrawal of the BAOR.[60] In the German parliament, Brentano met the attacks of the opposition by arguing that it had been a test of Germany's international reliability. He stated that he had left the allies in no doubt that these would be the last payments.[61] The monetary consequences were minor, and the sterling problem remained. Troop costs, however, had become an increasingly disturbing factor. The poisoning of mutual relations therefore was the most important consequence of the whole affair, "which bid[s] fair to do more damage to Anglo–German

---

56 Minutes on Brentano trip to London, June 5, 1956, PA-AA, Dept. 304/31.
57 CM(56), 45th conclusions, meeting of June 21, 1956, PRO CAB 128/30. The talks were concluded quickly to spare Adenauer a discussion on this problem during his June visit to the United States. For the results of these talks, see U.S. aide-mémoire to AA, June 6, 1956, PA-AA, Dept. 301/95; France received $66 million after having to admit that 30,000 of its troops destined for NATO were engaged in Algeria; see note, May 28, 1956, PA-AA, Dept. 301/95. This relatively generous treatment was criticized in the British press and parliament. Belgium, Denmark, the Netherlands, and Canada also secured small amounts.
58 Finance Ministry memorandum, June 8, 1956, BA, B126/51521.
59 U.S. aide-mémoire to federal government, June 29, 1956, PA-AA, Dept. 301/95; Brentano to British Embassy, Bonn, June 29, 1956, PRO FO 371/124616.
60 Hansard, House of Commons, 5th series, Vol. 555, 866–70. The press echoed this criticism. *The Times* called the agreement "deeply disappointing" (June 30, 1956) and *The Economist* denounced the negotiations as a "sad effort," July 7, 1956, 14.
61 *VDB*, 2. period 1953–57; 155th meeting, 8416 B.

relations than any single issue for a long time."[62] It would have been tolerable if the problem had disappeared. But it persisted, and the proposed weapon purchases proved to be an empty promise. The delay in German rearmament increased Allied discontent with the agreement.

The Germans, however, felt that the agreements had done little to secure a stable Allied troop presence.[63] Furthermore, they felt obliged to continue payments that closely resembled occupation costs and as such were highly criticized by the public. The fact that the German government had been defeated on the issue points to another characteristic of postwar policy for which the support-cost negotiations are an excellent barometer: They became a continuing reminder of Germany's status as a "semi-sovereignty" after 1955. It was not only the restrictions of the Paris Accords but also the fact that Germany had voluntarily accepted dependence on continued Allied troop presence that were to foster Germany's compliance with the Allies in other areas, usually in the area of economic concessions. Until the formulation of Ostpolitik in the late 1960s Germany coped with the fact that, compared with its Cold War rhetoric, its actual contribution to defense remained relatively low. This discrepancy became obvious almost immediately after West Germany formally became part of the transatlantic security system.

GERMANY'S COLD WAR POLITICAL ECONOMY AND
THE REARMAMENT CRISIS OF 1956

The support-cost problem had hardly been solved when West Germany was once again in the hot seat: This time the reason was the delay in its rearmament program. The German government had to openly admit that its ambitious plans were unrealistic and that the creation of a German army would proceed much more slowly than promised. This failure became the foundation of the Allied argument for a continuation of German payments to support their military commitment to the defense of Europe. How was it possible that prospering and fervently anticommunist West Germany displayed such a conspicuous lack of urgency in its rearmament effort, even though it had taken so long to put all necessary contractual arrangements in place? My answer concentrates less on the details of the rearmament process and the protracted practical prob-

---

62 An account . . . , Aug. 3, 1956, PRO CAB 134/129.
63 Report by Ambassador Herwarth, London, July 4, 1956, PA-AA, Dept. 301/95.

lems that accompanied it;[64] instead, my intent is to outline the broader political and economic reasons for the delay, to show how they influenced the troop-cost debate, and to point to some of the fundamental political and economic factors underlying West Germany's remilitarization in the 1950s.

The rearmament plans drawn up during the EDC negotiations had foreseen the buildup of a fully equipped 500,000-man army from 1955 to 1959. Despite deep doubts of the West German Finance and Defense Ministries as to the practical feasibility of this endeavor, in 1955 Adenauer personally promised the Americans that the schedule would be kept as agreed.[65] By the end of the year, it had become obvious to many experts in Bonn and elsewhere that this was a very optimistic commitment. Publicly, however, the government incessantly reaffirmed its intention to create the promised forces within three years, although it had no coherent overall plan for financing the rearmament effort. Instead, it clung to the cost estimate of DM 9 billion ($2.143 billion) a year that had been fixed during the early 1950s, despite great uncertainty about whether this sum was adequate. Not surprisingly, the financial planning for rearmament was revised continually during 1955 and 1956. For example, the projected overall cost shrank from DM 45 billion ($10.7 billion) to DM 32 billion ($7.6 billion) from January to June 1956. Some earlier estimates had predicted figures of DM 60–80 billion and more.[66] These downward revisions reflected the pessimistic view of the Finance Ministry regarding availability of funds and the time schedule of the enterprise. At no time were the Allies able to obtain a clear picture of German financial planning. No wonder; the German government itself had no real idea of how much rearmament would cost. In any case, German hopes that American aid would cover much of the cost were wiped out by a sharp U.S. aide-mémoire in early 1956. It stipulated the end of grant aid to the Federal Republic on the grounds that the Germans themselves were not doing enough for their own defense.[67]

One fact seemed particularly galling: The delay obviously was not due to a lack of money. In 1954 the German government earmarked the

64 On these issues, see *MGFA I–IV*.
65 Schäffer to Adenauer, Aug. 31, 1955; Schäffer-Tuthill conversation, July 23, 1955; Adenauer to Conant, Sept. 5, 1955; all in BA, B136/2163.
66 BMF memorandum on defense planning, Jan. 25, 1956, BA, B126/51520; BMF memorandum: military budget, June 28, 1956, BA, B126/51521; Abelshauser, "Causes and Consequences," 317–18.
67 U.S. aide-mémoire to Germany, Mar. 15, 1956, BA, Blankenhorn papers, 61b/1.

following funds to be spent on defense for the successive four years: the so-called *Juliusturm* ($1.2 billion),[68] U.S. grants ($950 million), and a provision for four years from the federal budget ($8.57 billion).[69] Only a fraction of that amount ($194 million) was spent before the end of 1956. Occupation costs and support-cost payments amounted to $1.267 billion.[70] The rest of the appropriated funds were simply added to the *Juliusturm*. In view of these figures and the growing monetary reserves of the Federal Republic, German arguments that rearmament might seriously damage its economic progress and that the continuation of support-cost payments would endanger the creation of a German army seemed quite exaggerated.

In mid-1956 the German government realized that it would have to admit the awkward truth about the delay. Adenauer looked for a scapegoat. In the summer of 1956 the minister of defense, Theodor Blank, had promised NATO in writing that all force goals would be met as planned. At the end of October, at NATO's annual review meeting, the Germans had to put their cards on the table. To "spare" Blank embarrassment, a new defense minister was installed shortly before the meeting. This was the former minister for nuclear questions, Franz Josef Strauss, who had coveted the job for years. In the NATO meeting Strauss told Germany's partners what they had already suspected. The German conscription period would be reduced from eighteen to twelve months. Publicly, the government justified this with alleged Allied troop-reduction plans. Strauss stressed the difficult psychological situation of a demilitarized and defeated country that rendered military service unpopular.[71] The step, publicly announced without prior consultation with Bonn's NATO allies, met with strong criticism from the Americans and British.[72] Furthermore, Strauss informed his colleagues, procurement planning for the German forces would be stretched to take into account the requirements created

<hr>

68 The *Juliusturm* was a growing amount of unspent funds accumulated by the federal government due to unexpectedly high tax revenues and the delay in rearmament. It was named after the tower in Berlin where the German Reich deposited French reparation payments after the 1870–1 war.

69 Abelshauser, "Causes and Consequences," 316; Christian Greiner, "Die militärische Eingliederung der Bundesrepublik Deutschland in die WEU und in die NATO, 1954–57," in *MGFA III* (Munich, 1993), 641–58.

70 Finance Ministry memorandum on defense expenditures, Dec. 7, 1956, BA, Blankenhorn papers, 70/3.

71 Draft of speech at NATO Council meeting, Oct. 22, 1956, ibid., 68/2.

72 Blankenhorn to Adenauer, Oct. 9, 1956, ibid., 67/1; memorandum of discussion at the 284th NSC meeting, May 10, 1956, in FRUS 1955–57, IV, 80. The Americans tried in vain to warn the Germans against a shorter conscription period. See Brentano–Dulles conversation, May 4, 1956, and Strauss–Elbrick conversation, May 14, 1956, in FRUS 1955–57, XXVI, 93–8.

by new strategic developments and the latest technological advances. He had in mind the discussion about the "New Look" in the Eisenhower administration and the massive equipping of U.S. forces in Europe with tactical nuclear weapons. The most sensitive announcement was the admission that due to practical problems the buildup of the promised conventional army would be considerably delayed, despite the well-known stockpile of unallocated money Schäffer had accumulated. The federal government informed the United States before the NATO meeting that manpower targets were to be reduced to "80,000 instead of 96,000 by the end of 1956 and to between 175,000 and 200,000 by the end of 1957."[73] Strauss, in his speech, gave an even smaller figure.

The admission of failure put the German government in an awkward position. After all, rearmament had been the price for the Federal Republic's sovereignty. It appeared that, after having achieved its political objectives, it now was shirking its political and economic commitments. NATO Ambassador Herbert Blankenhorn wrote: "At all events, we should avoid the impression that the delays in the buildup, which we cannot deny, are taking place only because we don't want to impede the extraordinary economic progress of the Federal Republic. It will be difficult, in any case, to counter the argument that in this and the next year we will make much less of a sacrifice for defense than other nations and that therefore the support-cost question should be dealt with again."[74]

Blankenhorn was right: West Germany's NATO partners reacted angrily. The official German arguments did not convince them. Partly supplementing their own conventional troops with German forces had been a major aspect of the EDC debate, and this prospect was, at least temporarily, postponed to a future date. Frustration understandably ran high, fueled by the high performance of the German economy while other NATO partners struggled with the defense burden. Whereas the United States and Great Britain seemed stuck with their troops in Europe, Germany appeared to be concerned mainly with accumulating foreign exchange reserves instead of creating a strong conventional army. It comes as no surprise that this situation had a decisive impact on the support-cost debate.

What were the real reasons for the rearmament crisis? The causes for the failure were more complex than the official announcements suggest. It is true that one important factor was the delay in the decision about

---

73 American Embassy, Bonn, to DOS, Oct. 16., 1956, in FRUS 1955–57, XXVI, 168.
74 Blankenhorn to Adenauer, Oct. 9, 1956, BA, Blankenhorn papers, 67/1.

the whole political organization of the defense effort, caused by the defeat of the EDC project. As a result, previous plans for the practical implementation of rearmament became obsolete.[75] Even in 1955 blueprints for the structure of the German military contribution were extremely sketchy. Necessary legislative action by the federal government had to be rushed through parliamentary procedures. This was not easily done. The whole rearmament process was heavily criticized by the Social Democrats, who were backed by a strong popular movement against Germany's remilitarization.[76] It is also true that practical problems abounded, such as delays in building barracks, difficulties in acquiring land for them, and the slow process of recruitment.[77] Allied troops occupied much of what remained of the prewar barracks and training areas. Considerable disorganization existed within the German defense ministry and in the cooperation between the other ministries. All these bottlenecks contributed to the delay; in the end, however, they were not decisive.

The major causes of the rearmament crisis lay in the German government's fundamental doubts regarding the economic and military conditions of a conventional buildup. On closer view it comes as no surprise that conventional rearmament no longer was a high priority for West Germany. Germany was now integrated into and protected by the Alliance. Thus, it had achieved its basic foreign policy goal without having to pay the price, German manpower, beforehand. Conventional rearmament was neither popular with the people nor did it fit into the general strategic trend of the Alliance, which increasingly stressed nuclear deterrence. The German government adopted its own version of Eisenhower's New Look policy, which aimed at replacing expensive conventional armaments with cheaper nuclear weapons. This change was symbolized by the replacement of Blank by Strauss. Strauss, now in the post for which he considered himself the ideal man, immediately set "new priorities." His plans to equip the German army (Bundeswehr) with nuclear delivery systems, and possibly with nuclear weapons, incited violent public debates in Germany.[78] "Quality instead of quantity" became his often-

---

75 Abelshauser, "Causes and Consequences," 312.
76 On domestic opposition to German rearmament, see Hans-Erich Volkmann, "Die innenpolitische Dimension Adenauerscher Sicherheitspolitik in der EVG Phase," in *MGFA II* (Munich, 1990), 235–604; Hans Ehlert, "Innenpolitische Auseinandersetzungen um die Wehrverträge 1954–56," in *MGFA III* (Munich, 1993), 235–560.
77 Strauss speech at the NATO meeting, Oct. 22, 1956, BA, Blankenhorn papers, 68/2; see also Greiner, "Militärische Eingliederung," 674–5.
78 The exact extent of Strauss's intentions is still hotly debated. For an assessment, see Pertti Ahonen, "Franz Josef Strauss and the German Nuclear Question, 1956–62," *Journal of Strategic Studies* 18 (1995): 25–41.

cited slogan, not only with respect to his nuclear plans but also regarding the conventional buildup.[79] He was unwilling to finance the application of outdated strategic concepts when Germany's allies were putting increasing emphasis on nuclear warfare, rocket technology, and sophisticated air power. Delaying rearmament, even at the risk of provoking a crisis with the Allies, was a logical move under these circumstances.

This reasoning was decisively reinforced by economic considerations. The money saved because of the delay was spent partly in politically more opportune ways, such as social expenditures.[80] A costly reform of the pension system was undertaken. Refugees, veterans, and victims of the Nazi regime received generous financial aid. After all, 1957 was an election year. The rest was stockpiled to cover future burdens, on which Schäffer tirelessly insisted. Blank, during his tenure, was not able to prevent funds not used for rearmament from being diverted to these purposes, despite his protests against Schäffer's tightfisted attitude.[81] Schäffer supplied the economic rationale behind the rearmament crisis and felt that remilitarization could easily interfere with the phenomenal economic progress of the Federal Republic. He feared above all that spending the billions in the *Juliusturm* on defense would foster inflation, which was a distressing prospect for both German financial experts and the public. The president of the Bundesbank, Wilhelm Vocke, supported Schäffer's arguments: "[The] fact is that an acceleration of defense expenditures in combination with the release of billions for new federal programs plus tax reductions, and all that in connection with continuing demands for higher wages . . . is enough to damage the strength of the currency."[82] The danger of inflation was aggravated by the fact that industrial production in Germany had almost no free capacity. This was one motivation behind Schäffer's promotion of arms purchases abroad.[83] They unburdened the booming economy and transferred surplus foreign exchange abroad. Even most industrial leaders agreed with the government.[84]

---

79 Greiner, "Militärische Eingliederung," 822–5; Wolfgang Krieger, *Franz Josef Strauss: Der barocke Demokrat aus Bayern* (Göttingen, 1995), 34–42.
80 Otmar Emminger, *D-Mark, Dollar, Währungskrisen: Erinnerungen eines ehemaligen Bundesbankpräsidenten* (Stuttgart, 1986), 78. On the expansion of welfare benefits, see Hans-Günter Hockerts, *Sozialpolitische Entscheidungen im Nachkriegsdeutschland: Alliierte und deutsche Sozialversicherungspolitik 1945 bis 1957* (Stuttgart, 1980).
81 See, e.g., the controversy in Blank to Chancellor's Office regarding stationing costs in 1956, July 13, 1956; and Schäffer to Chancellor's Office, July 18, 1956; both in BA, B126/34100.
82 Vocke to Adenauer, Apr. 20, 1956, BA, B136/3320.
83 Finance Ministry memorandum on defense planning, Jan. 25, 1956, BA, B126/51520.
84 Federation of German Industrialists (BDI) memorandum, Jan. 16, 1956, BA, B102/57514; note on meeting Erhard, Strauss, BDI, Jan. 22, 1957, ibid. It might also have been detrimental to the

Labor shortages also made the shortening of the conscription period a reasonable step, and this was a major aspect of the decision.[85] In the cabinet, Adenauer stated his own purpose: He was well aware of the unpopularity of long military service in West Germany and undertook the move with a view to the next elections.[86] Domestic priorities rated higher than regard for alliance affairs. It was the *Wirtschaftswunder* (economic miracle) and not *Westintegration* (integration into the West) that now became the major factor of identification and rehabilitation in the eyes of the German public. The necessary security framework had been put in place. Now the policy of economic growth took priority, conflicting with the economic exigencies of rearmament. This shift in policy priorities from the search for security in the alliance to a promotion of economic growth within the European framework became a source of potential conflict with the United Kingdom and, later, the United States, whereas the search for military security, resulting in the re-creation of a German army, had tended to worry France. The French profited from the economic rise of Germany within the framework of the European Community, from which Britain was excluded. This was the background to the Anglo-German problems and to French-German harmony during the successive years, and the troop-cost conflict was to illustrate that clearly. In fact, the French seemed not much troubled by the delays in German rearmament – contrary to the Americans and the British.

After the NATO meeting in December 1956 Washington and London exerted increasing pressure on Strauss and the German government. They succeeded in putting new steam into the stuttering effort, although when Strauss tried to get more money released for rearmament, he, like Blank, met with Schäffer's resistance. The finance minister was not willing to commit funds from the *Juliusturm* prematurely and stubbornly defended his reserve. Strauss consequently identified him as the main culprit in the slow progress of the buildup.[87] He was not the only one to criticize Schäffer's tight financial policy. Adenauer and Brentano had already blamed his resistance on the question of support costs for the strained relations with England. Schäffer's insistence on restricted public spending

willingness of the industry to produce weapons when they were clearly told that arms production would remain under the tight control of politicians.
85 Andrew Birtle, *Rearming the Phoenix: U.S. Military Assistance to the FRG, 1950–60* (New York, 1991), 323–5.
86 Günther Buchstab, ed., *Adenauer: Wir haben wirklich etwas geschaffen; Die Protokolle des CDU-Bundesvorstands 1953–57* (Düsseldorf, 1990), 1031.
87 Schäffer memorandum, Sept. 18, 1957, BA, Schäffer papers, 34; Schäffer memorandum on formation of the cabinet 1957, Oct. 1957, ibid., 37.

and on holding reserves for future problems made his stance within the cabinet increasingly unpopular and finally cost him his job in October 1957.[88] Although the most fervent "antispending" minister had disappeared, it still took some time and much trouble before the creation of the German army gained momentum. The delay began to be overcome at the close of the 1950s, although probably not fully until after the Berlin Wall Crisis in August 1961, and the strength of the German army never reached the level of allied expectations.

Not unexpectedly, the delay in German rearmament was seen as an incentive to make new support-cost demands on the Federal Republic. The United States and the United Kingdom felt trapped by the immobility of the political situation and by the temporary foundering of their hopes that a German army could provide alternative conventional manpower. One solution to this dilemma was a continued German financial contribution to the conventional effort of Britain and the United States. Another was to increase reliance on the cheaper, "more bang for the buck" nuclear deterrent. In this sense, the support-cost debate paralleled the discussion that started during these years about the nuclearization of the Alliance. Both were sparked by a will to economize in military budgets and to alleviate the burden of Europe's defense on the British and American economies. If the Germans would not provide the necessary conventional forces, they had to pay for Allied troops and accept the defense of their territory by nuclear weapons, over which they had little control. This bitter pill was not easily swallowed, as shown by the incessant debate during the late 1950s and throughout the 1960s about the nuclear status of Germany and the financial management of the alliance.

---

88 Note from June 30, 1957, on a cabinet meeting of June 19, 1957, ibid., 39; Hans-Peter Schwarz, *Adenauer: Der Staatsmann* (Stuttgart, 1991), 354.

2

The British "New Look" and Anglo–German Relations

Indications that the British government would reopen the debate on troop costs multiplied during the late summer of 1956. In addition, rumors about impending reductions in British forces in Europe circulated widely. Overshadowed as those reports were by German rearmament problems and later by the Suez and Hungarian crises, they did not receive much attention. However, the contradictions between Britain's security policies, its monetary objectives, and its relations with Europe, the Commonwealth, and the United States were bound to emerge in the issue of British troops in Europe. This chapter discusses the support-cost negotiations of 1956–7 against the backdrop of the British defense review initiated in 1956. London saw itself confronted with difficult choices regarding its relations with the rest of Europe if it wanted to bring its economic resources in line with its security commitments. The consequences of these choices, which were reflected in the troop-level and support-cost debates, as well as in the failure of British arms exports to Germany, had a deep impact on British-European relations.

At the meeting of ministers of the North Atlantic Council in December 1956 the United Kingdom started a new round of support-cost negotiations. Macmillan, then chancellor of the exchequer, personally attended the meeting and gave a candid summary of Britain's situation. He emphasized the foreign-exchange problem facing the United Kingdom, the enormous resources it employed for defense worldwide, and compared this with West Germany's deficient military effort. Macmillan urged NATO to undertake a strategic reappraisal that in theory might have led to less reliance on conventional troops and to a stronger emphasis on nuclear weapons. He left no doubt as to the seriousness of his

45

statements: "We are prepared to pay the budgetary cost of appropriate forces to be maintained on the continent. But we cannot accept responsibility for payments across the exchanges. . . . I must . . . make it quite clear that unless our overseas costs can be met, the future of our overseas contribution to NATO forces will be jeopardized."[1] Thus, the British government openly declared its view that its security commitment in Europe was to a large degree dependent on the status of sterling. Nobody, least of all the U.S. government, was really surprised by Macmillan's statement. In July 1956, as the American government discussed similar ideas, Anthony Eden wrote to President Eisenhower to propose revising NATO strategy in a way that might enable the United Kingdom to cut its troop deployments on the continent.[2] Arguing the increasing importance of nuclear weapons in modern warfare and citing Britain's difficult balance-of-payments position, he urged a reappraisal of NATO's military policy and suggested that costly conventional forces be replaced by cheaper nuclear weapons. However, the Americans, after a debate along the same lines within the U.S. government, were impressed by the strong negative reaction within the Alliance to U.S. plans to reduce troops in Europe. They concluded that the political consequences of a military policy that relied solely on nuclear weapons would be very undesirable.[3] But the American debate had left the British with the impression that the United States was ambiguous on this issue and would not totally oppose a revision of the British defense posture. Thus, even when the Americans became more outspoken in their criticism of British blueprints for NATO reform, the British decided to continue with their initiative. The major reason for their determination was the Suez crisis.

In late 1956 Britain and France were pressured by both the United States and the Soviet Union to retreat from the canal zone, which they had occupied militarily after it was nationalized by Egyptian President Gamal Abdel Nasser. Not only Britain's military but also its economic vulnerability were made clear during the crisis. The United States had reinforced its arguments against a continuation of the occupation with a temporary refusal to support the British currency.[4] Apart from the blow

---

1 For the full text of Macmillan's statement, see record of NATO Council meeting, Dec. 13, 1956, BA, Blankenhorn papers, 71/1. A telegram-style version is in FRUS 1955–57, IV, 151–5.
2 FRUS 1955–57, IV, 92.
3 Dulles memorandum to Eisenhower: U.S. position on review of NATO strategy and force levels, Oct. 1, 1956, ibid., 96–8.
4 For Washington's use of financial pressure during the Suez crisis, see Alan P. Dobson, *The Politics of the Anglo–American Special Relationship* (Brighton, U.K., 1988), 166–73; Lewis Johnman, "Defending the Pound: The Economics of the Suez Crisis, 1956," in Anthony Gorst, Lewis Johnman, and

to British prestige, Suez had provoked a run on the pound and a tremendous loss of foreign exchange reserves. In November and December, Britain lost $410 million of its reserves, an enormous drain on pre-Suez reserves of about $2.25 billion.[5] To stop the run the British government borrowed $1.3 billion from the IMF and took up a loan of $700 million from the Export-Import Bank. The loans were approved by the Americans only after Britain had agreed to a cease-fire in the canal zone. The repayment of these debts weighed heavily on Britain's external balance in the following years.

However, even before Suez, apprehensions had mounted in the British government that principal foreign policy objectives – to sustain Britain's role as third power in the world and to preserve sterling's role as a reserve currency – were seriously prejudiced by the pressing burden of military expenditure. In March 1956 Macmillan and Defense Minister Sir Walter Monckton urged on Eden "a reappraisal at the highest level of the whole basis on which our defense policy should rest."[6] This reappraisal was to bring British resources and its defense posture into line. The *Report on the Future of the United Kingdom in World Affairs*, dated June 1, 1956, and prepared by treasury, foreign office, and defense officials, was the result.[7] The report stated that the United Kingdom had an overloaded defense structure, placing the economy under constant strain. A concentration on the essential political goals of defense policy was indispensable to avoid further damage. From these essentials – keeping the Americans in Europe, developing closer cooperation with North America, and maintaining the cohesion of the Commonwealth – continental Europe was conspicuously absent.[8] A reform of the traditional economic foundations of British military policy would, in particular, have to take into account the exigencies of the currency situation. Savings were to be achieved in places where foreign exchange losses were high in proportion to political and military gains. The foreign exchange cost of the forces assigned to NATO was now estimated to be $190.4 million a year for the BAOR and the Second Tactical Air Force.[9] According to the report, this was too high a price for the political gains of troop stationing in Europe. Therefore, reductions in

W. Scott Lucas, eds., *Postwar Britain, 1945–64: Themes and Perspectives* (London, 1989), 166–81; Diane B. Kunz, *The Economic Diplomacy of the Suez Crisis* (Chapel Hill, N.C., 1991).

5 The December losses were obscured in official announcements by adding the first part of the IMF loan to Britain's reserves; see KCA 1956, 15239; and KCA 1957, 15307.

6 Defence Policy: Macmillan and Monckton memorandum to Eden, Mar. 20, 1956, reprinted in Goldsworthy, ed., *Conservative Government*, 60.

7 Ibid., 61–81.   8 Ibid., 67.

9 CP(56)269, minister of defence memorandum: U.K. forces in Germany, Nov. 28, 1956, PRO CAB 129/84.

defense expenditure "must be found largely in our expenditure on our defense in Europe. It is there that the greatest scope exists for reducing demands on our engineering industry, our military manpower, our technical and scientific resources and our foreign exchange, in the interests of re-establishing our economic strength."[10]

The problem was how to achieve such a reform and the corresponding reduction without embarrassing the United States or damaging British relations with third countries too much.[11] If NATO had adopted a new strategic concept based mainly on nuclear weapons and requiring just a "tripwire" force of conventional troops on the Cold War border, the task would have been much easier. This was the background of Eden's letter to Eisenhower. As outlined above, it soon became clear that the Americans were less than enthusiastic about the British proposals.[12] They informed London that a strategic discussion in the alliance at that moment would endanger congressional legislation on foreign aid as well as the legislative procedures concerning rearmament in the German parliament.[13] They therefore urged London to delay presenting their plans for review in NATO committees. The tense international climate, marked by the Suez Crisis and the Hungarian uprising, made a fast British move difficult anyway, and the British also feared that premature reduction announcements would seriously impair the further payment of support costs by Germany. There was no hope that reductions could be started before late 1957, and the previous agreement ended in May 1957. A follow-up agreement therefore seemed necessary in any case. All these considerations slowed down the British initiative.

Prior to the NATO meeting in December 1956, the British discussed their problem with the U.S. delegation headed by Dulles. British Foreign Minister Selwyn Lloyd stated that they "could not keep troops in Germany unless a way was found to reimburse the British for this expense." After Dulles asked: "Unless the Germans pay for it?" Lloyd replied: "Unless someone pays for it!"[14] Ignoring this broad hint, Dulles acknowledged the gravity of the situation and agreed with Britain that Germany was not doing enough for its own defense. However, he warned of the effect of reductions on the German electorate. He also declared

10 Defence Policy: Macmillan and Monckton memorandum to Eden, Mar. 20, 1956, reprinted in Goldsworthy, ed., *Conservative Government*, 60.
11 Cabinet Policy Review Committee minutes, June 9, 1956, CAB 134/1315, reprinted in Goldsworthy, ed., *Conservative Government*, 86.
12 Cabinet meeting minutes, June 19, 1956, PRO CAB 128/30.
13 U.S. memorandum to U.K., June 29, 1956, in FRUS 1955–57, IV, 87–8.
14 Anglo-American meeting, Dec. 11, 1956, in FRUS 1955–57, IV, 123n2.

himself against reliance on the British version of the "tripwire" strategy that, in the opinion of the United States, placed too much emphasis on nuclear deterrence. This did not impress the British, and they threatened openly to break the WEU treaty, hinting that American technological support for the British nuclear program might be a solution.[15] This plea was a further consequence of the defense review being conducted by the British government. If the United Kingdom, despite the projected cuts, was to retain a military capability compatible with its self-perception as the third power in the world, recourse to increasing its nuclear potential seemed the only way.[16] However, U.S. financial and technical support was necessary. Particularly regarding missile technology, the United Kingdom had fallen far behind. Mischievous jokes suggested that the next British rocket should be constructed in such a way as to allow highly trained athletes to carry it into enemy territory.[17] In December 1956 the U.S. delegation remained ambivalent regarding assistance in this area. Soon afterward, however, the Americans began to expand their nuclear cooperation with Britain.[18] It is unlikely that this was linked to a British promise to limit their defense cuts in Europe. The quid pro quo was base rights for the Americans in Britain, and the important objective was to repair Anglo-American relations after Suez. However, the troop connection would soon play an increasing role. At the end of the aforementioned meeting, both sides agreed that it would be better to wait for the German reaction to the new support-cost demands before the British committed themselves to a fixed position on reductions in Europe.[19]

THE SUPPORT-COST NEGOTIATIONS, 1956–1957

The British position on approaching the Germans was clear: The reform of their defense structure was not negotiable, but the readiness to compromise on particular points would be influenced by the German willingness to contribute to the foreign exchange cost: "Decisions concerning withdrawal of our troops were therefore not primarily dependent on the

---

15 Ibid., 130–1; see also Anglo–American talks, Dec. 11, 1956, PRO PREM 11/1270.

16 For an excellent treatment of this topic, see Ian Clark, *Nuclear Diplomacy and the Special Relationship: Britain's Deterrent and America, 1957–62* (Oxford, 1994).

17 Quoted from Andrew N. Porter, "Downhill All the Way: 13 Tory Years," in Richard Coopey, Nick Tiratsoo, and Steven Fielding, eds., *The Wilson Governments, 1964–70* (London, 1993), 21.

18 An Anglo–American agreement on the proliferation of medium-range missiles was signed in July 1958. See Timothy Botti, *The Long Wait: The Forging of the Anglo–American Nuclear Alliance, 1945–58* (New York, 1987), 234; Christopher J. Bartlett, *"The Special Relationship": A Political History of Anglo–American Relations Since 1945* (London, 1992), 88; Clark, *Nuclear Diplomacy*.

19 FRUS 1955–57, IV, 134.

outcome of the negotiations concerning stationing costs, although these negotiations would influence the extent to which we should wish to withdraw our troops."[20] A favorable agreement seemed fairly unlikely under these circumstances. Indeed, strong political arguments against a new round of negotiations had been raised in the Foreign Office after the embarrassing experience of the previous year. But when the full extent of the delay in German rearmament became known in late 1956, those reservations were discarded.[21] The Germans were not surprised by the new request. Conscious of their shortcomings in the military field and aware of the disastrous repercussions of the negotiations in 1955–6, they immediately accepted the invitation to a new round of negotiations. Moreover, they now saw support-cost payments as a means in the fight against suspected British troop-reduction plans.[22]

At the meeting with the British on December 12, Foreign Minister Heinrich von Brentano and Franz-Josef Strauss presented a figure of $286 million as an upper limit for all support-cost requests and promised preferential treatment for Britain because of its special currency problems.[23] It was decided to set up an Anglo–German economic committee as a forum for support-cost negotiations. During the discussions in this committee, for the first time the Federal Republic proposed monetary measures as an offset for troop costs.[24] These comprised a premature repayment of postwar debts, investment in U.K. Treasury papers, and an expansion (from £20 to £30 million) of Germany's account at the Bank of England, which was earmarked for arms purchases and hardly ever used.[25] The offer was an expression of the increasingly strong reserve position of the Federal Republic, which it slowly learned to use for its political aims. Furthermore, the German delegation offered $120 million as direct support-cost payments. The British demanded $182 million. The talks were complicated by requests that dribbled in from the rest of the stationing countries. Those requests were answered with German offers

20 MAC(G)(1957), services cost in Germany, first meeting, Jan. 4, 1957, PRO CAB 134/2223.
21 An account of the 1957 negotiations is found in MAC(G) note on the negotiations leading to the Local Defence Cost Agreement with the FRG, 1957, Gore-Booth memorandum (M 101/234), Oct. 15, 1957, PRO CAB 134/2223.
22 Excerpt of cabinet meeting, Dec. 8, 1957, BA, B126/34103; diary note, Dec. 17, 1956, BA, Blankenhorn papers, 71/2; Brentano to Adenauer, Dec. 6, 1956, PA-AA, Dept. 301/96.
23 Meeting of U.K.–FRG delegations, Dec. 12, 1956, PA-AA, Dept. 301/96.
24 The committee was headed by the undersecretaries of foreign affairs. The first meeting took place on Jan. 14, 1957; extensive documentation is in PA-AA, Dept. 301/96 and Mutual Aid Committee: Subcommittee on Germany 1957, PRO CAB 134/2223.
25 AA circular telegram, Jan. 28, 1957, PA-AA, Dept. 301/96; cabinet memorandum by foreign minister: Anglo–German financial talks, Jan. 4, 1957, BA, B126/34103; note on negotiations . . . , Oct. 15, 1957, PRO CAB 134/2223.

of half the amount agreed on in the previous year.[26] By far the greatest complication was Britain's public announcement in February 1957, when the talks were almost concluded, of its intent to reduce its troops. Widespread speculation on the subject had affected the negotiations from the start. The Germans were particularly disturbed by Britain's plans at a time when their own army was just a blueprint. Thus, the plans implied a serious military weakening of NATO front lines. Furthermore, Bonn feared a combined move toward a nuclearization of Western defense, with Germany supplying the "foot soldiers" because it had renounced the use of nuclear arms.[27]

The Germans added to their bargaining position in the support-cost negotiations by stating that "German concessions [will] be made dependent on guarantees for the maintenance of previous force levels and combat capabilities."[28] They requested the insertion of a clause in the prospective agreement that coupled payments to a British guarantee of stable troop levels. This was exactly what the British wanted to prevent. Macmillan, who became prime minister in January 1957, insisted "that there should be nothing written in the agreement, which prevents us from making the reductions we have in mind, or which would entitle them to reduce their money payment correspondingly."[29] He angrily wrote Adenauer: "In effect, therefore, your negotiators appear to be trying to bring financial pressure upon us to delay giving effect to reductions which we regard as essential to our economy, by leaving in doubt what contribution we could count on in 1957–58."[30] Adenauer, in his answer, promised that he would do everything to find a solution, but he also expressed his dissatisfaction with the plans for troop reduction.[31] Finally, a somewhat diluted version of the clause, which stipulated that the negotiations could be reopened only in the case of deep cuts in the British forces during the current year, was accepted by the Germans. The negotiations were concluded in March. Germany agreed to pay $140 million cash, to deposit £75 million at the Bank of England as prepayment on postwar debts, and to enlarge the account for military purchases to £30 million. The final signature was delayed at the last minute by the arrival of an official U.S.

---

26 France was excluded from this harsh treatment, but it nevertheless was offered considerably less on the argument that French forces in Germany were seriously under strength due to the Algerian war. For documentation on these negotiations, see PA-AA, Dept. 301/97 and 301/100.
27 For a German assessment of the British plans, see BMVg memorandum: military evaluation of British white paper, Apr. 25, 1957, BA, Blankenhorn papers, 75b/1.
28 Brentano to Adenauer, Feb. 22, 1957, BA, B126/34103.
29 Macmillan to Lloyd, Feb. 8, 1957, PRO PREM 11/1842.
30 Macmillan to Adenauer, Feb. 22, 1957, PA-AA, Dept. 301/97.
31 Adenauer to Macmillan, Feb. 23, 1957, ibid.

support-cost request for a sum much larger than expected. Arguing the necessity of preferential treatment for Britain and the need for the funds in its own rearmament effort, the Federal Republic, after some discussion, managed to get the United States to agree to $77.5 million, half the amount of the year before. Yet it had to accept a clause that granted the United States the right to reopen the case within six months if the German rearmament effort was still behind schedule at that time.[32] After these negotiations were concluded, the Anglo-German agreement was finally signed.[33] Thus, the support-cost problem was resolved and attention focused on the British troop-reduction plans.

THE BRITISH WHITE PAPER, APRIL 1957

Prime Minister Macmillan and his new minister of defense, Duncan Sandys, were impressed by the constraints Britain's financial position placed on its foreign policy. The Suez Crisis hardened the determination of the British government to continue with its controversial defense review, including plans to trim the BAOR. This proved a thorny endeavor, given the obligations of the WEU treaty and the expected resistance of the WEU member countries. Britain could not claim any overseas emergency, which was the first escape clause from its troop commitment. It had to base its plea on financial reasons. This required the consent of the WEU members. The conflict would not remain an isolated issue, as some in the British government realized beforehand. Sandys's immediate predecessor, Anthony Head, wrote to his colleagues when the December meeting of NATO approached: "The problem facing us can, I think, be summarized as follows: How large a reduction should we propose to our Allies in the interests of our economic position, bearing in mind that if we go too far we may provoke a general reduction in military contributions to NATO, and indeed endanger the very stability of the alliance as well as damaging the prospects of the closer relationship with Europe which we have in mind in other fields."[34] It soon became obvious during

32 For the U.S.-German discussion, see U.S. aide-mémoire to Germany, Feb. 25, 1956, BA, B126/34104; Wilson to Eisenhower, Mar. 22, 1957, DDRS 1987/149; Adenauer to Eisenhower, Mar. 23, 1957; Dulles memorandum to Eisenhower, Mar. 27, 1957; memorandum of conference with the president, Apr. 2, 1957; Eisenhower to Adenauer, Apr. 12, 1957; all in FRUS 1955–57, XXVI, 220–9. For the agreement on June 7, 1957, see *BGBL* 1959, II, 410–11.
33 Exchange of notes concerning local defence costs of U.K. forces in the FRG, June 7, 1956 (HMSO, Cmnd. 256, 1957).
34 CP(56)269, Defence Ministry memorandum, Nov. 28, 1956, PRO CAB 129/84.

the NATO meeting that the other WEU members would not be pleased. When, in February 1957, the British officially presented their plans for a reduction of their troops in Europe at the WEU council meeting, the dilemma between Britain's attempts to preserve its influence in Europe and the anti-European impression that the reduction plans conveyed became very clear, although meanwhile the United States had resigned itself to limited British reductions. The full extent of Britain's plans was finally made known in the famous Ministry of Defense white paper of April 1957, provoking further apprehensions on the part of Britain's military allies.

The major changes the white paper proposed were general reductions in manpower, the end of national service in 1962, cuts in arms research and development, and an increased emphasis on international cooperation in the development of new armament systems. These ideas were not entirely new, and the white paper only summarized an ongoing discussion that had taken place throughout the 1950s.[35] Thus, it was no radical change in policy but rather an attempt by Britain to devise strategies that limited the obvious erosion of its prestige and freedom to act as a world power. The basic cause was the perceived economic strain that the military posture put on the British economy. This was summarized in the opening section of the white paper:

Britain's influence in the world depends first and foremost on the health of her internal economy and the success of her export trade. Without these, military power cannot in the long run be supported. . . . Over the last five years, defence on average absorbed 10 per cent of Britain's gross national product. Some 7 per cent of the working population are either in the Services or supporting them. One-eighth of the output of the metal-using industries, upon which the export trade so largely depends, is devoted to defence. An undue proportion of qualified scientists and engineers are engaged in military work. In addition, the retention of such large forces abroad gives rise to heavy charges which place a severe strain upon the balance of payments.[36]

The section establishes a clear causal link between Britain's military expenditures and its overall economic problems. The assertion of the white paper that military spending was primarily responsible for British

---

35 The most recent account is Martin Navias, *Nuclear Weapons and British Strategic Planning, 1955–58* (London, 1991), 134. See also Christopher J. Bartlett, *The Long Retreat: A Short History of British Defence Policy* (London, 1972); Philip Darby, *British Defence Policy East of Suez, 1947–68* (London, 1973); Wyn Rees, "The 1957 Sandys White Paper," *Journal of Strategic Studies* 6 (1989): 215–29.

36 HMSO, Cmnd. 124, Defence: Outline of Future Policy, 1957, 1.

economic problems was prevalent in the British government and widely
shared by contemporary commentators.[37] The issue of the foreign
exchange losses of British troops in Europe from the 1950s until well into
the 1960s was embedded in this interpretation. According to this argument, the high concentration of investment and labor in defense industries diverted resources from fast-growing industries, such as consumer
goods, that were the linchpin of the postwar boom in Europe and thus
damaged British exports. Together with military expenditure abroad, this
was also seen as a central factor in British balance-of-payments problems.
The fact that the crisis of British postwar recovery in 1951 coincided
with the Korea rearmament seemed to underscore the argument:
"Britain's incalculated act of sacrifice during the crisis at the start of the
Korean War in embarking on a defence program which used up all the
resources in sight and more, continued to exercise an unfavourable influence on economic development long after the event."[38]

It has already been suggested, however, that such a straightforward
interpretation might be too simple. The foreign exchange cost of the
troops must be put into perspective. The failure of British arms exports
to Europe, as I show more fully at the end of this chapter, was due mainly
to the fact that such exports were not consistent with the basic lines of
British foreign policy. This argument can be extended to the whole sector
of British exports. Complaints about surrendering markets to the Europeans during the rearmament period often ignore the fact that Britain at
that time was not necessarily willing to direct its trade toward Europe but
rather toward the United States and the Commonwealth.[39] The crucial
interest in earning dollars and the unfavorable trade balance with the
United States rendered exports there a priority and does not need much
explanation. British trade with the Commonwealth was of a much higher
value than trade with Europe, although its level was stagnant compared
to the breathtaking growth of intra-European trade. However, it took the
whole of the 1950s until this realization began to dawn on the British
government. For political and ideological reasons Britain defended its
imperial links despite the huge cost of doing so. A brusque revision of

37 For a vigorous critique of British defense spending, see Andrew Shonfield, *British Economic Policy
    Since the War* (London, 1958). See also Bartlett, *Long Retreat*, 105–6; *The Economist*, Jan. 5, 1957.
    The argumentation is still influential and sustained by critics of British policy in the 1950s. See,
    e.g., Chalmers, *Paying for Defence*; for further references, see Till Geiger, "The Next War Is Bound
    to Come: Defence Production, Supply Departments, and Defence Contractors, 1945–57," in
    Anthony Gorst, Lewis Johnman, and W. Scott Lucas, eds., *Contemporary British History, 1931–61:
    Politics and the Limits of Policy* (London, 1991), 96.
38 Shonfield, *British Economic Policy*, 56.
39 Peter Burnham, *The Political Economy of Postwar Reconstruction* (New York, 1990), 150–76.

traditional foreign policy would have been almost impossible to explain to the British public. The abandonment of European markets was a necessary consequence of these policies, not of the claims on resources made by defense spending.[40]

The difficult question of whether military spending is a gain or a loss for an economy has to be answered by tedious sector studies rather than by sweeping statements, and the military burden is only one of the many arguments in the great debate about the British postwar decline.[41] Whatever the final result, it is safe to say that the blanket assertion of the white paper was overly simplistic. The monocausal linkage of high defense costs and economic decline is not so clear as the public discussion in Britain suggested. The argument advanced here is that economic considerations in defense matters, as they were pushed forcefully in the support-cost question and in the defense review of 1957, were shaped by underlying political choices, with economic reasoning often following them. What were these political choices?

In the wake of the political and economic shock of the Suez crisis, the British government was convinced that its economy and its military posture no longer were compatible. Choices had to be made, and these choices were politically and economically significant. The emphasis Britain put on its nuclear potential as the simplest and least expensive way to maintain its beleaguered power in the world was in many ways beyond its economic and technological resources.[42] The maintenance of a useful nuclear potential was not possible without international cooperation.

40 It is not surprising that the prevailing view of the effects of British defense costs on the economy (and the balance of payments) was soon challenged. It is even possible to argue that "the rearmament program *strengthened* [original emphasis] Britain's ability to earn reserves in the years thereafter." See William P. Snyder, *The Politics of British Defence Policy, 1945–62* (Oxford, 1964), 214–15. In support of this statement, Snyder cited the receipts of U.S. foreign aid (1952–6: $1 billion), the foreign exchange expense of U.S. and Canadian troops in Britain (about $182 million a year in the 1950s), and military exports ($577 million until 1959). One might add that U.S. support for the pound was motivated not only by economic reasons but also by the intent to enable Britain to keep its military commitments. However, Snyder acknowledges the commonly presented bottlenecks of the rearmament program: the pressure on metal-using industries, the concentration of research on defense, and the outlays for overseas troops. Other analysts twist the traditional argument and maintain that the economic weakness was not produced by the effects of high defense costs, but rather that Britain was no longer able to bear the expense because of economic weaknesses deriving from other factors. See Werner Abelshauser, "Rüstung, Wirtschaft, Rüstungswirtschaft," in Maier and Wiggershaus, eds., *Das Nordatlantische Bündnis*, 103. More detailed research confirms that the impact of rearmament was confined to a temporal check on exports, whereas economic problems allegedly resulting from rearmament already existed beforehand; see Burnham, *Political Economy*, 176.
41 One example is Peter Burnham, "Rearming for the Korean War: The Impact of Government Policy on Leyland Motors and the British Car Industry," *Contemporary Record* 9 (1995): 343–67.
42 The changes in British nuclear strategy are described in detail in Navias, *Nuclear Weapons*.

Whereas the French, with similar problems, turned halfheartedly to Europe, the British chose to accept an increased reliance on the United States and valued the "special relationship" more than the European connection. In a paper from January 1957, titled "The Grand Design," British Foreign Minister Lloyd proposed to his colleagues a pooling of the British nuclear program with European resources within the framework of the WEU.[43] The paper was an attempt to escape a too-pronounced dependence on the United States, which became evident during the Suez Crisis. When it was discussed in the cabinet, however, a majority opposed Lloyd's idea, citing in particular the importance of Anglo-American cooperation.[44] This robbed Britain of the principal incentive it could have offered the Europeans in exchange for cooperation in other areas. When Macmillan in March 1957 went to meet the U.S. president in Bermuda, his overriding concern was a broad expansion of Anglo–American cooperation.[45] Cooperation with the Europeans on nuclear-arms matters was – for the time being – ruled out during cabinet discussions on the white paper.[46] This choice, subsequently reaffirmed on many occasions, would seriously impede the British realignment toward Europe.

A further choice the British made was very much in line with the first. It meant going ahead with a substantial reduction of forces in Europe, that is, cutting the European commitment to preserve the stability of sterling. The exact figure to which the army was to be reduced was 165,000 men (down from about 400,000). This figure was kept secret. The 77,000 men in the BAOR in particular were targeted. The support-cost negotiations of 1957, which covered only 75 percent of the cost, seemed to make heavy cuts necessary, particularly in view of a rapid decline of German payments in the future. However, even a more acceptable result would not have deterred the British, although the Foreign Office clearly emphasized the political risks of troop reductions. Apart from the foreseeable negative reaction of Britain's allies, there was the danger of a loss of British prestige in Europe and of the progressive enlargement of Germany's role on the continent.[47] Furthermore, the appearance of a reversal of policy so shortly after the 1954 WEU pledge was awkward. To a majority in the government, however, these political

43 "The Grand Design" (Co-operation with Western Europe). Cabinet memorandum, Jan. 5, 1957, CAB 129/84, reprinted in Goldsworthy, ed., *Conservative Government*, 102–7.
44 Ibid., 107–10.
45 For documentation on the meeting, see FRUS 1955–57, XXVII, 704–67.
46 Cabinet meeting minutes, Feb. 22, 1957, PRO CAB 128/31.
47 Brief for Committee on Service Costs in Germany, May 14, 1956, PRO FO 371/124622; undated FO note on troop reductions, ibid.

risks did not outweigh the perceived economic strain. The British announcement at a meeting of the WEU in February 1957 that it would reduce the BAOR to 40,000 and halve the Second TAF by the end of 1958 triggered a long diplomatic battle in which Britain was constantly on the defensive and which cast a long shadow over Britain's attempt to adjust to the evolving European integration process. The main problem was that the British government was not able to offer a politically acceptable alternative to troop maintenance or any other credible commitment to the Europeans.

Either one of the aforementioned choices alone might not have been interpreted negatively in Europe. Both, however, and the manner in which they were pushed through, dealt a serious blow to Britain's European policy. This is well illustrated by the analysis of a core issue in all troop-cost negotiations until the 1970s: arms sales to Germany and the conspicuous failure of British efforts in this field, particularly during the decisive period of German rearmament.

CENTURION AND THE FAILURE OF BRITISH WEAPONS EXPORTS

The Federal Republic in the 1950s and 1960s was among the largest arms importers in the world. Hampered by the lack of a domestic arms industry, multiple restrictions on arms production imposed by the victorious World War II alliance, and an economy that was already running at full capacity, Germany was unable to produce more than the most basic equipment for its nascent army, particularly in the high-technology sectors. The Allies competed aggressively for this market of utmost economic and political significance. Moreover, the United States and the United Kingdom saw German arms purchases as a principal way of balancing the foreign exchange cost of their troops in Germany. It would have been an elegant solution to the problem if the dollars and pounds the Germans earned from the presence of British and American troops had been reinvested in the arms industries of the stationing countries. Arms purchases became a recurrent theme in all support-cost and, later, offset negotiations.

As we have seen, a considerable amount of time passed before German rearmament was able to relieve the NATO partners of some of their defense burden in Europe. The British and the Americans quickly became impatient. When the Germans somewhat impertinently asked the United States in early 1956 for more financial assistance for rearmament, they received a blunt response: In a memorandum dated March 15, 1956, the

Americans accused them of spending far less than the average of other NATO countries on defense matters, despite the excellent state of the West German economy. Therefore, any additional aid would be precluded.[48] Washington urged Bonn to complete its defense procurement plans and demanded that much higher arms orders be placed in European countries. This was a broad hint regarding the ongoing support-cost negotiations between Britain and Germany. The Eisenhower administration saw American grant aid to Germany as increasingly anachronistic, given the economic situation in the Federal Republic. The last big item was the so-called Nash list of 1953. It was worth about $900 million and consisted mainly of loans of military materiel, military training, and exchange programs.[49] It was the only aid commitment made by the United States after the March 1956 memorandum. This and earlier American military aid programs had one important lasting consequence: They provided the German forces with their basic equipment in the most important categories, for example, tanks. Thus, the Bundeswehr developed a structural dependence on American materiel in many areas. This situation tended to perpetuate itself because newly bought U.S. arms were more compatible with existing stocks than materiel from any other source.

In the first years after 1955 the Germans fully agreed with the American suggestion that they buy equipment for the Bundeswehr abroad for several reasons. First, West Germany lacked its own armaments industry; advanced military materiel was only available abroad. Second, as outlined in Chapter 1, there were apprehensions of a macroeconomic nature brought forward by Finance Minister Fritz Schäffer and by Strauss, including the danger of domestic inflation in the case of massive government investment, the possible curtailment of German export capabilities, and the disturbingly high balance-of-payments surplus.[50] According to Strauss, "Apart from the advantage that arms and equipment from allied NATO countries originate from current production and have therefore – partly – considerable price advantages, ordering weapons abroad also affects trade policy. By buying abroad we correct payments imbalances caused by the German export surpluses in deficit countries. In particular, we are able to

48 German memorandum, Jan. 10, 1956, BA, B 126/51520; the response: U.S. memorandum to FRG, Mar. 15, 1956, BA, Blankenhorn papers, 61b,1.
49 For U.S. aid to Germany, see Birtle, *Rearming the Phoenix*.
50 *FAZ*, Mar. 6, 1956. This was precisely the hope of some sectors of the British government and industry.

reduce our surplus in the EPU."[51] Most German industrial leaders shared the government's sentiments and argued that for the moment they were working at capacity.[52] The production in such a short time of equipment for the planned twelve divisions was regarded by both government and private business as impossible. It also could damage export prospects and lead to tax increases and incalculable conversion costs. In addition, German industrialists still vividly remembered the dismantling of many of their factories by the victorious powers after 1945 and the vehement attacks on them for producing weapons for the Nazis. Therefore, they were not eager to re-enter the politically sensitive arms business. The competitive advantage of weapons industries in other countries also played a role in the initial reluctance of German industry to fight for a piece of the armaments pie.[53] Although this restraint by German industry in producing weapons was to change relatively quickly, in 1955–6 German and Allied objectives appeared to be in accord. The major question now was where Germany would get the equipment for its military forces. Would it cooperate mainly with the United States or with Western Europe? How large was domestic production to be? What role would the United Kingdom play? These decisions not only had economic consequences – they were also to be of considerable political importance.

France, the United Kingdom, and the United States were the main competitors for German orders. Soon after the international agreements that set the rules for German rearmament were signed, these countries moved into high gear. For example, in October 1956 the United States concluded an agreement that laid out the framework of defense procurement by Germany.[54] The U.S. government would act as an agent for military sales, and payments were to be transferred to a specific account maintained by the U.S. Treasury. Despite pressure from all sides, however, the Germans felt no urgent need to choose among the competitors. The rearmament crisis made the final form of the German army difficult to foresee. Therefore, procurement plans were extremely preliminary. The strategic debate in the Alliance, which diminished the importance of conventional weapons, added another factor of insecurity. If the Federal Republic invested in conventional weapons while all its major allies were equipping their armies with nuclear arms, the Bundeswehr would be

---

51 BPI 1958, 330–1.
52 Gerhard Brandt, *Rüstung und Wirtschaft in der Bundesrepublik* (Witten, 1966), 148–51.
53 Ibid., 86–7; 175–8.
54 Exchange of notes: Mutual Defense Assistance, Oct. 8, 1956, TIAS 3660, 2787–802.

relegated to second-class status from the start. It seemed wiser to defer massive investment until the outcome of the debate within NATO over the relative importance of nuclear versus conventional weapons was clearer.

In April 1956, Herbert Blankenhorn, the German ambassador to NATO, was informed by the Ministry of Economics that the previously earmarked sum of about $600 million for military purchases in Europe over the whole rearmament period would have to be increased to $1.43–1.67 billion as a consequence of the support-cost negotiations.[55] However, the authors of the memorandum added, military experts did not expect orders of this size to be feasible. This was a sound judgment. In the questionnaire the Federal Republic had to answer and submit to the annual review meeting of NATO in October 1956, the announced target figures for orders in Europe turned out to be considerably lower than the allies expected. At earlier NATO meetings, the Germans had made suggestions to order weapons to the tune of about $595 million from European sources and $2.143 billion from the United States in the period 1957–9. Strauss explained at the meeting, however, that only $286 million could be expected for Europe and $548 million for the United States in 1957–8, adding that even these figures might be too high.[56]

Despite these delays, American leadership in the German market grew quickly. Various French efforts to get Germany to agree to their repeated proposals for a bilateral arms-cooperation scheme failed, most spectacularly with the famous Franco–Italian–German Trilateral Agreement (FIG). Almost immediately after the EDC had been voted down by the French parliament, the French suggested to Bonn a bilateral armaments organization that would act independently of the WEU armaments committee. The Germans initially stalled.[57] In late 1956 Adenauer suddenly came out as a supporter of the French plan.[58] Strauss, who was the major German driving force behind the idea of European armaments cooperation, was also well disposed toward the French idea. In 1957 the French extended their proposals to the nuclear sphere.[59] A protocol was signed that stipu-

---

55 Ministry of Economics memorandum, Apr. 7, 1956, BA, Blankenhorn papers, 61a/1.
56 NATO review meeting: questionnaire on German military buildup, Oct. 29, 1956, ibid., 68/1.
57 Fauré–Adenauer conversation, Sept. 17, 1956, DDF 1956, II, doc. 188, 392–6.
58 Couve de Murville to Pineau, Nov. 3, 1956, doc. 104, 164–5; notes for visit by chancellor: Franco-German cooperation, Nov. 3, 1956, doc. 123; both in DDF 1956, III; Werner Abelshauser, " 'Integration à la carte': The Primacy of Politics and the Economic Integration of Western Europe in the 1950s," in Stephen Martin, ed., *The Construction of Europe: Essays in Honour of Emile Noel* (Dordrecht, 1994), 12–16.
59 Fauré–Adenauer conversation, Nov. 16, 1957; Strauss–Chaban-Delmas conversation, Nov. 20, 1957; both in BA, Blankenhorn papers, 81b.

lated French–German cooperation in the field of military production, including nuclear weapons.[60] Shortly afterward Italy joined the agreement. In the end, however, France was not ready to share its nuclear secrets and feared a violent Soviet reaction if Germany were to acquire nuclear weapons. On becoming head of state, Charles de Gaulle canceled the ominous third part of the agreement concerning nuclear cooperation.[61] Soon afterward, the Germans retaliated by buying the American Lockheed Starfighter aircraft for their air force instead of the French Mirage, despite intense lobbying by the French.[62] The German decision was based not only on Strauss's annoyance at the cancellation of the FIG: Coproduction of some components in the Starfighter gave Germany access to high-tech know-how, and the U.S. fighter was technologically superior. Another factor was high-pressure American lobbying combined with subtle hints about future help in upgrading the Starfighter to nuclear capability.[63] In any case, the French were furious. They considered the German decision a heavy blow to any future effort at European arms cooperation.[64] In fact, Franco–German cooperation in the field of armaments was to trail behind German–American cooperation for a long time.

Where did all this leave the British? As it turned out, they were left in the role of odd man out, although they offered substantial know-how and a vast selection of military hardware. From the beginning, armaments trade as a means to reduce the imbalance in the bilateral payments account had been an issue in British–German support-cost negotiations. The British government, however, regarded arms trade as a rather ambiguous business. A big share of arms in British exports was considered a mixed blessing. The Bank of England had noted this as early as 1950. Dealing with the conversion of large sectors of British industry to arms production during the Korean War, the bank warned the Treasury "that if we concentrated wholly on armaments and made up the resulting shortages both at home and in the Sterling Area by buying civilian equipment from

---

60 Pineau to Bonn and Rome embassies, Nov. 20, 1957, DDF 1957/II, 717–18; protocol, Nov. 25, 1957, DDF 1957/II, 762–3.

61 Wormser–Laloy–Strauss conversation, Nov. 19, 1958, BA, Blankenhorn papers, 92b/2; the episode is now quite well researched; e.g., see Peter Fischer, "Das Projekt einer trilateralen Nuklear-kooperation: Französisch-deutsch-italienische Geheimverhandlungen 1957/58," *Historisches Jahrbuch* 112 (1992): 143–56; *Revue d' histoire diplomatique* 104 (1990): 77–158.

62 Catherine M. Kelleher, *Germany and the Politics of Nuclear Weapons* (New York, 1975), 103.

63 Wormser–Laloy–Strauss conversation, Nov. 19, 1958, BA, Blankenhorn papers, 92b/2; AA memorandum: German–French military cooperation, Nov. 26, 1958, ibid., 94/1; Kelleher, *Germany*, 103.

64 Seydoux to Couve de Murville: Adenauer–Joxe conversation, Oct. 28, 1958, DDF 1958/II.

Germany, Germany at the end of the rearmament period would find herself with a firm foot in the markets which we had given up to her, and without the reconversion problem with which we ourselves would be faced."[65] This argument became commonplace in the British government. Despite these reservations, however, during the period 1950–2 Britain embarked on an ambitious rearmament program triggered by the Korean War and greatly expanded its arms-production capacity. The British metal-producing industry, which accounted for about 40 percent of the country's exports, was especially affected.[66] The Treasury observed in 1955 that the "concentration of defence claims on the metal using industries has led to a direct conflict with exports and investments."[67] By this time the rearmament boom had long been over. Unlike the Federal Republic, however, Britain had large portions of its production capacity bound up in armament industries. Apparently, the Bank of England's prediction had come true. The Treasury wrote: "The absence of any defence expenditure making claims on the economy, which compete with the claims of exports and investment, has been of great benefit to Germany during the period of reconstruction since the war and has given the German economy a relative advantage over that of the UK, particularly in the export field."[68] The major negative factor in Britain's rearmament drive might indeed have been the surrender of markets in Europe to Germany at a time when the latter's industry was still relatively weak. However, it has been said before that this was only consistent with the overall trend of British policy, namely, the concentration of economic policy on the Commonwealth and the United States.[69] In any case, in the mid-1950s the United Kingdom continued to have huge capacities in arms production. Its defense expenditures were falling. Therefore, the British either had to sell abroad or had to accelerate a costly reconversion of these industries.

When, during the NATO meeting in 1955, Schäffer offered German arms orders to offset the foreign-exchange drain resulting from British troop maintenance in Germany, his proposal was received with some indignation, particularly within the British Treasury:

We shall be tying up our manpower and industrial capacity on defence to the advantage of our strongest export competitor. The Germans do not conceal that

65 Bank of England to Treasury, Sept. 25, 1950, PRO T 234/30.
66 Peter Burnham, "Rearming for the Korean War," 343–67; Cairncross, *British Economy*, 100.
67 Brief for a meeting with German ministers at NATO, Dec. 1955, PRO T 234/24.
68 Treasury memorandum, Dec. 13, 1955, PRO T 234/24.
69 Milward, *European Rescue*, 396–408.

they have no intention of disrupting their civilian industry and export potential. Dr Schäffer indeed offered that if it was the balance-of-payments that particularly worried us Germany would be prepared to buy arms from us. We shall have to consider in any case what advantages we can derive from the German policy of buying arms abroad. We shall however sell arms to Germany anyway. We have no spare materials or idle capacity to produce additional tanks and aircraft whose export would be a pure gain to our balance of payments, offsetting our DM expenditure.[70]

London therefore concentrated its diplomatic efforts in the support-cost negotiations on obtaining direct payments. However, the Treasury's ambiguous stance on arms trade was not shared by other departments, notably the Foreign Office,[71] the Ministry of Supply, and the embassy in Bonn, which "had long considered that German purchases of British arms were the only long-term palliative to the balance-of-payments problems with which we are faced; not only in 1956, but for some years to come."[72] This view was reinforced by the disappointing result of the first round of support-cost negotiations. Apparently there was no alternative to arms trade. The ambiguity with which the government regarded this business would, however, prove to be a considerable disadvantage to its sales promotion efforts.

Estimates by the Ministry of Supply for German arms orders ran from £80 million ($224 million) to £250 million ($700 million) a year.[73] These hopes were confirmed by a letter of intent from the West German government in June 1956 in the context of the support-cost agreement, wherein Brentano promised German orders to the tune of $524 million in 1956–7.[74] No major new orders were received that year, however. The German account at the Bank of England, which consisted of prpayments for arms as agreed to in the support-cost negotiations, remained almost untouched. Of the $157 million of arms orders that were registered until March 1957, $120.5 million were for Hispano-Suiza armored track vehicles, an order of dubious value, as it turned out later.[75] The

70 Treasury note, Jan. 2, 1956, PRO T 234/25.
71 The Foreign Office also cautioned, however, "that it is not necessarily in our interest to encourage the Germans to buy rather than to make arms, and thus encourage them knocking us for six in the export markets"; see Warner to British Embassy, Bonn, Apr. 12, 1956, PRO FO 371/124613.
72 FO note to Treasury, Feb. 24, 1956, PRO FO 371/124612.
73 MAC(G)(1956), Ministry of Supply memorandum, Jan. 10, 1956, PRO CAB 134/1291; Bonn to FO, no. 415, May 30, 1956; Bonn to FO, no. 477, Aug. 13, 1956; both in PRO FO 371/124615.
74 Brentano to U.K. Embassy Bonn, June 29, 1956, PRO FO 371/124616.
75 FO brief for prime minister, May 1957, PRO FO 371/130727. Bundesbank member Emminger

British government grew more and more uneasy about the situation.

A particularly heavy blow to British expectations was the case of the British-made Centurion tank, which the British government had high hopes of furnishing to the German army. The value of the prospective order was estimated at £50 million ($140 million), which theoretically would have disposed of more than one-tenth of Britain's accumulated EPU deficit.[76] The importance of a sale of Centurions is illustrated by the fact that Prime Minister Eden twice wrote Eisenhower seeking the president's support for the British model against American competition.[77] The particular urgency in this case was caused by the highly critical economic situation of the Royal Ordnance Factories in Dalmuir, where the tanks were produced. Of the four factories, three were kept working in the hope of obtaining German orders.[78] The German decision, however, kept being delayed, and in September 1956 the case already seemed lost. Especially embarrassing for the British was that the Americans had given the German army 1,000 M-47 tanks free of charge as part of the Nash list. Strauss evoked renewed hopes that additional needs might possibly be filled by Britain. In May 1957 Macmillan, in a last desperate pitch, wrote once more to Eisenhower: "Both for the sake of European cooperation, and in order to lessen the need for dollar end-items, it is most desirable that some of these requirements should be supplied by Britain."[79] But although Eisenhower promised support, the German decision was made in favor of the new American M-48 tank. A final protest by Macmillan to Adenauer achieved nothing.[80]

This was quite a fiasco. The British embassy in Bonn and the Foreign Office had wasted almost two years of strenuous effort on the issue and now blamed the Americans. "It is virtually useless for us to try to sell the Germans anything where we are in competition with the Americans. The

reported from a meeting of the OEEC that the British government was "embittered" that none of the German promises had been kept. See Emminger to AA, Nov. 10, 1956, PA-AA, Dept. 301/96.

76 Final report 1959, EPU, 36; Ministry of Supply memorandum, Jan. 26, 1956, PRO CAB 134/1291.

77 Eden to Eisenhower, Feb. 18, 1956, PRO PREM 11/3344; McElroy memorandum for president: tanks, Apr. 1957, DDRS 94/1319.

78 Arms Working Party meeting, Feb. 28, 1956, PRO FO 371/124612; minutes of cabinet meeting 49, Jul. 12, 1956, CAB 128/30, CM 49(56).

79 Macmillan to Eisenhower, May 17, 1957, PRO PREM 11/3344.

80 Adenauer to Macmillan, June 29, 1957, PRO PREM 11/3344; Macmillan to Adenauer, Jul. 28, 1957, FO 371/130794.

reason is, of course, that the Americans have in the shape of MAAG some 200 American business men dressed up in uniform who have a great deal of time and money to be spent in nobbling the Germans who count. . . . We have nothing comparable to offer."[81] The Pentagon, in fact, and contrary to Eisenhower's wishes, had not hesitated to offer its good offices in selling the M-48 – particularly because it was about to develop a successor model for which German funds were a welcome financial help.[82] Two other reasons were decisive for the Germans: First, the new U.S. tank was compatible with the M-47 tanks that the Bundeswehr already possessed.[83] Second, the M-48 appeared to be the newest model, whereas the British were about to replace the Centurion tank with a newer version that had not been offered to the Germans.[84] The Germans were always ready to suspect, not without some justification, that they were being used to get rid of outdated materiel at high prices.[85] The failure of the Centurion deal was followed by a similar case that involved the British P-177 aircraft. Again, Britain kept facilities open only in the hope of selling planes to Germany. The Royal Air Force (RAF) had expressed its lack of interest in the aircraft in the follow-up to the 1957 defense review.[86] Again, the deal fell through due to French and American competition, and production had to be stopped at the end of 1957, when the Germans refused to purchase any of the aircraft. This caused fierce protests at the Saunders-Roe Company, which was depending on the order and, moreover, was located in an economically weak region.[87]

Most damaging to the reputation of the British weapons industry was the case of the Hispano-Suiza armored track vehicles. The contract for the order, worth about $120 million, had been concluded under Strauss's

---

81 FO minute, Nov. 1, 1957, PRO FO 371/130775.
82 Memorandum of conference with the president, Apr. 2, 1957, in FRUS 1955–57, XXVI, 227; Eisenhower to Macmillan, Aug. 26, 1957, ibid., XVII, 782–3; McElroy memorandum to president, Apr. 1957, DDRS 1994/1319.
83 Record of a meeting between Macmillan and Strauss, May 11, 1959, PRO PREM 11/2704.
84 Embassy Bonn to FO, no. 49, Jan. 26, 1956, PRO FO 371/124632.
85 FO brief for prime minister's visit to Germany, May 1957, PRO FO 371/130727; Gore-Booth to FO, Jan. 29, 1958, PRO FO 371/137471.
86 "HMG have continued to finance development only in order to give the Germans time to make up their minds" (see briefing paper on arms sales to Germany in preparation for Adenauer's visit to London, Dec. 17, 1957, PRO FO 371/130773); FO briefing paper for prime minister's visit to Germany, May 1957, FO 371/130727.
87 FO brief for Harvey visit to Bonn, Jan. 15, 1958, PRO FO 371/137471; German Embassy, London, to AA, Dec. 24, 1957, PA-AA, Dept. 301/37; KCA 1957, 16020.

predecessor, Theodor Blank. The primary partner, the dubious Swiss firm Hispano-Suiza, had subcontracted the largest part of development and manufacture to British Leyland without the involvement of the British government.[88] Unfortunately, the vehicle proved to be of dreadfully poor quality, and there was evidence of bribery in the West German Defense Ministry when the order was placed. When Strauss realized this, he canceled 1,800 of the 2,800 vehicles ordered, thereby reducing Britain's biggest arms-export success in Germany to a third of its original size.[89] The loss of such a tremendous amount (about $84 million) was a considerable shock.[90] Although the British government was aware of the shady circumstances of the deal, it urged the German Defense Ministry to review its decision. Eventually, the Germans were willing to reinstate part of the order because of their disappointment with the Franco-Italian-German agreement and because of the need to use the arms account at the Bank of England.[91] However, the affair left a very bad impression.

The series of failures caused considerable annoyance in the British government:

> The Germans must realize that these disappointments and the way in which they have come about are having an adverse political effect in the United Kingdom and are seriously disturbing Anglo–German relations. In particular they strengthen the hands of those . . . who do not wish the United Kingdom to cooperate with Germany or, indeed, with Europe; . . . the view is gaining ground in some quarters that the Germans have been leading us up the garden path.[92]

Compared with the estimates of 1955, the result of the British efforts was miserable. In July 1957 the preliminary total for orders was $168 million, in March 1958 it was $213 million, and in 1961, after the Hispano-Suiza deal had been slashed, it declined to $138 million.[93] Frustrated, British civil servants contemplated the reasons for these failures. They produced

---

88 Embassy Bonn to FO, Aug. 29, 1958, PRO FO 371/137476.

89 A series of articles with essentially correct information on the affair can be found in *Frankfurter Rundschau*, Dec. 6–16, 1958; see also BMVg to AA, Nov. 6, 1958, PA-AA, Dept. IIA7/1202; meeting of departments, Nov. 6, 1958, PA-AA, Dept. IIA7/1202.

90 PRO CAB 129/86, Duncan Sandys memorandum: cancellation of German defense orders, Nov. 15, 1958, PRO FO 371/137476, Steel to Ministry of Supply, Aug. 28, 1958.

91 Embassy Bonn to Ministry of Supply on McFarlane–Hopf conversation, Apr. 19, 1958, PRO FO 371/137477.

92 FO no. 144 to Bonn, Jan. 21, 1958, PRO FO 371/137471.

93 Data derived from Ministry of Defence memorandum, July 15, 1957, PRO FO 371/130774; Mar. 31, 1958, PREM 11/3344; Finance Ministry memorandum, Mar. 18, 1961, BA, Etzel papers.

a tremendous variety of explanations: the anti-British attitude of Strauss; the possibility that British weapons were outdated and too expensive; the Franco–Italian–German Tripartite Agreement; Britain's reluctance to cooperate in arms production and its independent strategic policy; the secretiveness and absence of cooperation in British services; the reluctance of Britain to make government-to-government deals; and, of course, U.S. competition.[94] Although the last reason was grave, the political explanations are more important. All evidence points to German interest and British hesitation in becoming involved in a cooperative arms development scheme on the continent.[95] When it seemed to go ahead without Britain, as in the case of FIG, there was great indignation. As long as British policy seemed to be one of maintaining economic, military, and political distance from the continent, however, it was not surprising that the Germans felt it would be more politically efficacious to cooperate with the United States and France. Armaments trade was to a large degree a political business, and the political profit was greater when it was pursued with these countries. Thus, the main stumbling block in Britain's sales efforts was that they were not in line with the overall direction of its foreign policy. The level of British sales remained disappointing throughout the 1950s and 1960s.

Although the British government adopted a more cooperative attitude after 1958, this trend did not change, with failures such as the Hispano-Suiza deal contributing their mite.[96] American competition in high-tech weapons became the decisive factor during the 1960s. Regarding less sophisticated types of armaments, German industry caught up rapidly and expanded its share greatly. Changes in British policy came too late. The United Kingdom continued to trail far behind American and French sales, approaching the level of Italian sales to the Bundeswehr, as Table 2.1 shows. In the 1960s arms sales again became an integral part of German-

94 Ministry of Supply to prime minister on export of arms, Mar. 12, 1958, PRO PREM 11/3344; Bonn to FO, Apr. 17, 1956, FO 371/124613; Lloyd–Herwarth conversation, Feb. 18, 1958, FO 371/137374; McFarlane (Bonn) to Ministry of Supply, Jan. 29, 1959, FO 371/145946; Anglo–German Economic Committee: Arms Supply to Germany, Nov. 22, 1956, FO 371/124616.

95 E.g., from the start of rearmament the Germans had expressed their preference for government-to-government deals rather than negotiating directly with foreign firms, which they suspected would overcharge them. The United States had immediately agreed to this, but the government of the United Kingdom, mainly because of resistance from industry and the services, steadfastly refused. See brief on Adenauer visit, Apr. 29, 1958, PRO FO 371/137474; FO brief for defense minister's visit to Germany, Mar. 20, 1958, PRO FO 371/137474.

96 Summary of Strauss's remarks at Budget Committee meeting, Feb. 27, 1959, BA, B136/3105.

Table 2.1. *Foreign and domestic Bundeswehr expenditures for materiel, maintenance,
and R & D, 1956–67 (in millions of dollars)*

Year	Domestic	U.S.	U.K.	France	Italy	Others	Total
1956	339	126	—	13	—	18	496
1957	265	301	26	22	6	95	714
1958	530	276	9	32	2	18	867
1959	427	390	28	77	28	91	1,042
1960	504	147	17	74	18	173	933
1961	865	226	18	60	38	112	1,320
1962	1,250	367	50	82	40	177	1,966
1963	1,278	568	95	134	35	219	2,328
1964	1,198	530	19	172	51	167	2,137
1965	1,097	430	23	130	22	120	1,823
1966	1,162	156	39	106	22	66	1,551
1967	1,476	222	37	123	13	82	1,953

Note: The most plausible figures had to be chosen from among several widely divergent sources. Mendershausen's figures best correspond to the data found in disparate archival documents.

Source: Mendershausen, *Troop Stationing*, 132.

British offset agreements. But the continuing distance between Germany and the United Kingdom, underlined by quarrels about support costs, monetary policy, and troop levels, impeded closer military cooperation between the two countries.

3

Adenauer and "Perfidious Albion": Troop Reductions, Support Costs, and the Integration of Europe, 1957–1959

ANGLO–GERMAN DISCORD

In May 1959 the British ambassador to NATO, Frank Roberts, reported a quip by Konrad Adenauer he had picked up from his German colleague, Herbert Blankenhorn.[1] Allegedly, Adenauer remarked that he now had two main enemies: England and his own Foreign Office.[2] Whatever the source of this quote, it was typical of the state of affairs between Britain and West Germany in 1959. It seemed as if the conflicts of the previous years and all the fundamental differences in policy matters suddenly converged, culminating in a tense meeting between Harold Macmillan and Adenauer at the end of the year.[3] Numerous disagreements, whether they were about East-West relations, disarmament, the Free Trade Area (FTA), or support costs, were inextricably linked and reinforced each other to produce a postwar low in Anglo–German relations.

After the war the relationship between the United Kingdom and the Federal Republic seemed to develop much more auspiciously than Franco–German relations. However, Bonn and London never achieved the degree of collaboration that characterized the dealings between Bonn and Paris. This proved to be particularly harmful to Britain's attempts between 1957 and 1963 to work toward a form of European integration consistent with its basic foreign policy objectives. British politicians were slow to acknowledge that London's European policy had become dependent on German support. If Bonn had opposed the French policy of excluding Britain with the same determination as did The Netherlands, France at that time probably would have thought twice before taking the risk of

1 The Adenauer quip "Perfidious Albion" is related in Siegfried Balke to Peter Tennant, Oct. 29, 1959, PRO FO 371/145780.
2 Roberts to Steel, May 27, 1959, PRO FO 371/145775.
3 For the series of mutual recriminations during 1959, see the documents in PRO FO 371/145777.

antagonizing Germany and thus driving it into the Anglo–American camp. It must be kept in mind that the famous "axe Franco–Allemand" emerged only slowly in the late 1950s. To assume tacitly that its formation was somehow natural distorts reality. The situation was open as to whether European integration was to be more inclusive or exclusive, more "Gaullist" or "Atlanticist." When in the 1960s the institutions of the European Economic Community (EEC) and the member countries rapidly created a complicated web of mutual checks and balances, it became impossible for the United Kingdom to change the direction of the integration process. The late 1950s were decisive for the later shape of Europe, and this chapter concentrates on some of the factors that help to explain the critical choices of these years. It is argued that much of Germany's tacit support for French European policy originated in its disappointment with Britain in the security field. How were these security questions (and their financial dimensions) linked with the problem of Britain's position in Europe? The support-cost negotiations of 1957–8 and the debate about British troop reductions between 1957 and 1959 provide the empirical base for an answer to this question.

A simple comparison of dates already suggests a close interrelationship between British security policy and European integration. The six EEC countries had, soon after the EDC disaster, "relaunched" the integration process at the Messina conference in June 1955. At this time the feeling that prevailed in Britain was that the pledge in the WEU treaty to maintain troops on the continent and a loose cooperation with other European institutions were sufficient involvement in Europe for the time being.[4] However, it rapidly became clear that troops were no substitute for a consistent European policy. Contrary to British expectations, the Spaak Committee, which worked out the Messina proposals for the Common Market, overcame the huge obstacles that lay in the way. Britain had withdrawn its representative from the negotiations in November 1955 and saw itself completely excluded afterward. When the success of the six countries became evident, Britain reacted with the formulation of its own alternative to the Common Market, the design of a wider Free Trade Area (FTA). The plan was presented to the Organization for European

---

4 For Britain's European policy as it evolved up to the ill-fated application in 1961–3, Miriam Camps's *Britain and the European Community, 1955–1963* (Princeton, N.J., 1964) is still indispensable. More recent works include Sean Greenwood, *Britain and European Cooperation Since 1945* (Oxford, 1992); Gustav Schmidt, ed., *Grossbritannien und Europa: Sicherheitsbelange und Wirtschaftsfragen in der britischen Europapolitik nach dem Zweiten Weltkrieg* (Bochum, 1989); Jacqueline Tratt, *The Macmillan Government and Europe: A Study in the Process of Policy Making* (New York, 1996).

Economic Cooperation (OEEC) on February 13, 1957. One day later, British troop-reduction plans were made public at the WEU Ministers Council. This resulted in heated discussions between Britain and its WEU partners, which are described in some detail later in this chapter. The British FTA plans received less immediate scrutiny than their reduction plans. Serious negotiations took place only when the Six, at the end of March 1957, finally signed the Rome treaties, which established the EEC.[5] Soon afterward, a new round of support-cost negotiations began. It ended in early 1958, accompanied by further British troop reductions, and placed the usual strains on German–British relations. The discussion in the WEU about British troop levels lasted even longer, well into 1959. Meanwhile, the FTA negotiations continued in the so-called Maudling Committee. They were pursued in a worsening climate, although differing positions on specific issues seemed slowly to converge. When the French suddenly declared in November 1958 that further talks on the FTA were point-less, it came as a shock to Britain and a surprise to the five other EEC members. However, no decisive opposition was heard from Germany. Throughout these events Britain followed a parallel policy of trying to achieve the largest possible reductions of its Europe-based troops while attempting to convince the Six of the benefits of its economic pro-posals. The outright denial or deliberate disregard of the awkward fact that both policies were inseparably linked remained one of the most fun-damental flaws in British policy until its unfortunate applications for EEC membership in the 1960s.

THE NEGOTIATIONS OVER BRITISH TROOP REDUCTIONS IN 1957

When the British announced at the WEU meeting in February 1957 that they would reduce the BAOR from 77,000 to 50,000 men and halve the Second TAF (consisting of 466 aircraft and 15,000 men), they provoked a storm of criticism from their WEU partners.[6] It has been said before that the white paper of April 1957 indicated a political choice in favor of privileged relations with the United States and the Commonwealth, to the detriment of the British position in Europe. That is exactly how the proposed troop reductions and the white paper were perceived. The Europeans, and partly also the United States, refused to see the British problem as merely a financial issue. They strongly emphasized the

5 Both France and Germany insisted on this condition; see Dulles–Adenauer conversation, Bonn, May 4, 1957, in FRUS 1955–57, XXVI, 240.
6 Wilhelm Grewe, *Rückblenden 1976–1951* (Frankfurt am Main, 1979), 279–80.

political background, and this shattered all British hopes that their objectives would be accomplished without serious political irritation.

Initially, the French turned out to be particularly critical. British–French relations had suffered much because of the Suez crisis and the British decision to intensify nuclear cooperation with the United States. The WEU announcement was a further affront. The French government, which had accepted German rearmament partly on condition of the British troop-maintenance pledge and had emphasized this publicly, was shocked by the rapid erosion of this promise. When the French discussed the reduction plans with the British on March 9, 1957, their annoyance (and British intractability) "led rapidly to a dramatic turn in a very friendly discussion."[7] French Prime Minister Guy Mollet denounced the breach of the WEU pledge, which, he said, might lead to a recurrence of the situation of 1938. Macmillan pointed to Britain's financial problems and to the fact that France had long since moved large contingents of its forces in Germany to Algeria without consulting anyone. The conversation ended on a depressing note: "No agreement was reached, no compromise envisaged. Subsequently, it was indicated to the English ministers that, if they insisted on reaching a decision this week, it would be impossible to avoid initializing at WEU an action contrary to their intentions."[8] France's sharp reaction was very inconvenient and surprising to the British. Up to this point they had rather neglected the impact that their defense review would have on European political opinion, and in their preparations had concentrated on getting approval from American and NATO authorities.

Gaining this approval was not easy, either. The Americans realized the real extent of the British plans only very late, that is, during the bilateral consultations in early 1957. They were told by Duncan Sandys "that HMG was not prepared to spend any foreign exchange on the maintenance of troops in Germany next year and therefore put us clearly on notice that the issue of whether any British forces would be maintained in Europe would arise in acute form in a year's time."[9] Such precipitate action was unacceptable above all to the Supreme Allied Commander in Europe (SACEUR), Lauris Norstad, who complained that these reductions made any forward strategy in Europe illusory. Washington shared this interpretation and made it clear that, although it understood the financial situation of the British, it would oppose any rapid reduction. In that case, the

---

7 DDF, 1957, I, 429.   8 Ibid., 430.
9 U.S. Secretary of Defense Wilson–Sandys conversation, Jan. 29, 1957, in FRUS 1955–57, XXVII, 684.

Americans threatened, a U.S. disengagement from Europe could not be ruled out.[10] Both Norstad and the U.S. government demanded a phasing-out of the British plans. The British, who deemed U.S. support crucial, accepted this compromise to obtain American acquiescence to their plans. They agreed to delay their first 13,500-man reduction of the BAOR (from 77,000 to 63,500) until the end of 1957 and to continue with a second cut down to 50,000 in 1958–9.[11]

The confrontation with the French endangered this compromise. A French-sponsored resolution in the WEU against the British proposals was imminent, very probably leading to a major diplomatic row. If the WEU members refused to approve the British case, an open breach of the WEU treaty would have been necessary in order to effect the cuts. The dangers that lay in antagonizing France and the other members were obvious, as the British cabinet realized:

Moreover, the Paris Agreements and the current plans for the closer association of this country with Europe in a Free Trade Area had given great encourage-ment to our friends throughout Europe, and a faulty presentation of the with-drawal of British forces might do serious damage to our relations with European countries generally. We should therefore spare no effort to avoid a vote against us in WEU, which would leave us no alternative to breaking the WEU treaty.[12]

Britain offered another minor concession: to delay the discussion about the second part of reductions until October. Surprisingly, this proved to be helpful. The French backed down and refrained from a direct con-frontation. This conciliatory mood may not have been due to a reversal of their position but to relatively weak support by the other Europeans, especially the Germans.

This rather astonishing German position is explained by a behind-the-scenes gentleman's agreement between the United Kingdom and the Federal Republic. During those months Germany made strenuous efforts to formulate a review of NATO that promoted closer consultation of the smaller nations by the Americans.[13] Looking for allies in this matter, the Germans had approached the United Kingdom: "Mr. Lloyd said that the Germans attach great importance to their proposal for a review in NATO, and, although the British were unenthusiastic about it, they would support the Germans because the Germans had been so helpful to them

10 Ibid., 685.
11 Blankenhorn to Adenauer, Mar. 11, 1957, BA, Blankenhorn papers; Mager, *Stationierung*, 180.
12 Seventeenth meeting of the British Cabinet, Mar. 12, 1957, PRO CAB 128/31.
13 Detlef Felken, *Dulles und Deutschland: Die amerikanische Deutschlandpolitik 1953–1959* (Bonn, 1993), 350–3.

in the WEU meeting."[14] Apart from that, the German government was convinced of the inevitability of British reductions. It was also acquainted with the U.S. position of accepting a certain number of reductions in view of Britain's economic problems.[15] Thus, the initial resistance of the WEU members was overcome. On March 18 the WEU council approved the first slice: a reduction of the BAOR by 13,500 men (to 63,500) and of the Second TAF by 50 percent of its aircraft and 25 percent of its personnel.[16]

For the United Kingdom this was only the first step, however. The central aim of the British reduction efforts in the following years was a manpower ceiling of 165,000 for the army, to be reached in 1962, which was consistent with the abolition of national service that year. This long-term perspective was known only to the United States, SACEUR, and Paul Henri Spaak, the secretary general of NATO.[17] It was evident that, with such a manpower target, further reductions in Germany were unavoidable, even to less than 50,000, which had already been made known to the WEU partners.[18] The publication in April of the British white paper on defense removed any doubts about British plans for the future of its forces in Europe. The announced basic purposes and the exclusive focus on nuclear weapons evoked mistrust and apprehension. The Germans in particular felt deceived because this kind of surprise was exactly what they had wanted to avoid with their reform proposals.[19] When Macmillan visited Bonn in May 1957 he was lectured about the German view of Western defense strategy, that is, the importance of a conventional forward defense.[20] This pronounced criticism compelled the United Kingdom to issue reassuring declarations about its intention to

---

14 Memorandum on Dulles–Lloyd conversation, Bermuda, Mar. 22, 1957, in FRUS 1955–57, XXVII, 723. In the final result, the German efforts for more cooperation were not very successful. The United States made it clear that they reserved the right to act without consultation if the situation demanded it. See Adenauer to Dulles, Nov. 19, 1957, in FRUS 1955–57, IV, 187–90; Brentano–Dulles conversations, Nov. 21–4, 1957, in FRUS 1955–57, IV, 190–217.

15 Memorandum on Brentano-Dulles conversation, Washington, D.C., Mar. 5, 1957, in FRUS 1955–57, XXVI, 216–17; Dulles to Adenauer, Mar. 17, 1957, ibid., IV, 165–6.

16 The text of the WEU resolution can be found in KCA 1957, 15724–5.

17 Report: "Local Defence Cost Negotiations with Germany 1957–8"; prepared by Treasury, Oct. 16, 1958, PRO T 225/1128.

18 In January 1958, the British plans provided for 44,900 men in the BAOR by 1963 (and for 8,500 in the Second Tactical Air Force by 1961). See local defense costs in Germany: Report by officials, Jan. 8, 1958, PRO CAB 129/91.

19 AA memorandum on British policy toward NATO, Apr. 29, 1957, BA, Blankenhorn papers, 75b/1; diary entry, Apr. 24, 1957, BA, Blankenhorn papers, 75b/3; meeting with Chancellor Adenauer, Apr. 27, 1957, NHP.

20 Summary record of Adenauer and Macmillan conversations, May 7, 1957, BA, Blankenhorn papers, 84/4.

keep troops in Europe. The British government thought it wise to wait until the end of 1957, when the financial situation as well as the outcome of new support-cost negotiations were known, before starting deliberations on a second round of reductions in WEU and NATO.[21]

A NEW SUPPORT-COST ROW

Although Britain's Foreign Office objected to a new round of support-cost negotiations after the troop-reduction debate in spring, the prime minister and the Treasury prevailed. The reason was a new balance-of-payments crisis. Between July and September 1957, British reserves fell by £189 million ($529 million), from a level of about £860 million ($2.4 billion).[22] At the same time repayment of the debts incurred during and prior to the Suez Crisis made it very difficult to achieve a positive balance of payments.[23] The annual EPU deficits were an additional burden. In mid-1957, prompted by the Federal Republic's large surplus, talk about a possible DM revaluation against sterling began, and speculative money flowed to Germany in huge amounts.[24] At the OEEC meeting in June, German and British representatives clashed openly over differing interpretations of the imbalance. The British delegate called the German surplus "very disturbing and depressing" and accused the Germans of following an irresponsible monetary policy that took no account of the external situation.[25] According to the British, Germany had drained the system of reserves, hoarding them instead of reinvesting them, following the enlightened practice of the Americans and the English after the war. The Germans rejected this interpretation and saw the problem as one of varying rates of inflation; the British should first fight against the sources of inflation in their own country.[26] The Germans suspected that "behind

21 Mager, *Stationierung*, 181–3.   22 KCA 1957, 15770–1.

23 The commitments of Britain included £80 million a year repayments on U.S. and Canadian loans, the repayment of the IMF drawing of £200 million and of the EX-IM bank loan of £180 million. See the U.K. memorandum, Nov. 27, 1957, in which the NATO resolution of July 26 is invoked; PRO CAB 134/2223, MAC(G)(57)29.

24 Werner Wippich, "Die Rolle der Bundesrepublik Deutschland in der Krise des £-Sterling und des Sterling Gebiets 1956/57," in Gustav Schmidt, ed., *Zwischen Bündnissicherung und privilegierter Partnerschaft: Die deutsch-britischen Beziehungen und die Vereinigten Staaten von Amerika 1955–1963* (Bochum, 1995), 33–79.

25 Record of meetings of the OEEC's Working Party 19, June 17–18, and July 3, 1957, BA, B106/25878.

26 Preparatory meeting of German officials for OEEC conference, June 3, 1957, BA, B102/25878. West Germany did not have to worry about deficits undermining its currency. On the contrary, foreign money moving into the country greatly complicated the Bundesbank's efforts to keep prices under control, despite the booming economy. See Otmar Emminger, "Deutsche

those [British attacks] obviously . . . was the intention to prepare new demands on Germany in the framework of defense burden-sharing (NATO)."[27] Speculation against sterling calmed down only when German and English delegates came together at the IMF meeting in September and afterward announced their determination to maintain existing parities.[28] They also decided to stop public accusations and counteraccusations on the subject. However, the support-cost question soon led to a collapse of this uneasy truce. The monetary clash of 1957 paralleled emerging British–German conflicts in European and security matters.[29] From now on, international currency affairs became directly linked to these problems, a fact immediately apparent in the support-cost negotiations.

In connection with the currency crisis, Britain obtained a NATO resolution that allowed countries suffering from monetary difficulties incurred by troop maintenance abroad to request an examination of its problem by an independent team of NATO experts.[30] The United Kingdom was at first reluctant to initiate such a multilateral NATO procedure, fearing that public discussion would only heat up sterling speculation and that Britain's own receipts from American and Canadian troops would be taken into account.[31] Therefore, a bilateral approach to Germany was chosen once more and coupled with new discussions about troop levels that were to start in October 1957:

The main point to make is that our decision as to whether any concession can be made over the 13,500 men will depend on what can be done to relieve us of the DM costs of troops in Germany. The whole question of what forces we can maintain and in particular whether we can make any concession to meet the point of view of our Allies depends on finance.[32]

Any concessions, however, would at most apply to 5,000 of the 13,500 men who were to be removed. Oddly enough, the British nevertheless expected a conciliatory response from the Germans. This was based on

Geld- und Währungspolitik 1948–75," in Deutsche Bundesbank, ed., *Währung und Wirtschaft in Deutschland 1876–1975* (Frankfurt am Main, 1976), 485–552.
27 Excerpt of 248th ZBR meeting, June 26, 1957, BA, B102/25878.
28 Aide-mémoire UK to Germany, Sept. 18, 1957, BA, B102/25817; Emminger report on IMF annual meeting, Oct. 30, 1957, BA, B102/12660.
29 Unfortunately, there exists no comparative study on the impact of monetary policy on European integration during the 1950s and 1960s.
30 NATO document C-M(57)112, July 30, 1957, PA-AA, Referat IIA7/769.
31 Report: "Local Defence Cost Negotiations with Germany 1957–8," Oct. 16, 1958, PRO T 225/1128.
32 FO to British delegation at NATO in Paris, Oct. 30, 1957, PRO CAB 134/2223, MAC(G)(57)21. See also memorandum on Dulles–Lloyd conversation, Bermuda, Mar. 22, 1957, in FRUS 1955–57, XXVII, 723.

incorrect reports from the embassy in Bonn: "[There now is a] much better German understanding of our position and no inclination to have another knock-down drag-out row."[33] Yet, German resistance to negotiations proved as strong as two years prior. All the Germans offered was an augmentation of their arms account at the Bank of England and of the £75 million debt prepayment account, which had resulted from the last agreement. These offers underscored the fact that the Federal Republic was not prepared to extend any budgetary help in the future and would confine its efforts exclusively to the monetary aspect of the problem.[34] Of course, the German proposals were unacceptable to the British. They would have provided only short-term help for the balance of payments, at the cost of a long-term debt burden.

When the Germans refused to change their position, the British decided to invoke the NATO resolution of July, while offering to limit their reductions to 8,500 in the case of a satisfactory financial solution.[35] NATO appointed a panel of three experts to investigate the influence of the troops on the monetary problems in Britain. The German government made its disapproval known immediately: "There is no British balance-of-payments problem resulting from troop maintenance in Germany! . . . The British balance-of-payments situation has general monetary and politico-economic reasons. It is out of place to link this problem with NATO defense questions."[36] Only later did the British government learn of the reasons for this intractability. They were bluntly told that Germany expected the British to pull back anyway and saw no point in paying more.[37] Furthermore, the Germans argued, their military build-up was proceeding at full steam now, and estimates for defense appropriations in the following years showed sharp increases. New support-cost payments would open gaps in future budgets.[38] Bonn refused to accept the NATO procedure even when the NATO experts approved the British case in their report, presented in January 1958. With special regard to British efforts to strengthen their currency and, to this end, to hold their balance of payments in continuing surplus, the experts judged the British request for financial help legitimate. However, the Germans persisted in

---

33 Steel to FO, Oct. 1, 1957, PRO FO 371/130728.
34 Finance Ministry memorandum: "Mutual Aid (Art. 3, NATO Treaty)," Nov. 28, 1957, BA, B126/34103; Brentano to Adenauer, Feb. 12, 1958, PA-AA, Referat IIA7/769.
35 Memorandum on Dulles–Lloyd conversation, Oct. 22, 1957, in FRUS 1955–57, XVII, 804.
36 AA memorandum for NATO Council meeting, Jan. 17, 1958, PA-AA, Referat 301/98.
37 Lloyd–Herwarth conversation, Feb. 18, 1958, PRO FO 371/137374.
38 Memorandum prepared by the German delegation to NATO: "Financial Planning for Defence until March 1961," dated Nov. 9, 1957, BA, Blankenhorn papers, 80/2.

their argument that the British problem justified only monetary help, not budgetary payments.[39] This led to a stalemate that even Paul Henri Spaak, who at that time was secretary general of NATO and closely involved in the discussions, could not resolve. His visit to Bonn proved as useless as the repeated personal messages by Macmillan to Adenauer.[40] Concerted pressure applied by the Western NATO members was futile.[41] Spaak was stunned by the suspicion of Britain he encountered in Bonn.[42] The Franco–Italian–German agreement on military cooperation had been signed in November 1957, and Germany's willingness to work with Britain was at its lowest.[43] In late January 1958 the WEU council approved a reduction of 8,500 men in the BAOR, a decision doubtless eased by German resistance to accepting the report of the NATO experts.[44] This passed the buck back to the British. Their plans to withdraw another 5,000 men, a strategic reserve of special importance, met heavy resistance.[45] Norstad especially refused to accept this further weakening of his lines. The United States urged Britain to stop the reductions and accept a compromise in the support-cost question, while offering American aid to cover the burden not met by a German–British agreement.[46] The Americans proffered a further incentive: The intensification of Anglo–American cooperation in nuclear technology would proceed much more smoothly if the British were willing to maintain their military presence in Europe at roughly the same size.[47]

The British government finally decided to take a step that was long overdue. It accepted a long-term solution to the support-cost problem, coupled with a new pledge for a minimum level of troops. Earlier in the negotiations the British cabinet had realized that, due to the increasing

39 AA memorandum for NATO Council meeting, Jan. 17, 1958, PA-AA, Referat 301/98.
40 Note on Spaak visit, Jan. 31, 1958, PRO T 225/1128; record of Macmillan–Adenauer conversation, Paris, Dec. 15, 1957, PREM 11/2331; Adenauer to Macmillan, Jan. 4, 1958, PREM 11/2331; diary entry, Feb. 2, 1958, BA, Blankenhorn papers, 85a/3.
41 Record of a secret meeting of NATO ambassadors, Jan. 21, 1958, ibid., 85b/2; summary of NATO Council meeting, Jan. 8, 1958, BA, B126/34103.
42 Roberts to FO, Feb. 3, 1958, PRO FO 371/137374.
43 BA, B126/34102 contains a Finance Ministry note that reports a striking re-orientation toward France and Italy of German programs for military orders, Feb. 18, 1958.
44 French resistance was less rigid than the year before. France agreed to the new reductions, yet not without signaling "the very grave consequences which derive from the progressive weakening of the British presence on the continent, coming close to putting into question the foundations of common defense" (Foreign Minister Pineau to Ambassador Chauvel in London, Jan. 28, 1958, DDF 1958 I, 100–1).
45 UKdel Paris to FO, Apr. 8, 1958, PRO T 236/5099; chancellor of Treasury minute on conversations in Paris, Apr. 28, 1958, ibid.; memorandum on Dulles–Norstad conversation, Sept. 26, 1958, in FRUS 1958–60, VII, 1, 358.
46 Background notes: strength of BAOR, Oct. 30, 1958, PRO T 225/1128.
47 Clark, *Nuclear Diplomacy*, 222–4.

size of the German army, a continuation of support-cost payments after the current year was doubtful.[48] Furthermore, an uncompromising stance would have had grave political consequences: "a weakening of NATO; the frustration of our plans under the heading of interdependence, balance of collective forces, political consultation, etc.; more European Six Power activity, i.e., excluding the United Kingdom; serious prejudice to the prospects for obtaining the free trade area; [and] an increase, especially in Germany, in the desire to make some sort of a settlement with Russia."[49] In addition, further large-scale reductions became increasingly difficult to handle because of a lack of housing and facilities for the returning soldiers.[50] Based on these considerations the British transmitted new proposals to Spaak. In any case, they promised to keep 45,000 men until 1962 if Germany covered one-third of its foreign-exchange cost during this period and supported sterling by prematurely repaying postwar debts as well as depositing a further advance amount for arms orders at the Bank of England. For the first time Britain officially linked the FTA problem to troop costs. One of the conditions was that "the organisation of Europe in the economic field develops in a manner consistent with the political and military organisation of NATO and enables the United Kingdom to participate with its allies on equal terms."[51] The British informed the Germans that if their proposal was not accepted they would not hesitate to withdraw all their troops; the German foreign minister replied that this showed Britain's lack of interest in Europe.[52]

When the proposal reached the German government a struggle broke out between the supporters of an uncompromising stance and the more conciliatory advisers who were growing increasingly uneasy about Anglo–German relations.[53] The Germans even presented two different counter-proposals at the same time. Soon after Albert Hilger van Scherpenberg, who was state secretary of the Auswärtiges Amt and in charge of the negotiations, communicated a plan close to the British position, another official memorandum, influenced by Strauss, arrived in London entirely rejecting the British proposals.[54] It explicitly negated a connection between the organization of Europe and monetary problems arising from

---

48 Nineteenth meeting of the British Cabinet, Feb. 27, 1958, PRO CAB 128/32.
49 Report by officials: "Local Defence Costs in Germany," Jan. 8, 1958, PRO CAB 129/91.
50 Conclusions of Cabinet meeting 19 (1958), Feb. 27, 1958, PRO CAB 128/32.
51 Report: "Local Defence Cost Negotiations with Germany 1957–8," Oct. 16, 1958, PRO T 225/1128.
52 PRO PREM 11/2331, Lloyd–Brentano conversation, Mar. 6, 1958.
53 Diary entry, Feb. 2, 1958, BA, Blankenhorn papers, 85a/3.
54 Aide-mémoire to the U.K., Mar. 27, 1958, PA-AA, Referat 301/98.

the maintenance of British troops in Germany. A visit by Adenauer to London, planned for April 1958, gave new urgency to the support-cost problem. Finally, the Germans gave up their resistance to cash payments; after all, they wanted to secure the presence of a British force of at least some value, declaring slyly that "45,000 British soldiers were better than 50,000 French grandmothers."[55]

The United Kingdom, after discussions lasting more than six months, finally managed to achieve a solution by agreeing to the Scherpenberg proposals. The Germans paid $33.6 million a year until March 1961, they maintained an interest-free account for arms orders at the Bank of England (to the tune of $140 million), and they paid the 1962–4 rates of the 1953 London debt agreement, which regulated German postwar debts, ahead of schedule. The British government declared that it would keep its troops at 55,000 (including the strategic reserve) until the end of 1958 and at 45,000 until March 1961. SACEUR Norstad and the United States urged the British to postpone any further reductions below 55,000, however, and this interest was used by the British to lobby for additional dollar aid.[56] Receiving $25 million earmarked for joint weapons development, the British government agreed to keep the troop level stable in 1959.[57] This "deal" was kept secret in order to spare the U.S. government embarrassing questions from members of Congress. Washington's decision to put in its own money clearly displayed the concern of the United States about the never-ending quarrels among its allies. Again, the Americans had to put their own support costs last. The British told them in unequivocal terms that if the United States persisted in demanding a share, thereby limiting the funds available for them, the BAOR would have to leave Europe.[58] As partial compensation, the Americans agreed with the Germans on a premature repayment of postwar debts to support the weakening American balance of payments.[59]

The 1958 agreement calmed the support-cost front of Anglo–German relations for three years. However, it did not prevent the hidden political

55 Bonn embassy telegram no. 333 to FO, Apr. 12, 1958, PRO T 236/5099.
56 For this and the following, see background notes: strength of BAOR, Oct. 30, 1958, PRO T225/1128; U.K. embassy to Ministry of Defense on Sandys's talks in Washington, D.C., Sept. 27, 1958, PRO T 225/1128.
57 Dulles–Lloyd conversation, May 4, 1958, in FRUS 1958–60, VII/2, 327–8; FRUS 1958–60, VII/1, 348n1.
58 "The Foreign Secretary [Lloyd] said the question is simply this: Does the United States want to see Britain keep troops in Germany? They will not stay there unless their local costs are paid and a U.S. demand now for additional money would diminish this possibility" (memorandum on Dulles–Lloyd conversation, Oct. 25, 1957, in FRUS 1955–57, XXVII, 824).
59 Brentano to Chancellor's Office, Mar. 10, 1959, BA, B136/3132; AA memorandum on U.S. support costs, Sept. 10, 1958, PA-AA, Referat IIA7/1201.

tensions that made the problem such a hot issue between 1955 and 1958 from erupting in 1959 on the highest level.

THE ORGANIZATION OF EUROPE AND THE ANGLO–GERMAN CRISIS OF 1959

From 1955 on, Anglo–German relations deteriorated due to fundamental political differences in monetary and security issues. The British government was increasingly content with the Cold War status quo in Europe, judging the security situation to be essentially stable. For this reason it saw no need to continue undermining one of the most fundamental objectives of its policy, the strengthening of its currency, by maintaining troops in Europe. The Germans, however, still felt the need for direct military protection and forward defense. They also expected Britain to express continued allegiance to the long-term goal of German reunification and active British support against Soviet provocation. That Germany should pay for this by supporting the British currency policy, which it saw as flawed due to domestic mismanagement, caused deep resentment. Problems such as support costs tended to expose these differences and thus came to acquire a disproportionate potential for conflict. These conflicts had serious repercussions on other fields of mutual relations in general and on the question of Britain's place in Europe in particular.

The British FTA proposal of 1956 was an attempt to create an economic and political environment that would prevent the prolongation of the crises that plagued Britain after World War II by coming to an accommodation with the economically thriving European countries. However, after the creation of the Common Market, with its relatively strong integrative clauses and the common external tariff, it was obvious that Britain would need strong support from within the EEC to reconcile its proposals with the already existing arrangements. The success of the British proposals depended much on the German attitude, especially when the French position became more and more intransigent. Initially, the prospects for a functioning German–British collaboration in this field seemed good. In his famous Brussels speech in September 1956 Adenauer publicly emphasized his support for a close British alignment with the continent. In 1957 he made plain to Macmillan his support for the FTA.[60] It was well known that the German economics minister, Ludwig Erhard,

---

60 Hans-Peter Schwarz, ed., *Adenauer: Reden 1917–1967* (Stuttgart, 1975), 327–32; Macmillan diary, May 8, 1957; quoted in Alistair Horne, *Harold Macmillan* (London, 1989), 33.

was a fervent proponent of greater economic cooperation beyond the limited Common Market. He was supported by public opinion and the majority of German industrial leaders because the Federal Republic would have profited economically from a wider European solution.[61] In addition, Charles de Gaulle's rise to power in 1958 provoked deep apprehension and mistrust in Germany, not least in Adenauer.[62] One of de Gaulle's first actions was to propose a "world directorate" composed of the United States, Britain, and France, which infuriated the Germans and gave the British an opportunity to score easy points.[63] Thus, Britain had every reason to hope that its supporters within the German government might overcome the advocates of a narrow European solution. How was this chance lost?

The neglect of relations with Germany in the preceding years exacted a heavy toll. An important segment of the German political establishment had come to regard British policy with deep mistrust. Adenauer's aide Felix von Eckardt, in a conversation with the British ambassador, listed as a German complaint Britain's failure to join the EDC, its subsequent military policy, its distant attitude toward the Common Market, and the hostile attitude of the British press toward Bonn. As for FTA, it was seen as an attempt by the British not to be excluded from the economic benefits of the EEC.[64] When Australian Prime Minister Sir Robert Menzies mentioned this trade agreement to Adenauer, the chancellor elaborated on Britain's unreliability in the security area.[65] The feeling of suspicion peaked in early 1959 when Macmillan announced a trip to Moscow without consulting Adenauer. The chancellor feared that the Americans and British were working toward disengagement from Europe and deeply resented their disarmament plans.[66] The British embassy in Bonn woefully reported that the "Chancellor's suspicions of us are not only still

---

61 Thomas Rhenisch and Hubert Zimmermann, "Adenauer Chooses de Gaulle: The West German Government and the Exclusion of Britain from Europe," in Richard T. Griffiths and Stuart Ward, eds., *Courting the Common Market: The First Attempt to Enlarge the European Community* (London, 1996), 83–100.

62 Adenauer, Brentano, and Blankenhorn meeting, May 19, 1958, BA, Blankenhorn papers; Blankenhorn to Adenauer, May 23, 1958, ibid.

63 For de Gaulle's proposal, see FRUS 1958–60, VII/2, 81–3. The polite but firm rejection of de Gaulle's memorandum by all NATO member countries marked the beginning of the long decline in France's relations with NATO, and, particularly, with the "Anglo–Saxons." See Eisenhower to de Gaulle, Oct. 20, 1958, in FRUS 1958–60, VII/2, 108–9.

64 Steel to Lloyd: note on Anglo–German relations, Apr. 10, 1958, PRO FO 371/137375.

65 Van Scherpenberg to Brentano on a conversation between Adenauer and Menzies, June 19, 1959, BA, Brentano papers, 179.

66 Steel to FO, Feb. 3, 1959, PRO FO 371/145773. The attraction of disarmament for Britain at that time also stemmed, of course, from the prospect of some defense economies. See Chauvel to Pineau on conversation between Moch and Lloyd, Mar. 3, 1958, DDF 1958 I, 257.

alive but more rampant than they have ever been. . . . [He] is convinced that we are preparing to sell Germany down the river."[67] During 1959 the attitude of the British and German leaders toward each other went from bad to worse. When the British warned the Germans of the dangers of a narrow European solution and urged them to use their influence against France, they resorted to the threat of British disengagement from Europe, which, as it turned out, was a counterproductive move.

Even at that time Adenauer's suspicious attitude was not shared unanimously in the German government. Erhard had repeatedly encouraged the British to pursue their FTA plans.[68] Prior to Adenauer's visit to England in November 1959 one of his own ministers, the minister of atomic questions, Siegfried Balke, had urged the British "not to be so polite that he [Adenauer] comes back still believing that Britain is a negligible quantity." With astonishing frankness Balke criticized the Treaty of Rome as "a Catholic alliance reviving the Carolingian empire in the form of a third force."[69] The Bundesbank transmitted the same message. Its representative at the Bank of International Settlements (BIS) meeting in Basle, Karl Blessing, counseled the British to be tough with Adenauer to convince him of the dangers inherent in an economic division of Europe.[70] The British, however, had not much in hand to be tough with. Nuclear cooperation had been ruled out, a wholehearted commitment to German reunification was very unpopular in England, and in the economic field Bonn and London were competitors rather than collaborators. The British capacity to influence German politics therefore was quite limited. At this point the function of British troops in Germany as guarantors of its security seemed the only means of pressure left. Internally, Macmillan had repeatedly made this link.[71] He even employed the troops to impress de Gaulle. "If this negotiation [on the FTA] does not succeed, a very dangerous situation would result. . . . I recall to your mind that we have made a big effort for Europe. For this reason we have four divisions in Germany. If, however, the issue of the [free trade] area does not progress

---

67 Bonn to FO, Mar. 31, 1959, PRO FO 371/145774.
68 Erhard understood the Rome treaties as only a first step toward a much larger economic framework. He did not share Adenauer's predominantly political attitude toward European institutions and therefore vehemently supported the British FTA proposals. See Ulrich Lappenküpper, " 'Ich bin wirklich ein guter Europäer': Ludwig Erhards Europapolitik 1949–1966," *Francia* 18 (1991): 85–100.
69 Confidential letter of Peter Tennant (overseas director of the Federation of British Industries) to Maudling, Macmillan, and Lloyd, Oct. 29, 1959, PRO FO 371/145780. A remark on the letter says that the prime minister was "impressed" by it.
70 Roger Makins to FO, Nov. 12, 1959, PRO FO 371/145781.
71 Macmillan note to foreign minister and Treasury, June 24, 1958, PRO PREM 11/2315.

in a satisfactory way, we would have to look for new friends."[72] Presumably de Gaulle was not very impressed by this attempt at intimidation. To him, Britain had already chosen its friends: They were in Washington.

The Americans, who adopted a very hesitant attitude toward British requests for help in the European question, were confronted with the same argument. Selwyn Lloyd explained that "the continued economic and political division of Europe would, for example, make it difficult for the U.K. to keep its troops in West Germany."[73] Nevertheless, the United States indicated clearly to the Germans and the British that they preferred the Common Market to a wider, possibly discriminatory, free trade area.[74] This did not prevent Macmillan from repeating his threats even more explicitly in Washington:

If exports fall, there will be a pressure on sterling of a sort which inexorably demands countering measures such as deliberalization and other backward steps. The British people would not be prepared under these circumstances to continue to spend across the exchanges, year after year, 50 or 60 million pounds to keep troops in Germany, as they would feel their economic distress was caused by German discrimination and would see no justification for continuing to help defend Germany.[75]

The threat of disengagement was used with increasing intensity against the Germans. In November 1959 it became an open means of pressure against Adenauer to induce West Germany to adopt a more cooperative European policy. The relevant passage of the Adenauer–Macmillan talk is worth quoting at length because it makes the use of troops for politico-economic aims extremely clear. After the chancellor had expressed his deep concern over a British disarmament proposal for a denuclearized zone in Europe, Macmillan retorted harshly by calling nto question the British WEU commitment:

Frankly, had the British government of that day thought of the Six Powers of the European Economic Community forming an economic grouping from which Britain would be excluded, they would not have accepted such a commitment. Nor could it be expected that any British parliament would continue those obligations under such changed conditions. In this matter economics and politics run together. He hoped that Dr. Adenauer would realise that for an island people like the British, maintaining troops abroad for a long period was unprecedented and would be very difficult to continue if there were two economic

72 Record of Franco–British talks, June 29, 1958, DDF 1958 I, 870.
73 Lloyd–Dillon conversation, Dec. 8, 1959, in FRUS 1958–60, VII/1, 176.
74 Conversation among Dillon, Adenauer, Erhard, and others, Dec. 11, 1959, ibid., 196.
75 Memorandum on Macmillan–Herter converation, Mar. 28, 1960, ibid., 273.

groups in Europe engaged in a sort of economic war. The proposals for a common tariff for the Six meant a permanent discrimination against the UK. It would be almost impossible to honour the West European Union commitments while simultaneously conducting a tariff war. Therefore it was essential either to bring down discrimination to negligible proportions or to negotiate some other arrangements.[76]

The meeting, which had started with mutual recriminations, brought both sides no closer to those "other arrangements."

What is especially striking in retrospect is the fact that the British did not realize that the worth of their security guarantee had been devalued by their own actions in previous years. The troop commitment had been presented as a liability that Britain had no intention of carrying further if the cost was not offset. Whenever British politicians cited the danger of an economic division in Europe, they were confronted with the effects of their defense policy, and whoever wanted to attack the British FTA plans was free to cite the defense policy as evidence of Britain's dubious reliability. Thus, the political capital London had won by becoming part of the defense structure in Europe was squandered within a few years.

It was an additional irony that the reduction threat in 1959 was a mere bluff because the United Kingdom had quietly decided to stop the reductions. Several circumstances worked together to induce the government to take this step, which stabilized the troop level in Germany at about 55,000 men. First, in November 1958 Nikita Khrushchev's Berlin ultimatum had greatly raised the temperature of the Cold War. Second, the British were forced by a drawn-out guerrilla war in Cyprus to give the country its independence and to reduce their garrison there by 20,000 men to a mere 5,000. Upon their return, these troops and those coming from Europe encountered a serious lack of housing and other facilities. This posed difficult administrative problems and forced the government to halt the reductions in Europe.[77] The arguments of the Foreign Office against reductions gained new weight: "Nothing would suit Dr. Adenauer and Herr Strauss better than to see our troops in Germany reduced while theirs are being augmented. They want a larger share of the NATO commands . . . [and would be] able to say . . . that we were of less use as allies

76 Record of Adenauer–Macmillan conversation, Nov. 19, 1959, PRO FO 371/145780.
77 "Informed opinion in the Ministry of Defence is that in view of the Berlin crisis and the rundown in Cyprus it is likely that this [i.e., the stop] is the line which will be recommended" (note, Apr. 29, 1959, PRO T 225/1129). See also record of Strauss–Macmillan meeting, May 11, 1959, PRO PREM 11/2704; Treasury brief for Etzel visit, June 10, 1959, PRO T 225/1391; Macmillan to Heathcot Armory, chancellor of the exchequer, July 9, 1959, ibid.

and that there was less need to meet us over the FTA because we were pulling out of Europe anyway."[78] Finally, the Americans would certainly have been distressed by further reductions. To use the stabilization of troop levels in 1959 as a demonstration of European-mindedness therefore was slightly anachronistic.

Summing up all the evidence, the powerful influence of security questions on Germany's attitude toward British European policy is evident in many ways. Certainly, the British FTA proposals posed difficult economic questions, and Britain's desire to exclude agricultural products from the FTA, to sustain preferential treatment for Commonwealth members, and to resist a common external tariff was hard for the Europeans to accept. However, these economic divergences might have been overcome or at least mitigated by a more thorough search for compromises. Germany, for example, would have benefited economically more from the FTA than from the Common Market. Compromise formulas might have been found by concerted pressure on France from the other five countries. But when the moment approached for strong intervention to overcome the obstacles, the German government exerted little if any pressure on France. This unwillingness to search for a compromise or to support Britain more forcefully was due to conflicts over security. It was a clear misjudgment by the British government to use its security guarantee in economic and monetary conflicts with Europe while simultaneously depriving this guarantee of much of its credibility. What spoiled the FTA for the Germans was the lack of a political commitment. The proposal seemed designed more to contain than to cooperate with Germany. Seen as a whole, the conflicts in the security field and British proposals for Europe did not match. Thus, British policy was seen as contradictory and confused at best, and as deliberately destructive at worst.

78 Lloyd to Macmillan, July 8, 1959, PRO T 225/1391.

4

The Radford Plan: America and Its Troops in Germany, 1955–1958

During the 1950s the American GIs in Germany were, in sharp contrast to the controversies surrounding the British troop commitment from 1955 onward, not a source of serious conflict between stationing and host countries – apart from one significant episode, which forms the subject of this chapter. Within a few years after the end of World War II, the American military presence became an integral feature of the European postwar settlement. Divergences on their military and political roles were usually fought out in internal strategic debates that did not significantly affect troop levels. This relative calm and stability does not indicate, however, that in U.S. government circles preoccupations similar to British ideas were nonexistent. On the contrary, the principle of a seemingly unlimited presence of its troops in Europe was never accepted by the American government as a whole nor by Congress and the American public. However, in the absence of powerful financial counterarguments, such as balance-of-payments problems, the political arguments for an undiminished commitment to the defense of Europe carried the day in discussions within the government. This changed only in 1959 and 1960, when the American dollar came under pressure just as the English pound had.

Allied force levels in Europe were influenced by changes in strategic thinking and revised war plans. However, this influence was felt mainly at the planning level. When the plans were to be implemented, financial and political considerations proved to be stronger than strategic doctrines. To understand the debate about force reductions, it is necessary to recapitulate briefly the basic lines of the strategic discussion within the Alliance during the 1950s.

87

This debate was mainly about the most appropriate balance between conventional and nuclear weapons.[1] The basic lines of NATO's military strategy were set by the United States, which also retained, due to its exclusive possession of a huge nuclear potential, the ultimate decision about the actual use of nuclear arms. However, the established concepts of deterrence were challenged continuously, not only by the Europeans but also from within the U.S. administration and from many semiofficial strategic thinkers. Technological progress, political considerations, revised estimates of Soviet military power, and above all, economic limitations led to frequent doubts regarding the wisdom of the strategic doctrine of the day.

A stable factor in strategic thinking after the war was the feeling that conventional NATO troops were inferior to those of the Warsaw Pact. In the first years of the Cold War it therefore was tacitly accepted by American and British military planners that in case of a full-scale attack, the Soviet Union would conquer large parts of continental Europe.[2] With the help of air power and nuclear strikes, the occupied territory was then to be liberated, closely following allied strategy in World War II. However, the experience of the Korean War (1950–1) clearly showed the uselessness of atomic weapons in liberating occupied territory. In addition, the prospect of Soviet occupation was completely unacceptable to the Europeans. The implementation of a forward strategy became a political necessity. Its expression was the huge conventional buildup program that was adopted at the NATO Council meeting in Lisbon in February 1952. It provided for ninety-six divisions as the force goal, and it was clear that without German resources and manpower, this goal was impossible to achieve. To close the gap until German forces were available was one of the reasons why the United States formally approved the stationing of a large number of American troops in Europe.[3] But even given the existence of a German army, the NATO countries soon realized that the Lisbon plans were utopian, especially from a financial point of view. A way out of this dilemma was provided by the development of tactical nuclear weapons for use on the battlefield. The Eisenhower administra-

---

1 For an excellent review of the American strategic debate, see the articles in Trachtenberg, *History and Strategy.*

2 Wolfgang Krieger, "Die Ursprünge der langfristigen Stationierung amerikanischer Streitkräfte in Europa," in Herbst, Bührer, and Sowade, eds., *Marshall-Plan,* 373–99; Bernd Greiner, "Zur Rolle Kontinentaleuropas in den alliierten strategischen Planungen," in Maier and Wiggershaus, eds., *Das Nordatlantische Bündnis,* 147–50.

3 See Chapter 1; see also Gregory F. Treverton, *America, Germany, and the Future of Europe* (Princeton, N.J., 1992), 64–91.

tion adopted a corresponding military policy from 1953 onward, termed "New Look," based on an almost complete reliance on nuclear deterrence to decisively reduce the cost of defense. With tactical nuclear weapons, and by keeping the advantage in nuclear technology, it seemed possible to entrust deterrence mainly to the nuclear threat, avoiding the expensive maintenance of large conventional forces. Consequently, the United States' nuclear stockpile was increased dramatically (from 50 nuclear warheads in 1948 to 18,500 in 1960), and tactical nuclear weapons were stationed in Europe.[4] During the 1953 NATO Council meeting the Allies were informed of the new strategy.[5] They were assured by the United States that an attack on them would be answered immediately by atomic weapons. This was made credible by the presence of American troops on the front line, which would force the Americans from the first day to take part in any hostilities.

The so-called sword (strategic ballistic weapons) and shield (conventional troops reinforced by tactical nuclear weapons) strategy, which was the result of the New Look and was approved by NATO in document MC 48, assigned the troops the role of tripwire.[6] How strong this tripwire should be, however, was never established and was subject to heated debates. The military value of conventional troops was called into question when seen in those strictly strategic terms. Continuous pressure rose in various countries during the 1950s to save as much as possible on military budgets, notably in the United States and Britain. The Eisenhower administration and the Macmillan government never abandoned the hope of soon being able to reduce their commitment decisively. The Europeans, however, saw these commitments as politically and militarily essential for the postwar European security architecture. Thus, the political implications of conventional troops turned out to be a huge obstacle to reductions. Even when reliance on nuclear deterrence was paramount, troop reductions (or reduced-force goals) became hotly contested issues. Whatever strategic thinking was predominant at the time, its practical implementation would be dependent mainly on political and economic circumstances. This is demonstrated by the first German-American dispute on troop levels in 1956–7, which created considerable diplomatic discord. German and American strategic and political views of the troops differed

---

4 David A. Rosenberg, "The Origins of Overkill, 1945–1960," *International Security* 7 (1983): 3–71.
5 Klaus A. Maier, "Amerikanische Nuklearstrategie unter Truman und Eisenhower," in Maier and Wiggershaus, ed., *Das Nordatlantische Bündnis*, 234–40.
6 Marc Cioc, *Pax Atomica: The Nuclear Defense Debate in West Germany During the Adenauer Era* (New York, 1988), 7.

increasingly, and these differences were intensified by economic considerations. The crisis surrounding the so-called Radford Plan made this
abundantly clear.

On July 13, 1956, the *New York Times* published an article that reported
that the chairman of the U.S. Joint Chiefs of Staff, Admiral Arthur
Radford, planned a reduction of American conventional manpower by
800,000 men, nearly one-third of the total strength of the U.S. Army.[7]
Obviously, the European theater would be affected by reductions of this
magnitude. Adenauer was highly alarmed by the report, and he initiated
a major diplomatic effort to counter what he considered a dangerous
development with potentially disastrous consequences. The German
ambassadors in Washington, London, Paris, and at NATO headquarters
in Brussels were summoned to Bonn for consultations, emissaries went
to Washington, NATO, and the WEU, and Adenauer himself wrote an
impassioned letter to his "dear friend" Dulles.[8] In this letter he painted
an apocalyptic picture of the future world situation should the American
disengagement plans prove true. What lay behind this extraordinary response to an unconfirmed newspaper account?

Adenauer's reaction clearly underlined the importance he attached to
the U.S. troops in Germany. For him these troops were the fundamental
symbol of the American commitment to Europe. They were not only the
principal condition under which the other Europeans accepted German
sovereignty, they also literally guaranteed protection against a Soviet
Union that most Germans held to be extremely expansionist. The principal deterrent, the American nuclear umbrella, was effective and credible
for Germany only in combination with the strong conventional troop
presence of the NATO members. Without this "hostage function" of a
force that could pursue forward defense, Germany would have been confronted with two very inconvenient situations in the event of war: either
occupation or nuclear war on German soil. Thus, a strong and credible
conventional force level was essential. This was one of the main reasons
for the German government to pursue the establishment of a German
conventional army so shortly after the war, in direct opposition to a large
part of the West German population. To make this army acceptable to the
rest of Europe, the controlling force of the United States, represented by
its troops, was crucial, as Adenauer well understood.

7 *New York Times*, July 13, 1956.
8 Adenauer to Dulles, July 22, 1956, IFZ, Krekeler papers, 39; State Secretary Hallstein to Ambassador Krekeler, July 20, 1956, ibid., 47; conversation between Deputy Undersecretary Murphy and
  Ambassador Krekeler, July 17, 1956, in FRUS 1955–57, XXVI, 131–3.

Apart from these strategic and political reasons, domestic reasons were responsible for the uncompromising stance of Adenauer and his successors on stable troop levels. Any sign of American disengagement might have revived the bitter debate about rearmament and *Westintegration* (economic, military, and political integration with the West) that had dominated German politics in the early 1950s.[9] The opposition movement had heavily criticized Adenauer's policy of achieving sovereignty within the Western framework by rearming Germany and silently delaying the prospect for reunification. For if the Federal Republic was to be rearmed, any chance of an understanding with the Soviet Union over Germany as a whole seemed impossible. Another argument of the antimilitaristic movement, led by the Social Democratic Party (Sozialdemokratische Partei Deutschlands, or SPD), was the fear that German soldiers would, in the case of war, serve only as cannon fodder. The implementation of the New Look strategy in the United States, with its reliance on strategic and tactical nuclear weapons, made this interpretation somewhat plausible. The possible redeployment or reduction of American troops therefore played on Adenauer's worst fears, perhaps driving the Germans toward neutrality by undermining the credibility of *Westintegration*.[10] He had staked his credibility on this policy, and his "Grand Design" was threatened by the possibility of American disengagement. An additional galling detail of the whole affair was that it came just after the chancellor had returned from a visit to Washington, where he had not been informed of the government's plans.

The U.S. government was well aware of Adenauer's fears; and even if it did not know until the *New York Times* story, it knew perfectly well afterward thanks to Adenauer's tireless efforts to communicate his disapproval. Was the *New York Times* report credible? It was well known that Eisenhower basically supported the view that the American manpower commitment in Europe was only temporary, and he mentioned this frequently.[11] Indeed, a reduction of expensive conventional manpower would have been an essential element in putting the economizing aspects of the New Look strategy into force. But because they feared negative

---

9 Konrad Adenauer, *Erinnerungen (1955–1959)* (Stuttgart, 1967), 197–214; Hans-Gert Pöttering, *Adenauers Sicherheitspolitik 1955–1963: Ein Beitrag zum deutsch-amerikanischen Verhältnis* (Düsseldorf, 1975), 62–90.

10 These arguments are summarized in a speech that Brentano gave to the hastily convened WEU Council on September 15, 1956; for the text, see BA, Blankenhorn papers, 67/3.

11 "The president said he had always insisted that the Europeans should develop ground forces to replace ours" (memorandum on conference with president, Oct. 2, 1956, in FRUS 1955–57, IV, 100). For Eisenhower's views on this matter, see Marc Trachtenberg, *A Constructed Peace: The Making of the European Settlement, 1945–1963* (Princeton, N.J., 1999).

repercussions on the debate over the EDC, Eisenhower and Dulles never seriously planned such a risky move during the first half of the 1950s.[12] On the contrary, the Paris Accords were supplemented by a solemn declaration by the president that U.S. troops would remain in Europe as long as they were needed.[13] Soon, however, the economic consequences of this commitment became an issue in the Eisenhower administration, particularly after German support-cost contributions petered out.

The U.S. Treasury warned frequently of the foreign exchange losses implicit in long-term troop maintenance abroad.[14] Prior to 1958, however, these warnings did not have the weight to overcome the political counterarguments of the State Department. The focus of the administration's efforts to reduce costs therefore was on budgetary savings. Cost-saving studies were a common exercise for U.S. military services in these years. It seems that the Radford Plan was part of such a cost-saving study that had been leaked.[15] These studies were also an expression of the deep dissatisfaction felt by large parts of the administration regarding the slow progress the Allies were making toward achieving greater self-reliance in defense matters, thus failing to relieve the United States of the heavy burden of its worldwide commitments. Although proposals the size of the Radford Plan apparently survived only in the lower levels of government, a lively discussion, fed by the need to economize and suggested by new strategic priorities, nevertheless was going on in the higher ranks about the possibility of "streamlining" the forces. These discussions were reinforced by British intentions to reduce the BAOR. There also were considerable struggles going on among the different branches of the U.S. forces over the question of what the most appropriate strategy would be in employing conventional and atomic weapons. The Radford Plan indicated a certain preference for the Air Force's view to the detriment of the Army, whose influence shrank with the diminishing importance of the large troop contingents in Europe. It is quite possible that army officials were responsible for the leak to the *New York Times*.[16]

---

12 Thoss, "Presence of American Troops," 417–20.
13 The pledge stated that the government of the United States intended to "continue to maintain in Europe, including Germany, such units of its armed forces as may be necessary and appropriate to contribute its fair share of the forces needed for the joint defense of the North Atlantic area while the threat to that area exists, and will continue to deploy such forces in accordance with agreed North Atlantic strategy for the defense of this area" (FRUS 1952–54, V/2, 1345).
14 Memorandum of discussion at the 280th NSC meeting, Mar. 3, 1956, in FRUS 1955–57, XIX, 272–3.
15 Two hundred and forty-ninth NSC meeting, Aug. 17, 1956, in FRUS 1955–57, XIX, 349.
16 Rosenberg, "Overkill," 42–3; Felken, *Dulles*, 366.

During August and September 1956 the American government discussed different approaches to the problem. There was overall agreement
on the desirability of cuts in troop deployments abroad:

It should be our purpose to seek to establish a situation that would permit the
withdrawal of a considerable amount of U.S. ground forces from Europe as soon
as this can be done without undue risk. The creation of the German divisions
and the imaginative use of military manpower may afford that opportunity. The
sole question presented is whether circumstances at this time permit us either to
withdraw forces, or even publicly to disclose a trend in that direction.[17]

According to the State Department, such a political situation was not yet
extant. German pressure apparently worked. The prospect of an SPD
victory in the 1957 German elections alarmed the Americans more than
necessary. For the time being the principal interest of the State Department was "to avoid undercutting Adenauer," and Eisenhower agreed. He
"felt very definitely that we cannot take divisions out of Europe at this
time. The effect on Adenauer would be unacceptably damaging."[18]

Moreover, France supported the German position. Mollet, the French
prime minister, informed Dulles that his country still insisted on the
absolute necessity of the American troop presence:

Mr. Mollet explained to Mr. Dulles that the French understanding of the European defense problem rests on three principles: (1) Necessity of an American
presence in Europe. . . . It is indispensable that [the U.S.] is represented physi-
cally: The importance of the troop-levels derives from that; (2) Impossibility to
rely only on nuclear weapons. Conventional armaments are still indispensable . . . ;
(3) Necessity that atomic weapons, particularly tactical weapons, are stored
at the line where . . . the defense is organized.[19]

U.S. Senator Walter F. George was sent on a goodwill tour of Europe to
smooth ruffled feathers. He assured Adenauer that there would be no
withdrawal or reduction as long as the allies welcomed the U.S. presence.[20] This firm position was also meant to deter the United Kingdom
from bringing forward proposals for a reduction of its forces in Europe
during the NATO Council meeting in December 1956. The "job of
changing the German psychology from the present feeling that if we did
make any reduction whatever, we are abandoning them," as Dulles put it,

---

17 C. Burke Elbrick and Douglas MacArthur II to Dulles, Sept. 27, 1956, NSA, NHP, oral history
    sources compiled by Robert Wampler, box 5.
18 Two hundred and forty-ninth NSC meeting, Aug. 17, 1956, in FRUS 1955–57, XIX, 349;
    memorandum on conference with president, Oct. 2, 1956, ibid., 99.
19 Dulles–Mollet meeting, May 6, 1957, DDF 1957, II, 740.
20 George–Adenauer conversation, Sept. 28, 1956, in FRUS 1955–57, XXVI, 161–3.

would have to be sustained.[21] The convenient moment for large-scale U.S. troop reductions was expected to lie somewhere in the near future – an assumption that proved to be wrong. The Americans tried a more subtle method to reduce troops, suggested by the president: "The President asked why we cannot streamline divisions and cut down backup troops without public announcement. It could be done on a worldwide basis, avoiding the connotation of pulling out of Europe."[22] So it happened. The available data show that manpower in Germany fell from 262,000 in 1956 to 235,000 in 1958.[23] The departing troops were mostly Air Force units whose functions were made obsolete by tactical nuclear weapons arriving in Europe.[24] Large-scale reductions, however, were ruled out for the time being. During military budget discussions the subject was brought up regularly, but only at times of a sharply deteriorating balance of payments, such as 1959–60, did serious debate start anew.[25]

The persistent rumors about the debate within the American government were enough, however, to influence Adenauer's policy to a considerable extent. He was by no means reassured: In every conversation with American politicians in late 1956 he returned to the subject and complained about U.S. policy, incessantly demanding more consultation.[26] When Germany's failure in its own rearmament became clear, these complaints naturally caused a great deal of annoyance in Washington. The United States suspected that the turmoil caused by the Radford Plan was used by Adenauer to deflect American criticism regarding the planned reduction of the German conscription period from 18 to 12 months.[27] This motive cannot be ruled out completely, considering Adenauer's style of policy making, but his grievances had a very real background, as we have seen. German misgivings about the U.S. commitment to Europe remained. The German government considered it highly probable that the United States would redeploy its troops in due course. In the following

---

21 Memorandum on meeting at the White House, Aug. 12, 1956, in FRUS 1955–57, IV, 94n4.
22 Memorandum on conference with president, Apr. 2, 1957, in FRUS 1955–57, XXVI, 226.
23 See Appendix 1, Table 2.
24 Memorandum on conversation between president and Norstad, Oct. 28, 1957, in FRUS 1955–57, IV, 184–5; NSC memorandum: "U.S. Security Effort Overseas," Dec. 19, 1957, DDRS 1992, doc. 372.
25 E.g., see Cutler memorandum for president, July 1, 1957, in FRUS 1955–57, XIX, 533–5; 332d NSC meeting, July 25, 1957, in FRUS 1955–57, XIX, 556–65; 345th NSC meeting, Nov. 14, 1957, in FRUS 1955–57, XIX, 681.
26 Conversation between Adenauer and Quarles, Sept. 10, 1956, BA, Blankenhorn papers, 63/3; message from SACEUR (Alfred Gruenther) to Andrew Goodpaster, Nov. 19, 1956, in FRUS 1955–57, XXVI, 174–5; Schwarz, *Adenauer*, 320.
27 Telegram from U.S. Embassy, Bonn, to secretary of state, Oct. 16, 1956, in FRUS 1955–57, XXVI, 167.

years Adenauer frequently cited the Radford Plan as evidence of the United States' unreliability. Any new sign of shrinking U.S. troop levels would revive this mistrust.

The Radford Plan also had immediate repercussions on German foreign policy. In a speech in Brussels in September 1956 Adenauer emphasized as strongly as ever before the importance of the European integration process.[28] Implicitly criticizing the United States, he gave strong approval to the "relaunching" of European integration, initiated by the meeting of the foreign ministers of France, Germany, Italy, and the Benelux countries in Messina in June 1955. The Radford Plan played a prominent role in making Adenauer an outspoken European at this time, as the French noted gleefully: "At present, the chancellor regards the American policy with strong reservations and this also applies to statesmen and diplomats of the United States. . . . To counter this, he considers it absolutely necessary that the European countries are united. From there derives his will to revive European policy in a situation that he thinks is the last opportunity."[29] During a famous meeting with Mollet at the height of the Suez Crisis he appeared to be almost hysterical about the danger of a Soviet–American condominium over the world.[30]

The Radford Plan also played a role in the reconsideration of German abstinence in the nuclear field pursued by Adenauer and parts of the German political establishment in the following years.[31] Adenauer gave Defense Minister Strauss free rein in talks on nuclear cooperation with France and Italy, as mentioned previously.

The Radford Plan thus forced West Germany to see the limitations and problems of too strong a reliance on the United States. It made abundantly clear that the U.S. presence and its role as a pacifier were not to be taken for granted. It was, however, only a foreshadowing of the debate about the permanence of American troops in Europe, which was to escalate during the 1960s.

---

28 Adenauer, *Reden*, 329.
29 Foreign Minister Couve de Murville to Ambassador Pineau, Oct. 10, 1956, DDF 1956, III, 1990, doc. 261, 553.
30 Adenauer–Mollet conversations, Paris, Nov. 6, 1956, DDF 1956, III, 1990, doc. 138, 237.
31 Cabell, CIA acting director, memorandum to secretary of state, Aug. 28, 1956, in FRUS 1955–57, XXVI, 148; see also Greiner, "Militärische Eingliederung," 731–6.

5

The Political Economy of U.S. Troop
Stationing in Europe

THE CAUSES OF THE DOLLAR PROBLEM

In November 1960 Robert B. Anderson, the U.S. secretary of the treasury, and Douglas Dillon, the U.S. undersecretary of state, paid a visit
to Bonn that has been called "a striking symbol" of the changing nature
of European–American relations.[1] Whereas in the first postwar decade
European delegations crossed the Atlantic to negotiate economic help
with their American counterparts, the mission of Anderson and Dillon
was aimed at rallying the Europeans to the defense of the American currency, which had been under pressure since 1958. Germany was the main
target, and the negotiators' agenda included a request for a direct contribution toward the cost of maintaining U.S. troops in Germany. Press
commentators on both sides rushed to the event. The German press commented on the visit with particular malice. Anderson and Dillon were
portrayed as begging for money and, to underline this characterization,
the German news magazine *Der Spiegel* printed a photo showing the stout
German minister of economics, Ludwig Erhard, lecturing the skinny
Anderson.[2] The Anderson–Dillon mission illuminates the increasingly
intertwined nature of security and monetary problems in German–
American relations. The visit signaled a new framework in which
European–American relations were to evolve: The limits of American
economic power became visible and contrasted sharply with the success
of the European recovery, particularly in the monetary field. This change,
partly perception, partly reality, had enormous political consequences.
Monetary questions were to affect American–German relations (and
American–European relations in general) deeply during the 1960s. A

---

1 Robert Solomon, *The International Monetary System, 1945–81* (New York, 1982), 33.
2 *Der Spiegel* 49 (1960): 27.

closer look at the causes for and consequences of the visit will help us to understand the real changes taking place and their political significance.

The developments in the international monetary system prior to 1960, particularly the emergence of large American balance-of-payments deficits, were widely seen as the most conspicuous sign of a fundamental change in U.S.–European relations. Later on, commentators usually referred to the decline of the dollar when speaking of a supposed "decline of U.S. hegemony."[3] In the early 1950s the annual American deficits stayed close to $1 billion; in 1958–60 they suddenly rose to more than $3 billion. American gold reserves declined from $22.86 billion in 1957 to $17.8 billion in 1960.[4] Nobody had expected this to happen, and these alarming figures moved rapidly to the center of public and official attention. In order to understand why this development occurred and why it caused such alarm in the United States and in financial circles all over the world, it is necessary to outline briefly the basic features of the international monetary system as it evolved during the postwar period.

Already during World War II various blueprints for a postwar monetary system had been drawn up in Great Britain and the United States. The common ground in these plans was the conviction, especially strong on the American side, that the chaos in international financial markets during the 1930s had had a decisive influence on the catastrophic events that followed.[5] The conclusion drawn was that the most developed coun-

3 The concept of "hegemony" is problematic yet dominates the political science literature focusing on the international monetary system. There is no agreement on whether U.S. hegemony was actually declining or whether this hegemony was benign or repressive. This ambiguity illustrates the problem of using this concept as an analytical tool in historical research. Another drawback is that an emphasis on U.S. hegemony fosters a tendency to portray European policies as essentially reactive. Historians of U.S.–European relations during the 1950s have questioned the extent of American influence in shaping European affairs, for example, during the debate over the Marshall Plan. See Charles S. Maier, "Introduction," in Charles S. Maier, ed., *The Marshall Plan and Germany: West German Development Within the Framework of the European Recovery Program* (New York, 1991). The use of "hegemony" in analyzing transatlantic relations is critically assessed by Anthony T. Gadzey, *The Political Economy of Power: Hegemony and Economic Liberalism* (London, 1994).
4 See Appendix 1, Table 2. Again, as in the British case, we encounter the difficulty of evaluating balance-of-payments statistics. How to measure the balance of payments correctly has always been a bone of contention among economists. Every country has its own accounting method. Moreover, governments have numerous opportunities to manipulate the statistics by changing their methods. The present study is not meant to contribute to this debate. The officially announced figures, used in diplomatic dealings and in major financial statistics, are accepted as the basis on which decision makers founded their policies. The so-called liquidity balance, equating liquid liabilities to foreign governments and private holders as well as changes in official reserve assets, was regarded by the U.S. government until 1966 as the overall measure for the balance-of-payments position.
5 C. Fred Bergsten, *The Dilemmas of the Dollar: The Economics and Politics of United States International Monetary Policy* (New York, 1975), 329; the classic study on the creation of the postwar monetary system is Richard N. Gardner, *Sterling-Dollar Diplomacy: The Origins and the Prospects of Our International Economic Order* (New York, 1969). Recent assessments include Harold James, "The IMF

tries had to cooperate closely in their monetary policies to prevent a return to the disastrous monetary practices of the interwar period. Moreover, a closer control of market forces by state authorities seemed necessary. This conviction was a fundamental driving force in postwar American economic policy toward Europe. The central role accorded monetary policy in the stabilization of postwar Europe and in creating an economically liberal Atlantic system, protected by a U.S.-dominated security system, is an important factor for understanding the American reluctance regarding changes in the system. The monetary system and the security system were two sides of the same coin, and changes in one sphere invariably affected the other, as we shall see.

To avoid the unilateral currency devaluations and the massive trade restrictions that had characterized the "beggar thy neighbor" policies of so many interwar governments, American and British officials devised, at the 1944 Bretton Woods Conference, a system of fixed exchange rates for the major world currencies. The values of these currencies were pegged to the dollar, and this made the dollar the center of the system. Exchange-rate fluctuations were to be limited to the extreme circumstance of *fundamental disequilibrium*, a very vague term. The value of the dollar was expressed by a fixed rate to gold ($35 per ounce). Dollar holders were given the guarantee by the U.S. government that they could exchange their dollars for gold at this rate at any time. The U.S. gold stock thus provided the keystone for exchange-rate stability in this system. The objective was to make all major currencies convertible with each other and with the dollar, thus guaranteeing an undisturbed flow of goods and capital in the world economy. In case a country experienced balance-of-payments difficulties, it would draw on the resources of the newly created body, the IMF. This system, negotiated by Britain and the United States but perforce also accepted by the rest of the industrial countries (apart from the Communist Bloc), had another important consequence that made it different from prewar practices: The participating governments "formally committed themselves to the principle of collective responsibility for the management of the international monetary order."[6] In international organizations such as the IMF, the OEEC, the EPU, and the BIS, among others, monetary policy was discussed and common solutions were sought.

and the Creation of the Bretton Woods System," in Barry Eichengreen, ed., *Europe's Postwar Recovery* (Cambridge, 1995), 93–126; Georg Schild, *Bretton Woods and Dumbarton Oaks: American Economic and Political Postwar Planning in the Summer of 1944* (New York, 1995).

6 Benjamin C. Cohen, *Organizing the World's Money: The Political Economy of International Monetary Relations* (London, 1977), 93.

This was particularly important when the rules of the Bretton Woods system revealed themselves to be out of tune with the severe realities of the postwar world and the rapidly changing economic circumstances. The major problem was the immense need for capital and goods to recon-struct the war-ravaged European economies. Only the United States was able to provide such capital and essential commodities. Thus, it became by far the biggest supplier of goods to world markets, and the need for dollars to pay for these goods soon made the dollar a rare asset. Most governments had to impose heavy restrictions to prevent conversion runs from their currency to the dollar. The ill-fated attempt by the United Kingdom to return to convertibility in 1947, for example, resulted in such a run. It made clear that a longer transitory period than expected would be necessary before full convertibility could be achieved. Meanwhile, U.S. economic programs and military aid fueled the European economies with liquidity in the form of dollars. This provided Europe with the possibil-ity of building up its reserves and also kept the European market open for American business. What emerged was a fixed-rate dollar standard dif-fering in many aspects from the plans envisaged at Bretton Woods.[7] Among the features remaining were the gold–dollar link and the U.S. promise to guarantee the value of the dollar with its gold reserves. This actually was not necessary for the functioning of the fixed-rate dollar system and ultimately proved fatal for it. However, in the late 1940s it was hardly possible to foresee that the Cold War would last as long as it did and that the corresponding outflow of dollars to finance U.S. com-mitments abroad would continue, transforming the dollar gap into a dollar glut. In any case, the system worked very well for most of the 1950s. At the end of 1958 most European countries had achieved the goal of closing the dollar gap and had built up respectable monetary reserves, held mainly in dollars. De facto convertibility was introduced. The sudden emergence of huge U.S. balance-of-payments deficits, however, almost immediately threw the system into crisis.

THE DEBATE OVER THE BALANCE-OF-PAYMENTS DEFICIT

The debate on the causes and consequences of the American deficit pro-duced innumerable reports by governments, journalists, and scholars.[8] The

---

7 Ronald I. McKinnon, "The Rules of the Game: International Money in Historical Perspective," *Journal of Economic Literature* 3 (1993): 1–44.
8 The contributors to the extensive literature on monetary problems in the 1960s divide roughly into four categories: economists, political scientists, historians, and participants in international

most influential contribution was a study published in 1960 by the Belgian-American economist Robert Triffin. In *Gold and the Dollar Crisis* Triffin pointed to an inherent paradox in the dollar–gold system, which later became known as the "Triffin Dilemma."[9] His analysis focused on the international monetary system's dependence on the dollar as the main source of liquidity for the world. This was a consequence of the liquidity gap after the war that had put countries in reconstruction on a de facto dollar standard. The role of the dollar as reserve currency and transaction unit implied, according to Triffin, that the United States necessarily had annual balance-of-payments deficits caused by the outflow of dollars into the growing world economy. However, as the numbers of dollars in the reserves of major industrial countries and those accumulating in the system mounted, the U.S. gold reserves, which guaranteed the value of the dollar, no longer were able to cover all the claims on the U.S. government. Consequently, confidence in the value of the dollar waned, and dollar holders exchanged their holdings for gold, draining the U.S. gold stock. The necessary measure to restore confidence would have been to restrict the outflow of dollars. This, however, would have resulted in a shortage of liquidity for world trade. (Gold as a rare raw material was not able to cover the expansion of world trade.) Thus, the system was undermining itself. The solution Triffin devised for this problem was a type of world bank where the rich industrial countries could pool their reserves, which would then become the source of liquidity.

However, like most of the ingenious mechanisms economists contrived, this proposal was out of step with political reality. The surrender of sovereignty to such a body was hardly acceptable to any nation at that time.

monetary diplomacy. Examples of accounts by economists include Michael D. Bordo and Barry Eichengreen, eds., *A Retrospective on the Bretton Woods System: Lessons for International Monetary Reform* (Chicago, 1993); Leland B. Yeager, *International Monetary Relations: Theory, History, and Policy*, 2d ed. (New York, 1976). Political scientists tackle the problem mostly by scrutinizing the power structure behind international monetary relations: see, e.g., Fred L. Block, *The Origins of International Economic Disorder: A Study of United States International Monetary Policy from World War II to the Present* (Berkeley, Calif., 1977); Bergsten, *Dilemmas of the Dollar*; Cohen, *Organizing the World's Money*; Stephen D. Cohen, *International Monetary Reform, 1964–1969* (New York, 1970); John S. Odell, *U.S. International Monetary Relations* (New York, 1982); Strange, *International Economic Relations*. Historical accounts based on archival research are rare: William S. Borden, "Defending Hegemony: American Foreign Economic Policy," in Thomas G. Paterson, ed., *Kennedy's Quest for Victory: American Foreign Policy, 1961–1963* (New York, 1989), 57–85; Kunz, *Butter and Guns*; James, *International Monetary Cooperation*. Policy makers concerned with monetary problems also contributed to the debate. Among the best known are: Milton Gilbert, *Quest for World Monetary Order* (New York, 1980); Solomon, *International Monetary System*; Robert V. Roosa, *The Dollar Problem and World Liquidity* (New York, 1967); Charles A. Coombs, *The Arena of International Finance* (New York, 1976).

9 For the following discussion, see Robert Triffin, *Gold and the Dollar Crisis: The Future of Convertibility* (New Haven, Conn., 1960).

As usual, governments looked not for the most rational solution to the monetary problem but for the politically most opportune. Corrective actions in the monetary field entailed – as they still do – very unpopular measures. This was a strong incentive to perpetuate the dollar–gold standard by treating the symptoms and neglecting the causes. After all, the Triffin dilemma had been there since the end of the war and the system nevertheless had worked to mutual advantage.[10]

The different elements of the American deficit were easily identifiable. Apart from temporary factors, four causes of a structural nature were mainly responsible: (1) U.S. military expenditure abroad (including foreign aid). The maintenance of military facilities on a worldwide basis and the expansion of foreign aid to stabilize friendly governments were essential parts of American Cold War foreign policy. In the case of Europe the implicit outflow of capital coincided positively with the European need for dollar liquidity during the 1950s. This need vanished, as we have seen. The U.S. military posture, however, remained essentially the same, as did the dollar drain associated with it. (2) U.S. investments abroad and long-term capital outflow. As the European recovery proceeded, investment in the European market became very attractive for American business. Factors such as low labor costs, the lowering of tariffs within the Common Market, the proximity of markets, and so forth, made this an obvious strategy for U.S. investors.[11] (3) The shrinking American trade surplus, closely connected with re-emerging European competitiveness and output. (4) Short-term capital movements. The pegged exchange-rate system made speculation against currencies under pressure good business without much risk. Sterling, and subsequently the dollar, repeatedly became the target of speculative attacks that then required costly rescue actions. (See Appendix 1, Table 2, for figures on the U.S. balance of payments.)

A rapid correction of these factors would have required revolutionary changes in U.S. foreign and domestic policies, such as a reappraisal of its security policy, the introduction of currency controls, direct controls over American investment abroad, or curbing the domestic economy to keep prices down. The last option was hardly considered in the United States, contrary to the British case. To balance its external account, Britain resorted repeatedly to restrictive domestic policies. There were hardly any

10 This inertia was one of the main reasons that flexible exchange rates were ruled out for such a long time; see also Milward, "Origins," 135–51.
11 Thomas L. Ilgen, *Autonomy and Interdependence: U.S.–Western European Monetary and Trade Relations, 1958–1984* (Totowa, N.J., 1985), 27.

other options available, apart from devaluation and large-scale borrowing abroad. The United States, however, was able to exert enough influence to get other countries to hold large parts of its reserves in dollars and not exchange them for gold. The Americans were also able to induce other countries, including Britain, to accept a monetary policy that actively supported the reserve-currency role of the dollar. Britain lacked this bargaining power. Everyone except the Sterling Area countries was free to cash in surplus sterling for dollars and thus add to the rampant speculation against the pound.

Devaluation, the most logical way of adjustment for any country with a persistent deficit, was ruled out by the American government as long as the dollar was not seen as fundamentally overvalued. Moreover, without the acceptance of this measure by Washington's major trading partners, such a move might be neutralized by devaluations in other major countries. It was also very likely that a change in the dollar–gold parity would end an international monetary system that held considerable advantages for the United States. It had been instrumental in building up a "free world" that was economically and militarily compatible with American policies, it had helped to finance long-term military commitments abroad without balance-of-payments constraints or domestic inflation, and it made the United States the issuer of the world's principal monetary vehicle and reserve currency.[12] Further reasons against devaluation were notions of prestige and national pride. Until the early 1970s U.S. presidents saw devaluation as humiliating for the nation and disastrous for themselves on the domestic front. It is not by accident that militaristic language like "the battle for the dollar" or "war against the deficits" was used so often by the U.S. government.

Thus, radical solutions were ruled out. Other, less grave measures were sought, often requiring active cooperation by other countries. The U.S. government did not see the deficits as its sole responsibility. The view became prominent in Washington that American policies that had helped to rebuild and protect Europe were the main cause of the deficits and that the beneficiaries should take over part of the burden of adjustment. This basic, underlying conviction is fundamental to understanding American

---

12 This argument was brought forward forcefully by European critics of U.S. monetary policy, such as Susan Strange: "The United States had used its exorbitant privilege as the centre-country of a gold-exchange system to run a perpetual balance-of-payments deficit and to finance a distant and expensive war in Vietnam by inflationary credit creation rather than by a transfer of resources from the civilians to the military by means of taxation"; see her "Interpretations of a Decade," in Loukas Tsoukalis, ed., *The Political Economy of International Money: In Search of a New Order* (London, 1985), 11.

international monetary policy in the 1960s. It also partly explains the emphasis many American politicians put on the foreign-exchange cost of U.S. troops, although they were only a limited part of the problem. Much of the political argument between Europeans and Americans on the payments deficit was due to a structural omission in the framework of the international monetary system. Nowhere was it stipulated that surplus or deficit countries should take the necessary steps in case of a persistent imbalance.[13] On a global level there were no formal procedures to settle such imbalances. The conflict had to be decided by interstate bargaining, and a basic economic problem thus became a highly politicized issue. Monetary adjustment in a fixed-rate system has strong repercussions on the domestic economy and politics of the adjusting country, and is therefore risky for any government. It was much safer to get other countries to adjust. The result was various political and economic pressures that led to the kinds of linkages that the troop-cost issue exemplifies.

The disagreements about the responsibility for adjustment found their expression in the profoundly different views held by the United States and the European governments. This fundamental divergence is well summarized in an exchange of letters between Marius Holtrop, president of the Dutch central bank, and Eduard Bernstein, a high-ranking American IMF official.[14] Both made very clear who they thought should take the principal steps to solve the problem. Holtrop concluded his letter by stating that "the solution of the American balance-of-payments problem has fundamentally to be found in the internal economic policies of the United States. This conclusion is not different from the one we arrived at when balance-of-payments troubles, after the period of reconstruction was over, still harassed many European countries." Bernstein retorted: "If the United States continues to bear an excessive share of the expense of defense within Europe . . . and relieves the European countries of meeting an adequate part of the cost of their own defense, it is inevitable that these wealthy countries will save too much . . . this is the central part of the U.S. payments problem . . . the U.S. cannot solve its payments problems through its own financial policies." These key positions were to be repeated during the 1960s and formed the background of a debate that became increasingly acrimonious.[15]

---

13 Erik Hoffmeyer, *The International Monetary System: An Essay in Interpretation* (Amsterdam, 1992), 70.
14 The letters are in the archive of the Dutch Foreign Ministry: Holtrop to Bernstein, July 26, 1960, MF/GT/891/EEG/E/Algemeen/4; Bernstein to Holtrop, Aug. 17, 1960, MF/GT/891/EEG/E/Algemeen/4. The author thanks Ynze Alkema for making these documents available.
15 A concise summary of European–American differences in monetary matters is provided in Harold van B. Cleveland, *The Atlantic Idea and Its European Rivals* (New York, 1966), 75–95.

In the late 1950s, however, both sides agreed that they had better find some common ground and coordinate their monetary policies to a greater extent than they had previously. The introduction of convertibility for European currencies in 1958 had vastly increased the amount of capital movement, and the negative American balance of payments caused large-scale speculation. The Europeans first pointed out the dangers of this development. They had rebuilt their reserves, yet dollars were still accumulating in their accounts. The temptation to transfer them back to gold was strong, but it was a two-edged strategy, given the dangers to the international monetary system this implied. There was general transatlantic agreement on the desirability of continuing with a system that had served the participants well since the end of the war and whose breakup would have unforeseeable consequences. The major questions were what action should be taken and, above all, who should take it.

GETTING OUT OF EUROPE OR PAYING THE BILL

It is difficult to trace the exact point at which the balance of payments began seriously to trouble the American administration and the public. There had always been deficits during the 1950s, apart from an exceptional year in 1957, when the Suez Crisis pushed raw materials prices up and produced a small surplus. Shortly afterward, the American economy slumped into a brief recession, characterized by low investment rates and rising unemployment. When it recovered, parallel to a period of stagnation in European economies, the trade balance of the United States was unsettled by an import boom and a slowing down of exports to Europe. The traditionally high American trade surplus with Europe, which had balanced capital export and government expenditure abroad, shrank considerably.[16] At the same time, the drain on the U.S. gold stock rose to record levels. The recession also led to a loss of confidence in the dollar.

The convergence of these temporary factors with the structural factors outlined above caused the high 1958–60 deficits. In November 1958 President Eisenhower and Robert Anderson informed the Senate majority leader, Lyndon B. Johnson, about warnings from abroad concerning the dollar's stability. Eisenhower set the tone of the later debate, stating that "the stability of our currency is an absolute necessity to our security and our economic development,"[17] but serious discussion started only in

---

16 For these developments, see background paper: "U.S. Balance-of-Payments Position," Nov. 16, 1960, NA, RG 59, lot files: BEA, OGA, box 5.
17 NSA, NHP (Fred Kaplan Donation), box 1, folder 61, Nov. 18, 1958.

mid-1959. From the outset, the solution of raising the price of gold, which meant a devaluation of the dollar, was ruled out as contradicting basic U.S. postwar policy.[18] Foreign economic policy was still a prerogative of the State Department, and in a short paper of July 1959 it laid out its proposed course: The authors acknowledged that the present trend in the balance of payments could not be allowed to continue. The sharp decline of the trade balance and large military expenditures abroad were identified as the fundamental problems.[19] Rejecting explicitly restrictive measures in the domestic economy, the paper proposed the removal of trade restrictions of all kinds, the substitution of U.S. foreign aid by European aid, and a reduction of military expenditures. The cabinet approved a program of action along those lines in August 1959. Subsequently, Washington intensified its efforts toward trade liberalization, in particular vis-à-vis Europe, and toward a more equitable sharing of the foreign-aid burden.[20]

Divergences within the administration emerged on the reduction of military expenditures. A recurrent theme in European–American relations in the 1950s was that Washington felt that it bore a disproportionate share of the cost of common defense. Time and again, Eisenhower criticized European reticence toward shouldering more of the burden:

We should ask when the hell these other people are going to do their duty. We have got to get tougher with them. . . . These other NATO powers cannot go on forever riding on our coat-tails. . . . All of these nations seem to be trying to figure out how little they themselves can do and how best to leave us to do the rest of the job.[21]

The gold outflow and the deficits added to this sentiment: "The President said he would have no objection to new measures in Berlin and Germany. He commented that, for example, it is time to pull out some of our forces now located in Europe. He cited the balance-of-payments difficulties the U.S. is experiencing at the present time."[22] The foreign exchange cost of American forces in Germany had risen sharply through-

18 U.S.–British meeting, June 10, 1958, in FRUS 1958–60, IV, 7–28; minutes of cabinet meeting, Mar. 13, 1959, in FRUS 1958–60, IV, 103.
19 Paper prepared by DOS: "U.S. International Payments Position," July 24, 1959, ibid., 115–20.
20 Record of actions on items presented at cabinet meeting, Aug. 19, 1959, ibid., 53–4. A U.S. initiative at the 1958 session of GATT led to the lifting of many quotas in European-American trade. The so-called Dillon Round, negotiating mutual tariff reductions, started only in 1961. For the American effort to get their allies to share the foreign-aid burden, see Burton I. Kaufman, *Trade and Aid: Eisenhower's Foreign Economic Policy, 1953–1961* (Baltimore, 1982).
21 Memorandum on discussion at the 390th NSC meeting, Dec. 11, 1958, in FRUS 1958–60, VII, 368–9.
22 Memorandum on conference with president, Oct. 16, 1959, ibid., IX, 70.

out the 1950s, particularly after the termination of occupation and support-cost payments. In FY 1953–5 it had been $250 million, in 1956, $316 million, in 1957, $425 million, in 1958, $545 million, and in 1959, $686 million, a level that was expected to remain stable.[23] Compared with the liquidity deficit, it seemed as if troop stationing in Germany contributed to about 20 percent of the deficit. As illustrated in earlier chapters when discussing the cost of British troops, it is very difficult to establish the real impact of troop maintenance abroad on the balance of payments of the stationing country. There is little doubt, however, that American troops contributed considerably to the accumulation of reserves by the Federal Republic and, correspondingly, to the American deficit. This factor and the growing dissatisfaction with the intractability of the political and military situation in Europe sparked a contentious debate within the U.S. government that centered on the question of whether monetary and military developments required a reduction of the U.S. military commitment in Europe. The arguments used during this debate will be outlined in some detail in the following; they were to come up again and again in subsequent discussions within later American administrations.

In late 1959, during the budget discussions, a series of high-level meetings were devoted to the problem. The initiative seems to have originated – like the Radford Plan – in the Department of Defense. The secretary of defense, Neil McElroy, thought that troop cuts in Europe were now possible and desirable for military reasons. These were, first, the diminished importance of conventional troops due to the gigantic nuclear capability the United States had built up during the 1950s in both the strategic and tactical ranges, and second, the improved mobility of combat forces. McElroy predicted that

the U.S. is going to have to begin withdrawing forces from Europe and otherwise cutting back in FY 1961. This is necessary not so much because of a desire on our part to reduce our defense expenditures . . . but because of our deteriorating foreign exchange position. . . . At the same time, it would give us a great deal more flexibility to have the principal body of our troop strength in the U.S. where they could be dispatched quickly to any trouble spot.

McElroy added that "it seems likely that West Germany would soon be in a position to take over the U.S. role as chief defender of Western

23 Briefing paper for the Anderson-Dillon mission: "Support Costs," Nov. 1960, NA, RG 59, BEA, OGA, box 14. To give an illustration of how this foreign exchange was used: The 1959 figure ($686 million) comprised $295.5 million for contractual services, $243 million for military pay, and $109 million for materials and supply.

Europe."[24] He was strongly supported by Anderson, who argued that the balance-of-payments problem was as vital as defense matters. In his opinion, this problem could not be solved by conventional means and urgently required action on military expenditure abroad.

Against this, Thomas S. Gates, the deputy secretary of defense, pointed out that "he did not see how we could balance our budget unless we completely revolutionized our military strategy."[25] His position was supported by the State Department, as expressed by Acting Secretary of State Gerard Smith:

> There seems to me to be no greater problem facing this government than whether or not to warp our military doctrine and stunt our military establishment to meet temporary economic pressures. We face the alternative whether to run an uncertain risk of some loss of confidence in the dollar or the certain risk of a loss of confidence in America's determination to make common cause with its allies and maintain a rational and credible deterrent to communist aggression. If this happens, the standing of the American dollar and a great deal more besides will inevitably be prejudiced.[26]

The president took a position between the two views. Although he was increasingly frustrated with the fact that the United States' troops seemed to be stuck in Europe and was deeply worried about the gold drain, he was also highly sensitive to any action that could unsettle NATO. At the beginning of November he met with SACEUR, General Norstad, who argued strongly against force cuts because of the dangerous situation provoked by Nikita Khrushchev's 1958 Berlin ultimatum, which sparked the second Berlin crisis. After once more denouncing the Europeans for "making a sucker out of Uncle Sam," the president agreed in the end "that we cannot take ruthless actions simply for financial reasons."[27]

Soon afterward he convened a meeting of the National Security Council (NSC) in which the opponents in the debate once more presented their arguments.[28] The director of the budget, Maurice Stans, pointed out that the whole NATO commitment cost the United States $4 billion a year in budgetary terms, of which $1.2 billion were relevant

---

24 Excerpt from a memorandum on a conversation between Burden and McElroy, attached to a memorandum from Deputy Undersecretary Livingston Merchant to Secretary of State Herter, Sept. 25, 1959, NSA, The Berlin Crisis, doc. 1666.
25 Conversation among Anderson, Herter, McElroy, and others, Oct. 24, 1959, in FRUS 1958–60, VII/1, 488–94.
26 Memorandum from Gerard Smith, acting secretary of state, to Christian Herter, Oct. 29, 1959, ibid., 496.
27 Memorandum on Norstad–Eisenhower conversation, Nov. 4, 1959, ibid., 497–500.
28 Memorandum on a discussion at the 424th NSC meeting, Nov. 12, 1959, ibid., 504–15.

for the balance of payments. He doubted whether he could ever balance the budget with this burden. Representatives of the State Department and the Central Intelligence Agency, however, warned of political destabilization in Europe in case of troop cuts. They believed that reductions should be effected only if there were corresponding moves by the Soviet Union. The president apparently had decided against reductions beforehand. He stated, grudgingly, that the time was not yet ripe for reductions. The final decision was "that there would be no significant cuts in calendar year 1960 in the forces committed to NATO for that year, unless agreed to through negotiations [with the Soviet Union]."[29] Eisenhower's rather timid disarmament proposals, however, never came close to mutual force reductions. This was due partly to Konrad Adenauer's resistance to any such scheme. The idea that mutual, balanced force reductions were a solution to the problem was to surface again, particularly during the Johnson administration.

The outcome of the debate signified that the balance-of-payments crisis would, for the moment, remain separated from the issue of troop levels in Europe. After all, the dollar difficulties were widely seen as temporary, manageable, and even self-correcting because costs and prices were rising faster in Europe than in the United States. The political rationale behind a stable troop commitment was still perceived as strong enough to overcome short-term economic difficulties. Washington's activism therefore centered on trade liberalization and foreign aid. Germany was asked to create its own foreign-aid program.[30] The Germans, relieved by the absence of troop-cut threats and support-cost demands, promised vigorous efforts. But the results were poor. One year later, during the annual meeting of the IMF and the World Bank, the Germans were the targets of strong criticism directed at their failure to initiate a foreign-aid program that might have helped to correct their high surplus.[31] At the same meeting, the Americans were confronted with widespread anxiety in international financial circles about the future of the international monetary system if the dollar deficits continued. This was no surprise. Despite a remarkable recovery in the trade balance, another high balance-of-payments deficit was expected at the end of 1960. It was clear that the first efforts of the Eisenhower administration had not yielded the expected

---

29 Ibid., 515.
30 Anderson memorandum to president, Dec. 2, 1959, in FRUS 1958–60, IV, 357; Dillon–German government conversation, Dec. 11, 1959, in FRUS 1958–60, VII/1, 196–201.
31 *New York Times*, Sept. 27, 1960, 5; *Financial Times*, Sept. 28, 1960.

results. The gold outflow continued with irritating regularity, and U.S. liabilities came perilously close to the point where they were no longer covered by U.S. gold reserves.

The American government also became aware of a possible spillover into other policy fields. This was true, above all, for relations with those allies who were the main recipients of outflowing dollars or gold. In the case of serious conflict – and Charles de Gaulle's actions since his ascendancy to power were ominous – this factor could possibly be used as a tool against the United States.

[State Secretary Christian A.] Herter said that a report, almost a rumor, had come to him that, during the conversations of de Gaulle and Adenauer, they talked about shifting the currency base from dollars to gold, in part as a means of putting pressure on the United States to accede to some of their ideas affecting NATO. The President said that if this were to happen, our immediate and necessary action would be to pull our forces out of Europe and that this would destroy at their very heart the security arrangements in Europe.[32]

The exchange almost prophetically shows the hidden political conflict in the balance-of-payments question and its emerging linkage to the context of security policy in the alliance.

As the gold losses continued, despite the United States' recovery in the trade balance, more drastic action than the export-promotion program advocated by the State Department was obviously necessary. The options seemed limited. Restrictive action in the domestic economy was hardly considered, given its unpopularity in the middle of Richard M. Nixon's election campaign against John F. Kennedy and the fact that the economy had just come out of a recession. Interest rates remained low for this reason, and what was decisive, they remained lower than the rates in Europe.[33] Thus, in the autumn of 1960 attention focused again on U.S. military commitments. This time, the feeling that the monetary problem would be temporary had been shattered. Anderson informed his colleagues that "this large outflow and accumulation by financially strong Western European countries and Japan was more likely to create a crisis both for the United States and the Free World than any other set of existing circumstances."[34] He accused the State Department and the Pentagon of having blocked all burden-sharing initiatives by citing various political

32 Memorandum on conversation, Aug. 12, 1960, in FRUS 1958–60, IV, 127.
33 From June to August 1960, the U.S. discount rate was lowered from 4 percent to 3 percent. The Germans, struggling with a booming economy, raised their rate from 4 to 5 percent and thus massively attracted speculative capital. See Emminger, "Deutsche Geld- und Währungspolitik," 502.
34 Memorandum on meeting with president, Oct. 4, 1960, DDRS 92 (408).

obstacles. According to Anderson, it was time "to negotiate on a bilateral basis with the European countries, and especially Germany, for the payment of the cost of maintaining United States forces abroad."[35] This time the president acknowledged the need for firm measures, and an action program for further study was formulated that included the removal of the troops' dependents from Europe, support-cost negotiations with Germany, force reductions, and further trade liberalization. Simultaneously, Eisenhower wrote a letter to Adenauer in which he pointed to the need for German action in the area of international monetary policy and announced that Anderson and Dillon would visit Bonn to pursue corresponding negotiations.[36]

The alarm felt in the U.S. government grew close to panic when an unforeseen event in October 1960 rocked the foundations of the international monetary system. In the span of a few days a wave of speculative gold acquisitions drove up the price of gold on the London market from the official \$35 per ounce to \$40.[37] The danger of a run on the U.S. gold stock, freely available at \$35 per ounce, was obvious. In view of the absence of sufficient gold sales by the producing countries, it was up to the United States to furnish gold to satisfy the demand. U.S. authorities supplied the Bank of England with gold from its reserves to enable it to keep the price down.[38] The alarming result of the London gold crisis was that it revealed the shaky foundation on which the international monetary system was built. The whole system rested on the certainty that the United States would guarantee the exchange value of the dollar with its reserves, and around 1960 it became clear that the reserves in Fort Knox were not adequate to cover foreign liabilities. The slightest hint that the United States would in these circumstances increase the official price of gold was met with an immediate run from dollars to gold. The 1960 presidential race caused this type of speculation because of Kennedy's uncertain intentions were he to be elected. Huge amounts of short-term capital were moved into European accounts in anticipation of a change in monetary policy. Only after Kennedy firmly pledged on October 31

35 Ibid.
36 Eisenhower to Adenauer, Oct. 7, 1960, in FRUS 1958–60, IX, 692–4. Adenauer ostentatiously welcomed the prospect of a visit. He urged Eisenhower not to request anything like support costs, however, citing the well-known argument of an impending election campaign; Adenauer to Eisenhower, Oct. 20, 1960, ibid., 694–6.
37 Eighty-five percent of all newly mined gold was traded on the London gold market, by either central banks or private dealers. The Bank of England had assumed responsibility for controlling the market price. Yet, under the pressure of the gold speculation of October 1960, its reserves for intervening in the market were soon exhausted.
38 Strange, *International Economic Relations*, 76.

to defend the dollar–gold exchange rate did markets slowly calm down. For the Eisenhower administration the London gold crisis was the last straw, and any impediments against drastic action were thrown overboard. "We can't afford to let our monetary system break down before Mr. Kennedy is even sworn in,"[39] Eisenhower remarked, and he added in a telephone conversation with Herter that "when you are going into a war – and this is in effect a kind of war – you take lesser objectives and put them aside."[40] Anderson struck an equally apocalyptic note: "We had not been faced by a problem as serious as the one facing us now. Moreover, this was a unique experience; it had never happened to the United States before."[41]

The government hastily put together an emergency program. Two weeks later, Eisenhower issued a directive outlining steps with respect to the U.S. balance of payments.[42] This was the first in a long series of presidential action programs dealing with the balance-of-payments threat. Eisenhower's directive contained no analysis of the deeper causes of the deficits, nor was there an attempt to evaluate its implications for future policies. The only new step, apart from restating well-known remedies – trade liberalization, domestic economic stabilization, tying foreign aid programs to purchases in the United States – was a sharp reduction in the number of dependents of U.S. military personnel abroad. There were, in fact, not many actions by which the outgoing Eisenhower administration could show its determination to resolve the problem. During another tense discussion, Anderson ruled out restrictive trade measures as inimical to U.S. interests and monetary remedies as catalysts of speculation. The only field where the government could act rapidly and unilaterally was in military commitments abroad. This was the background of the dependent decision.[43] The directive identified military expenditures abroad in general as a major cause of the balance-of-payments deficit but limited its concluding paragraph to the wish "that our friends and allies accept their full share of the costs of maintaining the security of the free world."[44]

---

39 Memorandum of conference with president, Nov. 15, 1960, in FRUS 1958–60, IV, 138.
40 Nov. 15, 1960. Paul Kesaris, ed., *Minutes of Telephone Conversations of the Secretaries of State, 1953–61* (microfilmed), reel 10.
41 Memorandum of discussion at the 465th NSC meeting, Oct. 31, 1960, in FRUS 1958–60, VII/1, 529.
42 American foreign policy, current docs. 1960, 786–92.
43 Memorandum of conference with president, Nov. 9, 1960, in FRUS 1958–60, IV, 130; telephone conversation Anderson–Herter, Nov. 11, 1960, in Kesaris, ed., *Telephone Conversations*, reel 11.
44 American foreign policy, current docs. 1960, 789.

THE ANDERSON—DILLON MISSION OF NOVEMBER 1960

In the aftermath of the London gold crisis the announced Anderson-Dillon visit was narrowed in scope. What had originated as a proposal to discuss various measures to resolve the balance-of-payments problem now became an outright demand for funds to balance the foreign exchange cost of U.S. troops. The question of whether the U.S. delegation should demand support costs, that is, straight budgetary help, or some kind of transaction that would offset the dollar drain was decided in favor of Anderson's position. He announced that he "would ask Adenauer for $650 million a year as payment for keeping our troops on their soil. Drastic action is necessary here."[45] Throwing overboard all political arguments, Anderson pressed his position through against resistance in the State Department and to the surprise of most participants in the U.S. embassy in Bonn and the German government.

In the midst of the preparations for the visit, Kennedy won the presidential elections. This deprived the delegation of much of its bargaining power. Anderson and Dillon therefore tried to enlist Kennedy's support for the initiative. All they achieved, however, was an explanatory meeting with one of Kennedy's advisers.[46] Kennedy was clearly unwilling to commit to a step that might have far-reaching political consequences.[47] This reflected the judgment of the State Department, which had moved to the sidelines of the discussion. Dillon himself was less than enthusiastic about the mission.[48] He was in a precarious position as a possible candidate for a post in Kennedy's cabinet. All in all, things did not bode well for a successful mission.

Meanwhile, the Germans tried to prepare themselves, assuming that they would be asked mainly for more foreign aid and not for support

---

45 Memorandum on conference with president, Nov. 15, 1960, in FRUS 1958–60, IV, 138; see also Karen E. Donfried, "The Political Economy of Alliance: Issue Linkage in the West German–American Relationship," Ph.D. diss., Fletcher School of Law, 1991, 61–5.

46 Paul H. Nitze–Anderson conversation, Nov. 16, 1960, JFKL, PPP, transition files: Task Force reports, box 1073.

47 One indication that Kennedy's people did not approve of the mission is a memorandum on the subject by an unidentified official, addressed to vice president–elect, Lyndon B. Johnson. It complained that Anderson had become "almost obsessed" with the gold outflow and that "gold outflow, troop-reductions, and NATO atomic arms plans are moves which really ought to await the transfer of powers" (LBJL, VPSF, box 9). After the American delegation had returned from Germany, the German ambassador in Washington, Wilhelm Grewe, reported that Acheson had ridiculed their effort and that Kennedy had felt insufficiently informed; Grewe to AA, tel. 2447, Nov. 30, 1960, PA-AA, state secretary files, 79.

48 Leddy to Dillon, transmitting an Anderson memorandum on the troop-cost issue, Nov. 4, 1960, NA, RG 59, DF 1960–63, 762a.5/11-460; *New York Times*, Nov. 27, 1960, 3.

costs.[49] If the latter were requested, the demand would be rejected outright as a revival of occupation costs.[50] In a German cabinet meeting on November 15, a big foreign-aid program was finally approved. It amounted to about one billion dollars, of which more than a quarter would be supplied by German industry.[51] This large capital export program has to be seen not only as an attempt to take the wind out of America's sails but also in the context of Germany's efforts to get rid of the surplus capital streaming into the country. In addition, the Germans planned to accept a larger share in NATO infrastructure costs and possibly the prepayment of postwar debts.

Although the complete records of the actual conversations at the Anderson–Dillon–Adenauer meetings are not yet available, detailed accounts from both sides permit an accurate reconstruction of the issues. At the outset, Anderson and Dillon met with Adenauer. According to Dillon, the meeting only served to underline that the chancellor did not understand the problem "at all well" and just kept on repeating "that there is only one thing that worries him, and that is the possibility that we might redeploy some of our troops."[52] On this point Anderson remarked that Eisenhower was resolved to take any measure necessary to protect the dollar. After this short encounter the delegations met and the Germans presented their proposals.[53] These included the foreign-aid program, the NATO infrastructure costs, and the proposal for the prepayment of postwar debts, provided the Americans released German assets vested during World War II. There was also some talk about larger military purchases in the United States, and the Germans promised 100 percent prepayment to the existing Treasury account to which Germany transferred the payments for its military orders. As a last concession, Germany offered to negotiate on taking over some part of the cost of U.S. military aid to Turkey and Greece. The Americans, however, regarded the foreign-aid program as self-evident and possibly just self-serving, and the other measures as too small: "The U.S. Secretary of Treasury, Anderson, outlined in

---

49 In August, Dillon had written to Adenauer on this subject. The U.S. Embassy was advised to tell German authorities that "their first financial and moral obligation was to establish a significant long-term lending program" (see Dillon to Adenauer, NA, RG 59, 862a.0000, 8-260); Dillon to U.S. Embassy, Bonn, Aug. 1, 1960, NA, RG 59, 862a.10, 8-160.
50 Preparatory meeting of officials prior to U.S. delegation visit, Nov. 7, 1960, BA, B126/34104.
51 Excerpt of 129th cabinet meeting, Nov. 15, 1960, BA, B126/34104.
52 This account is based on a memorandum on a conference with the president, Nov. 28, 1960, in FRUS 1958–60, IV, 142–3.
53 Ibid.; Anderson to Eisenhower, Nov. 23, 1960, DDRS 87(2061); extract from the records of the 83rd ZBR meeting: Emminger report on U.S.–German financial discussions, Dec. 1, 1960, BBA, ZBR.

very drastic words the U.S. situation and its needs, and he hinted very broadly at German moral obligations in this respect. . . . It became clear that, in the end, a German budgetary contribution was expected."[54] The U.S. delegation presented the details of its proposal in a meeting of officials. It expected that Germany would pay $600 million to a fund at the U.S. Treasury that was to be used for direct payments to the United States and for additional purchases of military equipment to be delivered to poorer NATO allies.[55] State Secretary Volkmar Hopf from the Federal Defense Ministry responded that it was impossible to add such a large amount to the German defense budget. He also rejected the notion that the foreign exchange losses in Germany were responsible for the U.S. deficits. The Americans suggested "that an increased contribution to the United States defense effort could be explained to the German public as a contribution toward Germany's own defense." At this point the representative of the Finance Ministry fiercely rejected the American demands. He could "not see what practical significance there could be in having a joint fund if all the money was to come from German sources and if the main purpose was to distribute these funds to ease the U.S. balance of payments; . . . any payment of support costs was out of the question. Those times are gone forever."[56] The differences were irreconcilable. Subsequent negotiations on separate items in the agenda brought no results. As in earlier conflicts with the British, the Germans denied the existence of a link between military commitments and foreign exchange problems. Instead, they pointed to the large outflow of American private capital to Europe. A welcome example was the recent decision by the Ford Motor Company to purchase the shares of its British subsidiary, thus transferring $358 million abroad, much to the annoyance of the U.S. government. Later, Dillon commented angrily that "General Norstad had said it would be a long time before the GIs buy a Ford again." He suspected that "they [Ford] are doing this to get their money out of the United States in anticipation of real trouble here. . . . The Europeans, who have a large experience in this kind of thing, certainly recognize it as just that."[57]

The Germans welcomed the additional argument, which would later become part of de Gaulle's repertoire in countering U.S. hegemony. After more bickering about the causes of the balance-of-payments deficit the

54 Eighty-third meeting, Emminger report, Dec. 1, 1960, BBA, ZBR.
55 Memorandum of conversation U.S.–German officials, Nov. 22, 1960, NA, RG 59, lot file, BEA, OGA, box 5.
56 Ibid.
57 Memorandum on conference with president, Nov. 28, 1960, in FRUS 1958–60, IV, 144–5.

Americans broke off the negotiations, to the surprise of the Germans. Anderson summarized the results in a telegram to the president:

For practical purposes there is very little relief either to our budget or balance-of-payments position that will result from our discussions. . . . We made clear to the Chancellor and his associates that in view of these circumstances and in view of the key position which the U.S. dollar occupies in the international financial system we will be required by irresistible logic to make whatever decisions we deem appropriate both in our domestic and foreign policies, including both military and economic matters as are necessary and appropriate to our firm resolve that we will not allow the dollar to deteriorate.[58]

After Bonn, Anderson and Dillon went to France, where they received a noncommittal statement of support for their monetary policies, and then to London. The British consoled the American delegation with their own dismal experiences over the issue. Lloyd called the German proposals "chicken food" and expressed his difficulties in understanding the German psyche.[59] It is difficult to see, however, how Anderson could have expected the Germans to take such far-reaching steps when dealing with a lame-duck administration. It even seems that the Germans were informed beforehand that the newly elected president did not approve of the position taken during the talks.[60] Thus, they leaned back and waited to see what direction the new administration would take. There was also heavy U.S. press criticism of the American delegation and its clumsy negotiating tactics.[61] When the Eisenhower administration took stock of the mission, it had to acknowledge that the results had been poor and that "anything the Germans really do they will want to do for the new administration, so as to get maximum credit with them."[62] Nevertheless, Eisenhower did not want to leave his post with such a failure and with the Atlantic Alliance in disarray. In his last two months in office he tried to leave his mark on three major issues related to U.S.–European relations: balance-of-payments talks, troop reductions, and the problem of NATO nuclear sharing.

The talks with the Germans were continued at a lower official level after Anderson and Dillon went home. The demand for outright support costs was quietly dropped, due to the reaction of the Germans.[63] Shortly after the U.S. delegation had returned, a group of Pentagon and State

---

58 Anderson to president, Nov. 23, 1960, DDRS 87/2061.
59 Memorandum of conversation Lloyd–Anderson, Nov. 25, 1960, NA, RG 59, lot files, BEA/OGA, box 5.
60 Germany Embassy, Washington, D.C., to AA, Nov. 22, 1960, BA, B126/34104.
61 See, e.g., *New York Times*, Nov. 24 and 25, 1960.
62 FRUS 1958–60, IV, 144.
63 On November 28, Press Secretary David Hagerty said that the issue of support costs would not be taken up again because "the Germans are not prepared to discuss it" (KCA 1960, 17955).

Department officials met to discuss the prospect of a huge increase in the German defense budget, which promised to result in much higher levels of procurement abroad. The officials agreed that, because France and Britain were also eager to obtain a portion of these contracts, the main concern was "where the prospective business goes."[64] The Americans lost no time. Beginning on November 29, Pentagon officials, in collaboration with the U.S. embassy, pursued negotiations regarding military purchases with German officials in Bonn. The Germans remained noncommittal, citing budgetary problems as well as possible protests by third countries and German industry in the case of increased procurement from U.S. sources.[65] There was also little progress on the questions of debt pre-payment as linked to vested German assets, infrastructure costs, and the assumption of military aid. Decisions on all issues were made only after Kennedy took over. The outgoing administration would get no concessions from the Germans at this point.[66] Eisenhower and Anderson, in turn, spared no effort to impress on the new president the importance of the issue.[67]

Discussions on the issue of troop levels continued during the last weeks of the Eisenhower administration. Pentagon and Treasury officials, in the wake of the Anderson–Dillon mission, argued in favor of immediate reductions.[68] There was much debate over whether the United States should announce such a reduction at the NATO Council ministerial meeting in December 1960. It was finally decided to introduce the following sentence into a speech that State Secretary Herter gave to the meeting: "Some redeployment may become necessary unless our balance of payments can be brought into a more reasonable equilibrium."[69] A clear statement in favor of reductions was not possible given Kennedy's well-known disinclination to commit himself on such an important issue before he was sworn in.

64 Memorandum: "German Assistance to U.S. B/P Problem," Nov. 29, 1960, NA, RG 59, DF 1960–63, 811.10/11-2960.

65 U.S. Embassy, Bonn, telegram nos. 824, Dec. 2, 1960, Bonn 825, Dec. 2, 1960; Bonn 848, Dec. 6, 1960; Bonn 870, Dec. 8, 1960; and Bonn 891, Dec. 13, 1960, documentation in NA, RG 59, 811.10, box 2286; see also Donfried, "Political Economy of the Alliance," 83–4.

66 U.S. Embassy, Paris, telegram no. 2508: Anderson, Dillon–Erhard meeting, Dec. 15, 1960, DDRS 92 (1330); Carstens memorandum on German–American financial talks, Jan. 11, 1961, PA-AA, state secretary files, 79.

67 Anderson memorandum: "Meeting with Kennedy," Dec. 6, 1960, in FRUS 1958–60, IV, 147–51; memorandum for the record, Jan. 19, 1961, in FRUS 1961–63, IX, 1–2; Dwight D. Eisenhower, *Waging Peace, 1956–1961: The White House Years* (Garden City, N.Y., 1965), 715.

68 Memorandum on conference with president, Nov. 30, 1960, in FRUS 1958–60, IV, 543–7.

69 FRUS 1958–60, VII/1, 681; for the debate on this statement and the German reaction, see Herter to Eisenhower, Dec. 14, 1960, NA, RG 59, DF 1960–63, 811.10/12-1460; White to Merchant, Dec. 23, 1960, ibid., 12-2360.

Herter's speech at the NATO meeting also announced another project that would, like the troop-cost talks, long outlive the administration that initiated it, namely, the plan for a multilaterally manned NATO atomic force. The scheme was intended to give the Europeans a say in nuclear matters, to prevent the development of independent atomic capabilities, and to solve NATO's credibility dilemma, which lay in the question of whether the United States would really wage nuclear war for Europe, particularly after the Soviets had demonstrated that they were able to reach U.S. territory with their nuclear weapons. As an initial contribution to this multilateral force (MLF) Herter offered five submarines equipped with *Polaris* missiles.[70] The plan was to meet the European demand for more participation, while leaving the final decision to the Americans. Apart from the protracted practical problems, this ambiguity was to plague the MLF project until its hardly glorious end in the mid-1960s. When Eisenhower handed over the presidency to his successor in January 1961 he had only taken some tentative steps concerning American monetary problems and Europe's demands for equality, particularly in the nuclear field. Transatlantic relations in the 1960s were to be dominated by these issues. The balance of payments was to play a central role in the game, and consequently, so too did the troop-cost problem.

The deeper cause of the problems outlined in this chapter, however, lay in the simple, fundamental fact that the monetary system and the Atlantic security system, which had largely been two sides of the same coin, showed increasing signs of incompatibility. The monetary system, which was, as critics such as Robert Triffin and others have pointed out, in itself irrational, had functioned well during a period of unprecedented American commitments abroad. These had included not only direct military commitments, military intervention, foreign aid, military aid, and other material help, but also the enormous expansion of American "cultural" activities abroad. The monetary system had allowed this expansive policy without undermining the external value of the dollar and disrupting the domestic economy, which would have led to an erosion of domestic support for American foreign policies. The monetary system also had been of considerable advantage to America's principal allies. It had fostered (or at least not impeded) economic growth at home and abroad, and at the same time had made the financing of the Cold War possible. But this advantageous situation slowly and inexorably changed. The strains

---

70 For the discussion and the proposal, see the documentation in FRUS 1958–60, VII/1, 611–82; a recent analysis of the MLF story is Haftendorn, *Kernwaffen*, 107–48, with references to the extensive literature on the subject.

that American commitments abroad put on the world's financial structure became increasingly evident. The principal way out was either to reform the security system to relieve the strain on the monetary system (and this would have amounted to a fundamental change in Cold War policies) or vice versa. If neither of these far-reaching steps was taken, a third possibility was to look for temporary expedients in the hope that the monetary situation would move back into equilibrium. This is precisely what happened. The next chapter looks at the origins of probably the most important of these expedients: offset.

6

Offset and Monetary Policy During the Kennedy Administration, 1961–1962

INTERNATIONAL MONETARY POLICY

Since the first accounts of Kennedy's presidency were published it has become common knowledge that the president took a keen interest in monetary matters and that he considered the dollar–gold problem one of his most serious challenges, to the point of comparing it with the nuclear threat.[1] Contrary to the initial expectations of the Kennedy team, balance-of-payments matters became an ongoing preoccupation that turned up on the agenda with irritating regularity. Most academic research has interpreted these monetary problems as an expression of the decline of American hegemony and viewed Kennedy's policies as a fight against this decline.[2] Unfortunately, these interpretations lack serious empirical underpinnings. A thorough historical account of how Kennedy managed his international monetary policy, how it evolved over time, where exactly the points of debate lay, and what strategy he pursued regarding the surplus countries still needs to be written. In this chapter I summarize and supplement previous research, outline briefly the rationales behind U.S. monetary policy toward Europe, particularly toward Germany, and show how the link between American security policy toward Europe and the monetary problem became increasingly tighter.

Kennedy's first balance-of-payments message to Congress, shortly after his inauguration, made it clear that he contemplated no radical departures from existing policies for solving the dollar problem. After the

---

1 Arthur M. Schlesinger Jr., *A Thousand Days: John F. Kennedy in the White House* (Boston, 1965), 654; Theodore Sorensen, *Kennedy* (New York, 1965), 405; Walt W. Rostow, *The Diffusion of Power: An Essay in Recent History* (New York, 1972), 136; Roosa, *Dollar Problem*, 3.
2 See, e.g., Borden, "Defending Hegemony," 57–85; David P. Calleo, *The Imperious Economy* (Cambridge, Mass., 1982); Allen K. Matusow, "Kennedy, the World Economy, and the Decline of America," in J. R. Snyder, ed., *JFK: Person, Policy, Presidency* (New York, 1988), 111–22.

appointment of Douglas C. Dillon as secretary of the treasury, this came as no surprise. The central point of Kennedy's message was: "The United States' official dollar price of gold can and will be maintained at $35 an ounce. Exchange controls over trade and investments will not be invoked. Our national security and economic assistance programs will be carried forward."[3] The Kennedy administration denied any need for far-reaching reforms in the international monetary system and saw the balance-of-payments deficit as a manageable problem that it was confident of solving within a relatively short period. The recommended policies included a more sophisticated use of available monetary instruments, further removal of trade barriers, and strong domestic efforts to improve the competitiveness of American goods.[4] Proposals from within the administration for more radical solutions, such as a change in the gold price, capital controls, or restrictions on tourism, never prevailed.[5] The Treasury Department held on to its leadership regarding monetary issues. The two main elements of its policy were a more vigorous domestic economic policy than Eisenhower's and increased participation by other industrialized powers in the management of the international monetary system. This second element was based on the optimistic assumption that these countries, mostly affluent members of the Atlantic Alliance, were willing to cooperate on a larger scale.

The idea that European countries were obligated to help the United States was as deeply rooted in the thinking of Kennedy's administration as it had been in Eisenhower's. It stemmed from the conviction of Kennedy and his advisers that the surplus countries bore at least an equal part of the responsibility for the crisis of the monetary system and that it was generous American policies that had enabled the Europeans to acquire their huge currency reserves. The prepresidential Task Force on Foreign Economic Policy stated in its report on the balance-of-payments deficit that it "resulted principally from the failure of other major

3 "The Balance of Payments and Gold Outflow from the U.S.: Message of President Kennedy to the Congress," Feb. 6, 1961, in *DAFR* 1961, 30.
4 This approach was suggested by a special task force on the balance of payments, which produced a comprehensive report on the problem in December 1960; see JFKL, PPP, transition files: task force reports, box 1073. One of the ongoing conflicts within the administration was whether economic policy should be pursued with little regard to balance-of-payments objectives, as the CEA demanded, or whether economic policy, particularly short-term rates, should be dominated by monetary considerations, as the Treasury maintained.
5 Dillon and Roosa warned that plans for radical changes would create additional large-scale speculation as long as the position of the dollar was not safe. Kennedy accepted this argument; see Roosa, *Dollar Problem*, 6–13; Odell, *U.S. International Monetary Relations*, 106–8.

industrialized powers to pursue adequate policies of growth."[6] The main target of this reproach was Germany, which had built up its economy with the help of American aid and was now allegedly shirking its obligation to help the United States in times of monetary trouble. "To some significant degree . . . Germany's ability to maintain its export volume can be attributed to liberal U.S. policies on trade, aid, and investment," Undersecretary of State George Ball wrote in early 1961. Secretary of State Dean Rusk echoed him: "The Germans have an obligation to make a contribution to the solution of this problem without need for any compensatory action on our part."[7] Dillon thought that the German "balance-of-payments surplus was the counterpart of both the U.S. and the U.K. deficits. Actions by us alone to correct the situation would merely result in shifting our deficit to the British, and therefore the primary need was for the Germans to take appropriate action."[8]

Many remarks by the president show that he fully shared this sentiment.[9] When Charles de Gaulle vetoed the British accession to the Common Market in January 1963, an event that blatantly exposed the weaknesses of U.S. foreign policy toward Europe, this factor became a dominant theme in the ensuing discussions. Kennedy voiced his frustration in a series of remarks that were typical for the German–American burden-sharing debate in the 1960s.

We have been very generous to Europe and it is now time to look out for ourselves, knowing full well that the Europeans will not do anything for us simply because we have in the past helped them. No longer dependent on the U.S. for economic assistance, the European states are less subject to our influence. If the French and other European powers acquire a nuclear capability they would be in a position to be entirely independent and we might be on the outside looking in. We must exploit our military and political position to ensure that our economic interests are protected.[10]

Similar statements were made frequently during the 1960s – by journalists, members of Congress, and officials of the U.S. government. They

---

6 Report, Dec. 31, 1960, JFKL, PPP, transition files, box 1073; for a similar statement, see Gregh–Nitze discussion on NATO strategy, May 25, 1961, NSA, Berlin Crisis Collection, doc. 2054.
7 Ball to JFK, no date (Feb. 1961?), JFKL, POF, countries: Germany, box 116a; Rusk to Dillon, Feb. 1, 1961, in FRUS 1961–63, IX, 107. For similar statements, see Walter W. Heller to JFK: "The Future of the Dollar," Sept. 15, 1961, JFKL, POF, depts. & agencies: CEA, box 73; Carl Kaysen to Kennedy, Sept. 18, 1962, in FRUS 1961–63, IX, 151.
8 Memorandum of Stikker–Dillon conversation, June 16, 1961, in FRUS 1961–63, IX, 117.
9 See, e.g., his discussion with the French minister for cultural affairs, Malraux, on May 11, 1962, in FRUS 1961–63, XIII, 695–701.
10 Remarks of President Kennedy to the NSC meeting, Jan. 22, 1963, ibid., 486.

demonstrate not only a strong moral dimension to American arguments; they also indicate that the balance-of-payments problem was not regarded as an isolated matter but was rather an integral and essential part of political relations within the alliance. In this matter, the governments of the United States and the United Kingdom saw eye to eye. In his first meeting with Kennedy, Harold Macmillan placed the blame for the American and British payments problems on the Europeans (in particular the Germans), who had failed to reinvest the foreign exchange they had acquired via Anglo–American aid and military expenditure in Europe after the war.[11] Both heads of government strongly emphasized the need for adequate compensation for their foreign exchange losses. Thus, a clear split in monetary policy emerged between the European surplus countries and the deficit countries. This split mirrored differences in security matters (between nuclear and nonnuclear members of the alliance) and in trade policy (between EEC and non-EEC countries). Although these lines of conflict were often blurred when it came to specific issues, Germany was frequently caught in the middle.

The Kennedy administration expected active participation by its European allies in two main areas: first, the intensification of monetary cooperation between the major monetary powers by a series of multilateral agreements, which were vigorously pursued by Dillon and Undersecretary of State Robert Roosa; second, the reduction and sharing of the defense and foreign-aid burden, with an offset of military expenditure in Europe as the most important component. This policy was strongly pursued by Secretary of Defense Robert S. McNamara. Although these two policies were pursued by different departments and in different institutional settings, they had the same overriding objective: the elimination of the American balance-of-payments deficit. Therefore, they have to be seen as a whole.

MILITARY STRATEGY AND THE BALANCE OF PAYMENTS

Kennedy made it clear from the outset that he assigned a very high importance to military burden sharing.[12] This derived not only from his determination to defend the dollar and his conviction that America's allies had to carry a larger share of the defense burden; changes in military strategic thinking also suggested a more assertive burden-sharing policy. The new administration immediately started revising American military

11 Macmillan–Kennedy meeting, Apr. 5, 1961 (CAB 133/244), NSA, Berlin Crisis Collection, doc. 2024.
12 JFK to Rusk, Feb. 20, 1961 (NSAM 22), JFKL, NSF, meetings & memoranda, box 328.

and strategic policy, resulting in a heavier emphasis on conventional forces. The strong inclination of the preceding administration to reappraise the military commitment in Europe for balance-of-payments reasons was not shared by the Kennedy administration, at least not during its first year. Because of its supposedly negative impact on GI morale, the military sharply criticized Eisenhower's directive to drastically curtail the number of dependents of American forces maintained overseas. Under Kennedy, the directive was rescinded.[13]

Simultaneously, the Americans sought to educate the Europeans on their new strategic ideas. These ideas, subsumed under the heading "Flexible Response," expanded on ideas formulated during the closing stage of Eisenhower's presidency, most notably by people such as Robert Bowie and Maxwell Taylor.[14] Appalled by what they saw as an irresponsible reliance on the immediate use of nuclear weapons in the case of a limited conflict, and based on a more balanced estimate of Warsaw Pact forces, strategic planners in the Kennedy administration tried to shift the emphasis of military strategy away from nuclear weapons and toward an improved conventional capability in order to have a broader range of options. The Berlin crisis underscored this need. A corresponding commitment by the Europeans to provide conventional troops in order to make Flexible Response credible became a top priority of U.S. security policy in Europe. A study group, headed by Dean Acheson, summarized these ideas in a policy paper, and the so-called Acheson Report became a policy guideline approved by Kennedy.[15] In April, Acheson went to Europe and told Adenauer (and de Gaulle) that "the new administration wished to correct some harmful impressions created toward the end of the old one . . . American troops were not to be withdrawn from Europe, nor would there be any threat to do so."[16] As Acheson recalled later, however, he

was never quite sure how completely [Kennedy's] mind was sold on this . . . the thing that continually seemed to bother the president about this was the continuation of so large a body of American troops in Europe without any plan that they should come home at a specific date. . . . Surely we do hope to bring them home, but the point was to bring the Europeans into such a state of confidence

13 JCS–president meeting, Jan. 27, 1961, JFKL, NSF, Clifton–Kaysen memoranda; McNamara to JFK, Feb. 1, 1961, JFKL, POF, depts. & agencies: Defense, box 77; oral history interview with Roswell Gilpatric, JFKL.

14 For the Bowie Report, see FRUS 1958–60, VII/1, doc. 266; Maxwell D. Taylor, *The Uncertain Trumpet* (New York, 1960). On "Flexible Response," see Stromseth, *Origins of Flexible Response*.

15 FRUS 1961–63, XIII, 285–91.

16 Telegram U.S. Embassy, Bonn, to DOS: Adenauer-Acheson conversation, Apr. 10, 1961, ibid., 270. Kennedy repeated this reassurance during his first meeting with Adenauer; ibid., 273.

and growing capabilities that this time would come. It would never come if you keep saying, "If you don't do exactly what we want, we'll go home." This was the wrong way to act. I don't think he was ever quite with me on this.[17]

Kennedy's ambiguity is not surprising because Flexible Response, with its inherent continuation or even augmentation of American troop presence in Europe, conflicted with balance-of-payments objectives. What made sense in military and political terms did not at all coincide with perceived economic necessities, contrary to the situation until the mid-1950s. One way to square the circle was to get the Europeans to assume more of the burden of conventional defense. Another possibility was to negotiate financial compensation for the American foreign exchange losses wherever possible. To achieve this, the threat of disengagement was the obvious means of pressure. Such threats, however, undermined the credibility of America's new strategic ideas. There is little doubt that Kennedy and his advisers felt this dilemma acutely. From 1962 onward the government was divided by an intense debate that led to a slow but steady erosion of the Acheson policy of a strong conventional defense.

THE FIRST OFFSET AGREEMENT

The Kennedy administration wasted no time in preserving the momentum of the financial talks initiated by Anderson and Dillon. Even before Kennedy's inauguration Dillon sent Secretary of State designate Dean Rusk a memorandum urging immediate action by the new government.[18] The question of the offset of American foreign exchange losses in Germany became the first of many German–American disagreements during Kennedy's tenure. The German government, in order to get a good start with the new administration, decided to table new proposals without delay. Counting on a more relaxed attitude in the new team, the Germans made almost no changes to the offer they had already presented to Anderson and Dillon.[19] The American reaction was indignation at the impertinence of the West Germans trying to sell the same offer twice. Kennedy, at a press conference, said that the proposals did not "meet the problem or the opportunity."[20] The first high-level visit from Germany by Foreign Minister Brentano, provided him with the chance to communicate his

17 Oral history interview with Dean Acheson, JFKL.
18 Dillon to Rusk, Jan. 13, 1961, 105, in FRUS 1961–63, IX.
19 U.S. Embassy, Bonn, telegrams nos. 1174 and 1175, Feb. 2, 1961, NA, RG 59, DF 1960–63, 811.10, 2–2/61; BPI 1961, 258.
20 PP Kennedy 1961: press conference, Feb. 8, 1961, 72.

disappointment directly. The Americans impressed on the Germans their view of the balance-of-payments problem. It was based on the assumption "that a general condition of economic imbalance exists in the Western world which can only be rectified by continuing and concerted measures which members of the Alliance should take . . . and which calls for sustained action by the Germans as the major surplus country of the West."[21] Obviously, the United States aimed for a long-term commitment from Germany to help relieve the American balance-of-payments problem. This expectation derived from America's long-term commitment to Europe's security. Not surprisingly the Germans resisted this approach, which would have deprived them of much of their autonomy in monetary policy-making. A fundamental conflict emerged between the Americans' interest to enlist German monetary powers for the defense of the dollar and the Germans' attempt to retain as much freedom of choice as possible. The outcome of the offset negotiations would reflect the first solution to this conflict.

The Brentano visit brought no resolution. The U.S. government provided the visitor with an aide-mémoire that set out its basic position on the balance-of-payments problem. It stated that the deficit existed mainly because of the American commitment to the defense of the free world and that this burden, as well as the foreign-aid burden, had to be shared equally among the members of the Alliance. The proposed German measures were deemed inadequate because they did not meet the conditions of a sustained program.[22] The aide-mémoire suggested a multilateral solution to the burden-sharing problem. Walt Rostow maintained that after the Brentano visit "Kennedy considered and tentatively supported a multilateral approach in the Alliance to the offset problem."[23] He added that concerted pressure by the Department of Defense and the Department of the Treasury subsequently killed that proposal. In any case, it would have taken long and protracted negotiations to integrate all of NATO into a comprehensive burden-sharing system. The Kennedy administration, looking for fast solutions, was hardly prepared for such a major diplomatic effort. The idea was to come up again from time to time, but it never came close to implementation.

On some of the lesser German proposals, agreement was achieved very soon after the Brentano visit. The German share of the NATO

21 Rusk memorandum for president, Feb. 15, 1961, JFKL, POF, countries: Germany general, box 117; record of conversation between Dillon and Scherpenberg, Feb. 17, 1961, PA-AA, state secretary files, 79.
22 BPI 1961, 322.   23 Rostow, *Diffusion of Power*, 236, 395.

infrastructure cost was raised from 13.72 to 20 percent, whereas the American share fell from 37 to 30.85 percent.[24] The foreign-aid problem was separated from the offset discussions and referred to the Organization for Economic Cooperation and Development (OECD). The major reason for this was that the Americans wanted to avoid a situation wherein uncertain foreign-aid efforts would be played off against other burden-sharing issues, thereby negatively affecting both areas.[25] The issue of trade liberalization was defused by some smaller German measures and for the time being lost its relevance within the context of offset. It was clear, however, that the U.S. government regarded all these matters as peanuts. The core objectives in American financial talks with Bonn from 1961 onward were to win extended German cooperation in international monetary negotiations and a full financial offset for the foreign exchange cost of U.S. troops in Germany, to be achieved in bilateral negotiations. The first part of this agenda was pursued mainly in a multilateral (OECD, IMF, BIS) context, and it led to cooperative undertakings such as the gold pool and the General Arrangements to Borrow (GAB).[26] At various points this monetary collaboration blended into the bilateral German–American negotiations on troop costs.

As mentioned previously, the Kennedy administration gave up on Anderson's request for direct budgetary payments and concentrated on achieving arrangements that, by means of German investment in U.S. assets, were to bring about a financial offset of the foreign exchange cost of U.S. troops. Talks on these arrangements started almost immediately after Anderson and Dillon had left, and the intervening change of presidents caused no interruption.

Most of the talks were held on a lower official level, by officials of the Federal Defense Ministry (BMVg), the Federal Finance Ministry (BMF), the U.S. Treasury and Defense Departments, and the U.S. embassy in Bonn. The participants split the large agenda into several issues assigned to three working groups. The first working group dealt with premature repayment of German postwar debts owed to the United States. The new American administration categorically refused to link this issue to that of German assets vested by the United States during the war, fearing that

24 BPI 1961, 294. The total annual cost of NATO infrastructure programs was $676 million between 1957 and 1960, and $733 million between 1961–4.
25 DOS circular telegram, Mar. 18, 1961, NA, RG 84, post files: Bonn embassy, 1959–61, box 17, 320: U.S. policy.
26 In 1961 the United States and eight other countries created the gold pool to supply or buy gold on the London gold market in order to keep prices stable. The GAB was a mechanism formed by ten industrial countries to expand the lending facilities of the IMF in times of crisis.

such a deal might require a long and uncertain ratification debate in Congress.[27] The Germans were bluntly told that the new administration would take no action whatsoever on this issue. This was a painful defeat for the German government, which had hoped to score a popular success on a highly sensitive issue. Endless bilateral discussions on vested assets had gone on during the 1950s.[28] After the Dillon-Anderson mission the United States had seemed ready to compensate the former owners of the assets, linking this with premature debt prepayment by the Federal Republic. The German government had already prepared draft treaties, and disappointment ran high when this hope was quashed.[29] At that point the Germans probably began to suspect that, in terms of the offset question, they had jumped from Eisenhower's frying pan into Kennedy's fire. Despite the lost opportunity Germany agreed, after more discussions, to prepay $587 million of its postwar debts as an offset measure, without conditions attached.[30] In any case, this was a convenient way to transfer back the surplus dollars that had flowed into German accounts during the speculative waves in 1960 and 1961. Short-term capital had continued to move into the country as rumors of a DM revaluation made their way to the public. These rumors were doubtless intensified by the fierce struggle on that question within the German government. Adenauer and Erhard repeatedly clashed on the issue, and industry, consumer organizations, and financial experts bombarded the government with recommendations for and against; opinions were divided even at the Bundesbank's highest levels.[31] Although there is no doubt that the United States was in favor of a revaluation, they apparently put no direct pressure on the German government and stayed clear of this hornet's nest. When the British urged them to press the Germans toward revaluation, Dillon answered that the United States accorded this question a lower priority than bilateral payment negotiations.[32] When in March 1961 the deutschmark was revalued from DM 4.20 per dollar to DM 4 per dollar, Ball committed a minor blunder by calling the revaluation a "useful but

27 Memorandum: "Prepayment of U.S. Postwar Aid," Mar. 20, 1961, BA, Etzel papers, vol. 18; Ball to Rusk, Jan. 30, 1961, and Rusk to Dillon, Feb. 1, 1961, both in NA, RG 59, DF 1960–63, 811.10, box 2287; memorandum of conversation among Ball, Dillon, and Scherpenberg, Feb. 19, 1961, NA, RG 59, lot files, BEA, Office of German Affairs, box 12.
28 Hans-Dieter Kreikamp, *Deutsches Vermögen in den Vereinigten Staaten: Die Auseinandersetzung um seine Rückführung als Aspekt der deutsch-amerikanischen Beziehungen 1952–1962* (Stuttgart, 1979).
29 Note for cabinet meeting, Jan. 10, 1961, BA, B136/2125.
30 BPI 1961, 657.
31 The best account of this conflict is Daniel Körfer, *Kampf ums Kanzleramt: Erhard und Adenauer* (Stuttgart, 1987), 464–518.
32 U.S.–U.K. bilateral talks, Dec. 15/16, 1961, in FRUS 1961–63, IX, 111–12.

modest step."[33] Nothing illustrates the nervousness of the monetary markets during the 1960s better than the mass of funds that shifted to Germany following this statement, indicating the possibility of further revaluation. The German ambassador protested personally to Kennedy. The markets calmed down in mid-1961, after combined intervention by all major central banks. It was the pound that once more came under pressure during these weeks and that was saved only by one of the many multilateral monetary rescue actions of the 1960s.

The offset negotiations continued during the monetary turmoil. After the debt prepayment question was settled, the two remaining issues, increased German procurement of American weapons and common use of U.S. military facilities located in Germany, came to the fore. The West German Ministry of Defense and the Pentagon assumed responsibility for these talks, which increasingly promised to be the only way of coming anywhere close to the magnitude of the financial settlement the Americans envisaged. By the time Adenauer was scheduled for his first state visit in April 1961, American interest in offset talks concentrated exclusively on these issues. In a forceful memorandum Dillon urged the president to

talk with the Chancellor about the importance of prompt action by Germany to step up its military procurement in the United States for at least the present year. Less urgent, but also important, is our desire for a reduction in the cost of contractual services for our military establishment for which we now pay Germany . . . without active Federal Republic cooperation there is no way of bringing our expenditure in Germany down to a tolerable level short of troop withdrawal which we do not want to contemplate.[34]

Dillon estimated the amount of prospective German orders at about $430 million per year, which would bring the foreign exchange cost of the troops (inflated to $650 million because of the deutschmark revaluation) down to $220 million. Thus, the main objective of the United States during the talks was to get the West Germans to commit to vastly increased military procurement. This was pushed at the highest levels, particularly by the treasury and defense secretaries. Whether there were many dollars in vague proposals for the common use of military facilities and contractual services by the U.S. and West German forces, which was the theme of the third working group, was at first unclear. However, the U.S.

---

33 FRUS 1961–63, XIV, 21–5. For the quotation by Ball, see ibid., note 2.
34 Dillon to president: "Discussion with Chancellor Adenauer on Balance of Payments," Apr. 7, 1961, JFKL, POF, countries: France/Germany, box 116a. For the talks between Adenauer and Kennedy on Apr. 13, 1961, see FRUS 1961–63, IX, 114–16.

government apparently soon realized that this issue could provide additional leverage in the procurement issue and, in case of a satisfactory agreement, political advantages as well. The Germans proposed, and the Americans agreed, to undertake long-range studies on a large number of questions, including, for example, the sharing of logistic services, training facilities, and reserve stocks, and developing standardized military equipment.[35] Detailed talks on these issues started in May 1961.

However, progress in the working groups on procurement and common use of military facilities was slow. The first disagreement arose not on the level of orders but on the American demand that the Federal Republic commit itself to a high level of purchases for an extended period. This was unacceptable to the Germans. The proposed level of $450 million for arms orders in 1961 was dismissed as completely unrealistic.[36] The Americans suspected competition by France and Britain behind this intransigence.[37] Both sides therefore tried to keep the talks confidential. The U.S. embassy in Bonn warned that, in case of publicity, "the FRG would be subjected to difficult pressure, not only from other governments, but from German domestic industry as well."[38]

During the first seven months of 1961 the Germans dragged their feet on any long-term commitment to military purchases. This might well have been an expression of Franz Josef Strauss's insistence on buying the "most modern" material. In long and animated discussions with Henry A. Kissinger in May 1961 Strauss complained about the outdated equipment of the U.S. Army: "He would be willing to approve a huge increase in German procurement of military items in the U.S. but was reluctant to do so when the Germans could produce better weapons here. . . . If the U.S. would modernize her weapons to match qualitatively the German weapons, then the German orders would soon erase the American balance-of-payments problem."[39] Apart from the exaggeration

35 Brewster H. Morris to Scherpenberg, Apr. 14, 1961, and Scherpenberg to Morris, Apr. 18, 1961, both in NA, RG 84, Bonn embassy 1959–61, box 25 (322.3 Logistic Support).
36 Memorandum on conversation between FRG officials and U.S. embassy officials, Mar. 16, 1961, NA, RG 59, DF 1960–63, 762a.5, box 1903.
37 "British are applying extensive pressure to increase level of German procurement and Selwyn Lloyd will arrive next week to discuss matter with Strauss. Federal Republic also peculiarly dependent on France because of basic need for training areas and French tendency to relate procurement to rights for facilities creates fundamental political problem" (Bonn no. 1487, Mar. 18, 1961, NA, RG 59, 762a.56).
38 Conversation among officials from the U.S. embassy, the MAAG, and the BMVg, June 6, 1961, ibid., 762a.5, box 1903.
39 Enclosure to Bonn no. 1686, May 18, 1961, NA, RG 59, DF 1960–63, 762a.5, box 1903. Apparently, Kennedy heard about the conversation and ordered an investigation of Strauss's allegation. The charged officials expressed surprise at Strauss's remarks because the German army was almost

concerning the quality of the weaponry made in Germany, there was a barely hidden quid pro quo. If the United States were ready to sell the most recently developed products of its weapons industry, Germany's inclination to buy American would increase. Strauss still had lingering suspicions that Germany would be sold second-rate materiel, as had happened in the 1950s. He was also conscious of German technological backwardness and hoped for some spillover.[40] He and his officials clearly understood the leverage that the offset issue provided in two key areas: parity in the equipment of German and American forces, and access to advanced military technology considered at that time the spearhead of technological progress.

Furthermore, Strauss expected a clarification of the future course of American military policy before embarking on a large procurement program.[41] The strategic reorientation of the Kennedy administration had met with strong resistance in the Federal Republic. The Germans feared that increasing reliance on a limited conventional response would invite Soviet adventurism, lead to the loss of Germany in the event of war, and make the country a nuclear battlefield.[42] By gaining a stronger voice in nuclear questions and particularly by getting access to "hardware" the Federal Republic acquired much more influence over the formulation of military policy in NATO and came a big step closer to pursuing a forward defense of its own territory, thereby reducing its dependence on other countries for this task. Both Strauss and Adenauer wanted control over the use of nuclear weapons on German territory, and during the final years of the Eisenhower administration the president's intentions for nuclear sharing had reached the point of considering equipping West German forces with tactical nuclear weapons.[43] Eisenhower wanted very much to "bring the boys home," and the only way to do so seemed to be through European and particularly German self-sufficiency. Kennedy and his advisers took a strong position against nuclear proliferation, however, and, to the great disappointment of Strauss, decided that it would

exclusively equipped with U.S. weapons. See memorandum on alleged superiority of West German equipment, July 3, 1961, NSA, Berlin Crisis Collection, doc. 2121.

40 Kelleher, *Germany*, 90–1, 96–7.

41 "Basic decision: increase level of procurement in US dependent on Strauss' acceptance of new strategic viewpoints and agreement on precise balance between nuclear and conventional forces" (Bonn no. 2170, June 24, 1961, NA, RG 59, DF 1960–63, 033.62A11, 6–2461).

42 Schwartz, *Nuclear Dilemmas*, 154–5, 167–70. On the strategic disagreements between West Germany and the United States in the early 1960s, see Kelleher, *Germany*; Stromseth, *Origins of Flexible Response*; Christoph Hoppe, *Zwischen Teilhabe und Mitsprache: Die Nuklearfrage in der Allianzpolitik Deutschlands 1959–66* (Baden-Baden, 1993); Haftendorn, *NATO-Krise*.

43 Trachtenberg, *Constructed Peace*, 146–200.

be extremely dangerous to give the West Germans access to nuclear arms or bring them closer to getting them. The offset issue provided the defense minister with an excellent means to put pressure on the new administration. Under the given circumstances, acquiring nuclear delivery systems was the closest the Federal Republic would come toward a more direct influence over the use of nuclear weapons on its territory, and thus this became one of Strauss's conditions for agreeing to the gigantic amount of military purchases the Americans demanded. What his intentions basically amounted to was the use of Germany's strong monetary position to enhance its military potential and thus garner more political influence on vital defense questions.

The available records of the working group meetings reveal three further German objectives:[44] First, the Germans requested that the U.S. government act as purchasing agent in weapons procurement because of the lack of German personnel qualified to negotiate directly with U.S. firms. Second, the Germans emphasized the importance of joint use by the Seventh Army and the Bundeswehr of logistical facilities, training areas, airfields, and barracks in Germany. The West German Defense Ministry faced particular difficulties in these areas. The German rearmament effort had been hampered from the beginning by various shortages, due to the country's dense population and occupation by allied forces of the most convenient training, stationing, and storage locations. When the buildup accelerated in the early 1960s, these problems became even more pressing. Bonn's NATO allies were not very cooperative in this respect. According to Strauss, "arrangements for depots in France was [sic] completely dependent on German procurement in France."[45] In 1960 the West German government even negotiated with Spanish dictator Generalissimo Francisco Franco for the use of training areas in Spain. International and domestic protest quickly killed this project.[46] Third, the Germans insisted during the talks that the negotiations be kept confidential and that an eventual agreement be concluded in a form not requiring parliamentary approval.[47] A public debate on the issue had to be avoided at all costs.

All these requests complicated the negotiations, and in July 1961 they reached an impasse. The dollar amount of proposed German orders was

---

44 Bonn no. 1711: studies on procurement, joint use, and contractual services, incl. memorandum of conversation U.S.–FRG officials (May 15), May 24, 1961, NA, RG 84, Bonn embassy 1959–61, box 25.
45 Memorandum of conversation among Gilpatric, Hopf, and Strauss, Oct. 24, 1961, NA, RG 84, Bonn embassy 1959–61, box 26.
46 Cyrus Sulzberger, "A Foolish Project," *New York Times*, Feb. 23, 1960.
47 Bonn no. 1711: Logistic support, May 24, 1961, NA, RG 84, Bonn 1959–61, box 25, 322.3.

still far from forming a full offset.[48] The U.S. military balked at the idea of having to share its facilities in Europe with another country's army. The gap between American and German expectations remained insurmountable until an event took place that served as a catalyst in the offset talks: the erection of the Berlin Wall in August 1961. The consequences were many. After long discussions, and despite many misgivings about the gold drain that such an action implied, Kennedy decided to augment the American forces in Germany by 45,000 men, with the option for further reinforcements if the situation required it.[49] The additional gold drain was expected to be offset by the German government. The wall also evoked a feeling of vulnerability on the part of West Germans and demonstrated how much the Federal Republic depended on the Western alliance for its security. The Western response, deemed lukewarm by a large part of the German population, sparked renewed doubts about the Western security guarantee. In this situation, funds suddenly flowed abundantly for the further buildup and modernization of the Bundeswehr. The West German defense budget was increased by about $750 million to $4.15 billion annually.

The leverage of the United States in the offset talks increased considerably. To capitalize on the situation, the Americans decided to meet some of the German requests. According to Dillon, the United States was "approaching the strongest bargaining position since the negotiations began. Our negotiating leverage is increased by the possibility of major deployments to assist in the defense of Berlin and Germany, and also by the fact that the Department of Defense is prepared to provide the German forces with a cooperative logistics system for which the Federal Republic has been pressing."[50] This system included the provision of U.S. government procurement services, the exchange of selected common items and U.S. war reserves, on-call support for German forces (tying the Bundeswehr, as a customer, into the U.S. logistical system for providing spare parts), and maintenance services.[51] Equally important was the fact that the Americans now indicated that they were willing to continue

48 For the following, see memorandum on conversation between Dillon and Strauss, July 15, 1961, NA, RG 59, DF 1960–63, 811.10/7–1561; Bonn no. 211, July 29, 1961, RG 84, Bonn embassy 1959–61, box 26.
49 U.S. troop strength rose from 233,000 to 277,600. For details, see the archival collection of the U.S. Army Europe Headquarters: "The Replacement and Augmentation Systems in Europe, 1945–63," chap. 6, Mar. 1964, NSA, Berlin Crisis Collection, doc. 1942.
50 Dillon to JFK, Sept. 14, 1961, JFKL, POF, dept. and agencies: Treasury, box 89.
51 Bonn no. 694, Sept. 21, 1961; Tyler to Ball: U.S./FRG military offset negotiations, Oct. 9, 1961, both in NA, RG 59, DF 1960–63, 811.10/9–2161; Bonn no. A-403, Sept. 30, 1961, NA, RG 84, Bonn embassy 1959–61, box 26.

selling the Germans some of their most advanced weapon systems, including nuclear delivery systems. Armed with these concessions, they stepped
up the pace of the negotiations and achieved a breakthrough.[52] At an
October meeting of the procurement working group the Germans
informed a delighted U.S. delegation that the level of procurement would
rise substantially above previous estimates.[53]

The circumstances seemed to be propitious for a comprehensive understanding. The negotiations moved to a higher level. Kennedy informed
Adenauer that he would send Roswell Gilpatric, the undersecretary of
defense, to Bonn. He expected the West Germans to "work out with us
arrangements to insure that U.S. military expenditures in Germany
do not drain foreign-exchange reserves from the U.S. to Germany."[54]
The Gilpatric trip was given very low-profile public treatment to avoid
drawing attention to the wide-ranging issues to be discussed. The undersecretary of defense brought along with him an outline of the logistics
assistance actions that the Department of Defense was prepared to offer
the Germans.[55] He also assured Strauss that the United States would continue to furnish the Bundeswehr with modern missile systems.[56] The
condition the United States set for these offers was straightforward: a
formal commitment by the Federal Republic to offset the entire foreign
exchange cost of U.S. troops in Germany by purchasing American
weapons. Strauss certainly understood that the consequence was a far-
reaching commitment to the United States in the military–economic field
at the expense of other allies. He remarked to Gilpatric "that if he signed
the agreement as presently drafted the British ambassador would be in his
office the following morning to demand equal treatment."[57] This did not
prevent an eventual signature. The German defense minister, however,
insisted on limiting the agreement to two years and demanded multilateral
negotiations in case of renewed U.S. demands that might result from a
substantial augmentation of U.S. forces caused by the completely unclear
Berlin situation. After some discussion Gilpatric accepted these conditions,
and a brief memorandum of understanding was signed on October 24,
1961. The following text established the working principle of offset:

52 Martin to Ball: "Report on Meeting Between Dillon and Gilpatric on U.S.–German Financial
    Negotiations," Sept. 14, 1961, NA, RG 59, DF 1960–63, 862a.10/9–1461.
53 MAAG Germany to secretary of state, Oct. 13, 1961, NA, RG 59, DF 1960–63, 762a.5/10–1261.
54 Kennedy to Adenauer, Oct. 16, 1961, JFKL, POF, countries: Germany, box 117.
55 Bonn to DOS: summary statement by Gilpatric, Nov. 2, 1961, NA, RG 84, Bonn embassy
    1959–61, box 26.
56 *FAZ*, Oct. 27, 1961; *Frankfurter Rundschau*, Oct. 29, 1961.
57 Memorandum on conversation among Gilpatric, Hopf, and Strauss, Oct. 24, 1961, NA, RG 84,
    Bonn embassy 1959–61, box 26.

It is anticipated that under the proposed cooperative logistics system, payments by the Federal Republic of Germany to the United States for materiel and for research, development, procurement supply, maintenance and other logistics services, including the Federal Republic of Germany's share of the system's capital and operating expenses, will be sufficient to insure that military transactions of direct benefit to the U.S. balance of payments are large enough to offset the transactions of U.S. forces in Germany of benefit to the FRG balance of payments, on the basis of such forces presently stationed in Germany or heretofore announced for movement to Germany. In the event of further deployment of U.S. forces to Germany, the two governments will consider methods whereby the balance-of-payments effect of such movements can be adjusted to their mutual benefit.[58]

The memorandum would be in effect for a period of two years, during which the accumulated foreign exchange cost of U.S. troops in Germany was anticipated to be about $1.45 billion. This signified that procurement in the United States was to make up roughly one-sixth of the German defense budget. Strauss supplemented the memorandum with an official letter, setting forth: (1) a firm commitment beyond U.S. FY 1962 was not possible; (2) the impossibility of concluding a similar agreement with any other country; (3) the necessity of maintaining existing military-economic relations with other NATO countries; and (4) a demand for U.S. political support if the agreement were to create problems with other NATO allies.[59] As it soon turned out, Strauss's apprehensions were well founded. The immediate problem, however, was how to place the broad understanding into a more precise framework. This led to hectic discussions on financial, organizational, and procedural details, as well as on the elements of the cooperative logistics system. Talks commenced on the large number of items that the FRG would eventually buy.[60] The financial framework posed a particular problem, and the West German Ministry of Finance, which had been almost completely excluded from the talks, objected to its implementation at the last minute. But its intervention came too late to change the outcome. A payments procedure agreement was agreed on based on the example of the MSMS agreement of October 1956. The period for order and payments targets was split. Orders to the tune of $1.45 billion were to be placed in U.S. CY 1961 and 1962, and the equivalent payments were to be made in FY 1961–2 and 1962–3 (ending June 1963). A formal exchange of letters between Strauss and Gilpatric

58 FRUS 1961–63, IX, 132–3.
59 Strauss to Gilpatric, Oct. 30, 1961, NA, RG 84, Bonn embassy 1959–61, box 25.
60 MAAG to Office of the Secretary of Defense, Nov. 16, 1961, NA, RG 59, DF 1960–63, 762a.5/12–1661.

recorded the details.[61] The payments level was made contingent on the success of the logistics agreement. Once more the Germans requested that the letter exchange be held in strictest confidence to avoid difficulties with the United Kingdom.

Nevertheless, the ticklish problem of informing the British and French now became urgent. The Federal Republic was particularly worried that the United Kingdom, then pursuing its own offset talks with the BMF without much success, would react furiously and demand equal treatment. Another delicate question was the need to inform the French. First, the political scope of the agreement was certain to displease the French government; second, the provisions of the logistics arrangements on war reserves and on-call support entailed the presence of German materiel in France because the bulk of U.S. war stocks in Europe was deposited there. This, and the possible presence of German military personnel for control and inspection purposes, would very likely anger the French, who were known to react negatively on issues regarding their sovereignty.[62] As early as August 1961 the U.S. embassy in Paris had warned of difficulties because a U.S.–German logistics agreement might undermine a French–German agreement, thus robbing the French of an important lever in their dealings with the Federal Republic. The embassy also expressed doubts about whether the Franco–American agreements regarding the use of French facilities by U.S. forces permitted sharing these facilities with other countries.[63] The State Department cautioned against pushing through the agreements without informing the French, even if this meant that the French might veto important parts of them: "The core of the problem is that the U.S. Line of Communication in France will under the proposed agreements be used to supply and store materiel for FRG forces."[64] Finally, rather vague information was conveyed that avoided the mention of the crucial payments arrangements.[65] It took the French some time to figure out the scope of the deal.

MILITARY, POLITICAL, AND MONETARY ASPECTS

To evaluate the real significance of the 1961 Strauss–Gilpatric offset agreement, it is necessary to place it in the military, political, and monetary

---

61 Bonn no. 1774 (section I + II), Jan. 31, 1962; Bonn no. 1789, Feb. 1, 1961; Bonn no. 1796, Feb. 2, 1962; all in NA, RG 59, DF 1960–63, 762.0221.
62 Ball to William R. Tyler, Jan. 9, 1962, ibid.
63 Paris no. 69, Aug. 5, 1961, NA, RG 84, Bonn embassy 1959–61, box 26.
64 Tyler to Ball, Jan. 9, 1962, NA, RG 59, DF 1960–63, 762.0221/1–962.
65 DOS to U.S. embassies in Paris and Bonn, Feb. 13, 1962, ibid., 762a.5/2–1062.

contexts of overall German–American relations. These contexts are discussed separately for the sake of clarity, but it is self-evident that all these factors were inextricably intertwined.

The military importance of the agreement lay primarily in linking the American and German military efforts in Europe on many levels and, at the same time, rationalizing the military posture of both countries. By considerably expanding the production of military materiel, the Pentagon was able to reduce unit costs for their own procurement. The American weapons industry derived a huge profit. Planning figures for 1964 indicate that military exports to Germany made up roughly one-third of all American weapon sales abroad.[66] This made the Bundeswehr a mostly American-equipped army, and the Federal Republic gained access to some of the most modern weapon systems in existence.[67] The Americans guaranteed the delivery of high-tech systems that the FRG was not able or allowed to produce. This was an important step toward the modern posture of German forces for which Strauss so fervently fought. Above all, the agreement gave the Germans the opportunity to buy weapons capable of delivering nuclear warheads, an unwritten condition for Strauss. Nevertheless, the defense minister was not completely happy. In November 1961 his representative told the Americans that Strauss wished to discuss with McNamara "one of his greatest worries, that is, the availability of nuclear warheads for the expensive weapons systems being bought by the Bundeswehr."[68] Strauss told McNamara that he no longer was willing to buy missile systems if there was continued uncertainty as to whether the German forces would get access to warheads in case of a conflict.[69] How successful Strauss was with his request is still shrouded in secrecy.

Cooperation between the American and the German forces increased substantially due to the logistics arrangement. A memorandum jointly

---

66 "Summary of Military Sales: FY 64 Order Goals," July 8, 1963, NA, RG 59, SF 1963, box 3753, DEF 19–3 US. I have been unable to obtain precise information on the influence of American industry on offset. However, it seems that relations between the sales agencies at the Pentagon and private industry were cordial, to say the least. See Monika Medick, *Waffenexporte und auswärtige Politik der Vereinigten Staaten: Gesellschaftliche Interessen und politische Entscheidungen* (Meisenheim am Glan, 1976).

67 Included were: tanks ($104 million), two Pershing battalions ($126 million), Nike and Sergeant missile systems ($69 million), and so forth. For a lump-sum payment of $75 million, Germany acquired the remaining items on loan from the Nash list. See also talking points for visit of the West German defense minister to the U.S., Nov. 13, 1961, NHP.

68 MAAG to Office of the Secretary of Defense, Nov. 17, 1963, NA, RG 59, DF 1960–63, 7621.5/12–1661.

69 Memorandum on information provided by the BMVg regarding German-American military-economic relations, Dec. 28, 1961, PA-AA, B 150/1961 (declassified for AAPD 1963).

authored by the departments of State, Defense, and the Treasury and sent to Erhard in July 1963 listed the following areas: "Co-Production of common military equipment by German and U.S. sources, resupply and maintenance support for FRG forces through U.S. military logistics systems, training of FRG troops in U.S. military schools, joint usage of military facilities, and joint research and development projects."[70] The Federal Republic thus gained storage space and badly needed training areas, for example, the huge Grafenwöhr area. Eventually, German military personnel would be sent to the United States for training. U.S.–German cooperation along these lines had existed before, but there are few doubts that these arrangements, which expanded over the following years, "Americanized" the German forces to the point of outright dependence. The Germans realized this danger but at that time accepted it because of the benefits they derived.[71]

This leads directly to the political aspects of the agreement. The massive level of procurement and the close cooperation between West German and American forces pushed the prospect of European armaments cooperation far into the future. The Strauss–Gilpatric understanding was a clear option for the United States, even if that was not so obvious at the time. The much-debated military provisions of the Franco–German Treaty in 1963 were insignificant compared to the effects of the offset agreement. It fostered a closer alignment of West Germany with the United States in the monetary and security spheres at a time when serious doubts arose whether Germany would not team up with the French against the United States. In this sense the offset agreement was a direct continuation of American policy toward Germany after the war that had aimed at binding West Germany as tightly as possible to an American-led Western security system.

For the German government the offset agreement was of similar political importance: It virtually bought itself a continuation of the security structure of the 1950s, that is, the preservation of a large U.S. troop presence in Germany. Eisenhower's policy had cast deep doubts on the U.S. commitment. At the end of 1961 NATO military planners still foresaw the fallback of its forces to the Augsburg-Weser line in case of a war, which meant giving up half of Germany.[72] The Berlin Wall crisis appeared to the Germans to initiate a new, intensified phase of the Cold War,

70 DOS to Bonn embassy, July 17, 1963, NA, RG 59, SF 1963, FN 12, box 3451.
71 Talking papers for meeting with Gilpatric, Feb. 6, 1963, NHP.
72 Paris no. 3035: Norstad briefing of NATO Military Committee, Dec. 11, 1961, NA, RG 59, DF 1960–63, 762.0221/12-1161.

making American protection more valuable than ever. The offset agreement became a means of stifling U.S. inclinations to redeploy its forces. Later, when Erhard replaced Adenauer and abandoned his policy of seeking closer cooperation with de Gaulle's France in order to reduce Bonn's dependence on the United States, a stable U.S. troop level became essential for him to ward off his Gaullist adversaries on the domestic front.

Probably the most important consequences of the offset agreement lay in the financial field. Time and again the U.S. government referred to the offset agreement as the most important success of its monetary policy. By counting these military sales as balance-of-payments gains, the Kennedy administration achieved a large reduction in the U.S. deficit, from $3.9 billion in 1960 to $2.67 billion in 1963. Kennedy himself made clear that "it should be understood that under present circumstances military offset agreements enjoy a clear priority over increased development assistance because of the immediate and direct benefits which this objective can bring to our balance of payments."[73] This view of the importance of the offset agreement was based on an overwhelming consensus among departments in Washington, with particularly strong proponents in Defense and Treasury. The agreement provided the Treasury Department with a breathing space in which it was able to pursue its policy of surrounding the dollar with "peripheral defenses." Without the offset deal, higher deficits would have made this strategy much more difficult to justify, and the dollar–gold standard might have come down earlier than 1971.

One might ask – and critics of the agreements increasingly did so – how many of the military sales to West Germany were actually additional and would not have been made anyway. This is not an easy question to answer. What counts, however, is that these purchases were directly linked to the principle of offset, that is, the balancing of the foreign exchange cost of U.S. troops in Germany. Thus, it was a manifestation of the Federal Republic's policy of supporting the dollar. The offset agreement was used in this sense by the American government, and it was perceived in this sense by other governments. As a highly placed collaborator of de Gaulle recalls: "Every time there was a meeting of Europeans to concert their [monetary] policies, the State Department announced, as if by chance, that to reduce the U.S. deficit, a possible reduction of U.S. forces in Germany

73 DOS circular telegram, Aug. 8, 1962, NA, RG 59, DF 1960–63, 811.10/8-862. Accordingly, the United States made concerted efforts to achieve similar agreements with other stationing countries. They succeeded in the case of Italy, which agreed to purchase $100 million worth of equipment per annum from the United States.

was under consideration. Thus, the Germans told us: We have no chance, we have to support the American position."[74] It would take a long time before this link between the defense of the dollar and the maintenance of the U.S. commitment in Europe was dissolved. All in all, offset allowed the Kennedy administration to bring into accordance the two contradictory objectives mentioned at the outset of the chapter: the continuation of the American military presence in Europe to deter the Soviets and preserve American influence in European affairs, and the continuation of the dollar–gold system in a period when the Atlantic security system and the world's monetary system became increasingly incompatible. For these reasons the continuation of the offset agreement became a top priority in American foreign policy. There were few high-level German–American meetings in the 1960s during which the West Germans were not reminded of the essential importance of this fact. The German government managed to combine a number of advances toward the goal of military equality with the avoidance of large-scale U.S. reductions that would have precipitated a drastic change in the structure of transatlantic security. Support for the dollar was the price that had to be paid.

In hindsight it is easy to see that the agreement was possible only because a set of favorable factors coincided: the impact of Berlin; the availability of funds and the German need for advanced weapon systems; the U.S. willingness to provide advanced military materiel; the German forces' need for logistical help; the incessant pressure by McNamara and his associates; the absence of sizeable West German and European competition; and the almost complete exclusion of the finance and foreign ministries from the talks. The offset agreement was a bargain that may have made sense for only a short period; nevertheless, it soon became an institutionalized factor in German–American relations. Both sides showed very early signs of disenchantment with their end of the bargain. The question was when it would unravel.

74 Institut de Gaulle, ed., *De Gaulle et son siècle III* (Paris, 1992), 157.

7

The Bargain Slowly Unravels: Offset, Troop Reductions, and the Balance of Payments, 1962–1965

With the exception of the target figure, the offset agreement had been rather vaguely formulated. The question of its actual implementation has received no attention in the scholarly literature, although a closer look at the offset mechanism offers interesting perspectives on the management of the transatlantic alliance by the United States. Particularly conspicuous is the relative absence of the State Department and the Auswärtiges Amt in this context. In the United States offset was managed by the Pentagon, with some participation by the Treasury Department; only when problems raised the issue to a politically sensitive level did the State Department become involved. A team of highly motivated Pentagon and Treasury experts began to travel regularly to Germany to discuss projects and orders. These frequent trips to Bonn by Henry J. Kuss and Charles A. Sullivan, the Pentagon and Treasury officials in charge, soon caused considerable irritation at the U.S. embassy in Bonn, which felt bypassed and warned of the absence of political considerations in the multimillion-dollar deals concluded between the West German Ministry of Defense and the Pentagon salesmen.[1] In August 1962 officers at the American embassy concluded, somewhat resignedly, that "State is no longer trying to keep fully abreast of the machinations of Messrs. Kuss and Sullivan. We have neither the manpower nor the money."[2] Very soon a kind of military-industrial complex dealing with offset emerged at the Pentagon. Its existence was closely linked to the rise in German military purchases, but it soon expanded its activities to a global scale. From 1961 to 1966

---

1 Tyler to McGhee, Apr. 16, 1964; and McGhee to Tyler, Apr. 18, 1964; both in McGhee papers, 1988add., box 1.
2 C. Arnold Freshman to Dowling: your meeting with Dillon, Aug. 8, 1962, NA, RG 59, DF 1960–63, 862a.10/8–862, box 2658.

American military sales abroad rose from $630 million to $1.937 billion a year.[3] The Federal Republic alone purchased about one-third of all those exports.[4] A special sales agency, headed by Kuss and somewhat euphemistically called the Office for International Logistics Negotiations, was established in the Pentagon. This agency expanded its activities on an unprecedented scale and in close cooperation with about twenty major weapons-producing firms. Industry representatives accompanied Kuss on his sales missions to Germany.[5] In Germany the Military Assistance Advisory Group, with over one hundred employees, established day-to-day contacts with procurement officers in the West German Defense Ministry.[6] German military personnel were trained on U.S. weapons, German supplies were processed and placed in the U.S. supply system, weapons maintenance was provided, procurement services were extended, and so forth — all, of course, against payments of dollars.[7] Thus, the Pentagon was able to reap handsome profits and to curtail the tremendous balance-of-payments impact the intensification of the Vietnam War was having on its activities. The continuation of German orders became a core element in Robert McNamara's management of his department. This led to his strong insistence on offset by military purchases even when the Federal Republic claimed to have no further need. Douglas C. Dillon and McNamara were interested mainly in a constant flow of offset funds and did not care very much about what was sold and how. Once the agreement was concluded it quickly became an institutionalized factor on which McNamara counted for his military-economic policy, particularly regarding the foreign exchange component of military expenditures, and on which Dillon relied in his efforts to stabilize the American balance of payments. Little thought was given to the long-term aspects of the agreement.

---

3 *Armed Forces Management* (Jan. 1967): 36. Journals such as *Armed Forces Management* and *Defense Industry Bulletin*, partly financed by the Pentagon, served as a showcase for American weapons production. They clearly demonstrate the close cooperation between the DOD and the major arms-exporting firms. Most of these exports went via the Pentagon and as such were registered as gains in the account of the Defense Department. On this subject, see also Medick, *Waffenexporte*, and David J. Louscher, "The Rise of Military Sales as a U.S. Foreign Assistance Instrument," *Orbis* 20 (1977): 933–64. Only at the end of the 1960s did Congress become aware of the major foreign-policy implications of McNamara's sales offensive.

4 Memorandum by Kuss: "Summary of Military Sales FY 64 Order Goals," July 8, 1963, NA, RG 59, SF 1963, box 3753, DEF19-3US.

5 DOD/FMOD conference in Bonn: list of participants, May 22, 1963, McGhee papers, 1988add., box 1.

6 Bonn no. 3161, May 22, 1963, NA, RG59, SF 1963, box 3760, DEF19-2US-WGER.

7 "U.S. Foreign Sales Carry a Guarantee of Continued Logistics Support," *Armed Forces Management* (Jan. 1967): 71–2.

A similar pattern emerged in Germany. As previously stated, the negotiations were conducted and concluded by Defense Ministry officials, apart from a last-minute intervention by the Finance Ministry, which achieved only a short delay. It seemed a deliberate policy by the German Defense Ministry to keep other ministries out of the offset process. As long as the offset funds were covered by the defense budget, the Finance Ministry saw no reason to take up the troublesome issue. Its officials had their hands full coping with British demands for offset, a task they had assumed very reluctantly and after all other relevant ministries had declined to manage it. The involvement of the Auswärtiges Amt in the offset process was also conspicuously limited. At the end of 1962, when Foreign Minister Gerhard Schröder was questioned by Dillon about indications that the agreement would not be fully honored, he displayed an almost awkward lack of knowledge of the subject.[8] This is particularly striking when one considers the important role the Auswärtiges Amt played in the support-cost negotiations with the British after 1955. Even if we account for Schröder's unwillingness to discuss the complicated problem at this level, it might well have been true that he knew very little about the details, as he claimed. Relations between him and Franz Josef Strauss were not particularly cordial. Furthermore, offset was in line with Schröder's policy of close alignment with the United States. His concern was that the Defense Ministry take care of the issue so that it would not interfere with the general conduct of German–American relations. What the Auswärtiges Amt worried about was the maintenance of U.S. troop levels. Chancellor Konrad Adenauer was also unwilling to concern himself with such a technical matter. When McNamara tried to obtain Adenauer's comments on the issue, the chancellor responded that the Pentagon chief should discuss offset with Karl Blessing, the president of the Bundesbank, and with Hermann-Josef Abs, one of Adenauer's principal advisers in monetary affairs; both at that time were hardly experts on the matter.[9] Thus, the Defense Ministry was left with a highly sensitive political issue. This situation was not particularly harmful as long as Strauss was the defense minister; he was a powerful figure in the cabinet and on the domestic political scene; he was also not susceptible to American pressure. However, his dubious role in the *Spiegel* affair put an unexpected stop to his ministerial career in late 1962. He was replaced by Kai-Uwe von Hassel, who distanced himself from the impetuous and

8 Schröder–Dillon conversation, Nov. 15, 1962, in FRUS 1961–63, IX, 157–9.
9 McNamara–Adenauer talks, July 31, 1963, AAPD 1963, 864–5.

energetic style of Strauss and had much less standing in the German cabinet. Hassel failed to initiate a change of policy on the offset issue, which continued to be vigorously pushed by the Americans, particularly by McNamara. It is unclear when the defense minister realized the limited rationality of continuing with offset by military purchases and why he then did not put on the brakes. It might have been loyalty to Adenauer's successor, Ludwig Erhard, that prompted him to adhere to the principle of offset until it was too late.

When Erhard became chancellor in 1963 the alliance with the United States became his and his foreign minister's all-important objective. They had to defend this objective against powerful critics at home. They expected the management of offset to be accomplished in such a way as not to interfere with the German–American relationship. Hassel himself was very Atlanticist and thus had every intention of assuring continued American support for the Erhard government. Rolf Dahlgrün, the new finance minister, was no Schäffer. A member of the smallest party in the coalition, the Free Democratic Party (Freie Demokratische Partei, or FDP), he developed no particular profile and was not the man to challenge the chancellor and the foreign minister on policies they considered essential. As a result, no one in the government took the issue seriously enough to revisit negotiations with the Americans. This neglect was particularly blatant in the case of Erhard, whose carelessness in this regard helped to dig his own political grave. Numerous high-level interventions by U.S. officials should have warned him that some kind of a political time bomb was ticking or, at least, that the Americans placed more importance on the "hardware" of mutual relations than on declarations of friendship.

In summary, the striking fact appears that the management of offset was pursued by both sides with insufficient consideration for future political problems, in the interest of short-term political and economic objectives. Officials in the German Defense Ministry and McNamara's salesmen had considerable autonomy in pursuing their multibillion-dollar deals in a highly sensitive area of mutual relations and of transatlantic relations in general. Probably even more conspicuous than this was the absence of democratic control due to the secrecy surrounding the agreements. Only very few members of Congress or the German Bundestag were aware of the deals and had a vague knowledge of what was going on. When the problem surfaced in early 1966 the scope of the agreements caught most parliamentarians and the public by surprise. Until the signs of trouble there had been hardly any discussion of the agreements in the press.

THE SECOND OFFSET AGREEMENT

Shortly after the Gilpatric-Strauss letter exchange of February 1962 the Americans directed their thoughts toward a follow-on agreement providing for orders in CY 1963–4, and payments in FY 1964 and 1965. Somewhat to their surprise, the negotiations proved short and not very complicated. The Americans, again headed by Gilpatric, offered to extend their logistics cooperation to the Navy and the Air Force, involving mainly the training of German soldiers at American facilities. In addition, the Germans sought a commitment from the United States to extend logistics cooperation to comprehensive wartime support. This was to assure supplies for German forces from bases abroad in case of an attack.[10] The U.S. embassy saw several advantages in such a scheme. First, it would increase the dependence of West Germany on U.S. materiel and shield American sales against competition from foreign or German weapon producers. Second, it would allow the United States to sell some of its war stocks in Europe, which were to be reduced anyway due to a cost-saving campaign initiated by McNamara. Finally, "United States influence could also be exercised indirectly on significant FRG policy decisions, for example, as a counterweight to such remote, but nevertheless conceivable, factors as a Franco–German 'third force' approach to European defense or any future tendency of the FRG to pursue an independent (be it neutralistic or adventurous) military policy vis-à-vis the Soviet bloc."[11] The Americans clearly saw the offset agreement as an instrument to bind West Germany more tightly to their version of the Atlantic alliance.

The new features were embodied in a new memorandum of understanding, signed on September 14, 1962, again with very few public repercussions. The German side, however, already had second thoughts about the continuation of offset. Strauss insisted on inserting an additional clause stipulating that offset payments would be made "subject to the availability of funds."[12] This proved to be a bad omen. Already in August reports had arrived in Washington that the German defense budget might be affected by growing German uneasiness about future strategic trends in

10 Bonn no. A-1493, US/FRG wartime logistics support agreement, June 12, 1962, NA, RG59, DF 1960–63, box 1276, 611.62a/6-1262; MAAG to ambassador: DOD/FMOD conference, May 22, 1963, McGhee papers, 1988add., box 1; memorandum of understanding on the creation of a logistic system for wartime support, Aug. 1, 1963, PA-AA, B 150/1963.
11 Bonn no. A-1493, US/FRG wartime logistics support agreement, June 12, 1962, NA, RG 59, DF 1960–63, box 1276, 611.62a/6-1262.
12 Memorandum of understanding, Sept. 14, 1962, McGhee papers, 1988add., box 2.

NATO and about the country's economic prospects.[13] In October it became clear that the 1963 federal defense budget would be much smaller than both the U.S. government and the German Defense Ministry expected, and too small to fulfill the goals agreed to in NATO defense planning. In addition, the Defense Ministry specified that under these circumstances all new procurement orders would be stopped by January 1963 at the latest and that payments for orders already made would be delayed.[14] The uncertainty regarding the defense budget was part of a protracted political situation in Bonn. Against the opposition of part of his cabinet, Adenauer concentrated on achieving closer cooperation with De Gaulle's France. France had always been particularly interested in arms cooperation and sales, and it was only prudent for the Defense Ministry to wait with new orders until Adenauer's plans took concrete form. Furthermore, the German Finance Ministry was insistent on limiting further growth of the defense budget, which the Defense Ministry had counted on in its offset deals. Strauss was immobilized by the *Spiegel* affair and not able to put up a fight for more money. It is quite likely that the ministry officials who informed the Americans of the problem painted an exaggeratedly negative picture to get the U.S. government to exert pressure on Adenauer and the Finance Ministry.

If this was the reasoning, it worked very well. The Americans reacted quickly and vigorously. The embassy in Bonn urged the president to approach Adenauer himself during the chancellor's visit to the United States in November.[15] Dillon and McNamara fully concurred. They pointed out that the German decision to delay the payment of $225 million, expected to arrive before the end of 1962, would expand the U.S. payments deficit by that amount. Both advised Kennedy to hit Adenauer strongly on this point.[16] The president did not need much persuasion. Alluding to the Cuban Missile Crisis, he told the chancellor: "Since our difficulties in October we had had to draw on our dollar resources even more and had since then heard the disquieting rumor that for budgetary reasons the Federal Republic was expecting not to fulfill this agreement. . . . This would have a very bad psychological effect."[17]

---

13 Bonn no. 556, Aug. 23, 1962; Bonn no. 597, Aug. 28, 1962; both in NA, RG 59, DF 1960–63, box 2658, 762a.5.

14 Bonn no. A-1193, Nov. 30, 1962, ibid., box 1903, 762a.5/11-3062.

15 Bonn no. 1299: memorandum on conversation between Hans-Georg Schiffers and Morris, Nov. 8, 1962, ibid., box 1903, 762a.5/11-862; Schiffers–Sullivan talks, Nov. 10, 1962, ibid., box 2658, 862a.10/11-1062.

16 Dillon, McNamara to Kennedy, Nov. 9, 1962, ibid., box 2658, 862a.10/11-1362.

17 Adenauer and Kennedy talks, Nov. 14, 1962, in FRUS 1961–63, XV, 435–6.

One day later a strongly worded memorandum covered the points more specifically: Because the United States was maintaining its full force in Europe, it felt it should "have the right to expect Germany, in turn, to do its full share."[18] The United States therefore requested an augmentation of the German defense budget. Another memorandum, ten days later, listed German obligations under the offset agreement and warned of "disastrous consequences" in case payments were deferred as announced.[19]

This broadside apparently convinced Adenauer and provided enough ammunition to overcome the resistance of the finance minister. Two weeks later the chancellor informed Kennedy that the projected defense budget would be augmented by an additional $275 million and that the Strauss–Gilpatric agreement would be fully honored. He added that German defense expenditures had now reached their upper limit.[20] The U.S. government expressed its satisfaction with the steps taken. However, the peace did not last very long. At his famous press conference on January 14, 1963, de Gaulle effectively challenged Kennedy's European policy. The solemn signing of a Franco–German Treaty of friendship and cooperation only one week later appeared to the Americans to be an act of utter provocation by Adenauer. As a consequence, the Kennedy administration undertook a reappraisal of its European policy. The crisis of trust in German–American relations had no direct impact on the continuation of offset. Initially, the United States was deeply worried about a possible nuclear deal between France and Germany, and a diversion of German military procurement to French sources. The Germans hastened to reassure the Americans on these points.[21]

Internally, however, the Germans were extremely skeptical as to whether they would be able to fulfill the agreement. French pressure was only one aspect of their apprehensions. The difficult budgetary situation, the uncertainty regarding the future of NATO policy, and the danger of increasing military dependence on the Americans were additional reasons.[22] The German Defense Ministry therefore stubbornly declined to commit itself to more than $1 billion of payments during the term of the second agreement, using the safeguard clause. And the Americans tried to extract from the Germans an unambiguous, loophole-free commitment

---

18 Kennedy memorandum to Adenauer, Nov. 15, 1962, ibid., 444–5.
19 Kennedy to Adenauer, Nov. 25, 1962, Kennedy–Adenauer correspondence, JFKL.
20 Adenauer to Kennedy, Dec. 12, 1962, ibid.
21 Note on Hassel–Gilpatric talks, Feb. 13, 1963, NHP; Bonn circular telegram re: Hassel–Gilpatric talks, Feb. 20, 1963, BA, Blankenhorn papers, 152/1.
22 Briefing paper for Gilpatric visit, Feb. 6, 1963, NHP; Bonn no. 2176, Feb. 22, 1963, NA, RG 59, SF 63, DEF19 WGER.

to full offset payments. The Treasury and Defense Departments were particularly active. In mid-1962 the continuation of offset became, in the absence of other major successes against the balance-of-payments deficit, the highest priority at Treasury. Dillon noted that a large part of the improvement in the balance of payments was due to offset.[23] The Americans undertook initiatives to conclude military offset agreements with numerous other countries, including France, Italy, and Japan.[24] On the occasion of the president's trip to Bonn and Rome, Dillon under-lined the importance of military offset agreements that "contribute so sig-nificantly to meeting our balance-of-payments goals and which constitute from the balance-of-payments point of view our top priority financial objectives in these countries."[25] In the absence of other breakthroughs in the fight against the deficit or a political decision for large-scale reforms in the international monetary system, the offset mechanism had taken on the role of a palliative for coping with a fundamental monetary imbalance.

Apart from these monetary reasons the sale of military hardware was increasingly considered a political tool. Elaborating on the desirability of American–German coproduction of a new tank, the U.S. embassy in Bonn wrote that the "the co-production technique . . . offers [the] only realistic method for [the] future not only to get our share [of] German armaments orders but also, and more importantly, to keep [the] Fed[eral] Rep[ublic] closely tied to us in conventional weapons."[26] A similar argu-ment was used by Dillon: "We should move promptly to make sure that European countries place orders now for U.S. manufactured equipment, rather than make plans to meet their needs from their own production or from other foreign sources."[27] During a taped discussion with Kennedy about his impending trip to Germany, McNamara was even more out-spoken on this issue: "Joint research projects, production projects, logisti-

23 Dillon to Kennedy, Nov. 14, 1962, in FRUS 1961–63, IX, 155.
24 France refused to buy more U.S. weapons as long as the Americans refused to sell their nuclear technology to France. Italy agreed on September 19, 1962, to buy $100 million of military equip-ment annually from the United States, but this was coupled with U.S. credits to Italy. See Dillon to JFK, Oct. 9, 1962, JFKL, POF, depts. & agencies: Treasury, box 90. In connection with the Vietnam War, numerous Asian countries also assumed offset obligations; see the 1968 balance-of-payments program, doc. 9e, military account, Dec. 25, 1968, LBJL, NSF, NSC histories.
25 Dillon to Ball, May 31, 1963, NA, RG 59, SF 1963, box 3455, FN12WGER.
26 Apr. 20, 1963, NA, RG 59, SF 1963, box 3769, DEF12 Armaments, Bonn 2817.
27 Dillon to president, May 13, 1963, JFKL, POF, depts. & agencies: Treasury, box 90; see also mem-orandum by Kuss: "Summary of Military Sales FY 64 Order Goals," July 8, 1963, NA, RG 59, SF 1963, box 3753, DEF 19-3US.

cal projects, all designed to so integrate the Germans into our military planning and production that they will not be able to proceed unilaterally with their own domestic arms industry . . . will be the best possible insurance for a continuation of our offset agreements with them, which they are trying to squeeze out of."[28]

From 1962 to 1965 the Germans continued to buy heavily in the United States because of Erhard's foreign policy priorities and also because of increasing U.S. pressure. Among the largest items again were modern missile systems, such as Pershing and Sergeant. This led to a certain uneasiness in the State Department about the proliferation of these weapons: "If the Chancellor (or von Hassel) suggests that Germany could meet its offset obligations by purchasing more Pershing missiles beyond the four battalions now contemplated, it would be advisable not to make any commitment but simply to agree to consider the request in the light of other Allied strategic interests [that is, a continued conventional buildup]."[29] In the end those considerations were overcome by the need to meet the foreign exchange cost of the troops, estimated at about $1.35 billion in FY 1963–5.[30] Nonetheless, the Germans lagged consistently behind schedule with their offset payments. They refused to commit themselves to more than $1 billion of offset in the two years covered by the second agreement.[31] In July 1963 the United States sent a long memorandum to the German government listing the advantages of the cooperative logistics system and requesting a firm commitment to a payment target of $1.3 billion.[32] The same point was made by McNamara to Adenauer when the two met on July 31. Hassel, who was also present, said that because of increasing domestic production, Germany had to limit purchases abroad. He mentioned that the United States had abandoned a scheme already agreed on in April that would have allowed Germany to bridge the gap by investing in U.S. Treasury bonds. McNamara denied that such an agreement had existed and threatened that if the offset target was not met the United States would have to reconsider

28 JFK, McNamara, and Bundy meeting, July 30, 1963, JFKL, tape no. 2/A 38. My sincere thanks go to Marc Trachtenberg for bringing this tape to my attention.
29 President's European trip, June 1963: scope paper Germany, June 14, 1963, DDRS 1979, 305B; see also Gilpatric to Hassel, May 8, 1963, McGhee papers, 1988add., box 1.
30 Tyler to Rusk: "Sale of Pershings/Sergeants to the FRG," May 21, 1963, NA, RG59, SF 1963, DEF13 US-WGER.
31 Bonn no. 5, July 1, 1963, NA, RG 59, SF 1963, box 3451, FN12US; Bonn no. 374, July 27, 1963, ibid.; see also George McGhee, *At the Creation of a New Germany: From Adenauer to Brandt; An Ambassador's Account* (New Haven, Conn., 1989), 75–6.
32 State/Treasury/Defense message, July 16, 1963, NA, RG 59, SF 1963, FN12US.

its troop commitment. At that point, Adenauer cut short the quarrel by referring this subject to discussions by financial experts.[33] Nevertheless, McNamara's threat was taken very seriously by the German government. Disturbing signs were coming from Washington, including increasing rumors that threw doubt on the continuation of the U.S. troop presence. In fact, the years 1962 and 1963 saw a major debate within the American government regarding the future of its troop commitment to European defense.

THE TROOP REDUCTION DEBATE OF 1962–1963

For many reasons, the Strauss–Gilpatric agreement did not end the discussion in the U.S. government about the adequate level of American forces in Europe. The balance of payments remained deeply in deficit. After the erection of the Berlin Wall and the Cuban Missile Crisis, fears of direct aggressive acts by the Soviets subsided. A gradual acceptance of the status quo and a search for some kind of détente in Europe became prominent aspects of U.S. foreign policy. Apprehension about irresponsible acts by the Germans diminished as the Federal Republic became increasingly accepted politically, economically, and militarily, and more strongly linked to the West. All those trends, touching on the rationales that had led to the stationing of U.S. troops in the early 1950s, surfaced in the troop-reduction debate of 1962–3, the outcome of which was to be of great importance to European–American relations in general and the offset issue in particular.

As soon as the Berlin Crisis subsided, the rationale behind the Acheson report of April 1961 lost logical force and the day-to-day concern of the balance of payments came to carry more weight. It has already been mentioned that Kennedy himself was deeply skeptical about the wisdom of keeping so many troops in Europe. His frustration mounted when reports showed that the ambitious goal of eliminating the balance-of-payments deficit at the end of 1963 would not be met. His attacks on

33 McNamara–Adenauer talks, July 31, 1963, AAPD 1963, 864–5; see also Bonn to DOS on McNamara–Adenauer talks, Aug. 2, 1963, McGhee papers, 1988add., box 1. During the same meeting, McNamara proposed that the Germans should acquire the U.S. logistic facilities in France that the Americans were about to close. A corresponding memorandum was signed on August 1, 1963. (Bonn no. 971, Sept. 14, 1963, NA, RG 59, SF 1963, box 3766, DEF13 US-WGER.) This set the stage for a major German–French row. The French explained that "since Franco–U.S. LOC [line of communications] arrangements are on a completely different basis than Franco–German arrangements (facilities used by Germans were under French command) France did not see how U.S. facilities could be transferred to Germans" (Paris no. 1338, Sept. 19, 1963, ibid.).

the Europeans who were not willing to increase their conventional force levels multiplied, perhaps most virulently during a tense discussion with André Malraux, the French minister for cultural affairs, on May 11, 1962. An ill-tempered Kennedy repeated several times that the United States would be happy to leave Europe if that was what the Europeans wanted:

If it is desired that we should cease to carry the load in Europe, nothing would be better from our point of view – it has now cost us about $1,300,000,000 to maintain our forces in Europe and the savings on these forces would just about meet our balance of payments deficit. . . . We feel like a man carrying a 200-pound sack of potatoes, and other people not carrying a similar load, at least in potatoes, keep telling us how to carry our burden.[34]

The expression of such sentiments by the president encouraged those members of the administration who viewed the forces in Europe as a wasted asset and had supported Acheson's recommendation for a conventional buildup only reluctantly. They had their champions in McNamara and Dillon. Still opposed to reductions was the State Department (although Dean Rusk was very ambiguous), which saw the European theater as being of paramount importance to U.S. foreign policy objectives and therefore accorded the Seventh Army a political importance that went beyond military and financial considerations. The consequence of this split was a long-drawn-out controversy in the administration. Only a few months after the Berlin Wall had been erected and U.S. troops had been augmented by about 40,000 men, the Department of Defense tabled its first plans to bring the costly reinforcements back. The Army and the State Department saw this as much too early and weighed in successfully against such a precipitous action.[35] No reductions were effected in early 1962, but the planning in the Defense Department went ahead – not only regarding the reinforcements but also the regular forces. No one in the administration took the president's repeated orders to reduce the foreign exchange component in the expenses of their departments more seriously than McNamara. By mid-July he had compiled an impressive list of proposed cutbacks, called Revised Project VIII, which were to reduce the balance-of-payments impact of defense expenditures by about one

34 FRUS 1961–63, XIII, 695–701.
35 "While the messages received here do not expressly state so, it is believed that gold drain from the U.S. was central among considerations behind the orders to USAREUR." (USAREUR to Dowling, Jan. 11, 1962, McGhee papers, 1988add., box 1). See also Maxwell Taylor to president, Dec. 9, 1961, JFKL, NSF, depts. & agencies: DOD, box 275; telephone conversation Rusk-Foy D. Kohler, Jan. 15, 1962, in FRUS 1961–63, XIV, 760; Rusk to McNamara, Jan. 20, 1962, ibid., XIII, 356–7.

billion.[36] McNamara envisaged large-scale reductions of the regular Seventh Army, to the tune of 44,000 men, as part of a long-term perspective. Based on new assessments of the Soviet threat that set Warsaw Pact military capabilities much lower than previously estimated, McNamara thought large reductions possible with regard to the military situation and necessary from a balance-of-payments point of view.[37]

The Department of State was alarmed. In its view the Berlin Crisis was not yet over and advance consultation with the Allies was necessary before reducing any troops at all.[38] One fact was undeniable, however: Gold losses in the first half of 1962 reached dangerous levels.[39] Faced with this predicament the State Department fought a continuous rearguard campaign on the troop-level issue. During 1962, as long as the studies on the Project VIII list continued, the State Department managed to fend off Defense Department and Treasury pressure for large-scale reductions. In the meantime the Americans continued their concerted efforts to get the Europeans to build up their conventional forces. They pointed to the necessity of avoiding immediate recourse to nuclear warfare, whereas the Germans complained about the inferiority of their forces, which had no tactical nuclear weapons at their disposal.[40] The strategic ideas of the Kennedy administration were unconvincing to the Germans. First, because of its geographic position the Federal Republic had to insist on forward defense and the immediate use of all available weapons to deter any attack on its territory. Any doubts about American willingness to use all its firepower for the defense of Germany limited the credibility of deterrence and impinged directly on German security. For this reason, in the late 1950s and 1960s, the Germans consistently tried to obtain a stronger voice in planning for the use of nuclear weapons.[41] Second, economic reasons played an important role. Strauss informed Adenauer that the conventional program the United States wanted was

---

36 Total annual defense outlays entering the American balance of payments were about $3 billion/ year in 1961; Revised Project VIII, July 10, 1962, JFKL, NSF, meetings & memoranda, NSAM 171, box 337.

37 Alain Enthoven and K. Wayne Smith, *How Much Is Enough? Shaping the Defense Program, 1961–69* (New York, 1971).

38 Russell Fessenden to U. Alexis Johnson, May 17, 1962, NA, RG 59, DF 1960–63, 740.56311/5-1762; Johnson to Nitze, May 23, 1962, in FRUS 1961–63, XIII, 394–5.

39 Report by cabinet committee on balance of payments to president, July 27, 1962, in FRUS 1961–63, IX, 31.

40 The disagreement is well summarized in an exchange between Adenauer and Kennedy on Nov. 14, 1962; see FRUS 1961–63, XIII, 452–3.

41 For an argument that convincingly explains the Berlin crisis and stresses the Soviet fear of German nuclear ambitions, see Marc Trachtenberg, "The Berlin Crisis," in Trachtenberg, *History & Strategy*, 170–3.

not only strategically undesirable but also financially impossible.[42] The fundamental dilemma of German foreign policy throughout the 1960s is well illustrated in this context. The Federal Republic had renounced the possession of nuclear weapons and was politically unable to change that position. For economic reasons, however, it was unwilling to live up to its own Cold War rhetoric by building up its conventional forces. As long as it did not change its rigid stance in the East–West conflict and achieve some kind of accommodation with the Eastern bloc, it would consequently remain dependent on the United States, its nuclear weapons, and its troops. This created the political and military necessity to assure American troop presence by all means, including offset.

Whereas in 1962 Kennedy, despite McNamara's efforts, shied away from provoking a crisis with Europe over troop reductions, his thinking changed drastically in 1963. In a discussion with the military leadership in December 1962 Kennedy commented on the gold outflow and the limited military logic of forward-basing so many troops, and questioned the necessity of the U.S. effort.[43] McNamara immediately promised a plan to withdraw 50,000 to 70,000 men from Europe. The president's frustration was heightened by de Gaulle's veto of the United Kingdom's entry into the EEC on January 14, 1963, and the signing of the Franco–German Treaty soon afterward. All this came on top of an already pronounced unease in the administration about the handling of the Skybolt affair with the British.[44] Altogether, these events exposed the contradictions and

42 Strauss to Adenauer, Dec. 21, 1962, NHP; for the strategic dilemma and economic reasoning, see talking paper for meeting with president, Nov. 18, 1961, NHP; results of talks between AA and BMVg in Münstereifel, June 1962, ibid.; draft protocol on BMVg-AA colloquium, Feb. 1963, BA, Carstens papers, 620.
43 Memorandum on conversation among JFK, McNamara, and JCS, Dec. 27, 1962, DDRS 1995/1787.
44 Owing to technical difficulties McNamara canceled further development of the Skybolt rocket in mid-1962. The rocket had been promised to the British as a delivery system and was essential for maintaining an independent British nuclear deterrent. When Macmillan met Kennedy in Nassau shortly afterward, he emphatically asked the Americans to provide a substitute. Despite strong misgivings – the Kennedy administration pursued a policy of nonproliferation and would have liked to see a phase-out of the independent British nuclear force – Kennedy relented. Later on, Kennedy felt that Macmillan had pushed him into the corner, and even LBJ was still haunted by the fear that British Prime Minister Wilson would "do the Macmillan" on him. Opponents of the concessions to Britain thought that de Gaulle might take the implicit snub badly and retaliate with an assault on Britain's application for EEC membership. This did happen, but other reasons played a more important role in de Gaulle's veto. For the very interesting Kennedy–Macmillan talks, see FRUS 1961–63, XIII, 1088–115. Kennedy afterward commissioned a long study on the mistakes made in the Skybolt affair. See Neustadt report to president: Skybolt and Nassau, Nov. 15, 1963, JFKL, NSF, meetings & memorandum, box 322. An excellent study on the issue is Clark, *Nuclear Diplomacy*. On the British EEC application and related aspects, see the articles in Richard T. Griffiths and Stuart Ward, eds., *Courting the Common Market* (London, 1996). On the reasons for de Gaulle's veto and the ongoing debate on this issue, see Andrew

conflicts governing relations in the Western Alliance. Kennedy's European policy had resulted in the alienation of the three major U.S. partners in Europe and had brought Washington nowhere closer to its objective of a comprehensive burden-sharing agreement with the Europeans. The president reacted impetuously to this failure. During a meeting of the NSC Executive Committee on January 25, 1963, he requested a sweeping reappraisal of U.S. policy toward Europe, including American troop presence, based on a "cold, hard" attitude, in order to preserve U.S. interests, which he saw as increasingly endangered.

As soon as the French have a nuclear capability, the president continued, we have much less to offer Europe and the Europeans may conclude that continuing their ties with the U.S. will create a risk that we will drag them into a war in which they do not wish to be involved. If we are not vital to Germany, then our NATO strategy makes no sense. The president said that we must not permit a situation to develop in which we would have to seek economic favors from Europe. He thought we should think now about how we can use our existing position to put pressure on the Europeans if the situation so demands. . . . He thought we should be prepared to reduce quickly, if we so decided, our military forces in Germany.[45]

Bad news from the monetary front weighed heavily on the president's mind when he made these remarks. The situation at the beginning of 1963 was bleak. The Treasury Department expected further substantial gold losses during the succeeding months, and reaching the goal of a balance-of-payments equilibrium seemed highly unlikely before 1965.[46] French policy with regard to its huge dollar reserves was incalculable; de Gaulle might cash in his dollar reserves at any time and thus provoke a major currency crisis. Kennedy felt that America's monetary weakness was a major reason for the intractability of the Europeans, and he ordered the secretary of the treasury to assess the relative monetary strengths of France and the United States.[47]

In the weeks after the Franco–German Treaty the Americans undertook a vigorous effort to get the Federal Republic to agree to an unambiguous declaration of adherence to the principles of the Atlantic Alliance and German-American postwar relations. The result was a resolution by

Moravcsik, "De Gaulle between Grain and Grandeur," *Journal of Cold War Studies* 2 (2000): 3–43; and ibid., 3 (2000): 4–142.

45 For a record of the meeting, see FRUS 1961–63, XIII, 487–91. The quotation is on 488.
46 Kaysen to Kennedy, Jan. 21, 1963; Dillon to Kennedy, Jan. 16, 1963; both in ibid., IX, 43–4 and 159–60, respectively.
47 JFK to Treasury, Jan. 19, 1963, JFKL, POF, depts. & agencies: Treasury, box 90; for Dillon's answer stressing the need to get the non-French countries to agree to a cooperative policy regarding their dollar reserves, see Dillon to president, Jan. 24, 1963, ibid.

the German parliament that accompanied the ratification of the Franco–German treaty and stressed the importance of Bonn's transatlantic links, much to de Gaulle's annoyance. The Americans presented the German government with an enticement in the form of a renewed initiative concerning the Multilateral Force. Overshadowed by these diplomatic ramifications, the question of the future of the U.S. troop commitment in Europe remained open in Washington. The issue consistently appeared on the agenda during the discussions of these weeks and formed one of the questions Kennedy put before the NSC Executive Committee, which was to coordinate the reappraisal of Washington's European policy.[48] The principal differences were as large as ever. Whereas Dillon urged a reduction by arguing the balance-of-payments impact, Rusk remarked that "we are in Europe not because the Europeans want us there but because we believe our presence there is essential to the defense of the U.S."[49] This was the basic point, and it was on this point that Kennedy, supported by McNamara and Dillon, had serious doubts. To them, the U.S. troop presence in Europe represented more of a favor extended to the Europeans than a policy dictated by U.S. interests. Emphasizing this is the letter Kennedy wrote to Adenauer the day after this discussion. He mentioned the "$45bn and 16 years of American economic and military assistance" that had brought nothing but hostility and warned of a new isolationism in the United States.[50] There was a considerable amount of self-deception in these statements that was to become a common feature of the transatlantic dialog during the 1960s. The Europeans for the most part saw U.S. postwar policy not as dictated by altruism but as what could euphemistically be called "enlightened self-interest." If the continued presence of U.S. troops was consistently presented as a favor by and a burden to the United States, the hard-nosed Machiavellians Adenauer and de Gaulle were easily able to cast doubts on the sincerity of the commitment.

The president was not convinced by the State Department's argument that stationing troops in Europe was of continued importance. Soon after the debacles of January 1963 he voiced his doubts about the stalemate in Europe in a meeting with the Joint Chiefs of Staff (JCS). Kennedy urged the military to come up with plans "as to how much we can reduce our forces in Europe in the next 12 months." He denounced the insufficient defense efforts of the Allies, cited the reduced military threat in Europe

48 FRUS 1961–63, XIII, 156–7.   49 Ibid., 161.
50 Kennedy to Adenauer, Feb. 1, 1963, ibid., 164–5.

(calling it "about the eighth on the list of trouble spots"), and proclaimed it as "absolutely essential for us to protect our monetary position. . . . Eventually we will have to confront them [the Europeans] with the fact that either they must pay or we will have to cut back."[51] His remarks summarized the arguments of the reduction proponents: the unlikeliness of a crisis in Europe, based on an implicit recognition of the status quo (which was at variance with the German reunification postulate); the vulnerability of the dollar, interpreted as a sign of political weakness in the United States; and frustration regarding the unwillingness of the Europeans to accept American strategic views and to live up to an equitable sharing of the defense burden. Similar concerns were summarized in a memorandum by McGeorge Bundy in March 1963:

> One might conclude from a general perusal of these papers [that is, the results of the reappraisal of American policy toward Europe] that the twenty-year involvement of U.S. forces in Europe may well be extended another twenty years or even more. In spite of U.S. difficulties with the political, social and economic problems of Western Europe, its crushing burden of expenditures on armaments, and the potentially destructive erosion of the U.S. monetary position, little consideration is ever given to ways of reducing the impact or effects of these issues.[52]

Bundy conceded, however, that reductions without compensatory moves by the Soviet Union were dangerous and that thorough advance consultation with the Allies was necessary.

The State Department supplemented those counterarguments with a long list of its own. Reductions might heighten the present uncertainty in NATO regarding future military strategy – they might signify the abandonment of Flexible Response, play into de Gaulle's hands, weaken American political influence in Europe and particularly in Germany, and, finally, the balance-of-payments gain would be relatively small compared to other corrective measures.[53] An additional reason for avoiding precipitous moves in early 1963 was the impending Kennedy visit to Germany in June. This point carried the day, and Kennedy was careful not to commit himself to any specific action during his visit, which was a spectacular success.[54] But the emphatic reaffirmation of German–American

---

51 Memorandum for the record, Feb. 28, 1963, ibid., 516–18.
52 Burris to LBJ: McBundy on European policy, Mar. 13, 1963, LBJL, VPSF, box 4.
53 Johnson to Rusk: "Political Effects of Troop Withdrawals from Europe," May 17, 1963, NA, RG 59, SF 1963, DEF6US/NATO; Bruce to Rusk, May 21, 1963; Rusk to McNamara, June 7, 1963, 66–7; both in FRUS 1961–63, IX.
54 See his speeches at the Paulskirche in Frankfurt am Main, June 25, 1963, and in Naples, July 2, 1963, in DAFR 1963, 203–11; Kennedy–Adenauer talk, June 24, 1963, AAPD 1963, 670. The president, however, warned Adenauer that recent events in Europe had provoked doubts in the United States as to the wisdom of keeping troops there; ibid.

friendship during Kennedy's trip did not halt planning for reductions in the Defense Department. It continued along several tracks: First, a slow reduction of the Berlin reinforcements (from a peak level of 273,377 in June 1962, troop strength in Germany fell to 241,222 in September 1963);[55] second, a reduction in noncombat troops; and finally, highly sensitive plans to reduce a considerable portion of the combat troops over the long term. These plans had received a new boost when in the first half of 1963 the administration began to review not only its European policy but also its previous balance-of-payments policies. In April, Kennedy had a long meeting with his principal advisers to discuss new ways of solving the problem. When asked about possible actions by the Defense Department, McNamara replied that he expected a net adverse balance of $1.6 to 1.7 billion per year in the military account over the next few years, provided the offset agreement was continued at the present rate. McNamara thought that the "only way to improve our position was to reduce troop deployments . . . this can be done without reducing our effective military strength."[56]

After the meeting Kennedy charged the secretary of defense with a program that would achieve foreign exchange savings of $300–$400 million in the defense account. The proposals McNamara presented in July 1963 were coordinated with the State Department and contained only minor reductions in Europe.[57] As soon as the major part of McNamara's proposals was approved, however, the president requested another cost-saving program. This time, savings without real cuts in combat strength were no longer possible.[58] The response by the Department of Defense was on the president's desk in September. In the European theater, it proposed a removal of about 50 percent of U.S. combat aircraft (made possible by a greatly increased missile force), a reduction of the army to about 205,000 men, as well as other streamlining measures.[59] The plans were to be implemented by FY 1966 and were projected to produce estimated foreign exchange savings of $339 million. The State Department protested strongly and eloquently against such far-reaching

---

55 "The Replacement and Augmentation Systems in Europe," Mar. 1964, NSA, Berlin Crisis Collection, doc. 1924, 63.
56 Memorandum for the record: "Meeting with President on April 18," Apr. 24, 1963, in FRUS 1961–63, IX, 51–62.
57 McNamara to Kennedy, July 16, 1963, ibid., 68–73.
58 Robert J. Schaetzel to Jeffrey C. Kitchen, July 24, 1963, NA, RG 59, SF 1963, DEF6-8US/NATO, box 3749; Popper to Schaetzel, Sept. 19, 1963, ibid., DEF6US, box 3747; DOS to Averell Harriman, July 19, 1963, ibid., FN12US.
59 FRUS 1961–63, IX, 94–6.

cuts, arguing that they "would be the gravest sort of mistake, fraught with adverse political and psychological consequences, perhaps out of all proportion to the intrinsic military significance, but, nevertheless, carrying a real danger of jeopardizing our entire existing national security posture."[60] This strong counterattack proved successful. Kennedy accepted the State Department's arguments and effected only limited reductions, particularly in Britain and France. Germany was spared. Presumably, the offset agreement, along with vociferous German protests against minor reductions in the summer of 1963, played the central role in this decision.[61] However, the president's decision was accompanied by the wish that a political base be established from which they could proceed toward implementation of the steps not accepted.[62] National Security Action Memorandum (NSAM) 270 was the resulting policy guidance formulation.[63] Rusk was charged with publicly announcing that the government would undertake no combat force reductions in the European theater. At the end of October the secretary of state traveled to Europe and visited Germany. In a programmatic speech at the Paulskirche in Frankfurt am Main he outlined the government's position on troops in Europe in a phrase that would become the official line on the subject for several years thereafter: "We have six divisions in Germany. We intend to maintain these divisions here as long as there is need for them – and under present circumstances there is no doubt that they will continue to be needed."[64] Kennedy repeated the same statement in a press conference a few days later. The president reaffirmed that apart from some streamlining of noncombat personnel the United States would keep its six divisions in Europe "as long as they are required."[65] No specific definition of this "need" was given, and likewise, no specific conditions were attached to the pledge. The discussion within the government had stopped just short of directly linking the pledge with the continuation of offset, however. It was a very small step toward the establishment of such a link as official policy, although a majority in the U.S. government probably already adhered to this view. Large-scale plans to reduce the troops in Europe were blocked for the moment; the "streamlining" continued, however. At some point during 1965 the official line on

60 Rusk to Kennedy, Sept. 18, 1963, ibid.; this memorandum was based on Johnson to Rusk, Sept. 16, 1963, NA, RG 59, SF 1963, DEF1US, box 3746.
61 Dillon to LBJ, Dec. 2, 1963, in FRUS 1961–63, IX.
62 Bundy memorandum for the record, Sept. 23, 1963, ibid., 97–8.
63 NSAM 270, Oct. 29, 1963, ibid., 98–100.
64 Address by Secretary of State Rusk in the Paulskirche, Frankfurt am Main, Oct. 27, 1963, DAFR 1963, 220.
65 Ibid., 222–3.

the subject of U.S. troops in Europe changed slightly: The word "six" was replaced by "five."

When Schröder visited Washington in September 1963 Kennedy tried to reassure the Germans, indicating that the United States had decided against troop cuts at that time. Schröder repeatedly stated that the German government was not against minor reductions as long as there was consultation well in advance and time to prepare the public.[66] The president agreed with him on this point, but it may well be that both men had different definitions of consultation. Schröder would hardly have accepted Kennedy's definition of "consultation" outlined in NSAM 270: "Possible redeployments of U.S. forces under consideration within the government should not be discussed publicly nor with our allies until a decision has been made and a politico-military plan for action approved. Following these steps, we should consult as appropriate with our allies before any public announcement is made, and then proceed with our intended actions. Wherever possible, action of low visibility should be taken without public announcement."[67] Whatever reassurance the Germans gained from the Kennedy–Schröder talk was badly shaken soon afterward by a series of official and unofficial public statements in the United States. First, Eisenhower gave a widely publicized interview in which he recommended drawing down forces in Europe to one division.[68] Then, on October 19, Gilpatric delivered a speech that seemed to indicate reductions in connection with the military exercise "Big Lift," in which the United States practiced the moving of large forces from the United States to Europe and back: "By employing such a multi-base capability the United States should be able to make useful reductions in its heavy overseas military expenditures without diminishing its effective military strength or its capacity to apply that strength swiftly in support of its world-wide policy commitments."[69] These remarks were accompanied by similar statements from senators and other leading personalities, all of which made headlines in German newspapers.

The timing of these announcements was particularly unfortunate from the German point of view because they were made during the first weeks of Erhard's chancellorship. The former minister of economics had assumed

---

66 Kennedy–Schröder conversation, in FRUS 1961–63, IX, 86–7.
67 NSAM 270, ibid., 99.   68 Williams, *Senate*, 137–8.
69 AAPD 1963, 1365, note 3.

the post only after long and bitter resistance by Adenauer, who had consistently humiliated his rival. Erhard's arrival was linked with a distinct reorientation of German foreign policy toward repairing its damaged relationship with the United States and taking a more independent stance toward de Gaulle. Discontent with Adenauer's one-sided inclination toward France had been a major factor in increasing intraparty criticism of the aging chancellor. Adenauer was not so easily put off, however. He retained the chairmanship of the Christian Democratic Union (Christlich-Demokratische Union, or CDU) and thus remained a major voice in German politics. Together with other political heavyweights such as Strauss, he made no secret about his dislike of the Atlanticist orientation of his successor's foreign policy. Domestic debates on foreign policy during the following years were shaped mainly by this conflict between Atlanticists and Gaullists. News of impending U.S. troop reductions therefore reinforced the arguments of de Gaulle and his supporters in Germany and undercut the new chancellor's policy, which was founded on the assumed steadfastness of the U.S. commitment in Europe. The U.S. troop presence had always been a major domestic issue in Germany; now it was directly linked with the political fortunes of the chancellor.

Erhard and Schröder immediately voiced their concerns about the statements by Eisenhower and Gilpatric to the American ambassador, George C. McGhee.[70] The Germans repeated their apprehensions to Rusk during his visit in October. The secretary of state showed them the draft of his Frankfurt speech and repeated the assurances of the ambassador but also said that the Federal Republic should take a broader look at the worldwide responsibilities of the United States.[71] In his meeting with Defense Minister Hassel the secretary of state said that the U.S. position was influenced by two factors: "(1) If NATO does not meet its force goals – and most member countries have not – how can we explain it to our people and justify our continuing to meet our goals? (2) The offset. If our gold flow is not brought under control, the question could become an issue in next year's elections. The continuation of Germany's payments under the offset agreement is vital in this respect."[72] There was hardly any

---

70 Erhard–McGhee conversation, Oct. 22, 1963; Schröder–McGhee conversation, Oct. 22, 1963; both in AAPD 1963, 1359–71.
71 Erhard–Rusk conversation, Oct. 25, 1963; Schröder–Rusk conversation, Oct. 26, 1963; both in ibid., 1384–97.
72 Memorandum on Hassel–Rusk talks, Oct. 25, 1963, McGhee papers, 1988add., box 1.

doubt that this was a condition for continued U.S. troop presence. The German government did not feel reassured by Rusk's speech in Frankfurt. Talks with other countries affected by reductions reaffirmed their apprehensions.[73] The assassination of Kennedy in November 1963 evoked new uncertainty concerning the future course of American foreign policy. It therefore became Erhard's major objective to obtain a commitment from the new president to the assurances Rusk had given in his Frankfurt speech.

President Lyndon B. Johnson sought in general to follow the policies of his predecessor. On the issue of troop levels, however, he found a situation that was still in flux. Kennedy had given orders to develop plans for implementing the elements of the McNamara proposals that had not been approved in October.[74] Firm decisions were still pending. This was the situation when Erhard went to Washington shortly after Johnson's inauguration. Dillon had furnished the new president with several memoranda for the meeting emphasizing the importance of the balance-of-payments problem. He termed the deficit and the gold drain the most serious present threats to American political and military leadership. According to Dillon, these problems had been caused in large part by military spending overseas, and he felt the Germans should be made to realize their crucial role in this matter: "If Germany wants the United States to continue its commitments in support of the Alliance, Germany must be as helpful as possible in correcting pressures on our balance of payments."[75] He urged the president to press for lower German interest rates, for a continuation of the policy of not exchanging dollars for gold, and, above all, for a firm offset commitment.

In view of our recent public assurances of our intention to maintain the present level of our combat forces in Germany "as long as they are required," it would seem appropriate and important to obtain Erhard's assurance that the FRG will continue to fully offset U.S. dollar expenditures in Germany both in new orders

---

73 The Japanese foreign minister, Masayoshi Ohira, reported U.S. plans for deep cuts in U.S. forces in Japan, and the deputy of the British Labour Party, George Brown, claimed during a conversation with Schröder that Kennedy had personally given him the impression that the United States would soon withdraw. See Ohira–Schröder talks, Nov. 7–8, 1963; Carstens–Brown talks, Nov. 27, 1963; both in AAPD 1963, 1421–2 and 1507–9, respectively.

74 Background paper for Erhard visit: "U.S. Force Levels in Europe," Nov. 19, 1963, JFKL, oral history interview with Gilpatric, 83–4; Johnson to Rusk, Oct. 21, 1963, DDRS 1992/3513; NA, RG 59, SF 63, box 3749, DEF6-8US/NATO.

75 Dillon to LBJ, Dec. 13, 1963, LBJL, NSF, country file: Germany, box 190; see also Dillon to president: Late report on Germany and our payments deficit, Dec. 20, 1963, ibid.; Dillon to president, Dec. 18, 1963, DDRS 1980/435A.

and in actual payments for "as long as may be required." It would seem to me that failure of the FRG . . . to fully offset our defense expenditures in Germany would be as clear evidence as we could have that the current level of U.S. forces in Germany was no longer required.[76]

Johnson followed this advice, although he did not explicitly link offset with troop levels. In his talks with Erhard he did, however, repeatedly underline the importance he attached to the continuation of offset.[77] During a car trip on the grounds of the Johnson ranch the president pointed to mounting criticism in his country because U.S. troops had remained in Europe for such a long time despite modern airlift capabilities and because of the unfair division of burdens. Erhard insisted on the absolute necessity of maintaining existing troop levels and emphasized this with the remark that in his opinion the GIs felt very happy in Germany. Johnson quipped that he was sure they would feel even better at home.[78] The communiqué of the meeting contained a repetition of Rusk's assurance in Frankfurt as well as a commitment in principle by Erhard to continue offset.[79] The meeting made clear that the debate in the United States regarding troop levels in Europe would continue. The only change was one of emphasis: Whereas Kennedy was haunted by the fear of gold losses, Johnson was more receptive to congressional criticism of the American military commitment in Europe. The most important outcome of Erhard's visit was the implicit offset-troop level link that at that point became official policy for a majority in the U.S. government.

In April 1964 McNamara sent Bonn a draft memorandum for a new offset agreement covering the years 1965–6. He intended to sign this memorandum on his visit to Germany in May. German officials felt uneasy about formalizing the chancellor's promise made in December 1963.[80] The Finance and Economics Ministries expressed doubts about whether the defense budgets of the succeeding years would be high enough to continue the practice of offset by military procurement. However, as officials from the Auswärtiges Amt and the chancellor's office

---

76 Dillon to president: "German Offset Agreement," Dec. 13, 1963, LBJL, NSF, country file: Germany, box 190; see also Francis Bator to Bromley Smith outlining the president's position on offset: "1. The U.S. prefers the status quo. 2. The status quo, however, has two components: offset purchases in the previously agreed amounts and force levels. 3. If the Germans unilaterally alter the status quo by not living up to their offset commitments, we shall certainly be forced to reconsider the question of force levels" (May 6, 1964, DDRS 1995/199).

77 For the talks on Dec. 28–9, see AAPD 1963, 1672–713; esp. 1673–4, 1696.

78 Erhard–Johnson conversation, Stonewall, Texas, Dec. 28, 1963, ibid., 1699–701.

79 *DOS Bulletin*, Jan. 20, 1964, 74–5.

80 Interdepartmental meeting of German ministries, May 4, 1964, AAPD 1964, 504–6; memorandum for cabinet meeting, May 5, 1964, BA, B136/3133.

explained, the political importance of continuing with the agreement had priority over financial concerns. At the lower levels of the German government no illusions existed about the American insistence on a continuation of offset, although the Germans hoped they would be able to avoid a direct link between troop levels and offset.[81] A line of text emphasizing the uncertainty of future military procurement levels was to be inserted in any new memorandum of understanding. In May 1964 McNamara arrived in Bonn with two major objectives: to conclude the third offset agreement and to urge the federal government to come forward with tangible help in Vietnam. Erhard was noncommittal with regard to Vietnam. He added that it would be problematic to continue offset on previous levels due to budgetary problems and increasing competition from German domestic industry for arms orders. McNamara remarked that Germany would do better to manufacture for export than to shift to the production of military equipment. He concluded the exchange by emphasizing that the United States "just cannot continue to maintain [its] forces in Germany without full offset payments."[82] In his conversation with Hassel the secretary of defense was even more outspoken: "He wished to make clear that he was making no threats, but it would be absolutely impossible for the United States to accept the gold drain caused by the U.S. forces in Germany, if Germany did not assist through continuation of the Offset Agreement." Hassel responded with "yes, yes" and reminded McNamara that the German cabinet would dislike such a link. The secretary agreed that the link should not be made public, but "privately there must be an association."[83]

This was the bluntest reminder of the offset–troop level link the German government had ever received, and afterward it should have been under no illusions regarding the conditions for maintenance of U.S. troop levels. Whether this threat was decisive in the signing of a further memorandum of understanding on the same day is difficult to determine. In any case, the Erhard government accepted the commitment to preserve its overriding foreign policy priority: undisturbed relations with the United States. The payment target for the years 1965–6 was fixed at $1.35 billion. The memorandum contained a proviso that the contracting parties were aware of the difficulties regarding fulfillment of offset by

---

81 Memorandum Dept. II (II6): Link between troop maintenance and weapons purchases, Apr. 24, 1964, PA-AA, B150/1964.
82 McGhee, *At the Creation*, 143–5; Bonn no. 1514, offset agreement, May 11, 1964, McGhee papers, 1988add., box 1.
83 McNamara–Hassel talks, May 11, 1964, DDRS 1995/3179.

military payments. This would only be possible if a corresponding need for weapons existed for German forces and if satisfying this need from U.S. sources made economic sense. In case a full military offset was not possible, negotiations would take place to determine other methods of offset.[84]

The United States tried to have the commitment reaffirmed on the occasion of Erhard's next visit, in June 1964. Only the State Department still resisted the rapid erosion of the rationales that had once led the U.S. government to station more than 300,000 men in Europe. In a memorandum for the president, Bundy expressed the new logic bluntly:

> I myself agree with Dillon and McNamara, who argue that we should closely link the offset agreements and our ability to maintain troop levels. The secretary of state – or his advisers – say that this linkage would be "short-sighted and untrue." I doubt if he is right, since our troop levels in Germany are justified, finally, more by the psychological needs of the Germans than by strategic necessity. If the Germans will not pay for psychological comfort, why should we?[85]

When the president mentioned the problem in his talk with Erhard and expressed his expectation of full offset, Erhard reassured the president and again emphasized the pre-eminence of the German–American alliance in all his considerations.[86] He had few choices left between an unbending Cold War policy and an equally unflinching repudiation of Gaullist policies. Internally, however, the German government was increasingly preoccupied. Soon it became all too obvious that Erhard's promise was far from easy to fulfill.

OFFSET AND THE GERMAN DEFENSE BUDGET

During 1965 German offset payments fell further behind schedule. When the Americans received the first reports about the lag in meeting the offset commitment they interpreted it as a recurrence of the problems with previous agreements, which, despite many complaints by the Germans, had always been fulfilled in the end. This was a mistaken assumption. It was precisely the fulfillment of the previous agreement that had heavily mortgaged the 1965–7 offset schedule. To meet the payment goal of the second memorandum of understanding on time, the German Defense Ministry had made huge advance payments to the U.S. Treasury.

84 For excerpts from this third offset agreement, see AAPD 1964, doc. 125, note 2.
85 June 11, 1964, LBJL, country file: Germany, box 191.
86 Johnson–Erhard conversation, June 12, 1964, AAPD 1964, 656–9.

Many of these payments were on orders that would be delivered much later and even on orders not yet placed.[87] The German Defense Ministry had thus reinitiated the policy of advance payments on armaments orders that had been so common in the 1950s. The problem was that this time a major buildup phase was nowhere in sight. Both military and economic reasons worked against a further increase in the equipment of the Bundeswehr. The American embassy was advised of these problems during several briefings by Defense Ministry officials. According to these officials, the German forces had reached their "consolidation phase" after the rapid buildup during the Berlin Wall crisis.[88] They were fully equipped with modern materiel, to the point that they lacked trained personnel to use the weapons and storage sites to protect them. Numerous indications show that the saturation point might have been reached in 1963–4 when Germany began to give away surplus military materiel on a large scale. Countries "benefiting" were Israel, Greece, and Turkey, in addition to numerous developing countries.[89] Another structural problem accompanying the consolidation of German forces was the rapid increase in operating costs, such as wages, social benefits, repair of equipment, and so forth. This was intensified by heavy competition for manpower in German industry in a labor market that was close to full employment, leading to a general increase in German wages during these years. Consequently, the share of funds earmarked for procurement declined in the German defense budgets of the mid-1960s. According to Defense Ministry officials, the discontinuation of the immense procurement program of the early 1960s was also suggested by the unclear military–strategic situation in the Alliance. The debate provoked by the strategic ideas of the Kennedy administration was still unresolved in 1965. The intricate discussion about future NATO strategy almost paralyzed NATO military planning; the French completely refused to cooperate, and the British pursued their own agenda, which was largely dictated by economic objectives. The MLF had been in a state of limbo since the end of 1964, and only the German government still stood firmly behind the idea. Force-planning exercises were volatile and superficial in this situation, and nobody knew exactly on what kinds of forces and on how many the

---

87 Bonn no. A-341: "Review of Recent Trends and Future Prospects of the German Defense Program and the Offset Agreement," Aug. 30, 1965, McGhee papers, 1988add., box 1.
88 Arthur T. Blaser to McGhee: "Outlook for the Offset Agreement as Revealed by the Attitude of the Germans During Mr. Kuss's Visit," Oct. 8, 1965, ibid.
89 The old M 48 tanks, for example, were transferred to Israel via Italy, as a result of an understanding between Erhard and LBJ; see DOS to Bonn embassy, June 18, 1964, DDRS 95/924.

NATO Alliance would agree in the end.[90] Therefore, the German Defense Ministry was well advised to wait for a clarification of NATO strategy before buying new weapons systems. The trend toward détente with the Eastern bloc also added little incentive to invest in new arms. The absence of a crisis situation in Europe made rapid agreement on strategic concepts and heightened military preparation very unlikely.

Even if the circumstances described above had been more conducive to a continuation of offset, the German government would still have faced another major problem: where to get the money to pay for new purchases. The years 1965 and 1966 saw the Erhard government desperately struggling to balance its budget. During the 1965 election year the government greatly expanded social programs for veterans, families, farmers, and the elderly; it lowered taxes and introduced a broad array of subventions amounting to over $4.5 billion.[91] The elections in October 1965 were a triumph for Erhard. The investment had paid off; the bill for payment was presented immediately, however. Required by the constitution to present a balanced budget, the government had to cut back government programs on all levels and go back on some of its election promises. The damage to Erhard was considerable. The defense budget had been particularly affected by the cutbacks. Allocations stagnated at about $4.4 billion.[92] From mid-1965 onward, almost no new orders or payments were made. The American government realized that intervention on the highest level was needed. Erhard's visit in December 1965 presented the obvious opportunity. The State Department again disagreed with the Treasury and Defense Departments on how strongly offset was to be linked to troop levels; all agreed, however, that the president should press the chancellor to fulfill the agreement.[93] According to McGhee, Johnson spared no effort. "Towering" over the chancellor and "gesticulating and speaking in a strong strident voice," he lectured Erhard as if he were a schoolboy.[94] The president was already incensed at the lack of German support for Vietnam. On top of that, the Germans now would not even honor their offset commitments.[95] Johnson demanded an immediate

90 On these debates, see Haftendorn, *Kernwaffen*.
91 Klaus Hildebrand, *Von Erhard zur Grossen Koalition 1963–1969* (Stuttgart, 1983), 123–6.
92 For comparison: 1962, $3.75 billion; 1963, $4.6 billion; 1964, $4.8 billion; 1965, $4.3 billion; memorandum on Dahlgrün–McGhee conversation, Nov. 9, 1965, McGhee papers, 1988add., box 1; Blaser to McGhee, Oct. 8, 1965. These figures should not be confused with actual German defense expenditures detailed in Table 1, Appendix 1.
93 Position paper on offset for Erhard visit, Dec. 15, 1965, DDRS 1995/200.
94 McGhee, *At the Creation*, 183–5; see also memorandum on Erhard–LBJ conversation, III of III, Dec. 20, 1965, and McGhee to Leddy, Jan. 13, 1966; both in McGhee papers, 1988add., box 1.
95 Erhard–Johnson conversation, Dec. 20, 1965, AAPD 1965, 1938–42.

lump-sum payment of $100 million. Erhard emphasized his own diffi-
culties and promised to do what he could. In their last meeting, after the
communiqué had already been formulated, the president returned to these
points. He "asked the chancellor if he understood correctly that the FRG
would honor the (offset) agreement. The chancellor nodded agreement."[96]
The communiqué stated that the offset "agreements were of great value
to both governments and should be fully executed and continued."[97]
This rather unenthusiastic approval of Erhard's was interpreted by the
Americans as a new fixed commitment.

All this raises the question: Why did the German government not try
to renegotiate the agreement instead of committing itself to new payments that it knew it would hardly be able to make? Certainly, the
Germans would face a storm of disapproval if they approached the United
States with such a proposal, but it surely would have been an alternative
preferable to the certain risk of major embarrassment when the cards had
to be put on the table. The paucity of German sources allows only hypo-
thetical answers to this question. Preparatory efforts for renegotiations
were apparently made. Already by the end of 1964 the Auswärtiges Amt
had planned to approach the Ministry of Defense, formally responsible
for offset, with such an initiative. The project was repeatedly delayed,
however, and nothing happened.[98] This was probably due to the prospect
of a major row with the Americans during an election year. Erhard would
not open this Pandora's box. After his triumph in October he might have
entertained hopes that he could get some concessions without a major
crisis; these hopes were quickly deflated by his treatment during his
December visit to Washington. Rather than take the initiative, the German
government hoped that the situation would resolve itself. It could hardly
foresee that during 1966 circumstances would propel offset to a central
place in German–American relations and in the domestic discussions of
both countries.

---

96 Memorandum on LBJ–Erhard conversation, Dec. 21, 1965, McGhee papers, 1988add., box 1.
97 *PP Johnson 1965*, 2:1165–7.
98 Note by Political Director Hans-Georg Sachs, Dec. 28, 1964, AAPD 1964, 1565–7, esp. note 13.

8

The Culmination of the Burden-Sharing Conflict: Chancellor Erhard's Visit to Washington in September 1966

At no point in its long and convoluted history did the troop-cost conflict become visible to the public with such spectacular consequences as during Chancellor Ludwig Erhard's desperate mission to Washington in September 1966. All the problems embedded in the never-ending controversy about the sharing of the conventional defense burden in Europe emerged and reinforced each other, resulting in a postwar low in German–American and German-British relations. In hindsight, the failure of Erhard's visit seems almost inevitable. Why did offset become such an explosive issue? The reasons for the inability of politicians on all sides to defuse the bomb in time are central to the understanding of transatlantic relations in the 1960s.

The offset crisis did not come as a bolt from the blue. Most German experts concerned with the execution of the offset agreements knew, even in early 1965, that a continuation of full offset through German purchases of American weapons after 1967 was practically impossible. Furthermore, it soon became apparent that even the targets for 1965–7, agreed on in the Hassel–McNamara protocol of 1964, would be reached – if at all – only by counting nonmilitary purchases or other substitutes. This was something the Americans had always resisted. During a cabinet meeting in March 1966 German ministers together with Bundesbank officials, who now took part in the deliberations concerning offset, noted that without a federal supplementary budget later in the year it would be impossible to honor the agreement with the United States.[1] The ministers foresaw

---

1 Military diary of Hassel, entry of Mar. 25, 1966; minutes of cabinet meeting, Mar. 25, 1966, BA, B136/3135; Horst Osterheld, *Aussenpolitik unter Bundeskanzler Ludwig Erhard 1963–1966: Ein dokumentarischer Bericht aus dem Kanzleramt* (Düsseldorf, 1992), 304.

a gap of about $700 million in orders at the end of 1966, and of $1.13 billion in payments in June 1967. The decision to initiate the supplementary budget was postponed, however, because it would have required difficult compromises on the part of the already strained governing coalition in Bonn. It seemed more propitious to first sound out the Americans about their receptiveness to alternatives to arms purchases.

In a May 1966 meeting between Kai-Uwe von Hassel and Robert McNamara in Washington, the German defense minister disclosed that he expected a huge payment gap in 1967, when the term of the agreement ended, and that the German government hoped to replace the strict formula of offset by military orders with another method. Hassel's appeal was not well received. McNamara retorted that in this case the United States would reduce its forces in Germany in proportion to the payment gap.[2] The exchange became public, provoking a strong reaction in the press and angry comments in the Federal Republic. Chancellor Erhard personally complained to the visiting U.S. secretary of state, Dean Rusk, that announcements such as McNamara's were highly embarrassing for the government.[3] Despite the protests, McNamara's threat achieved its main objective. Questioned by parliament on offset, Hassel asserted once more that the German government had every intention of fully honoring the agreement.[4] Subsequently, the Americans tried to smooth ruffled feathers and denied having any plan to withdraw a significant number of troops from Europe.[5] Both sides knew very well that, given the debate within their governments, the value of their reaffirmations was extremely doubtful. The stage was set for diplomatic conflict. What neither Americans nor Germans anticipated was that the issue would get out of control within a few months and develop into a veritable crisis. After the McNamara–Hassel row the public increasingly took note of the problem, and speculation regarding troop levels and offset continued all through the summer of 1966. Offset, which until then had played only a marginal role in public debates, suddenly became a big issue. The press and parliaments in both countries regularly brought up the matter. This came at a time

2 "The Secretary stated further that he must point out, as he has in the past, that unless a full offset agreement is attained with the Federal Republic, the U.S. would be required to reduce its forces to the level of the offset goals" (background paper: U.S.–German military offset relationship, Nov. 1966, LBJL, NSF, NSC histories: Trilaterals, box 51). See also Hassel note on talks with McNamara and Acheson, May 15, 1966, NHP; Knappstein to AA, May 24, 1966, AAPD 1966, doc. 161, 680; *New York Times*, June 6, 1966, 40; Christopher S. Raj, *American Military in Europe: Controversy over NATO Burden-Sharing* (New Delhi, 1983), 220–3.
3 Rusk-Erhard conversation, June 9, 1966, McGhee papers, 1988add., box 2.
4 Hassel in parliament, July 1, 1966, *VdB*, 5th per., 54. sess., 2609–13.
5 "Press Conference Rusk, May 27," *DOS Bulletin*, June 13, 1966.

when both the offset and troop-level problems were approaching the critical point at which top-level bargaining and difficult compromises were required to escape deadlock. Under observation by suspicious publics, both governments gradually found it more difficult to compromise. The offset system, which linked vital elements of transatlantic security and monetary policy, was clearly in trouble.

THE NATO CRISIS AND INTERNATIONAL MONETARY PROBLEMS

McNamara's public troop-reduction threat came at a particularly inconvenient moment for the Erhard government. In March 1966 the withdrawal of 30,000 combat personnel from the U.S. Seventh Army in Germany had become public. The German government had not been consulted, and American reassurances that the forces would be replaced to the last man by recruits failed to reassure the German public. Moreover, the progressive thinning out of U.S. forces in Germany had been going on for quite some time. The State Department cabled its missions abroad to remain silent on the issue and to "avoid to the extent possible further categorical statements on the maintenance of present composition and number of our forces."[6] The changes could not go unnoticed, however, particularly because the reductions mainly involved highly trained personnel.[7] Most observers came to the logical conclusion that the moves had something to do with the growing intensity of warfare in Vietnam. The U.S. government denied this charge with increasing vehemence.[8] Persistent questioning in Senate hearings, however, provoked a comment by McNamara that the reductions would "probably not" have been effected without Vietnam.[9] Such contradictions hardly calmed the suspicions of the German government. The substantial reductions of American forces – in both quality and quantity – became the subject of extensive discussion in the media. Particularly galling for the German government was that, promises notwithstanding, the Americans had not consulted Erhard. Foreign Minister Gerhard Schröder took up the issue in a long conversation with the U.S. ambassador, warning that "certain circles"

6 DOS to U.S. Mission at NATO, Dec. 9, 1965, in FRUS 1964–68, XIII. For the German reaction, see talking paper for meeting with General Wheeler, Apr. 9, 1966, NHP; Haftendorn, *Kernwaffen*, 227–8.
7 Cleveland to Rusk and McNamara, May 19, 1966, DDRS 1995/2652.
8 See McNamara's reaction at a press conference on Mar. 2, 1966: "It is absolutely not true and you are the first that ought to know it. I am sick and tired of having implications made that we have drawn down the forces in Western Europe when we haven't. The 7th Army . . . will not be affected . . . by our operations in Southeast Asia" (*PSSD*, XIV, 1396).
9 Hearing before the Senate Committee on Foreign Relations, Apr. 20, 1966, ibid., 2127.

exploited every indication of German-American disharmony.[10] The certain circles that Schröder mentioned were not the Communists but rather the "Gaullist" wing of his own party that in 1965–6 criticized, more outspokenly than ever, Schröder's policy of distance from France and close alignment with America.

Despite Bonn's protestations, however, the stream of alarming rumors from across the Atlantic regarding U.S. troop levels continued. Internally, the Erhard government resigned itself to the unavoidability of large-scale reductions in the near future.[11] Due to its beleaguered domestic position in foreign-policy issues, however, it felt unable to abandon a stance that had been part of German foreign policy since 1955: the insistence on an undiminished U.S. troop presence. Some critics of the German government's policy felt that the United States was about to shift its foreign policy concentration to Asia and to search for accommodation with Soviet Russia in the European arena. These critics took U.S. reductions as a confirmation of their suspicions. Thus, the Erhard government tried to postpone the inevitable withdrawal as long as possible – and to keep offset from becoming a convenient excuse for the Americans to draw down their troops.

The progressive weakening of American combat power in Germany was overshadowed by another event that rocked the foundations of NATO: the French withdrawal from the military arm of NATO and de Gaulle's announcement that all foreign forces and installations would have to leave French territory by April 1, 1967.[12] Apart from its political and military consequences, de Gaulle's move also played an important role in the escalation of the offset conflict. The United States had long been expecting a French assault on NATO. When the emergency actually occurred in March 1966, it met a relatively calm reaction, memorably summarized by Johnson: "If a man asks you to leave his house, you don't argue; you take your hat and go."[13] Walking out of France even had some

10 Schröder-McGhee conversation, Apr. 29, 1966, AAPD 1966, doc. 125, 545.

11 "In the long run, U.S. troop reductions are inevitable. However, it is essential to insist during the negotiations with the U.S. that troop reductions should take place only when the strategic, operational, and military-political preconditions are more favorable than at present" (talking papers for chancellor–minister talks in Washington, Sept. 20, 1966, NHP). See also personal diary of Hassel, entries of July 23 and Aug. 3, 1966.

12 Richard N. Gardner, "Lyndon B. Johnson and de Gaulle," in Robert O. Paxton and Nicholas Wahl, eds., *De Gaulle and the United States: A Centennial Reappraisal* (Oxford, 1994), 257–78; Institut de Gaulle, ed., *De Gaulle et son siècle*, 5 vols. (Paris, 1992), vol. 4; Maurice Vaïsse, Pierre Mélandri, and Frédéric Bozo, eds., *La France et l'OTAN 1949–96* (Paris, 1996).

13 Lyndon B. Johnson, *The Vantage Point: Perspectives of the Presidency, 1963–1969* (New York, 1971), 305.

advantages: Some of the 75,000 U.S. personnel located in France were redeployed to the United States.[14] Air Force units were relocated to British bases and helped the British gain some additional foreign exchange earnings.[15] The United States' economic "gains" however, were offset by the interruption of the U.S. logistics system concentrated in France and the forced move of NATO headquarters, both of which involved heavy expenses estimated at between $175 and $275 million.[16] The German–American payments balance was affected, too. Certain military installations, such as the U.S. Army headquarters, were moved to Germany, and provisions and supplies rerouted to German and Benelux ports. The Bundesbank estimated that this reorganization would increase the U.S. forces' foreign exchange need from the $1.35 billion envisaged in the 1964 offset agreement to $1.575 billion. This precipitate rise in cost, exacerbated by pay and wage increases, obliterated all the savings the forces in Germany had achieved in the previous years. This naturally lessened the Americans' willingness to compromise on offset payments.

De Gaulle's move had not only financial and logistical consequences; it also cast grave doubts on the rationale of the Western security structure. The NATO troops stationed along the Iron Curtain lost their hinterland. The reaction in the United States and Great Britain was that the political and military rationale for large-scale conventional troop maintenance in Europe, already undermined, was further damaged. In West Germany, however, the effect was the reverse: The dependence on conventional protection offered by the United States and Britain increased. The status of the French forces in Germany (about 71,000 men), which were withdrawn from SACEUR command after July 1, remained in limbo until the end of 1966. Initially the German reaction, mainly advocated by Schröder, was to insist on a clear NATO commitment for these troops, particularly in wartime operations. The French refused and, in the end, a more conciliatory attitude was pursued by Erhard, tacitly supported by the Americans.[17] Overall, the French withdrawal from NATO's integrated command deepened the Germans' feeling of insecurity and, like many of de Gaulle's policies, underlined West Germany's dependence on U.S. protection. It also heightened America's frustration with the situation in

---

14 Reductions included 18,000 military personnel and 21,000 dependents. The foreign-exchange savings were estimated at about $110 million per annum; talking paper prepared by DOD, July 1968, in FRUS 1964–68, XIII, 729.

15 Fowler to president: "Sterling Crisis," July 18, 1966, LBJL, NSF, Bator papers, box 3.

16 Summary notes of 566th NSC meeting, Dec. 13, 1966, in FRUS 1964–68, XIII.

17 This was a major political defeat for Schröder, who was to play a rather passive role in the final months of the Erhard government.

Europe. It became a major argument for those who thought that Europe not only did not need but actually did not want a direct commitment from the United States.[18] If the Federal Republic was not prepared to accept reductions in troop levels, however, it would have to pay. This was the reasoning of an influential group in Washington, most visibly represented by the secretary of defense.

The main reason for the growth of this isolationist sentiment was the escalation of the war in Vietnam. During 1965 the American military involvement in Southeast Asia expanded. The war increasingly absorbed public attention and dominated the activities of the government. Europe became a distant arena with no major crisis expected.[19] The effect on U.S. combat power in Europe was serious: The quantitative thinning out of American forces has already been mentioned. A parallel development was the precipitate fall in the quality of the troops in Europe. The Seventh Army suffered from a serious lack of officers and specialists, criminal incidents abounded, and drug use and racial conflicts became major problems.[20] Vietnam also played a major role in Washington's attempts to formulate a détente policy toward the Soviet Union, summed up in Johnson's bridge-building speech in October 1966.[21] The U.S. government became increasingly interested in some sort of accommodation with the Soviet Union in Europe, whereas Bonn still clung to the reunification postulate, opposing most American moves to reduce tensions in Europe. Speculation about a reorientation of American policy toward the Pacific became the preferred issue of political commentators on both sides of the Atlantic.

Washington's willingness to support the German viewpoint was not strengthened by the European response to the new base of containment strategy, the Vietnam War. In the United States frustration about Europe's lukewarm response to the effort in Vietnam ran high. Angry memoranda by the U.S. government did nothing to change Europe's aloof stance, and a perception of European ingratitude permeated comments in the government, Congress, and the press.[22] In addition, Vietnam had a strong impact on the U.S. balance of payments. The rise of the foreign exchange

---

18 Williams, *Senate*, 140–1.
19 For the impact of the Vietnam War on U.S.–European relations, see Lloyd C. Gardner, Andreas W. Daum, and Wilfried Mausbach, eds., *America's War and the World: Vietnam in International and Comparative Perspectives* (forthcoming).
20 Nelson, *History of U.S. Military Forces*, 1987, 83–4.
21 *PP Johnson 1966*, 1125–30; Hanrieder, *Germany*, 90.
22 For an aide-mémoire to the FRG requesting a list of possible German aid projects for South Vietnam, see July 6, 1964, McGhee papers, 1988add., box 1.

cost directly related to escalation was impressive: From 1964 to 1967 outlays in Southeast Asia rose from $847 million to $2.318 billion.[23] Part of this loss was offset by various agreements similar to the ones concluded in Europe, but the burden remained immense nonetheless. As an administrative history of the Treasury Department during the Johnson administration summarized it: "There was tacit recognition during 1966 that the efforts to achieve equilibrium in our balance of payments would not be successful as long as the hostilities in Vietnam continued on such a large scale."[24] This statement also reflects the indirect effect of the war. The rapid rise of government spending on defense, supplemented by the cost of Johnson's "Great Society" program, which provided for increasing expenditure on welfare, stimulated an economic expansion that, in the absence of tax increases, led to price inflation.[25] These developments produced increasing apprehension in the Treasury Department that the balance of payments might soon get out of control. Estimates of the year-end deficit went up to about $2 billion, despite "cosmetic" operations to the tune of $1.5 billion.[26] In addition, there was the incalculable risk of a run on sterling, which usually implicated the dollar as well. On top of this came heavy American gold losses, particularly in 1965.

The main reason for these losses was a new tool in de Gaulle's strategy to roll back the American influence in Europe: During a press conference in February 1965 he denounced the dollar-gold system as an instrument of American hegemony enabling the United States to buy up foreign industries with cheap money.[27] De Gaulle urged all dollar-holding countries to present their dollars at the U.S. Treasury to undermine the

---

23 Cora E. Shepler and Leonard G. Campbell, "U.S. Defense Expenditure Abroad," *SCB* 12 (1969): 44. Countries with the biggest increases between 1964–7 were Vietnam ($64 million to $564 million), Japan ($321 million to $538 million), Thailand ($34 million to $286 million), and Korea ($91 million to $237 million). The liquidity deficit in 1967 amounted to $4.89 billion.

24 LBJL, administrative history, Treasury, vol. 1, pt. 2, chap. IX: Balance of Payments.

25 On the economic policy of the Johnson administration, see Donald F. Kettl, "The Economic Education of Lyndon Johnson," and Burton I. Kaufman, "Foreign Aid and the Balance of Payments Problem," both in Robert A. Divine, ed., *The Johnson Years*, 3 vols. (Austin, Tex., 1987), 2:54–109.

26 The "cosmetic" operations consisted mainly of switches by foreign central banks from liquid dollar holdings to longer-term securities. Bator to president: Balance of Payments, July 6, 1966, LBJL, NSF, memos to president: Walt Rostow, box 9. It was enough to extend 12-month bonds to 13 months in order to make them disappear from the statistics for liquid liabilities, which formed part of the liquidity balance (the overall measure for the U.S. balance of payments until the late 1960s). See Gilbert, *Quest*, 140.

27 Charles de Gaulle, *Discours et messages, 1962–65* (Paris, 1969), 330–4. For de Gaulle's attack on the gold standard, see David P. Calleo, "De Gaulle and the Monetary System: The Golden Rule," in Paxton and Wahl, eds., *De Gaulle*, 239–255; Institut de Gaulle, ed., *De Gaulle et son siècle*, vol. 3: *Moderniser la France* (Paris, 1992); Michael D. Bordo, Dominique Simard, and Eugene White, "France and the Bretton Woods International Monetary System, 1960–1968," in Jaime Reis, ed., *International Monetary Systems in Historical Perspective* (London, 1995), 153–80.

dollar-gold standard. In the first quarter of 1965 the U.S. Treasury lost $3.244 billion of gold ($1.928 billion of it to France), and another $1.198 billion in April to June (French quota: $0.592 billion).[28] The only reason the United States was able to withstand the challenge was that almost all major countries with large dollar reserves reacted with disapproval to de Gaulle's suggestion. If they had followed the French example, the monetary system would have collapsed. Its preservation was still in the best interest of most countries, however, not least because the decisive countries were almost all linked in a security partnership with the United States. This was the case particularly of the Federal Republic, which, due to its large reserves, played a pivotal role.[29] Refraining from gold conversions was not particularly difficult for the Germans because from 1963 to 1965 they had balance-of-payments deficits that were financed by reducing their dollar reserves.[30] Immediately after the de Gaulle challenge the U.S. government issued a new statement committing itself unswervingly to the $35 per ounce ratio. The maintenance of the dollar value became more than ever a matter of national prestige. This stifled internal voices calling for parity changes.[31] However, the new treasury secretary, Henry Fowler, knew that determination and piecemeal measures à la Dillon–Roosa would not work. The United States took the lead in proposing a new reserve unit, initiating years of discussions with the Europeans that eventually led to the establishment of the so-called Special Drawing Rights.[32] The complicated negotiating process was constantly disrupted by the developments already discussed. It was clear that the dollar–gold system was on the brink of breakdown. These dangerous signals made the short-term balance of payments the prevalent con-

---

28 Odell, *U.S. International Monetary Relations*, 119. At the end of 1964, U.S. gold reserves stood at $15.47 billion.

29 In January 1965, on the occasion of Erhard's visit to Paris, de Gaulle repeated his main argument, namely, that the reserve role of the dollar freed the United States from monetary discipline and allowed U.S. firms to purchase foreign industries with cheap credit. He did not inform his visitor of the spectacular step he was to take only two weeks later; Erhard–De Gaulle conversation, Jan. 20, 1965, AAPD 1965, 150. The German government immediately dissociated itself from the move and yet expressed to the Americans similar concerns about the high level of U.S. investment abroad, which forced Germany to balance the monetary consequences by way of offset. See AAPD 1965, Erhard–McGhee conversation, Feb. 8, 1965, 270–3; Knappstein to Schröder on talk with the president, Feb. 9, 1965, 282.

30 The Bundesbank president, Blessing, informed Erhard that following de Gaulle's example as some economists had proposed made no economic sense under these circumstances. He assured Erhard that the Bundesbank had ways of converting its foreign exchange surplus to gold without drawing directly on U.S. reserves; see BA, B136/3322, Blessing to Erhard, Feb. 22, 1965.

31 Gilbert, *Quest*, 136–7.

32 The most comprehensive analysis of the creation of SDRs remains Cohen, *International Monetary Reform*.

sideration of U.S. officials in dealing with the question of offset during Erhard's visit in September 1966.

The Western Alliance reached a critical point in 1966 both in the monetary and the security field. The fundamental bases of transatlantic relations entered into a crisis at the same time that the offset practice ran into almost insurmountable practical difficulties in the German–American as well as Anglo–German contexts. Washington increasingly questioned the extent of its security commitment in Europe, whereas Bonn was forced to review its financial contributions to the Cold War. The situation was complicated even more by the contemporaneous escalation of the Anglo–German troop-cost conflict.

BRITISH OFFSET DURING THE 1960S

Compared with the amount of money and the serious implications for Western financial and security policy involved in U.S.–German offset, the British–German offset was a sideshow during the 1960s – although a very noisy one. The British took the issue as seriously as they had during the 1950s. A number of complicated questions were raised during the negotiations, and a complete, detailed account would go beyond the scope of this study.[33] I therefore survey the story and issues rather briefly, concentrating on the aspects that are important to my main argument. We left the British–German offset quarrel at the end of 1958 when, after tiresome complications, an agreement was reached covering the three years until March 1961. This removed the issue from the mutual agenda for some time. The basic causes of the conflict, however, had not disappeared: The British government continued to regard its continental troop commitment with ambiguity and the pound still remained weak, although in 1960 the British government was able to pay back large parts of the debts it had amassed during and after the Suez crisis. This was warmly welcomed by the Americans as they struggled with their emerging and persistent payments problem. One result of their efforts drew particular attention in London: the Anderson-Dillon mission. Because their three-year support-cost agreement was about to expire, the British were afraid – not without reason – of being left out in the cold by a large-scale

---

33 British–German offset in the 1960s is almost unresearched, despite the abundance of material available in German and British archives. The exception is Rosenbach, "Schattenseiten," 196–231, and my own "The Sour Fruits of Victory: Sterling and Security in Anglo–German Relations," *Contemporary European History* 9 (2000): 225–44. Further details can be found in Gustav Schmidt, "Die Labour-Regierung, die Bundesrepublik und Europa, 1964–67," in Schmidt, ed., *Grossbritannien*, 253–314.

German–American deal.[34] More important, the London gold crisis in October 1960 and the speculation following the revaluation of the German deutschmark in March 1961 vividly demonstrated the continuing weakness of sterling. A new agreement therefore seemed imperative, particularly because the government at the same time ruled out the possibility of further troop cuts. The political circumstances that would have facilitated a move did not pertain: First, the Berlin Crisis was still in full swing, necessitating a united Western front against the Soviet Union. Second, the BAOR was already understrength, drawing increasing criticism from NATO authorities and the U.S. government. Third, as even the British Treasury acknowledged, a reduction "could not fail to wreck such hopes as exist for a settlement of our European problems and it must bedevil our relations with the new American administration from the start."[35] These remarks hinted at Kennedy's request that the British live up to their conventional troop commitments to NATO, and at the need to obtain German political support for Britain's July 1961 application for membership in the EEC.[36] The three major political objectives behind British troop maintenance in Europe – containment of the Soviet Union, strengthening the "special relationship" with the United States, and enhancing Britain's leverage in Europe – once more proved stronger than the monetary argument against it.

The British were not prepared, however, to absorb the foreign exchange burden of their troops without a fight, just for the sake of these political gains. In March 1961 Selwyn Lloyd, now chancellor of the exchequer, arrived in Bonn for a new round of talks.[37] As during the Anderson-Dillon visit, the Germans resisted any attempt to force them to make direct payments. The British accepted that the support-cost concept was out of date. Thus, the negotiations took a turn similar to the U.S.–German talks. The German side promised to step up arms purchases in the United Kingdom (to about $70 million a year), to assume more foreign aid, to prematurely repay their remaining postwar debt, and to leave $70 million, which was the remainder of the German prepayments

34 "If we let the Americans get away with a deal in which our more real and pressing needs are overlooked, it will be a fatal blow" (Macmillan to Treasury, Nov. 14, 1960, PRO PREM 3773).

35 Report by Treasury officials on mutual defense costs, Dec. 5, 1960, ibid. Kennedy immediately informed Macmillan of the new U.S. emphasis on conventional troops that he expected the United Kingdom to follow. See Macmillan–Kennedy meeting, Apr. 5, 1961, NSA, Berlin Crisis Collection, doc. 2024.

36 Kennedy to Macmillan, Feb. 16, 1962, in FRUS 1961–63, XIII, 1059–61; Home to Macmillan, Feb. 14, 1962, PRO PREM 11/4217; meeting at Admiralty House, Mar. 12, 1962, ibid.

37 Anglo–German talks, Mar. 23, 1961, PRO CAB 129/105.

on arms orders, in the Bank of England.[38] Satisfaction with this non-binding promise did not last very long. In the summer of 1961 sterling again came under heavy pressure. In July 1961 Britain invoked the NATO resolution of 1957, which stipulated that NATO investigate and propose solutions for countries in payments difficulties due to troop stationing abroad.[39] The NATO experts supported the British case, and the Germans agreed to open formal offset negotiations. These were clearly prejudiced by the parallel German–American talks, which were in their final phase. The Strauss–Gilpatric agreement in October 1961 put the British and French in an even more disadvantageous situation on the German arms market than before. It soon became clear that the Germans could not formalize the promises made to Lloyd in March. They refused to offset the whole British troop cost, in contrast to what they had done for the Americans.[40] In the end, the British accepted less than full offset – a result that owed much to the political considerations outlined above. They also agreed, first, to count "civilian purchases" as offset and, second, to consider the assumption of British foreign-aid obligations by the German government as an offset measure.[41] Both provisions caused endless quarrels between officials from the Federal Ministry of Finance and the British Treasury on the kinds of projects to be credited against the German obligation.

The agreement was signed in March 1962.[42] Difficulties in reaching its targets soon arose. The Germans considered British weapons to be second-rate, not fit for the kinds of military operations German planners foresaw, and they were unhappy about Britain's reluctance to engage in common research projects.[43] In April 1963 German orders had reached only about

38 KCA 1961, 18002A.
39 Airgram no. A-11: U.K. statement at NATO Council meeting, July 27, 1961, NA, RG 84, Bonn embassy, 1959–61, box 16.
40 This put the Americans in an uneasy position that would last for many years. On the one hand, they wanted the British to keep their troops at full strength and the pound strong, and therefore supported the British offset efforts; on the other hand, they were not ready to share the German weapons market.
41 "Civilian purchases" meant orders for civilian equipment above normal levels by official German agencies; purchases of goods for the foreign-aid projects that Germany financed were to be placed in England.
42 Germany promised orders in Britain totaling $300 million, split into military purchases ($230 million), civilian purchases ($45 million), and foreign-aid projects ($25 million), to be placed between April 1962 and March 1964. A folder with extensive documentation on the negotiations is in BBA, A270/13168; an account by British officials is PRO FO 371/172175, Stationing Costs of British Forces in Germany: Report by Officials, autumn 1963. The agreement is printed in HMSO, Cmnd. 1766 (1962).
43 Interview by the author with Hassel, Aug. 17, 1994. BMV to Erhard: "Technological Cooperation with Britain in the Military Field," May 18, 1966, BA, B136/6894.

$95 million, further prospects were bleak, and the British government officially expressed its disbelief in the German capability to fulfill its promise.[44] The overall political situation in which the agreement operated also slowly changed for the worse. British admission to the EEC had been vetoed, and the Americans had second thoughts about the wisdom of a further conventional buildup. The British Defense White Paper of 1962 reflected this clearly and demonstrated the persistent doubts of the Conservative government about its European commitment.[45] Although the British Cabinet Defence Committee once more decided to avoid troop reductions in Germany, it was obvious that the firmness of this resolve hinged on the status of sterling.[46]

Britain's lingering hostility toward Germany in financial matters remained strong, as a handwritten note by Harold Macmillan, on a memorandum regarding a Schröder-Lord Home discussion, illustrates: "It is a very depressing story. The Germans have no sense of guilt and shame . . . there is nothing about the financial agreement, on which they are in default. What about the huge commitment to buy American? Every time they mention Eastern Germany, we ought to remind them of the intolerable financial situation."[47] This comment on the troop-cost problem, shortly before Macmillan left office, once more struck the emotional tone that had pervaded so much of the conflict in the preceding years. The trail of hostile remarks left by the prime minister in connection with this problem illustrates some characteristics of his policy toward Germany: a sense of frustration at the inexorable falling behind of Britain's economy; an unwillingness to cooperate with the former enemy, who had so rapidly been rehabilitated; a strong insistence on the symbols of British power, nuclear weapons and the reserve role of sterling; and annoyance at being stuck in Europe with troops whose military value seemed dubious, from whom Germany benefited economically, and whose political importance Macmillan saw mainly in relation to the United States but not to the Federal Republic. Thus, support costs and offset acquired a disproportionate role in determining the state of Anglo–German relations. Few steps were taken by the Macmillan government to get out of the political cul-de-sac in mutual relations.

Despite British apprehensions, the Germans fulfilled the 1962–4 agreement. This was probably due to the ascendance of leaders who were more

44 AA to Chancellor's Office: Cabinet memorandum, May 25, 1963, BA, B136/3133.
45 Darby, *British Defence Policy*, 223–7.
46 George E. Peter Thorneycroft to Macmillan, Apr. 24, 1963, PRO PREM 11/4726.
47 Macmillan to Lord Home, Aug. 21, 1963, PRO PREM 11/4259.

cooperative than the Macmillan–Adenauer duo. Erhard and Alec Douglas-Home both assumed office in October 1963. The offset success had been made possible only by large German prepayments on prospective military and civilian orders in Britain. (The civilian part of the agreement had turned out to be an almost total flop.) Thus, the next agreement was heavily mortgaged when negotiations for it commenced in late 1963.[48] They were concluded in a quite cooperative mood in April 1964, due to relatively calm monetary markets and the absence of troop-reduction threats. The Germans stated that they would try to offset the whole foreign exchange cost, estimated at $235 million, "as far as possible" by counting both military and civilian purchases.[49] The British acceptance that no fixed target should be set contrasted with the American–German agreement of May 1964. Early on, British officials had resigned themselves to getting less than the United States. An unspecified commitment seemed to be more acceptable to the public than a specified level far short of the actual cost, which would have been an easy target for attacks by the opposition.[50] A mutual working group was established that was to meet regularly to identify projects and review the progress made.

Shortly after the agreement was signed, general elections were held in Britain resulting in a Labour Party victory. The new government under Harold Wilson had hardly settled in when a new, violent currency crisis hit. The election campaign had been accompanied by speculation against the pound caused by political uncertainty and rumors of a prospective £800 million payments deficit in 1964. During November an unprecedented run on British reserves ensued. Within two days Wilson made up his mind, deciding firmly against devaluation.[51] The reasons were mainly political: apprehensions that Labour, which had devalued the pound in 1949, would retain the stigma of a devaluation party; the moral

---

48 The Federal Ministry of Finance waged and lost a fight in the cabinet to rid itself of responsibility for the talks. See Roberts to Patrick Reilly, Sept. 10, 1963; Eugene Melville to Reilly, Sept. 20, 1963; Bonn embassy to FO, Oct. 8, 1963 – all in PRO FO 371/172174; Dahlgrün to Westrick, Jan. 24, 1964, PA-AA, Dept. IIIA5, 384.

49 For the agreement, see HMSO, Cmnd. 2434 (1964). For the negotiations, see memorandum for cabinet meeting, Mar. 9, 1964; Dahlgrün to Erhard, Mar. 23, 1964; Dahlgrün to Erhard, May 15, 1964, all in BA, B136/3133; memorandum Carstens, Apr. 29, 1964, AAPD 1964, 495–6; Carstens to Dahlgrün, July 6, 1964, AAPD 1964, 796–7; memorandum Rolf Lahr (AA), July 24, 1964, AAPD 1964, 877–8.

50 CM 64(39), conclusions, July 17, 1964, PRO CAB 128/38; CM 64(41), July 23, 1964, PRO CAB 128/38; memorandum by Boyd-Carpenter, chief secretary to Treasury, July 22, 1964, CAB 129/118, CP(64)155.

51 Harold Wilson, *A Personal Record: The Labour Government, 1964–1970* (London, 1971), 5–7; George Brown, *In My Way* (London, 1971), 114; Cairncross and Eichengreen, *Sterling in Decline*, 166–7; Peter Browning, *The Treasury and Economic Policy, 1964–1985* (London, 1986), 5.

commitment to the Commonwealth and other dollar holders; and the belief that structural weaknesses in the British economy were causing the pressure on the pound and could be corrected by measures to improve the competitiveness of British goods. The diagnosis and the reactions were strikingly similar to Kennedy's response to the U.S. payments deficit some years earlier. Like the Democratic president, the Labour prime minister was seated on a very small margin and shied away from showing supposed weaknesses in monetary policy. Devaluation acquired the status of "the unmentionable"; an effective ban against even discussing the issue stifled debate within the government, and even the British press avoided speculation. On November 16 Wilson declared emphatically: "If anyone, at home or abroad, doubts the firmness of the government's resolve [to defend the pound] and acts upon these doubts let them be prepared to pay the price."[52] No speculator felt deterred, and the government found itself forced into a series of restrictive measures, such as a 15 percent surcharge on imports, which infuriated both EEC and EFTA countries and violated GATT rules. A belated rise in the interest rate did not help either and served only to annoy the United States, which had received solemn promises to the contrary.[53] The sterling crisis of 1964 was finally overcome by a hastily organized international credit of $3 billion, later supplemented by a $1 billion loan from the IMF.[54] The crisis clearly illustrated the British dilemma: They were forced either to take measures that irritated their major allies or to accept their "help" or "recommendations" and take vigorous action in the domestic economy (often among the conditions for help). Taking stock after the storm on the markets had passed, the Labour government, like its predecessors, subjected British overseas expenditures to closer scrutiny. Wilson probably had even less of a clear idea than Macmillan as to what purpose the BAOR still served. He considered the offset agreement he had inherited insufficient. The first meeting of the working group for the implementation of the offset agreement in December 1964 had shown the new government's discontent with the achievements of its predecessors. The British noted the absence of any significant German requests for British civilian or military goods and did not hide their disappointment.[55] One specific project acquired

52 Quoted from Cairncross and Eichengreen, *Sterling in Decline*, 169.
53 This step forced the United States to do likewise, and LBJ did not hide his irritation on the occasion of Wilson's first visit; FRUS 1964–68, XIII, Bundy memorandum on LBJ–Wilson conversation, Dec. 7, 1964, 137–9.
54 A vivid description of the international rescue action by one of the participants is provided in Coombs, *Arena of International Finance*, 110–23.
55 German embassy, London, to AA, Dec. 8, 1964, BA, B136/3133.

particular importance in this context. London pressed for a positive decision by the German Lufthansa to purchase the BAC 1–11 aircraft for its fleet, an order probably worth over $50 million. The British representatives said on the record that a "rejection would be regarded as an indication that the offset agreement meant little to the German side."[56] The Lufthansa order was deemed essential to the success of the aircraft on the European market, where not a single order had been placed until then. During his first meeting with Erhard, Wilson strongly pressed the case, citing the Germans' disappointing performance under the offset agreement.[57] Once more, the British had to compete against an American producer, Boeing. The U.S. ambassador in Bonn intervened on the highest political levels to support the American aircraft – a further illustration of the contradictory nature of U.S. policy regarding British financial problems.[58] In the end it was the alleged technical superiority of the U.S. aircraft that was decisive for the Lufthansa managers, despite an intervention by Erhard on behalf of the British firm.[59] Her Majesty's government was not amused. When Wilson visited Bonn in March 1965 he told Erhard that he was "profoundly disappointed, surprised and shocked" by the Lufthansa decision and that he regarded the whole offset agreement as "dirty work" that had to be renegotiated.[60] In a letter soon afterward the prime minister warned the German government against any "misunderstanding between us on the importance of this question for the future development of good Anglo–German relations." He added that the British had made the decision that whereas "naturally they wish to play their full part in the common defence of the West, they can no longer accept the very large share which they have to bear of the foreign exchange burden of maintaining British forces in Germany at its present level of £90 million a year."[61]

The acrimony that marked Anglo–German offset dealings during the Macmillan era continued. This is also reflected in a letter from Wilson to the American president in which he reviewed his meeting with Erhard. The prime minister displayed no intention of making any constructive

56 Record of meeting of Joint Committee in London, Dec. 8, 1964, BA, B126/34106.
57 FO brief for Bonn talks 1/1965: Offset Agreement, PRO FO 371/183099; record of PM–Erhard discussion, Jan. 30, 1965, PRO FO 371/183042.
58 Osterheld, *Aussenpolitik*, 125–6; BA, B136/3133, Federal Ministry of Transport to AA, Dec. 14, 1964.
59 Dahlgrün to Chancellor's Office, Feb. 25, 1965; Erhard to Abs, Mar. 4, 1965, both in BA, B136/3133.
60 Record of Wilson–Erhard discussion, Mar. 8, 1965, PRO FO 371/183046.
61 Wilson to Erhard, May 31, 1965, BA, B136/3133; Federal Ministry of Finance: Cabinet paper, June 11, 1965.

move toward ameliorating or deepening British relations with West Germany, despite the opportunity that the anglophile Erhard government represented. He assumed that the Federal Republic would continue its support for the pound in the international markets and that it also would offset the foreign exchange cost of British troops: "We had some very tough sessions on the offset agreement but since you have yourselves virtually equipped the German armed forces there does not seem much for us in that line. . . . We left the Germans in no doubt that if we did not get satisfaction on this part, we should be forced to agonizing re-appraisals."[62] The frustration resulting from the feeling of growing financial dependence on an ally protected by a British security commitment reached new peaks. The chief secretary of the treasury, John Diamond, expressed this frankly during the offset renegotiations in Bonn:

> In order that Britain should never again need to seek emergency assistance from its Allies, the British government needed to reorganise its affairs, and, in particular, its expenditure across the exchanges. In many respects British policies were directed and redirected by the balance of payments problem; it lay behind every Cabinet decision concerning economic affairs and defence, and the Government would never feel free to carry out its policies . . . until it had solved its foreign exchange difficulties.[63]

British Foreign Office officials became increasingly preoccupied with the emotional state of government thinking regarding Germany. Citing a top-level discussion at Chequers, Undersecretary of State Paul Gore-Booth wrote to his minister, Michael Stewart: "One may have what emotions and sentiments one likes about Germans – fair enough. But we cannot conduct . . . foreign policy like this."[64] The Foreign Office tried in the successive months to exert a calming influence on the prime minister and the chancellor of the exchequer without much success.

The German government could hardly refuse to reopen the negotiations, since it had failed to come anywhere near keeping its promises made to Douglas-Home. The talks started immediately after Wilson's visit to Bonn. In June Diamond and Dahlgrün agreed to extend the existing agreement by one year and to set fixed targets for the three years covered.[65] A German advance payment of $110 million, in addition to orders worth $80 million placed heretofore, brought the level for the first two years up to $190 million. For the third year the Germans undertook

62 Mar. 11, 1965, in FRUS 1964–68, XIII, 190–1.
63 Record of Dahlgrün–Diamond talks, June 28, 1965, PRO FO 371/183101.
64 Gore-Booth to Stewart, June 15, 1965, PRO FO 371/183044.
65 HMSO, Cmnd. 2731 (1965).

to offset $150 million. With this agreement the German government made two large commitments: first, to match the advance payment, borrowed from the Bundesbank, with orders until March 1966 or otherwise to repay it out of the Federal budget; second, to identify orders of $163 million in 1966–7. At the end of 1965, when problems in the Federal budget became apparent, the situation became critical. German officials desperately sought suitable projects to reach the targets. A Bundesbank memorandum on one of the meetings of the British–German commission recommended that before they were forced to pay *à fonds perdu*, the German ministries should equip their car park with Rolls Royce limousines.[66]

The British meanwhile struggled with other difficulties. The German advance payment was spent almost immediately during the next currency crisis, which escalated in the summer of 1965.[67] Again, the British turned to the United States for help only to hear that strings were attached. McGeorge Bundy wrote to the president in July 1965 that the

British are constantly trying to make narrow bargains on money while they cut back their wider political and military responsibilities. We want to make very sure that the British get it into their heads that it makes no sense for us to rescue the pound in a situation in which there is no British flag in Vietnam, and a threatened British thin-out in both East of Suez and in Germany.[68]

This shows the scope of the intense discussion that was taking place in Washington regarding the nature of those strings. The Treasury Department demanded a guarantee against devaluation of sterling, McNamara called for an increased British commitment in Southeast Asia, and the State Department wanted a more constructive policy toward Germany, including a stable BAOR level.[69] The rescue operation for the pound was

66 Memorandum dept. A21, Oct. 25, 1965, BBA, A270/13168.
67 Richard Crossman, *The Crossman Diaries*, 3 vols. (London, 1975), 1:290.
68 July 28, 1965, LBJL, NSF, memos to president: McGeorge Bundy, box 4.
69 Numerous documents in the LBJ Library relate to this discussion, e.g., telephone conversation Bator-Ball, July 27, 1965, Ball papers, box 1; Bundy to president: Sterling Devaluation, July 28, 1965, NSF, memos to president: Bundy, box 4; Ball on Pound Crisis, Aug. 6, 1965, NSF, country file: U.K., box 215; Gardner Ackley to president, Aug. 9, 1965, Fowler papers, box 4. Bator to Bundy: The U.K. Problem or "Thinking about the Unthinkable," July 29, 1965, DDRS 1978/211A. The British were deeply irritated by these requests. To quote from a letter by Wilson to Stewart dated Mar. 23, 1965: "Should the President try to link this question [Vietnam] with support for the pound I would regard this as most unfortunate. If the financial weakness we inherited and are in the process of putting right is to be used as a means of forcing us to accept unpalatable policies or developments regardless of our thoughts this will raise very wide questions indeed about Anglo–American relationships" (PRO PREM 13/693). For an assessment of British–American financial diplomacy in this period, see Diane B. Kunz, "Cold War Dollar Diplomacy," in Diane B. Kunz, ed., *The Diplomacy of the Crucial Decade* (New York, 1994), 80–114.

successful; there is little doubt that the Americans made their position known to the British, refraining only from asking for direct military support in Vietnam. In any case, the Labour government was surprisingly cautious regarding the European commitment. American pressure certainly was one reason for the absence of serious reductions in overseas defense expenditures in Wilson's austerity program of August 1965.[70] One further reason might have been that just before the 1965 sterling crisis broke out, the Wilson government had managed, as mentioned, to renegotiate the previous offset agreement. It would have been difficult to justify reductions so soon afterward.

The restraint lasted until the beginning of 1966. In February, London published a white paper that mentioned the possibility of troop cuts because the foreign exchange cost of the BAOR was insufficiently covered by the offset agreement.[71] Negotiations in early 1966 on the implementation of the agreement had become increasingly rough, with the British uttering dark threats and the Germans maneuvering around the issue. With vigorous efforts, including subsidies for German firms to induce them to place orders in Britain, the Germans reached the 1964–6 target.[72] Sighs of relief were premature, however. During Erhard's last state visit to London, Wilson and his chancellor of the exchequer, Jim Callaghan, demanded full offset for 1966–7 instead of 80 percent as agreed in 1965. This meant transferring an additional $125 million to the British Treasury. Erhard, in deep budgetary trouble, refused. Subsequent talks between Callaghan and Dahlgrün brought no results.[73] The sterling crisis that erupted in mid-1966 added urgency to the British case. Speculation reached new levels. Including the losses in these months, the total British foreign exchange losses in the currency battle since November 1964 reached a shattering $4 billion of owned and borrowed reserves.[74] Although even ministers now recommended devaluation, Wilson once more decided to hold the line. A huge program of deflationary measures (the so-called July program) was hastily pulled together, including a $280 million cut in overseas expenditures, a freeze in wages and prices, and

---

70 Cairncross and Eichengreen, *Sterling*, 178.   71 HMSO, Cmnd. 2901 (1966).

72 Memorandum on BMF–Treasury talks, Feb. 7, 1966; attachment to BMF cabinet memorandum, Feb. 25, 1966; memorandum on British offset, May 11, 1966, all in BA, B136/3134; AA note: Meeting of the mixed Anglo–German Commission on Offset, Apr. 6, 1966, PA-AA, Dept. IIA7/835.

73 Erhard–Callaghan talks, May 24, 1966, AAPD 1966, 682–8; Erhard–Wilson talk, May 24, 1966, AAPD 1966, 695–703; Blankenhorn to AA: Callaghan–Dahlgrün talks, July 1, 1966, AAPD 1966, 908–10.

74 Yeager, *International Monetary Relations*, 458.

deflation of domestic demand by various measures designed to check consumption. In his statement in the House of Commons on July 20, Wilson announced that expenditures for the BAOR "would be cut so that total foreign exchange costs were at a level covered by offset and other payments."[75] Callaghan was sent to Bonn with instructions to ask the German government to bring payments up to the full level of the British foreign exchange cost – to no avail. The Germans flatly told the British that no budgetary funds were available to fulfill their requests.[76] Departing, the chancellor of the exchequer said to the press that London would begin preparations to reduce its troops. The British government invoked the NATO and WEU procedures for a revision of its NATO commitment.[77] With de Gaulle's actions and the German–American problems this move seemed to foreshadow the end of the traditional structure of NATO, and therefore pushed the U.S. government to take the initiative to clean up the mess.

DOMESTIC CONSTRAINTS IN WASHINGTON AND BONN

Whereas in Britain, throughout the 1950s and 1960s, the troop-cost issue had led to caustic comments in parliament and the press concerning German stinginess, it had only rarely been a matter of public debate in the German–American context. The far-reaching consequences of the offset agreements were hardly discussed. These "fortunate" circumstances changed during 1966. The Johnson administration saw itself confronted with a serious motion by Congress to reduce the American commitment in Europe. One main argument in this debate was insufficient burden sharing by the Europeans. In the background hovered the nascent struggle between Congress and the executive branch caused by Vietnam, in which critics of Johnson's policy emphasized the overcommitment of the United States not only in Asia but also in Europe. Ever since the Great Debate in 1951 over the decision to send ground troops on a large scale to the European Cold War theater there had been voices in Congress criticizing the lasting commitment of the United States to Europe. Only in 1966, however, did this sentiment take on an organized form. What made this activity doubly inconvenient for the administration was that the initiative originated in the Democratic Party. In July the

---

75 Wilson, *Labour Government*, 258–9.
76 Interdepartmental meeting, June 27, 1966, BBA, A270/13168.
77 Memorandum by Political Director Hans Ruete: Defense minister conference in Paris, AAPD 1966, 1040.

Democratic Majority Policy Committee expressed its concern about the "excessive and unchanging" deployment of troops in Europe.[78] Shortly afterward a group of eminent senators introduced a sense of the Senate resolution to this effect, named for its main sponsor, Democratic majority leader Mike Mansfield.[79] Mansfield did not force his resolution to a vote, but the government had received a warning of what was to come. In early 1967 the resolution was reintroduced, and the issue of troops in Europe became a major subject of debate between the administration and Congress until the mid-1970s. The White House perceived the Mansfield resolution, quite correctly, as an attempt by the legislative branch to regain lost ground in the determination of U.S. foreign policy. As a result of the escalation in Vietnam, Congress had become increasingly restless about its limited influence on foreign policy formulation. The balance of payments, the pressure of military expenditures, the prospect of détente, and the prosperity of Europe all made the U.S. troops based in Europe an obvious target, because the majority did not dare to challenge Johnson's Vietnam policy directly.

The president reacted furiously to the initiative, and Senator Russell Long was subjected to a Johnson monologue during a telephone conversation about the Senate "playing president." LBJ assured the senator that despite Erhard's poor standing in recent public opinion polls he would ask "that poor devil" to "reimburse me for every dime." Johnson continued:

I had Rusk notify the Russians: "Would you be interested in reducing some of your 22 divisions if we would make a corresponding reduction in NATO." And they came back with a little indication – no commitment – emphasize, no commitment. But we got a response, a little feeler, that we thought was good. . . . And by God, right in the middle of it, so far as I can see without doing a bit of good to anybody, we've got every Democratic leader in the Senate, all 13 of them, to serve notice on the president that, by God, we ought to reduce. Now I'm just an old Johnson City boy, but when I'm playing bridge and I show the other fellow my whole hand, I can't make a very good deal with him.

LBJ instructed Long to impress on the Democratic Party that, in such a delicate international situation, they should stand behind their president:

And let them know that this is not going to be handled in the *New York Times*. And a goddamned sense of Congress resolution ain't worth a shit unless this president has some respect for the sense of it. And all it can do is notify every

---

78 Trilaterals background paper (DOS/EUR): Mansfield resolution, Nov. 17, 1966, LBJL, NSF, NSC histories: Trilaterals, box 51.
79 Congressional Records, Senate, Aug. 31, 1966, 20554.

enemy that we're just a bunch of un-unified folks running off like Bert Wheeler and Jeannette Rankin, in every goddamned direction.[80]

The flabbergasted senator was unable to focus the president's attention on the obvious fact that Moscow did not need the Mansfield resolution to realize the strength of the troop-cut proponents in Congress and, more important, in government policy circles. Thus, the very tentative American soundings for mutual balanced-force reductions in Europe came to naught.[81] The Soviet Union simply waited for the result of the debate in the United States.

Domestic conflict in Germany centered not only on the chancellor's authority regarding the formulation of German foreign policy, it also became directly linked to Erhard's political future. Offset was only a side issue in the acrimonious political controversies in the Federal Republic during the mid-1960s. But in the end it became an important element in Erhard's fall from power. It was predictable from the start that Erhard would not have an easy time as chancellor. Rivals such as former chancellor Adenauer, who was still the leader of the CDU, the main party in the government, and Strauss, the head of the Bavarian CSU, remained aloof from the government and kept enough power to exert a strong influence. This was particularly dangerous for Erhard because a deep rift on foreign policy issues ran through the governing parties after the last years of Adenauer's chancellorship. This rift separated the Gaullists from the Atlanticists. The former pleaded for a policy of closer alignment with France, more European independence from the United States, and resistance to American pressure to pursue their détente policy.[82] The Atlanticists – Erhard, Schröder, and Hassel led this group – emphasized the paramount importance of U.S.–German relations.[83] The debate was initially created and then intensified by domestic rivalries, and it can only be understood in this context. Most leading politicians saw Erhard as a transition chancellor and regarded Schröder as a main player in the struggle for succession. Foreign policy became one of the central battlefields. During 1966 Erhard was increasingly challenged by his opponents.

---

80 Johnson–Long telephone conversation, Sept. 1, 1966, in FRUS 1964–8, XV, 399–400.
81 Telegram from Moscow embassy, Nov. 12, 1966, in ibid., 448–9.
82 The most important protagonists of this "group" (characterized more by their common opposition to Erhard than by the similarity of their political views) were former Chancellor Adenauer, former Defense Minister Strauss, the CSU representative Theodor Freiherr zu Guttenberg, and Bundestag President Eugen Gerstenmaier. For a detailed portrayal of these men and their ideas, see Hans-Jürgen Grabbe, *Unionsparteien, Sozialdemokratie und Vereinigte Staaten von Amerika 1945–66* (Düsseldorf, 1983), 469–89, and Rainer Marcowitz, *Option für Paris? Unionsparteien, SPD und de Gaulle 1958–69* (Munich, 1996).
83 The Social Democrats were mostly "Atlanticists." See Grabbe, *Unionsparteien*, 540–88.

Adenauer continued to criticize publicly Erhard's and Schröder's policy toward de Gaulle. In an interview with *US News & World Report*, Strauss questioned one of the paradigms of German foreign policy, the insistence on a stable level of allied troops on German soil. He argued for a stronger European component in Western defense that would then allow the withdrawal of one or two U.S. divisions. These remarks were promptly cited by McNamara during congressional hearings as evidence of Europe's capacity to do more for its defense and, in case of unwillingness, to tolerate limited U.S. troop reductions.[84]

As a consequence of the ceaseless pressure, Erhard felt compelled to emphasize the importance of German–American relations in a much more strident way than he would have in the absence of domestic opposition. Unfortunately for him, American policy was not supportive. He had to take several snubs, all resulting from the questioning of traditional policies toward Europe that was taking place in Washington. Arguably the most severe blow was the quiet but inexorable dismissal of the MLF by the Johnson administration. Erhard and Schröder had risked their reputations for the scheme that was to secure the Germans some kind of say in the Alliance's nuclear affairs. Critics such as Strauss and de Gaulle saw it as just another means for the Americans to perpetuate their nuclear hegemony. In 1965–6 the project faded from the agenda, and the only government that tried to keep it alive was Bonn. Other sticking points that Erhard had to deal with were America's pursuit of détente without consulting the German government, conflicts on troop levels, and, last but not least, offset. What made the last issue particularly difficult for Erhard was that it also dovetailed with what turned out to be his most dangerous challenge: the battle about the 1966 and 1967 Federal budgets.

In 1965 Erhard silenced his critics temporarily with an impressive victory in the parliamentary elections. In order to placate and appease as many interest groups as possible, however, the government greatly expanded public expenditures prior to the election. More than $1.5 billion was spent in this effort.[85] The campaign pledges threatened to unsettle the 1966 budget; some of them had to be revoked almost immediately after the elections. Despite these cuts, government expenditure was running much too high, and a supplementary budget became necessary

---

84 "Time to Start U.S. Pull-back in Europe: Interview with F. J. Strauss," *U.S. News & World Report*, Apr. 18, 1966. For McNamara's statement, see hearing before Senate Committee on Appropriations: foreign assistance, 89th cong., 2d sess., Apr. 30, 1966, in PSSD, XIV, 2207.
85 Hildebrand, *Erhard*, 125.

to cover the government's commitments, including offset. The presentation of this appropriation to parliament was continually delayed. A parallel problem besetting Erhard's budgetary policy was that a balanced budget for 1967 seemed possible only if tax revenues grew or if tough spending cuts were effected that were politically very difficult to sell. At that time public opinion saw the balanced budget as a central task of the government; the Federal Republic had never practiced deficit spending.[86] On the contrary, it accumulated surpluses, like the *Juliusturm*. The hope for increased tax revenues proved fallacious. In 1965–6 prices began to rise perceptibly, endangering the main postulate of German economic policy, the stability of the currency. Consequently, the Bundesbank put on the brakes and pursued an increasingly restrictive credit policy, which was successful insofar as it decisively slowed down economic activity.[87] But problems such as low investment rates and a contraction of demand converged to produce the fear of a major recession. Although modest in its economic effects, the recession of 1966–7 had a strong impact on public perception because it was the first economic slowdown since the early 1950s.[88] An early effect of the slowdown was that tax revenues were much lower than expected. Erhard was confronted with a difficult dilemma; throughout 1966 the government struggled unsuccessfully to fight the recession while at the same time trying to reduce government spending. Erhard's authority in his own domain, economic policy, was seriously eroded, and all he could still draw on was his role during the *Wirtschaftswunder* (economic miracle). During the election campaign in North Rhine Westphalia, widely seen as a test for Erhard's government, the chancellor lost his temper and attacked a crowd of protesting steel and mine workers: "And before I go I'd like to tell you louts that you

---

86 Gerhard Fels, *1966/67: Anatomie einer Rezession* (Kiel, 1988), 10.
87 From January 1965 to May 1966, the central bank raised the discount rate step by step from 3 percent to 5 percent and repeatedly took the unusual step of criticizing the government publicly for its anticyclical spending policy. See the speeches by Bundesbank President Blessing on Dec. 8, 1964, and Feb. 24, 1966. See Karl Blessing, *Im Kampf um Gutes Geld* (Frankfurt am Main, 1966), 185–203, 275–87. See also Helmut Schlesinger and Horst Bockelmann, "Monetary Policy in the Federal Republic of Germany," in Holbik Karel, ed., *Monetary Policy in Twelve Industrial Countries* (Boston, 1973), 191–5.
88 It is probably more accurate to speak of a slowdown of growth than of a recession. The GDP sank by only 0.1 percent, unemployment rose to a modest 2.1 percent in 1967, and investment stagnated. Nevertheless, the political effect was powerful, first because certain branches (like mining and steel producing) were strongly affected and second because of a shaky political climate that tended to produce a flood of alarmed statements, leading to a feeling of crisis that was intensified by the government's inability to get a grip on its budget problems; see Herbert Giersch, Karl-Heinz Paqué, and Holger Schmieding, *The Fading Miracle: Four Decades of Market Economy in Germany* (Cambridge, 1992), 142–5; Christoph Klessmann, *Zwei Staaten, eine Nation: Deutsche Geschichte 1955–70* (Göttingen, 1988), 193–9; Fels, *Anatomie einer Rezession*.

would have perished in your nappies without me and my policy."[89] The exhortation did nothing to enhance Erhard's prestige, and on July 10, 1966, the elections resulted in a resounding victory for the Social Democrats. This blow made Erhard's domestic position almost untenable. His fate became dependent on the solution of the budgetary crisis and, as mentioned above, on a more convincing foreign policy. Offset had a strong impact on both issues.

As the British struggled with their monetary predicament and the German government slowly drowned in its budgetary morass, American apprehension about the continuation of its offset receipts grew rapidly. However, Washington did not take too seriously the alarming hints from Bonn regarding the current agreement. Every agreement had seen a critical phase, yet, in the end, funds had arrived (although the last agreement, as we have seen, was fulfilled only by huge prepayments on future orders). On July 5 Erhard wrote a letter to Johnson in which he urged different means of offset "than the purchase of weapons and military equipment alone. In my view, which I hope is shared by you, this set of problems should, however, not be linked with the question of the future presence of U.S. troops in Germany. This would all too easily give rise to an approach that would not do justice to the friendship between our two countries."[90] The letter sparked a heated debate in the U.S. government about the future of offset and also increasingly about the future of the commitment in Europe. This debate was overshadowed by the news from Britain and from Congress.

The front lines in the U.S. government were the same as they had been during the troop-reduction debate in 1962–3. McNamara's Pentagon and the Treasury Department under Henry Fowler were for a strict military offset approach and, in case of noncompliance by the FRG, a corresponding reduction of U.S. troops. A shrinking but still influential group in the State Department, the White House itself, and the ambassador in Bonn, McGhee, defended the traditional orientation of American policy toward Europe and did not want to see it endangered by a rigid offset policy. President Johnson and Secretary of State Rusk navigated somewhere in the middle until they were forced to take positions.

89 *Der Spiegel* 43 (1966), 50.
90 Erhard to Johnson, July 5, 1966, DDRS 1994/181.

The loudest voice in this debate, and the one generally held to be the most decisive, was that of McNamara, who, due to his rigid insistence on a continuation of offset by military purchases, subsequently earned himself the distinction of being a "tireless arms merchant with shockingly high-pressure sales techniques."[91] The roots and motives behind his policy are rarely analyzed adequately. Although McNamara had grave doubts about the possibility of continuing offset by weapons purchases in the long run, he had a real and deep interest in prolonging the military offset scheme as long as possible.[92] It has been noted before that soon after the first offset agreement was signed, a powerful coalition that benefited from it had formed in the U.S. government. This coalition included State Department members searching for arguments to preserve an undiminished U.S. presence in Europe, monetary authorities that needed offset to keep the payments deficit under control, and finally, a kind of military-industrial complex that developed out of the Pentagon's enormous sales activities in West Germany during the 1960s. These military sales were credited as a positive item in the traditionally negative military payments balance, which was the target of particularly energetic efforts by McNamara. At times of growing congressional unease regarding the huge defense budget, swollen with Vietnam-related expenditures, it became increasingly important to have guaranteed income and a counterweight to the growth of military expenditure in the balance of payments. The higher production numbers associated with successful sales of materiel abroad also made the Pentagon's own orders cheaper due to the lower cost of producing more output. Thus, a sudden reduction of foreign military sales would have undone many of the savings achieved by McNamara's vigorous managerial programs since the first days of the Kennedy administration.

McNamara's main concern in the mid-1960s was the conduct of the Vietnam conflict and the justification of this war at home. This conflicted with the allocation of resources for the European arena. Offset was vital

91 The phrase, repeated in many accounts of the events, was originally coined by Theo Sommer in "Bonn Changes Course," *Foreign Affairs*, Apr. 1967, 477–91. For McNamara's style, see his remarks on offset during a press conference on June 6, 1966: "This agreement was renewed under the instructions of President Johnson, confirmed by Chancellor Erhard, signed by Minister Hassel. We fully expect it to be met" (PSSD, pt. 3, reel XIV, 12), and just prior to Erhard's visit on September 15: Question: "Do you want to renew the offset agreement?" McNamara: "Oh, of course, we do!" Question: "For military equipment?" McNamara: "Yes . . . there is no question that they have a requirement for more military equipment" (PSSD, pt. 3, reel XVIII, 819–39).
92 "Realistically the FRG cannot continue indefinitely to provide a full offset," McNamara said during a discussion with British foreign and defense ministers, Jan. 27, 1966, in FRUS 1964–68, XIII, 304.

to balancing these contradictory objectives, particularly regarding the payments component of expenditures in Europe. Diversifying offset to include German investment in Treasury bonds, as Erhard had suggested, did not make much difference from an overall balance-of-payments perspective; it would, however, have made a huge difference to McNamara, who with one stroke would have lost about $700 million a year in foreign exchange terms. In McNamara's opinion whatever domestic problems the Germans cited were dwarfed by his own political and economic difficulties. It is for these reasons that McNamara was so insistent on continued weapons purchases by German forces. He left no doubt on this matter during congressional hearings on the Atlantic Alliance, when he was pressed by senators who demanded a reduction in U.S. forces in Europe.[93] Until the very end, he fought for a continuation of the old offset approach; in a straightforward memorandum to the president, prepared for the Erhard visit, he repeated his conviction that the Federal Republic's military posture was deficient, that it still had huge requirements for military hardware, and that German statements to the contrary were "clearly untrue."[94] He emphasized that the United States could not accept a different method for offset and that it could not accept the balance-of-payments drain if the Germans stopped their orders. Therefore, he recommended a troop reduction of about 50,000 men and the dual-basing (alternately in the United States and in Europe) of about half the U.S. Air Force in Germany if the Germans stopped ordering weapons.[95] Underlying this memorandum was the hope that if he kept enough pressure on the Germans they might in the end agree to American troop reductions. (Strauss's remarks had given him some encouragement in this regard.)[96] A telephone conversation between McNamara and the president on the second day of Erhard's visit makes this strategy very clear:

McNamara: "From a military point of view, Mr. President, I think substantial force adjustments are justified. Unless we handle it right, however, there would be a terrible political cost. And that's our problem."

LBJ: "Well, how do we handle that right?"

McNamara: "Well, I don't know. I think tonight and tomorrow we ought to . . ."

93 The Atlantic Alliance: hearings before the Subcommittee on National Security, Committee on Government Operations, 89th Cong., 2d sess., June 21, 1966, in PSSD, pt. 3, reel XV, 215.

94 Sept. 19, 1966, in FRUS 1964–8, XV, 413–16.

95 In a conversation with the British on Jan. 27, 1966, McNamara saw the solution in "first, a modification of our force structure, and second, a substantial increase in the FRG financial and force contribution" (Jan. 27, 1966, in FRUS 1964–68, XIII, 304).

96 Briefing memorandum Bator to LBJ, Aug. 23, 1966, ibid., 454–5.

LBJ: "Looks like to me, we ought to take advantage of this opportunity to make him tell us that he cannot afford to have our troops there."

McNamara: ". . . and he wants our troops out. That's what I think we ought to do, Mr. President. That's right. That's exactly right."[97]

The considerable risks inherent in this policy of brinkmanship did not go unnoticed: They included a prolonged deterioration of German–American relations, a further blow to the already shaky cohesion of NATO, a loss of U.S. prestige in Europe, and a weakening of the military position in Europe. These were the main points made by a group of advisers in the U.S. administration who became increasingly preoccupied with the state of European–American relations in the shadow of the Vietnam conflict. The members of this group included Walt Rostow, Johnson's national security adviser; Francis Bator, the deputy assistant of national security affairs; and George Ball from the State Department. A growing rift had developed between a more European-minded traditional group that had dominated U.S. foreign policy after World War II and others who, for better or worse, saw America's future in the Pacific.[98] The "Europeanists" argued for the overriding priority of keeping the traditional structure of the Alliance intact despite such pressures as the balance of payments, Vietnam, East–West détente, and domestic criticism. But they were up against a strong coalition made up of the Pentagon's civilian policy makers, the U.S. Congress, and the Treasury Department. The question of how to respond to Erhard's letter of July 5, in which the chancellor asked for reform of the offset system, led to a clash between these two groups.

The debate was complicated by the simultaneous public declaration of the British government that it intended to reduce its troops on the European continent. The hardliners in the American government wanted to send an immediate response to Erhard demanding full military offset for the period after June 1967.[99] When in early August the U.S. embassy in Bonn reported that the German cabinet was about to finalize its budget for 1967 and that there were rumors of heavy cuts in defense, McNamara urged a tough response. Ball, Bator, McGhee, and Rostow emphasized the dangers of this approach, which in all likelihood would

---

97 McNamara–Johnson telephone conversation, Sept. 26, 1966, in FRUS 1964–8, XV, 435.

98 See, e.g., the heated dispute between John J. McCloy, who accused the Johnson administration of having no European policy at all, and Harriman, who argued that no movements in Europe were possible without getting the Germans "in a stew" and saw the future in China, not in Europe. See note on a conversation with McCloy, Jan. 22, 1966, Library of Congress, Manuscript Division, Harriman papers, box 486.

99 Bator to LBJ, Aug. 23, 1966, in FRUS 1964–68, XIII, 453–5.

not convince Erhard to revise his spending program: "It would be a very poor trade for the U.S. to take serious risks with the stability of German and alliance politics, and hence with our security position in Europe, in order to make marginal gains on our balance of payments."[100] They recommended that the president postpone the reply to Erhard and bring together all principal actors before taking a firm position. Johnson agreed. This gave the proponents of a compromise two more weeks to formulate a proposal that dealt with both the German and British problems without putting further strain on German–American relations. The result was a plan to get all three nations together to work out a mutually acceptable offset framework trilaterally.[101] This general idea, originally a response to an expected action by de Gaulle against NATO, had been floated on and off by the State Department since mid-1965.[102] Only during the emergency situation in the autumn of 1966, however, was enough political impetus created to bring this plan to the fore and spur the U.S. government to make this major diplomatic move. The plan included proposals for comprehensive talks dealing with the actual threat in Europe, with necessary force levels, and with the nuclear problem. The intention was to delay, as long as such talks were in progress, an immediate British troop cut, which would have encouraged the Mansfield group in Congress. If, in the end, no compromise was reached, then the troop cuts could be legitimately based on the insolubility of the problem at hand. Johnson endorsed the proposal in a meeting on August 24.[103] The president wrote letters to Erhard and Wilson inviting them to participate in trilateral talks.[104] The letter to Erhard included a reminder on the current offset agreement: "I know that you and I are agreed that the current offset agreement will be fully met and provided for in your new budget and legislative program."[105] Erhard, in his reply, suggested that the Trilaterals be delayed until after his state visit in September.[106] The Americans

---

100 Bator to LBJ, Aug. 11, 1966, in FRUS 1964–68, XIII, 446.
101 John M. Leddy to Secretary Rusk: U.K. financial problem with BAOR, Aug. 23, 1966, LBJL, NSF, NSC histories: Trilaterals, box 50.
102 Leddy to Ball, Sept. 23, 1965, in FRUS 1964–68, XIII, 244–7. The British had already been approached with the idea; see FO brief for Stewart visit to Washington, D.C., Sept. 29, 1965, PRO FO 371/183103; excerpt Stewart letter to Lord Hood, Sept. 20, 1965. For the discussion within the American administration, see memorandum on conversation among Bundy, McNamara, Ball, and JCS et al., Oct. 8, 1965, in FRUS 1964–68, XIII, 253–7.
103 Bator notes on Aug. 23, 1966, meeting, ibid.
104 LBJ to Wilson, Aug. 26, 1966, in FRUS 1964–68, XIII, 457. Wilson, in his not yet declassified response, apparently requested preceding bilateral talks with the United States. This was denied by the U.S. government. See Johnson to Wilson, Sept. 1, 1966, ibid., 460–1.
105 LBJ to Erhard, Aug. 25, 1966, LBJL, NSF, NSC histories: Trilaterals, box 50.
106 Erhard to Johnson, Sept. 7, 1966, in FRUS 1964–68, XIII, 464–5.

displayed considerable activity in trying to prevent the participating governments from moves that would prejudice the exercise. LBJ wrote twice to Wilson to ensure that the British prime minister would not commit himself irreversibly to reductions in the BAOR.[107] At the same time the government tried to hold the line on the domestic scene, where the Mansfield resolution was introduced on August 31. A further blow disturbed the plan on the eve of Chancellor Erhard's visit to Washington: The German government notified the Americans that the current offset agreement was not going to be fulfilled.

POLITICAL AND ECONOMIC CRISIS IN GERMANY

The German government had been pondering for some time how to put its cards on the table. When it realized in March that the offset targets could be reached only with a supplementary budget for 1966, the government delayed a decision because of internal divisions, particularly between the CDU and the FDP. The former pleaded for tax increases, whereas the latter insisted on cuts in government spending. From mid-1966 on, the 1967 budget dominated government policy. All proposals submitted by the ministries were vigorously cut. This particularly affected the Defense Ministry. It had planned for a budget of $4.7 billion and ended up with $4.4 billion. In the cabinet Hassel stated that "in such a budgetary situation the offset agreement will be fulfilled neither with orders nor – even approximately – with payments."[108] In a letter to Erhard on September 12, he specified that the offset payments to the United States would total only $267 million at the end of 1966. The target for March 1967 was $1.392 billion. Orders placed to date would heavily mortgage future budgets, so the next offset agreements were to stay within a limit of $350 million for military and civilian orders, including a complete moratorium on orders in 1967.[109] Hassel added that the interests of German defense industries could no longer be neglected.

Hassel's approach was in step with mounting public criticism regarding the agreements. After Hassel's visit to Washington in May the Bundestag for the first time took up the offset issue. Hassel denied allegations that unnecessary materiel had been purchased. Helmut Schmidt (SPD)

---

107 Letters of Aug. 26 and Sept. 1, 1966, ibid., 457–8, 460–1; Rusk to Ball in London, Sept. 7, 1966, DDRS 1985/1008.
108 Military diary of Hassel, entry of Aug. 4, 1966, on cabinet meeting the day before; Carstens memorandum: "Meeting of Federal Defense Council," Aug. 24, 1966, AAPD 1966, 1098–101.
109 Military diary of Hassel, Hassel to Erhard, Sept. 12, 1966.

criticized the political and economic consequences of the agreements: "For reasons of security and alliance policy we can't permit ourselves to purchase all the heavy materiel we import from abroad exclusively from the United States. It just won't do. My preference would be to buy and jointly develop parts of this equipment in France, whenever possible, so that relations to France in this area would not suffer from the gigantic volume of payments we owe to America."[110] A further factor that increased public criticism of the military offset deals was the quality of the U.S. materiel: It was becoming increasingly questionable after a series of crashes involving the German air force's principal aircraft, the Lockheed Starfighter. Hassel had to face embarrassing questions in parliament regarding the wisdom of buying American.[111] Obtaining further authority for funds to fulfill the offset agreement was impossible under these circumstances.

Various ideas were floated as to how to avoid an open breach of the agreement and a major row with the Americans. Negotiations independent of offset were already under way on a premature repayment of the remaining German postwar debts to the United States. The U.S. Treasury refused to count that as offset, however.[112] Another idea, pushed by Erhard, was the possibility of increased cooperation in space technology, which might have made investment in U.S. technology possible. But the catch was that the expected sums were much too low to have any significance. The Americans also raised doubts about the "additionality" of this investment because, in their opinion, it would have been made anyway.[113] Using the same argument, they also refused to consider "civil" purchases, such as aircraft for Lufthansa. The only escape route seemed to be offset by financial measures, such as German investment in mid- or long-term U.S. treasury securities, thus transferring back the dollars received from the troops. In pursuing this alternative the Erhard government was confronted with two formidable factors: the first was that it was unclear whether the Americans would agree, and the second was the Bundesbank, which would have to advance the money because of the sad state of the government's budget. However, by law the Bundesbank was prohibited from extending credit to finance government programs. It was very likely that the bank's highest body, the Central Bank Council (Zentralbankrat or

---

110 *VdB*, 5th per., 44th sess., May 26, 1966, 2142. Schmidt's opinions were shared even by members of the governing parties, ibid., 2144–5.
111 *VdB*, 5th per., 43d sess., Mar. 24, 1966, 1510–17.
112 Memorandum: "Present Status of German Debt Prepayment Question," July 19, 1966, LBJL, Fowler papers, boxes 51–52.
113 Blaser to McGhee, July 16, 1966, McGhee papers, 1988add., box 2.

ZBR), would consider the government's request to be just that. Apparently, only major concessions by the Americans could help Erhard with the budgetary mess that threatened to bring down his government.

On September 9 Erhard informed the American ambassador that the German government was unable to fulfill its current offset obligation and that, during his forthcoming visit, the chancellor would request a payment moratorium on the agreement.[114] This came as a surprise to the Americans, who thought that only future offset agreements were endangered. The 1966–7 offset money had already been earmarked for various purposes, particularly in the Defense and Treasury Departments:

> The importance . . . of the past FRG offset receipts is indicated by the fact that the offset receipts of about $700 million in FY 1965 were equal to about one-half of the total Defense Department global military receipts. . . . The U.S. balance of payments deficit for CY 1965 was $1.3 billion on the over-all balance, liquidity basis. We rely heavily on those receipts in our total balance of payments program, and our CY 1966 and 1967 estimates are based on FRG honoring its commitments.[115]

These considerations were decisive for the United States' response to Erhard. Fowler and McNamara both saw their policies seriously endangered and urged the president to get Erhard to fulfill the present agreement by any means necessary. McNamara requested the authority to commence with troop cuts if the Germans did not keep their promises.[116] Various compromises were considered regarding the order commitments and the future offset pattern. The United States decided to remain steadfast on one essential point: The payments had to come through the exchanges, as planned. A joint memorandum on offset, agreed to by all departments, recommended that the president take a tough stance regarding the fulfillment of the offset obligation by any means, even if it included investments in Treasury papers; this clearly reflected the concerns of the Treasury Department. The order period was to be extended, with Fowler and McNamara insisting on eventual military orders and the Bator–Ball group arguing for substitution by other means.[117] The

---

114 Erhard-McGhee conversation, Sept. 9, 1966, AAPD 1966, doc. 280.
115 Treasury background paper: "Trilateral talks (U.S./German military offset relationship)," Oct. 24, 1966, LBJL, Fowler papers, box 69.
116 McNamara to president, Sept. 19, 1966, in FRUS 1964–68, XV, 413–16.
117 Bator to president: Erhard visit, Sept. 25, 1966, ibid., box 50.

essential consideration was the balance of payments. Fowler stated categorically that he could not "take a nickel's loss in the balance of payments this year."[118] The secretary of the treasury advised the president,
prior to the latter's meeting with the German chancellor, to refuse
Erhard's request for a payments moratorium under any circumstances: "We
need to have Erhard on the line that the financial requirement will be
met on time – that only the techniques need be worked out."[119] The last
instruction the president received prior to the meeting reflected this. He
was advised to insist on two things: an immediate start of the Trilaterals
to deal with the future of offset and the full honoring of the 1965–7
offset agreement within the agreed schedule.[120]

These instructions clearly showed how much the U.S. government
relied on the continuation of offset payments despite an awareness of its
character as a temporary expedient. Even if we take into account that
the U.S. government suspected Erhard's government was bound to fall
anyway, the decision to bluntly refuse his request was a risky one that
might poison mutual relations for some time to come. The contradictory
aims of an expansive Cold War policy, including Vietnam, the continuation of the dollar-gold standard, and the refusal to take drastic action in
the domestic economy were, to a considerable degree, held together by
the creation of offset. The U.S. government found itself trapped. One way
or another, it would have to compromise its policy by reducing its Cold
War commitments, diluting the monetary system, or initiating restrictive
measures in the domestic economy. For the moment, however, there
was still hope that Erhard would in some miraculous way come up with
additional funds.

Just prior to his departure for Washington, Erhard's domestic problems
took a dramatic turn for the worse. The coalition government agonized
over the budget disaster, and calls for the chancellor to resign were mul-
tiplying. The attacks were directed not only against the chancellor himself
but also against his advisers. Foreign Minister Schröder and Finance
Minister Rolf Dahlgrün had long been harshly criticized for their policies. Two of Hassel's chiefs of staff left office in protest over the issue of
union representation in the armed forces.[121] On September 21, 1966,
Hassel barely survived a vote of no confidence in the Bundestag. The dis-
organized functioning of the government also made Ludger Westrick, the

118 Rostow–Ball telephone conversation, Sept. 26, 1966, LBJL, Ball papers, box 1.
119 Memorandum from Fowler to Johnson, Sept. 25, 1966, in FRUS 1964–68, XV, 420.
120 Rostow to president, Sept. 26, 1966, LBJL, NSF, country file: Germany, box 193.
121 Hildebrand, *Erhard*, 211–15.

head of the Chancellor's Office and Erhard's closest aide, a target of incessant attack. He resigned in early September, and it turned out to be extremely difficult to find a successor. Nobody wanted to board a sinking ship. Erhard had been advised prior to the visit that it was better not to undertake this mission in such disadvantageous circumstances, but he brushed aside this advice. He and Schröder had refused American attempts to discuss the problems beforehand through lower official channels.[122] On the main issue, offset, the Germans had received no positive feedback. On September 23, during a NATO meeting, Hassel spoke briefly to McNamara. The secretary of defense told him that the U.S. government would probably be flexible regarding future offset, but there would be no compromise regarding current offset.[123]

As the state visit drew nearer Erhard saw no alternative but to ask Johnson, his friend,[124] to extend the current agreement, to change the rules for further agreements, to avoid immediate U.S. troop cuts, and to reaffirm American support for the MLF, although the chancellor had little to offer in return.[125] A diplomatic success on these issues, together with a reaffirmation of German–American friendship, might have given him some breathing space on the domestic scene. But Erhard was unaware of the strength of the American insistence on the agreed amounts of offset. Therefore, the German government had no concrete alternative plans for the offset agreement. Efforts to convince the Bundesbank to advance a short-term loan continued until the very last minute – and failed.[126]

Erhard's reception in Washington was not auspicious. Only Ball, who had already left government service, welcomed the German delegation. Strangely enough, the German finance minister was not present, which probably reflected the current state of the coalition; Dahlgrün was a member of the FDP. The first rounds of talks took place at the State Department. Erhard pledged prior bilateral consultation concerning the proposed trilateral talks. Regarding offset, he explained that the Federal Republic would not be able to fulfill the current agreement on time and needed an extension of the target date as well as diversification and a

122 Lilienfeld to Carstens, Sept. 13, 1966, AAPD 1966, 1182–3; Treverton, *Dollar-Drain*, 144. For a vivid description of the chaos preceding the trip to Washington, see Rosenbach, "Preis der Freiheit."
123 Military diary of Hassel, entry of Sept. 23, 1966.
124 Much has been made out of Erhard's alleged naïvetè and a quote of his "I love Mr. Johnson, and Mr. Johnson loves me" appears in almost all accounts of the events. If all of the sources cited for this remark are correct, Erhard must have made it on a number of occasions.
125 Talking points for Washington, Sept. 26/27, 1966, LES; Referat IIA7: chancellor's visit in Washington: problems of European defense, Sept. 17, 1966, NHP.
126 *Süddeutsche Zeitung*, Sept. 29, 1966; *Der Spiegel*, Oct. 3, 1966.

decrease in future offset payments.[127] His interlocutors responded that this problem would have to be dealt with in face-to-face talks with the president the following day. During this famous meeting of September 26, 1966, Erhard repeated his points, citing the cooperative attitude of his government in the whole field of bilateral issues.[128] He also hinted that if his government fell, the succeeding one might be less cooperative. Johnson did not take up any of Erhard's proposals and expressed deep disappointment at the fact that his German friends had broken their word and put him in an extremely difficult position. He suggested that experts on both sides start to work on the problem. There was no indication that the president would grant Erhard's basic request, a payment extension on the current agreement. When both rejoined their waiting delegations, Erhard, according to McGhee, looked "utterly dejected."[129] The German delegation, which had not formulated a consistent position in the event that Erhard's proposals might fail, worked feverishly to present an acceptable alternative. The only solution for filling the enormous order and payments gap was American acceptance of a large-scale German investment in Treasury papers and of premature repayment of the remaining German postwar debts ($214 million) as offset.[130]

The Bundesbank took a central role in the deliberations. Its president, Karl Blessing, was in Washington for the annual meeting of the IMF. In consultations with the German delegation, he stressed the stringent conditions that any Bundesbank loan to the federal government would entail. If the bank agreed to convert its short-term reserves to mid-term U.S. treasuries, thus depriving itself of flexibility in a potentially unstable monetary environment, then a supplementary budget for 1966 of DM 1 billion should be allocated, and an augmentation of the 1967 defense budget by another billion should be provided as well.[131] Those funds would allow the federal government to gradually acquire the bonds from the German central bank and repay the funds for the debt prepayment mentioned above. The hitch was that this offer was contingent on approval of the ZBR and that budget appropriations had to be approved by parliament. The German delegation informed the Americans that they would not be able to present more than suggestions for filling the $892 million

---

127 Erhard–Rusk talks, Sept. 26, 1966, AAPD 1966, 1237–42.
128 The complete text is found in FRUS, 1964–68, XIII, 471–7, and AAPD 1966, doc. 298, 1242–51.
129 McGhee, *At the Creation*, 193.
130 Estimated orders shortfall on December 31, 1966: $567 million; payments shortfall on June 30, 1967: $892 million. Both these figures were reached only by counting some questionable items. See minutes of U.S.-FRG discussion, Sept. 27, 1966, LBJL, NSF, NSC histories: Trilaterals, box 51.
131 Military diary of Hassel, entry of Sept. 25, 1966.

payments gap during their stay in Washington.[132] They suggested: a $428 million transfer of short-term Bundesbank funds to U.S. Treasury bonds, which would count as positive items in the American balance of payments; a $214 million prepayment of postwar debts; and $250 million in funds coming from an augmented defense budget. Regarding future agreements, the Germans suggested a level of $350 million per year on a five-year basis.

McNamara and Fowler swiftly rejected this last point as a question that had to be dealt with at the Trilaterals. Regarding the proposed purchase of treasury bonds, Fowler demanded that these be nonnegotiable, non-convertible, with a term of six to eight years and be settled later by arms purchases. This would in essence make them a prepayment on future military orders, preserving the military offset scheme. In the end, however, it was clear that Erhard was not able to agree to any precise method of effecting the payments because he needed the approval of either the parliament or the Bundesbank. Both delegations then tried to formulate a face-saving communiqué. The result was the longest of all post-war German-American communiqués, stating that the Federal Republic would "do its best" to meet the current agreement but would not be able to continue offset at the same level.[133] The Federal Republic also agreed to an immediate start of the trilateral exercise. The MLF was not mentioned.

The communiqué could scarcely veil the fact that the German delegation had fulfilled few objectives. Harsh criticism soon arose. Not only the press but also parliament and voices from Erhard's own party joined the clamor.[134] During Erhard's absence several conspiratorial meetings had taken place, but his rivals could not agree on a successor. Meanwhile, the budgetary chaos took on ever more disastrous forms. Shortly after Erhard returned, new estimates put tax revenues even lower than anticipated. The alternatives still were either cuts in government programs (which the

132 Carstens–Ball telephone conversations, Sept. 26, 1966, LBJL, Ball papers, box 4. See Hassel–McNamara meeting, Sept. 27, 1966, AAPD 1966, doc. 301, 1260–3; minutes of U.S.-FRG discussion, Sept. 27, 1966, LBJL, NSF, NSC histories: Trilaterals, box 51.
133 BPI 1966, 1017–19.
134 On Sept. 29, 1966, e.g., the *Frankfurter Rundschau* spoke of a "thinly veiled fiasco on all counts." For the debate in the parliament see *VdB*, 5th per., 60th sess., Oct. 5, 1966, 2939–70. Speakers for the opposition, such as Helmut Schmidt and Herbert Wehner, mentioned the absence of the finance minister, the secrecy surrounding the commitments, and the earmarking of enormous funds on the basis of insufficient budgets. FDP speakers joined this chorus, stating that present budgetary estimates were void in view of the offset commitment. Universally, the absence of a clause of best efforts was strongly criticized. Strauss attacked the same point and Erhard's naïve, one-sided reliance on U.S. policy; *Der Spiegel* 42 (1966), 31.

CDU/CSU resisted) or tax hikes (which the FDP abhorred). In October the FDP quit the government when the cabinet voted for tax increases. Erhard tried to cling to his chair with a minority government, but his fate was sealed. On November 8 a majority in the parliament passed a vote of no confidence. The CDU had to act fast. The following day the party named Kurt Georg Kiesinger, the minister president of Baden–Württemberg, as Erhard's successor. With the SPD, Kiesinger formed a "grand coalition" government of the CDU and SPD. On December 1 the Kiesinger government was confirmed by a vote of the Bundestag, with Willy Brandt as foreign minister, Strauss as finance minister, and Schröder now as defense minister.

The questions of how much his visit to Washington contributed to Erhard's fall and whether the U.S. government took this possibility into account are open to speculation. It is true that the United States was fully aware of Erhard's political problems and probably saw him as a lame duck. Any concessions would have been tactically unwise because Erhard's future was so uncertain. The danger was that the Americans might appear to be the culprits. As we have seen, however, the U.S. government was under strong pressure not to compromise and saw little choice. It did not escape all the blame for Erhard's fall, but the prevailing opinion was that Erhard's fate was sealed anyway and that the visit was just the last straw.[135] The indirect impact of the offset problem was more decisive than Erhard's visit to Washington. The exact role of offset commitments in the budget problem cannot be determined, due to the scarcity of available sources; it seems, however, that it was considerable.[136] Erhard's inept handling of foreign affairs became glaringly clear during this crisis. In the end, it was the budget that brought him down. Offset was a powerful symbol of Erhard's failure in both foreign and economic policy, and this made the issue a strong factor in the breakdown of his government.

Questions of responsibility, however, are only of secondary importance to the main argument of this book. The central purpose of this chapter has been to show the multifaceted nature of domestic and international, economic and political, and structural and temporary factors that shaped events and decisions on offset. During the Erhard visit the situation was exacerbated when a mélange of long-term factors (balance-of-payments problems, the British economic crisis, de Gaulle's challenge, détente, the

135 Theo Sommer, in his influential *Foreign Affairs* article in April 1967, wrote that "it was American insensitivity which brought Erhard down" (483). In the same vein, see Roger Morgan, *The U.S. and West Germany, 1945–1973: A Study in Alliance Politics* (London, 1974), 146–8.
136 *Süddeutsche Zeitung*, Oct. 27 and 29, 1966.

crisis in German foreign policy, Vietnam) was combined with the impact of short-term developments like the sterling crisis in July 1966, German budgetary problems, the sudden troop-cut resolution in the U.S. Congress, and the dim prospects for the U.S. balance of payments in 1966. Offset was the glue that kept all these disparate elements together. It had become institutionalized in a rather rigid form, particularly in Washington. When its further implementation became impossible, an immobilized German government was not able to change the modus and escape the commitment. Thus, the most important function of offset became temporarily unfeasible: It could no longer provide a protective shield for the currencies under pressure, the pound and the dollar, nor guarantee the continuity of Germany's military protection by its allies, symbolized by the troop commitments. The issue in the trilateral negotiations was whether another form of "glue" could be found to keep these positions intact or whether either Anglo–American monetary policies or German security policies must be revised. Such revisions would have signified the abandonment of the long-standing fundamentals of each country's foreign policy. It is no surprise that the trilateral negotiations turned out to be everything but smooth.

9

The Trilateral Negotiations of 1966–1967

FULFILLING THE MCNAMARA–HASSEL AGREEMENT

On October 11, 1966, President Lyndon Johnson announced that the governments of the Federal Republic, the United Kingdom, and the United States were about to

undertake a searching reappraisal of the threat to security and – taking into account changes in military technology and mobility – of the forces required to maintain adequate deterrence and defense in Central Europe. The reappraisal will also deal with: equitable sharing of defense and other comparable burdens, the impact of troop-deployments and force levels on the balance of payments of the United States and the United Kingdom, the effect on the German economic and budgetary situation of measures designed to ameliorate balance-of-payments problems.[1]

This program amounted to nothing less than a fundamental review of the Atlantic security system and its economic foundations. The trilateral negotiations are usually viewed as the first step toward the reform of NATO in the late 1960s, paving the way for NATO's so-called Harmel report on "The Future Tasks of the Alliance" at the end of 1967.[2] At issue was not only whether NATO would survive the crisis of 1966–7 but also whether the dollar-gold system could be preserved and whether a mechanism different from the previous offset practice could absorb the frictions between the monetary and the security systems. How this task was resolved and what factors determined the solution is a largely un-known story.

---

1 PP Johnson 1966, II: 1139.
2 The best analysis of this process is Haftendorn, *Kernwaffen*. On the Trilaterals, see Treverton, *Dollar Drain*; Wightman, "Money"; Georg F. Duckwitz, "Truppenstationierung und Devisenausgleich," *Aussenpolitik* 8 (1967): 471–5.

Before any serious negotiations about the future of transatlantic burden sharing and NATO force structures in Europe could start, several immediate questions required rapid solution. The most pressing was the ominous legacy of the unfortunate Erhard visit: the unfulfilled 1965–7 offset agreement. This issue was – by German–American agreement – to be dealt with separately from the trilateral exercise. The language adopted in the communiqué of the visit was that the German government would "do its best" to fulfill the agreement. The Americans took this as a binding commitment. Heated disputes among Ludwig Erhard, Gerhard Schröder, and the American ambassador, George C. McGhee, were the consequence.[3] The chancellor, who insisted that he had not caved in to American pressure in Washington, at one point furiously stormed out of a meeting. Schröder uttered thinly veiled threats that the Federal Republic might start a reorientation of its whole foreign policy. But those were only rearguard skirmishes by a desperate government. All parties in the German parliament acknowledged that Germany was obliged to honor the commitment if the United States did not grant a moratorium – and the Americans showed no inclination to do so. In what turned out to be his last weeks in office, Erhard faced the enormous challenge of obtaining the necessary funds. He complained bitterly to John J. McCloy, the chief U.S. negotiator at the Trilaterals, about Johnson's refusal to grant him an extension of the commitment and accused his defense minister of carelessness when concluding the May 1964 agreement with Robert McNamara.[4] However, it had been the chancellor's own imprudence that had prevented the exemption clause of the agreement from becoming effective. When, in his personal meetings with Johnson and McNamara, he should have insisted on a mutual revision of the agreement, he vacillated and was irresolute. Now, caught in a hopeless political situation, the

---

3 Erhard-McGhee meeting, Oct. 6, 1966, AAPD 1966, doc. 315, 1315; Schröder-McGhee meeting, Oct. 13, 1966, AAPD 1966, doc. 325, 1344–50.

4 Bonn no. 4833, Oct. 21, 1966, LBJL, NSF, NSC histories: Trilaterals, box 50; McCloy-Erhard meeting, Oct. 20, 1966, AAPD 1966, doc. 342, 408–13. Prior to the Erhard visit, the Germans and the Americans had disagreed on the interpretation of the McNamara-Hassel protocol. The Germans thought that the safeguard clause, on which Strauss had insisted as part of the 1962 agreement, was still valid. The Americans contested that. The German version of the protocol is ambiguous. Strauss had made the offset commitment "subject to the availability of funds," whereas the 1964 agreement coupled it to a German need for new weapons and to the economic competitiveness of the U.S. "goods." See McGhee papers, 1988 add., box 2; AAPD, 1964, 526n2. This is why McNamara, in his public statements, emphasized the insufficient equipment of the Bundeswehr as well as the competitiveness of U.S. weaponry. Erhard had committed himself several times to the full execution of the agreement without reservations, for example in the communiqué of the December 1965 meeting with Johnson. It is probably for this reason that the Germans did not attempt to dispute the safeguard clause during the talks in September 1966. A stronger German government could well have insisted on another interpretation.

chancellor was unable to offer more than vague suggestions. The only way out seemed to be help from the Bundesbank. But the bank balked. Its council (ZBR) refused to subscribe to the compromise formula that its president, Blessing, had proposed in Washington and informed the government that confidence in the German currency would be undermined if the bank were dragged into closing budgetary gaps. It was unwilling to tie up a huge amount of liquid funds in long-term (U.S. Treasury) bonds of a foreign country and thus lose a good deal of flexibility in its monetary policy. The members of the ZBR argued that in any case such an investment would be tantamount to the extension of a loan to the federal government, which was illegal according to Bundesbank rules.[5] The Bundesbank set two conditions the government had to fulfill before talks might even begin about possible ways around the impasse: first, parliamentary approval of a supplementary Federal budget for 1966, and second, increased defense appropriations for 1967 so the Bundesbank could be reimbursed if it provided any emergency help. Blessing later confirmed this to Ambassador McGhee, who reported to Washington: "Blessing had no desire to move to help Erhard until he took the necessary steps to help himself by an increase in the budget. . . . Blessing would not advance funds until he was assured of later repayments through the military budget."[6] Erhard's government neither was able to force the Bundesbank to moderate its conditions nor could it push through a hostile parliament an augmented budget with corresponding tax increases. The politically explosive idea of investing some German social security funds in U.S. Treasury bonds had to be abandoned as soon as the first rumors became public.[7] The only concession Erhard achieved was the Bundesbank's reluctant advance of funds for the prepayment of postwar debts, as it had done in 1961.[8]

The whole episode was the culmination of an increasingly assertive Bundesbank policy toward Erhard's government in 1965–6. The German central bank had repeatedly stated its disapproval of the government's spending policy. Confronted with a weak chancellor, it was easily able to withstand pressure by the government to relax its monetary principles. It

5 Records of 224th and 225th ZBR meeting, Oct. 6 and 20, 1966, BA, B 136/3327; Johannes Tüngeler (Bundesbank) to Carstens, Oct. 28, 1966, BBA, B 330/10245.
6 Bonn no. 6967: Meeting of McGhee with Blessing, Dec. 9, 1966, LBJL, NSF, NSC histories: Trilaterals, box 51.
7 Memorandum: Basic considerations in a solution of the current and future German offset problems, Oct. 15, 1966, McGhee papers, 1988add., box 2; *Süddeutsche Zeitung*, Oct. 19, Nov. 2, 1966.
8 Memorandum for the chancellor: ZBR meeting, Oct. 6, 1966; Blessing to Westrick, Oct. 10, 1966, both in BA, B 136/3135.

became and remained an important player in a question that had previously been the exclusive domain of the government: the financial management of the Western Alliance. Until then, the Bundesbank's policies regarding the defense of the dollar at the international financial meetings of the 1960s had been separated from the government's efforts to neutralize the U.S. troop cost, at least on the surface. The events of 1966–7 made the continuation of this rather artificial division impossible.

Kurt Georg Kiesinger's "Grand Coalition" of Christian Democrats and Social Democrats, which came to power on December 1, 1966, decided to honor Erhard's financial pledges. Its huge majority in parliament enabled it to prepare a supplementary budget for 1966 and effect spending cuts for 1967 without the furious opposition Erhard had encountered. To combat recession was the first priority for the new government. The economics minister, Karl Schiller, and Franz-Josef Strauss, back in the federal cabinet as finance minister, resorted to Keynesian policy and deficit spending for the first time in the Federal Republic's existence.[9] This made possible the fulfillment of the Hassel–McNamara agreement. Government bonds were placed on the market, which yielded enough income to pay $250 million to the United States at the end of the year and another $125 million in 1967.[10] These funds were to be covered by future defense budgets. The settlement of postwar debts, which, as a gesture of goodwill by the United States, did not have to be matched by military orders later on, amounted to $192 million. That left a gap of $325 million, which had been established during the Erhard visit ($892 million). Once more mortgaging future defense budgets with additional advance payments on prospective military purchases in the United States, the Federal Republic was able to transfer the final installment of the 1965–7 agreement in the first half of 1967.[11] As a consequence, the level of German advance funds on future military orders in U.S. accounts rose to almost $1 billion in June 1967. The German government knew that it would be unable to place any additional orders above this sum in 1967, which greatly reduced the options for the new offset agreement. For the moment, however, the advance payments were of great value to the American monetary position. In 1966 the liquidity deficit would have amounted to about $2.6 billion instead of the official $2.15 billion (which was only a slight drop

---

9 Giersch, Paqué, and Schmieding, *Fading Miracle*, 146–8.
10 *Süddeutsche Zeitung*, Dec. 28, 1966.
11 Background paper for Brandt visit: current US/FRG offset, Feb. 6, 1967, DDRS 1992/ 3537; Bonn no. 15302: Kiesinger visit: military offset, June 27, 1967, McGhee papers, 1988add., box 1.

compared to 1965). The payments were the major element in the "special transactions" that kept the deficit in the first half of 1967 at $1 billion rather than the $2.7 billion projected in the absence of these transactions.[12] Thus, the U.S. government managed to hide the increasing effects of Vietnam on the balance of payments.

The trilateral negotiations got off to a very slow start. The main reason was the German government crisis, which precluded firm decisions until January. The British, who had joined the exercise very unenthusiastically, posed another substantial difficulty because they had continued to pursue their bilateral offset talks with the Germans even after they had agreed to the Trilaterals. A gap of $125 million remained between the German offer and the British request for $215 million and, at the end of October 1966, the talks were suspended. The British government initiated preparations for troop reductions. Time was pressing because the measures were to take effect before the new budget was to be presented to parliament in April 1967. A comprehensive review of the strategic and military ramifications of the cuts was considered a luxury, and British representatives told the Americans openly that they were interested only in the financial aspect of the Trilaterals.[13] There was to be no mistake that for the British the commitment to sterling and to budgetary exigencies had absolute priority over any NATO strategic doctrines or cordial relations with Germany. The situation on the currency markets was so tight that the government saw no margin left for compromising on the troop-cost problem.

On closer examination, however, a series of political and practical problems inherent in immediate troop cuts emerged. The first was the old issue of where to house the returning troops.[14] Second, the "special relationship" interfered once more. Lyndon Johnson urged London in strong terms to refrain from any action that would prejudice the trilateral exercise.[15] Reductions in Europe therefore required careful advance

---

12 The figure also includes a $500 million purchase of U.S. Treasury bonds by the Bundesbank which was a result of the Trilaterals. See meeting in the president's office, Aug. 10, 1967, LBJL, Fowler papers, box 49–50.

13 Memorandum on Brown-Rusk conversation, Oct. 14, 1966, DDRS 1993/323; Leddy to Rusk, Nov. 8, 1966, LBJL, NSF, NSC histories: Trilaterals, box 51; memorandum on Healey-McNamara conversation, Dec. 14, 1966, LBJL, NSF, NSC histories: Trilaterals, box 50.

14 Bartlett, *Long Retreat*, 220.

15 LBJ to Wilson, Oct. 6, 1966, in FRUS 1964–68, XIII, 477–8.

preparation with the Americans. A third obstacle in the way of reductions was the new bid for EEC membership that the British government planned at the end of 1966. This placed the United Kingdom in an already familiar dilemma. Was it advisable to snub exactly those countries on whose support Britain would have to rely for EEC acceptance? These reasons appear to have convinced Prime Minister Harold Wilson that if he went ahead with reductions straight away he would find himself under attack from all sides. The catch was that the Labour government had already publicly committed itself to a firm position. A renunciation of cuts would have looked like backing down before foreign pressure. Wilson needed some compensation to solve the dilemma and placate his domestic critics. The Americans came to the same conclusion. They feared that if the British started to reduce, they would set in motion a wave that might well lead to irresistible pressure in the United States to follow suit. This would have rendered the Trilaterals moot before they even started. Thus, Johnson proposed an alternative to Wilson:

Would it help if I placed in the United Kingdom in the near future $35 million in orders beyond those already agreed to? I think I could do so on assurance from you that you will stay with us and the Germans in completing this fundamental review . . . making no change in your troop and supply dispositions there until after the completion of the review. . . . This procurement would supplement the accruals of dollars to you associated with the recent shift of our forces and installations to Britain from the Continent.[16]

This gave the British government a welcome opportunity to save face and the necessary time to prepare for the practicalities of a troop cut. Accepting the offer, the British announced a delay in any final decision for six months, at the end of which they would call on NATO and the WEU to set the reduction process in motion.[17] The Trilaterals could start.

The representatives chosen by the governments for the talks were McCloy on the American side, State Secretary Karl Carstens from the Auswärtiges Amt on the German side (he was later replaced by State Secretary Georg Ferdinand Duckwitz), and George Thomson for Britain. The choices signaled important institutional changes. McCloy, the former high commissioner in Germany, was a strong supporter of Atlanticist policy in

---

16 Johnson to Wilson, Nov. 15, 1966, in FRUS 1964–68, XIII, 492; on the genesis of the American offer, see Treverton, *Dollar Drain*, 123–4.
17 London no. 4234: Eugene Rostow talks in London, Nov. 22, 1966, in FRUS 1964–68, XIII, 499; memorandum on Healey-McNamara conversation, Dec. 14, 1966, LBJL, NSF, NSC histories: Trilaterals, box 50.

the U.S. government. The State Department acquired an important ally in the struggle against the seemingly inevitable reduction of the U.S. commitment in Europe. In Germany, the appointment of Carstens returned the principal responsibility for offset to the Auswärtiges Amt and removed it from the Finance and Defense ministry track. This assured that the broader objectives of German foreign policy would carry more weight than they had in the past. Finally, Thomson as cabinet minister had the necessary authority to defend the Trilaterals against the reduction front at home. The first meetings of the negotiators were devoted to setting the agenda for the talks and to silencing the protests from other NATO countries, which felt excluded from a very important strategic review. They had to be assured that they were not going to be presented with a fait accompli by the Big Three without being consulted.[18] For this reason the secretary general of NATO, Manlio Brosio, was allowed to participate in the talks. Three working groups were formed to look at the interrelated issues of Warsaw Pact military capabilities, NATO capabilities, and the balance-of-payments effects of troop stationing. This last group was tasked with establishing the real net foreign exchange drains and gains resulting from troop presence in Germany.[19] More crucial than the deliberations of these working groups, however, were the debates within the participating governments themselves.

THE AMERICAN DEBATE ON THE TRILATERALS

After Erhard's delegation had departed, the old rift in the U.S. government between troop-reduction supporters and their adversaries grew deeper than ever before. For the first time the discussion was strongly influenced by public debate. The essential question was whether the United States should continue its traditional European policy or give priority to the pressing political and financial exigencies of the moment. The Mansfield resolution and the end of the previous offset mechanism introduced important new elements into the debate. McNamara felt that he now, finally, would be able to effect a large reduction of U.S. forces in Europe. As we have seen, this was motivated not only by Vietnam, as most contemporary observers suspected, but also by McNamara's now six-year-old effort to achieve a modern and economically rational posture for U.S.

---

18 McCloy briefing for NATO representatives, Oct. 22, 1966, LBJL, NSF, NSC histories: Trilaterals, box 51, Paris 6006.
19 Terms of reference for working group on balance of payments, Nov. 19, 1966, ibid.; circular telegram, Dec. 5, 1966, AAPD 1966, doc. 386, 1583–6.

forces abroad.[20] Five days after Erhard had left, the secretary of defense circulated a memorandum on "NATO Strategy, Force Levels, and Balance of Payments," in which he argued for a reduction of U.S. forces in Europe by 50,000 men and the dual basing of almost all the U.S. Air Force personnel deployed in Europe.[21] Clearly, the U.S. government would not be able to participate meaningfully in the Trilaterals if it did not make a basic decision on the fundamental issues addressed in the McNamara memorandum. The debate dragged on for months. The first voice raised against McNamara's proposal came from the Joint Chiefs of Staff (JCS).[22] McCloy also immediately expressed his strong disagreement with McNamara's plans. In a lengthy report for the president on the basic issues of the Trilaterals, he emphasized the "historical" argument that the U.S. forces were the pacifiers of Europe and had prevented the outbreak of another European war. He argued that NATO was on the brink of falling apart and that American and British troop withdrawals would decisively accelerate this trend.[23] Both the JCS and McCloy realized that circumstances rendered some reductions almost unavoidable and included in their memoranda recommendations on the least damaging ways of effecting them. Their interventions had the desired effect of delaying the immediate decision McNamara sought. However, McCloy's effort to sever the link between troop levels and money by forcing first a purely political and military decision on troop levels failed.[24] The credo of the majority in the U.S. government remained as it had been for years: "The final decision on U.S. forces will inevitably depend in part on how much money McCloy can get out of the Germans."[25]

Time was pressing. The British government became increasingly nervous about the delay, and news from Germany bade ill. In January 1967 the German cabinet decided to put a virtual stop to military offset for both the United States and the United Kingdom. During a visit

20 A summary of DOD measures to reduce foreign exchange losses during McNamara's tenure is in "Statement Summarizing Actions by the DOD," FY 1961–7, LBJL, Fowler papers, box 1. Attempts to convince U.S. personnel abroad of the gravity of the balance-of-payments problem sometimes took quite unconventional forms. In 1966, for example, the GIs were subjected to a movie titled *Gold and You*, which described actions every army member could take to help alleviate the dollar drain.

21 The memorandum, dated October 4, is not yet declassified. Its contents can be deduced from the JCS response to it: JCS to McNamara, Oct. 27, 1966, LBJL, NSF, NSC histories: Trilaterals, box 51.

22 Ibid.

23 McCloy report: "Political Effects of NATO Troop Reductions; Military Effects of U.S. Force Changes in Europe," Nov. 21, 1966, LBJL, NSF, NSC histories: Trilaterals, box 50.

24 Treverton, *Dollar Drain*, 143.

25 Rostow to president, Nov. 23, 1966, LBJL, NSF, memos to president: Walt Rostow, box 11.

in London soon afterward State Secretary Klaus Schütz from the Auswärtiges Amt shocked his hosts with a public announcement that German payments would not reach the $350 million a year that had been the final offer to Britain in October 1966 and that British negotiators had at that time declared to be completely insufficient. When the British ambassador in Bonn delivered his official protest, he remarked that his instructions contained some of the strongest wording he had seen in his long diplomatic career.[26] The British government threatened that it might have to drastically cut its troops not only in Europe but also East of Suez. The Americans were told that Britain's preparations for its membership application to the Common Market were in danger.[27] It was clear that, unless the January decision of the German cabinet was altered, the whole trilateral exercise would fail. All observers agreed that the consequences would be disastrous. If the Americans wanted to avoid both the failure of their initiative and the risk of severe damage to both security and the monetary system, they had to keep this explosive situation under control by taking a position that demonstrated the intentions of the U.S. government. Would it put its full weight behind the effort to save the traditional structure of the alliance or would it take the lead in initiating far-reaching changes? McCloy pressed for the first position and for an unambiguous sign that the United States saw the preservation of the alliance as its overriding goal. Such a position required a positive statement on the future presence of American military forces in Europe. A presidential decision was needed.

The opposing sides in the U.S. government summed up their arguments in a whole series of memoranda. The Pentagon, tacitly supported by the Treasury Department, recommended the withdrawal of two of five divisions and a large part of the U.S. Air Force, that is, six of nine air wings in Europe. They were to remain allocated to the European theater and periodically be transferred there for training purposes. The State Department, the JCS, and McCloy brought up a familiar range of counterarguments: First, the relocations would save only relatively small amounts of foreign exchange; second, they would undercut the Flexible Response strategy; third, they would lead to deep cuts in European military expenditure; fourth, they would encourage Soviet pressure on Europe; fifth, they would result in declining American influence over

26 Foreign Minister Brandt–Ambassador Frank K. Roberts conversation, Jan. 25, 1967, AAPD 1967, doc. 30, 174.
27 German Embassy, Washington, to AA, no. 447: Trilaterals, Thomson visit to Washington, Feb. 17, 1967, PA-AA, B150/1967.

Europe; and sixth, they might destabilize Western Europe and NATO, and increase the danger of German nationalism.[28] The State Department therefore advocated a reduction/rotation of only one division and three air wings; McCloy was against any reduction. LBJ voiced his opposition to cuts in principle, not without pointing to the insufficient defense efforts of the United Kingdom and the Federal Republic, and, in particular, to domestic pressures. In mid-January, as a reaction to the slow progress of the talks with NATO, Mansfield had reintroduced his resolution calling for large-scale reductions. The president met with the congressional leadership to sound out the strength of the Mansfield group.[29] Faced with the arguments of the senators, Johnson hesitated to take a definite position, although he indicated that he preferred to remove as few men as possible. When, during the meeting prior to his departure for Europe for the next round of the trilateral negotiations, McCloy complained about his vague instructions, LBJ explained his position in a monologue colored by graphic, hill-country metaphors.[30] What emerged, apart from the president's asides about "stinginess" as part of the German national character and about ways to deal with the "babies" on Capitol Hill, did not satisfy McCloy: He should go to Europe and find out what the Europeans were ready to contribute.[31] Only then would the president make a decision on the troop-level issue.

McCloy was left with three basic guidelines for conducting the negotiations: "Force levels should be determined through agreement among the Allies on the basis of only security considerations, broadly construed; Germany should decide what levels of procurement in the U.S. and Britain it wishes to undertake in order to bring its military forces up to the appropriate strength levels; simultaneously, the Allies should deal with the remaining balance-of-payments consequences of allied troops stationed in Germany by cooperation in its management of monetary reserves."[32] These guidelines were probably not as precise as McCloy had

---

28 McCloy to Eugene Rostow, Feb. 9, 1967, and McCloy to president: Force levels in Europe, Feb. 23, 1967, both in LBJL, NSF, NSC histories: Trilaterals, box 50; JCS to secretary of defense: "Military Redeployments from Europe," Feb. 2, 1967, and Rostow, Bowie, Leddy, and Kitchen to Rusk: "OSD Proposals for Reducing U.S. Forces in Europe," Jan. 30, 1967, both in ibid., box 51.

29 Record of president's meeting with the congressional leadership, Feb. 27, 1967, LBJL, NSF, NSC histories: Trilaterals, box 50; Williams, *Senate*, 148–53.

30 Memorandum on president's conversations with McCloy, Mar. 1, 1967, LBJL, NSF, NSC histories: Trilaterals, box 50.

31 In February 1967 Kiesinger delivered a speech in which he used the phrase "atomic complicity" to describe U.S.–Russian negotiations on a nonproliferation treaty. This infuriated Johnson and poisoned relations between the two men.

32 President to McCloy, Mar. 1, 1967, in FRUS 1964–68, XIII, 536–7.

wished; however, they embodied important preliminary positions on several issues. The first principle indicated that the Allies would have a voice in the decision about troop levels. Therefore, it would be very difficult politically to reduce by as much as McNamara envisaged. That only "security considerations" were to decide future force levels, however, was – even broadly construed – wishful thinking. The second principle put an end to 100 percent military offset, formalizing a conclusion the American government had reached at the end of 1966.[33] Public criticism had been so outspoken in Germany that a continuation of the U.S. sales operations on the previous scale was impossible. Even in the United States, apprehension emerged. McNamara had to defend the operations of his sales division against mounting criticism in Congress.[34] The third principle pointed to the future solution of the offset problem: the wider field of monetary cooperation between the United States and the Federal Republic. In a cover memo to the president for one of the meetings on the troop-level question, Francis M. Bator had outlined the two major issues that Johnson was to consider before making a decision: "how the troop decision will affect German cooperation on money; and, most crucially, your judgment about the feedback on politics at home."[35] The president was particularly sensitive on the second issue and needed no reminder, faced as he was with an increasingly fractious Congress and elections drawing nearer. Bator even predicted that if NATO entered a deep crisis because of U.S. troop reductions this would give Republicans and Johnson's Democratic rivals (among them Robert F. Kennedy) a potent weapon for criticizing the president's conduct of foreign policy. These apprehensions were probably foremost in the president's mind when he hesitated to accede to McNamara's proposals. The problem was how to sell this restraint to Congress. To escape the dilemma of either becoming the president who had greatly weakened NATO or causing an uproar in Congress over a continuation of previous force levels without financial compensation, Bator recommended a monetary deal with the Germans. This might shield the president from domestic criticism, if he decided to keep the reductions to a minimum.

33 Egon Bahr memorandum: "Conversation with Ray S. Cline," Jan. 26, 1967, AAPD 1967, doc. 32, 180.

34 See, e.g., the remarks by Congressman Ellender and Senator J. William Fulbright, who accused McNamara of arming the world indiscriminately; PSSD, reel XV, House Committee on Armed Services, Jan. 1967, 32; 90th U.S. Cong., Senate Committee on Foreign Relations, Mar. 2, 1967, 137–40.

35 Memorandum for president: "U.S. Position in Trilateral Negotiations," Feb. 23, 1967, LBJL, Bator papers, box 4.

There is no hope for any sort of new 100 percent military offset deal with the Germans. However, we may be able to get them to agree to financial steps which would be far more valuable. Specifically: that they will not use their dollars, old or new, to buy gold; that they will join us in pushing the other Europeans, ex-France, to agree to the same sort of rules; to support us against France in negotiations on longer-range monetary reform; to neutralize the military imbalance by buying and holding securities which would count against our balance-of-payments deficit. If we can also get the Italians, Dutch and the Belgians, as well as the United Kingdom, Canada, Japan, to play by such rules, we will have negotiated the world onto a dollar standard. It will mean recognition of the fact that, for the time being, the U.S. must necessarily play banker of the world and that the continuing threat to convert to gold is simply unacceptable.[36]

In a conversation with the president one week later, Walt Rostow drew the same connection between monetary concessions by Germany and congressional acceptance of a continued stable troop level in Europe: "If we get a good money bargain with the Germans, which will really help stabilize the monetary situation and provide protection for the dollar, then perhaps we can turn the situation around in Congress."[37]

Bator's proposal was sweeping, openly combining the large security and money issues that formed the structural background of the offset complex. If it was implemented, the final decision regarding troop levels in Europe, with all its implications for Alliance policy and the European security structure, would depend on a basic pact between the Federal Republic and the United States regarding the continuation of the dollar-gold system. The idea of a formal no-gold-conversion pledge by Germany's government and central bank was to put an end to speculation that the Federal Republic might follow de Gaulle's example. Such a pledge would "crown" German monetary cooperation with the United States during the 1960s. The previously informal agreement between the Americans and the Germans regarding the structure of the alliance and international monetary relations would be moved to a new level, a clear quid pro quo that would allow each side to pursue – with the clear-cut support of the other – essential foreign policies that were crucial to the shape of international politics during the 1960s. The American government would support a security structure in Europe, the rationality of which was in serious doubt in both government and public spheres. The Federal Republic would help stabilize an international monetary structure it considered increasingly flawed. This was the core of the proposal Bator had outlined to the president.

36 Ibid.
37 Memorandum for the record, Mar. 2, 1967, LBJL, NSF, NSC histories: Trilaterals, box 50.

DEBATE IN GERMANY AND THE BLESSING LETTER

Similar proposals had occasionally been suggested by American planners since Kennedy's administration. A standstill agreement on gold conversion between Europe and the United States had been debated in 1962. Douglas Dillon and Robert Roosa, however, thought this would be an unnecessarily alarming signal and that the dollar problem could be brought under control by less drastic measures.[38] During deliberations at the State Department on how to continue offset after the Erhard visit, the proposal was tabled anew by the Treasury Department.[39] The Germans were informed that such a pledge would be of great help to the United States and probably very helpful with regard to the offset problem.[40] Not surprisingly, the Bundesbank refused to consider a commitment with such potentially enormous consequences. In late 1966 there was still hope for different solutions to the offset muddle. It soon became apparent, however, that the offset talks within the framework of the Trilaterals would lead nowhere. The trilateral studies on war capability and strategy, which had been concluded relatively quickly, played an increasingly secondary role compared to the pressing financial questions. One of the ambiguous goals of the Trilaterals had been to establish new ways for dealing with the foreign exchange cost of the troops. The first necessary step seemed to consist of establishing a commonly accepted measure for net drains and gains. The Federal Republic hitherto had accepted the figures supplied by the United States and Great Britain. It claimed, however, that its true gains were considerably less because of the numerous side effects of troop expenditures. The working group on balance of payments within the framework of the trilateral negotiations was to review this question comprehensively.[41] The result made it clear that arriving at precise figures was impossible as long as there was no agreement on economic methods and on the extent of the overall effects of military spending. How the German reserve position would have looked without foreign troops on its soil was ultimately incalculable. The Americans, for example, arrived at a considerably higher figure for German net balance-of-payment gains than the

---

38 Heller to Kennedy, Aug. 9, 1962, in FRUS 1961–63, IX, 138–41; Kennedy to Dillon and Ball, Aug. 24, 1962, in FRUS 1961–63, IX, 138–41; Wightman, "Money," 54–5.
39 Knowlton to McCloy: Treasury paper on future German offset agreements, Nov. 8, 1966, LBJL, NSF, NSC histories: Trilaterals, box 51.
40 Memorandum for the chancellor: Trilaterals, Nov. 28, 1967, BA, B 136/3135.
41 Treasury paper: "Net Balance-of-Payments Costs in the Military Accounts," Oct. 28, 1966, and "Terms of Reference for the Working Group on Military Balance of Payments," Nov. 19, 1966, both in LBJL, NSF, NSC histories: Trilaterals, box 51.

Germans themselves: $630 million as opposed to $350 million.[42] At the end of December the task of reaching a common position was declared impossible. The old practice of the stationing countries providing estimates was re-established, and the negotiations turned to the task of finding a compromise despite the differences and uncertainties. The American estimate for troop costs in 1967–9 was $850–$900 million a year.[43] The relatively simple objective was to have this sum covered by offset to the maximal extent possible. First priority was still accorded to military sales. A second possibility was civilian purchases, such as space equipment, foreign-aid projects, and so forth; but the Germans, because of their bad experience with the British and the strong protests of German industry, were reluctant to include civilian purchases in an offset agreement. More promising was a third option: German investment in U.S. bond issues. Negotiations on such transactions were pursued between the Bundesbank and the U.S. Treasury.[44] This would have been an extension of the various German investments in U.S. issues to support the American balance of payments, but the idea of German investment in interest-bearing certificates was difficult to sell to Congress as a concession. Thus, the idea of a nonconversion pledge remained the major hope for a solution. Whether Bonn would agree to this proposal in the end depended on basic decisions of the new government about the future direction of Germany's foreign policy.

One of the common policies of the coalition partners in the Kiesinger government was to avoid Erhard's mistake of getting locked into an agreement that could become a constraint and a liability in both foreign and domestic policies. Strauss, in particular, was against any material concessions to the United States and the United Kingdom. First, the mortgaging of future budgets caused by the previous agreement curtailed funds for any purchases. Second, he and many others thought that military orders should be redirected to German industry and to France.[45] This would have been a step toward escaping the clutches of the U.S. government in military matters. After the Erhard visit resentment about assertive American policies went beyond the Gaullists. The simple ques-

42 Attachment to McCloy report: "Balance-of-Payments Issues," Nov. 21, 1966, ibid., box 50; circular telegram by State Secretary Carstens: Trilaterals, Nov. 14, 1966, AAPD 1966, doc. 368, 1519–21; Duckwitz, "Truppenstationierung," 473.
43 White House background paper for Brandt visit, Feb. 6, 1967, DDRS 1994/3538.
44 The U.S. government wanted Kiesinger to put pressure on the "Bundesbank to play the kind of flexible game that is required for offsets in terms of long-term bonds" (Rostow to president, Nov. 23, 1966, LBJL, NSF, memoranda to president: Walt Rostow, box 11).
45 Memoranda for the chancellor, Dec. 13 and 28, 1966; memorandum for cabinet meeting, Dec. 28, 1966, all in BA, B 136/3135.

tion was whether the American security guarantee was still worth the sacrifices. The discussion on future offset in the Kiesinger government inevitably became embedded in a larger conflict about the future course of German foreign policy. The Kiesinger government attempted to reach a new understanding with France after the nosedive that German–French relations had taken during Erhard's tenure. It rapidly achieved an agreement with France on a question that had poisoned relations during the last months of Erhard's chancellorship: the status of French troops in Germany.[46] Technological cooperation was intensified. The Federal Republic made an effort to promote a common EEC position for the ongoing negotiations on the creation of new reserve assets for the monetary system. This effort was closely linked to European pressure for a reform of voting procedures in the IMF, which had until then given only the United States veto power, whereas the Six even united did not have enough votes to reject measures. This attempt at Franco-German rapprochement coincided with a phase of unprecedented mistrust in German-American relations sparked by the rude treatment Erhard had received in Washington, by U.S. overtures to the East, and, above all, by the proposed Nonproliferation Treaty that to many Germans seemed like a device to discriminate against Germany indefinitely.[47] It soon became obvious, however, that France and Germany still had deep differences, whether it was over European policy, French policy toward the East Bloc, or security policy. De Gaulle had nothing really substantial to offer, and many of his moves were gestures leading nowhere.[48] There was no way around the Americans, at least as long as reunification remained the centerpiece of German foreign policy and placed Germany in hostile opposition to the Warsaw Pact. Every softening of German policy would ultimately depend on American backing. The first tentative steps of *Ostpolitik* by Brandt needed a credible *Westpolitik.* These constraints underlined the necessity of putting a stop to the rapid decline of NATO that would certainly be accelerated by large-scale reductions of U.S. troops. The alliance with the United States remained vital for the Federal Republic and so did the U.S. troop presence, the major symbol of this

---

46 For the agreement, see BPI 1966, 1304. For details on the negotiations, see F. Roy Willis, *France, Germany, and the New Europe, 1945–1967,* rev. ed. (London, 1968), 353–6; Osterheld, *Aussenpolitik,* 309–26.

47 For a typical reaction to the NPT by German conservatives, see Wilhelm G. Grewe, *Rückblenden 1976–1951* (Frankfurt am Main, 1979), 689–702. A recent study on the NPT is Susanna Schrofstetter, *Die dritte Atommacht* (Munich, 1999).

48 Memorandum by Referat IIA7: "Intensification of Franco-German Cooperation – Possibilities and Limits," Jan. 3, 1967, PA-AA, B 150/1967.

alliance. The Kiesinger government, like its predecessors, could not escape the necessity of working toward a solution of the troop-cost problem.

Under very tight budgetary constraints, however, the government had at its disposal only very few resources for a solution. The defense budget, the source of previous offset payments, underwent deep cuts. The further amassing of public debt to serve U.S. offset demands was politically impossible. The only practical way out seemed to lie in the American proposals, and this meant placing the burden on the Bundesbank's broad shoulders. Thus, in a temporary alliance with the Americans, the government "strongly advised" the Bundesbank to be more forthcoming in its talks with U.S. officials, both on the issue of investment in U.S. Treasury bonds and on general monetary cooperation.[49] The Grand Coalition reasserted the government's leadership in macroeconomic policies, which had been lost by Erhard during his last year in office. In effect, it requested that the Bundesbank compromise its monetary principles in order to provide support for basic security policy objectives that the government judged to be more important at the moment.

As in the German case, U.S. policy in this respect can be understood only within the context of the general monetary and political circumstances in early 1967. The formation of the Kiesinger government was accompanied by much speculation in the United States about the course of future German foreign policy – a situation similar to the one existing after the Franco-German treaty was signed in 1963. Doubts about German policy also extended to monetary policy. As already mentioned, 1967 was the decisive year for the American effort to create a new form of liquidity, Special Drawing Rights, which should have relieved the pressure on the dollar. The French and American positions were diametrically opposed. In early 1967 leading American commercial banks openly voiced doubts about the future of the dollar-gold exchange guarantee. A lively public debate followed, reinforced by hints from Henry H. Fowler that the United States might take drastic steps if foreign central banks did not cooperate.[50] The pressure put on the American balance of payments by the Vietnam War and the government's expansive domestic spending programs was increasing. As deficits spun out of control, hidden only by dubious statistical tricks, and as Washington embarked on a major initiative in monetary diplomacy, formal support by the new German government for U.S. monetary policy would be doubly important. A further

49 Note by State Secretary Klaus Schütz on cabinet meeting, Jan. 26, 1967, AAPD 1967, doc. 30, 167n12; Haftendorn, *Kernwaffen*, 266.
50 Strange, *International Monetary Relations*, 245.

consideration was the Kennedy round of trade talks that was approaching its final phase and from which the Americans expected a positive impact on their external balance. The United States needed German support on this issue, too. These were essential interests, and a confrontational German policy would have posed a very serious challenge. McNamara's military and political arguments in favor of troop reductions had to wait. If the troops could again serve important economic objectives, particularly to shore up the monetary system, the Treasury Department would become an ally of the State Department on the issue of troop levels in Europe. Thus, in both the German and the American governments the nonconversion pledge was transformed from a technical proposal into the major hope for a way out of the difficult dilemma that the end of the previous offset arrangement had created.

Talks between the Bundesbank and the U.S. Treasury began in January 1967. The German government stayed out of the actual negotiations to avoid the impression of government infringement on the Bundesbank's authority over monetary policy. The question of German investment in U.S. Treasury bonds was settled quite rapidly.[51] The Bundesbank representatives declared themselves ready to acquire $400–$500 million of mid-term bonds. In fact, this was an extension of the bookkeeping investments in Treasury papers that had served to limit the extent of American deficits in the previous years. The difference was the longer term of four years. The Bundesbank demanded "that the transaction be cast in such a form so as not to make it appear that the Bank is directly or indirectly financing the government or assisting it in meeting a financial obligation for which it is responsible."[52] Internally, of course, the transaction was explicitly connected to the trilateral exercise. The decisive American concession was that the Bundesbank would be allowed to redeem the bonds prematurely if German reserves fell below a critical level. The Germans demanded furthermore that the bond purchases be counted as covering troop costs not offset by military orders. The Treasury Department accepted these conditions, although this "loan" presumed an amelioration of U.S. deficits when the bonds came due. The immediate effect on the balance-of-payments statistics for 1967 had priority. The Treasury also made its main interest very clear: "A large part of our difficulties relate to the public understanding of the Bundesbank's policy, and we would

---

51 Memorandum by State Secretary Duckwitz: "Final Report on Trilateral Talks," June 17, 1967, PA-AA, B 150/1967.
52 Frederick Deming (undersecretary of the treasury) to Tüngeler (Bundesbank), Feb. 24, 1967, BBA, Emminger papers, 237.

like – in fact, we need – clearer public recognition of this policy; only in this way can we assure our Congress and the American people that our liquidity position or, more basically, our gold reserve, is not endangered as a result of our expenditures on troops in Germany."[53] Only very sparse documentation on the further course of the negotiations between the Treasury and the Bundesbank, between the German government and the German central bank, and within the bank itself is available at the moment. On March 30, 1967, Blessing sent a letter that contained the nonconversion pledge to the U.S. Treasury. It opened with the somewhat euphemistic statement that the United States had "occasionally" expressed concern over the impact of its troop-dollar losses on its balance of payments. Blessing then stated his view that these costs were only one aspect of a much more complicated picture and pointed out that German reserves had not risen significantly over the past several years. However, he continued, the Bundesbank had for years refrained from conversion of dollars into gold and – the decisive phrase in the letter – the United States "may be assured that also in the future the Bundesbank intends to continue this policy and to play its full part in contributing to international monetary cooperation." The Bundesbank had rejected a U.S. version that replaced the phrase "intends to" with the word "will" and would have constituted a legal instead of a moral commitment.[54]

Blessing later regretted the letter. In a 1971 interview he remarked that he should have been "more rigorous toward the U.S. We simply should have agressively converted the dollars we accumulated to gold until they were driven to despair."[55] This statement certainly must be put into the context of the tumultuous events on financial markets after 1968 and German resentment of Nixon's unilateral monetary policy. It does, however, indicate the serious misgivings that existed in responsible German circles before the letter was sent. It is true that the letter only confirmed a policy that had been followed for years. Nevertheless, such a policy was open to reversal at any time. Indeed, in early 1967 the German government seriously discussed the option of joining de Gaulle in asking the United States for an increase in the price of gold.[56] This would have been a revolution in transatlantic economic relations. The disadvantages of signing a pledge of nonconversion were obvious from the

---

53 Ibid.
54 Blessing to William McChesney Martin (chairman of the Federal Reserve), Mar. 30, 1967, LBJL, NSF, NSC histories: Trilaterals, box 50; Blessing to ZBR, Mar. 17, 1967, BBA, Emminger papers, 237.
55 Leo Brawand, *Wohin steuert die deutsche Wirtschaft? Mit Analysen und Prognosen* (Munich, 1971), 61.
56 Memorandum: "Rise in the Price of Gold," Jan. 12, 1967, BA, B 136/3322.

German point of view. It would foster an increasing link of the DM with the dollar because of the danger of a progressive accumulation of dollar reserves in Germany. These reserves would be slashed in the event of a dollar devaluation. Germany would therefore have a strong incentive to support every action that helped avoid this. With the Blessing letter, the Bundesbank deprived itself of an important aspect of its monetary autonomy. A foreign country acquired an increasing influence over the value of Germany's reserves. Some years later, when the Nixon administration adopted its policy of "benign neglect" toward payments deficits and flooded the market with dollars, the Federal Republic, as a main recipient, was still bound by the pledge.[57] Probably even more important than these economic aspects were the political arguments against the letter. First, Germany would lose the ability to exert pressure on the United States, similar to that exercised by France, via monetary policy; second, with the pledge, Bonn hampered its chances of pursuing a common and independent European monetary policy.[58]

Why did those counterarguments not carry enough weight? The political base of German–American relations proved decisive: The deal assured the continuation of a large American troop presence, symbolizing American adherence to the basic principles of German foreign policy. In this interest the Bundesbank had to forfeit part of its autonomy, pressed by a strong German government and the dominant monetary power, the United States. It is not without irony that as the German government was looking for a political rapprochement with France, it effectively lined up with Washington in the vital field of monetary policy. This recalls the Strauss–Gilpatric agreement, which had condemned the military sections of the later Franco–German treaty to ineffectiveness. On the occasion of Adenauer's funeral in April 1967, both de Gaulle and Johnson emphasized the crucial importance of the monetary issue to mutual relations in their conversations with Kiesinger, and a few weeks earlier, American Vice President Hubert H. Humphrey had threatened a drastic American reaction if Germany lined up with France in monetary policy.[59] The Blessing letter signaled that the Americans were the clear winners in this contest for Germany's monetary soul. The German promise not to convert its accumulated dollars to gold has been termed "the most important

57 Hoffmeyer, *Monetary System*, 89.
58 Memorandum for chancellor: "Trilateral Talks in Bonn," Nov. 28, 1966, BA, B136/3135.
59 De Gaulle-Kiesinger conversation, Apr. 25, 1967, AAPD 1967, doc. 142; LBJ-Kiesinger conversation, Apr. 24, 1967, and Kiesinger-Humphrey conversation, Apr. 5, 1967, both in PA-AA, B 150/1967.

postwar step in insulating the United States from external pressure on its reserves."[60] In essence, the Blessing letter was the codification of the major factor behind all the offset agreements and monetary measures of German financial authorities to bolster the dollar: the effort to neutralize the huge amount of free-floating dollars that threatened the American gold stock. Would the Federal Republic have taken this step without American troops on its soil? Certainly, German monetary cooperation did not depend solely on Germany's interest in a guaranteed U.S. troop presence. The international monetary system had served the Federal Republic well during most of its existence; inflationary pressure was low throughout the 1950s and 1960s. The dollar-gold standard had given governments and central banks unprecedented control over currency markets, although the rising, uncontrolled money flow in the 1960s, particularly in the Euro-dollar market, seemed to erode this control. It was natural that governments and central banks should collaborate to avoid losing control over the use of monetary instruments. Thus, the Federal Republic had a residual interest in the preservation of the system and would rather take on some unpleasant commitments than assume responsibility for its breakdown.[61] However, the price that German monetary authorities had to pay for the continuation of the system continuously increased during the 1960s. In earlier years the government bore a huge part of the burden by committing itself to offset agreements, with all the intended and unintended consequences pointed out in the previous chapters of this book. At the same time, the Bundesbank assumed an expanding role in the various international monetary emergency activities during the 1960s, sometimes in collaboration with the government, sometimes independently. In the mid-1960s the German government's part in preserving the dollar-gold system – military offset – became increasingly burdensome on its foreign policy and its budget until it finally became impossible to continue; its emphasis changed to wholly monetary measures. Investment in U.S. Treasury bonds and the Blessing letter were expressions of this new reality. The fact that the Federal Republic pursued this policy, despite the increasing risks of supporting the dollar–gold system, even when it infringed on its monetary autonomy, cannot be explained by economic reasons alone. The security relationship with the United States was a major factor – probably *the* major factor – in West Germany's support of American monetary policy.

60 Bergsten, *Dilemmas of the Dollar*, 31.
61 For German monetary policy and German measures to support the dollar-gold system, see Thiel, *Dollar-Dominanz*, 137–50, esp. table on 147.

The U.S. government hoped that the Blessing letter would finally free the United States from some of the balance-of-payments constraints that had hampered Eisenhower, Kennedy, and Johnson so much since 1958. Bator wrote: "If we succeed – and after some serious education on the Hill and in the financial community – we will no longer need to worry about reasonable balance-of-payments deficits. This arrangement will not give us an unlimited printing press. But as long as we run our economy as responsibly as in the past few years, it will permit us to live with moderate deficits indefinitely."[62] These far-fetched hopes foundered on the impossibility of "moderate" deficits in the next years. Just one year later the United States had to suspend dollar-gold convertibility for the private market. The objective of the Blessing letter had been to prevent this. It thus is unlikely that the letter prolonged the dollar-gold standard significantly.[63] Its major impact was political, that is, a reaffirmation of the cooperation between the Federal Republic and the United States to preserve the monetary and security systems.

CONCLUSION OF THE TRILATERAL TALKS

With the conclusion of the talks between the U.S. Treasury and the Bundesbank it seemed as if the biggest obstacle to success in the Trilaterals was overcome. Other difficult issues awaited resolution, however, particularly the British offset. At the end of January 1967 the state secretary of the Auswärtiges Amt, Schütz, informed his hosts during a visit to London that the German cabinet had decided to make no offset payments to Britain in 1967–8. The British reaction was sharp: Such a decision would inevitably lead to a withdrawal of large parts of the BAOR,[64] and the trilateral negotiations hit their lowest point. The Americans reacted immediately and demanded that the Germans reconsider their decision in consultation with the Allies.[65] They were reassured that Germany would continue to participate in the talks; but an acceptable offer for Britain seemed impossible.[66] The main resistance to new

---

62 Bator to president: "Trilateral – Your Meeting Tomorrow with McCloy," Mar. 8, 1967, LBJL, NSF, NSC histories: Trilaterals, box 50.

63 It might even have had the paradoxical effect of impairing confidence in the dollar, as Hoffmeyer suspects: "That the United States felt it necessary to put so much political pressure on Germany in order to protect the gold reserves was taken as a sign of weakness" (Hoffmeyer, *Monetary System*, 63).

64 London to DOS on Schütz-Brown talks, Jan. 25, 1967, LBJL, Bator papers, box 4.

65 Bonn no. 8678, Jan. 26, 1967, McGhee papers, 1988add., box 1.

66 Bonn no. 8683: Cabinet decision on offset, Jan. 26, 1967, ibid.; Bonn no. 8747: McGhee meeting with Brandt, Jan. 27, 1967, ibid.

obligations came from Finance Minister Strauss. He thought the British would reduce their troops anyway and that it made no sense to make new commitments. Many in the German government agreed. Even the officials in the Auswärtiges Amt, who considered the refusal to help Britain a politically dangerous position, had no idea how to obtain the necessary funds and professed "general helplessness."[67] On returning to Europe in March after his consultations with the president, McCloy found his main task was to get the adversaries to compromise. At the first meeting with the British and German delegations at the trilateral negotiations he voiced the grave concern of the U.S. government regarding the unproductive attitude of the other participants.[68] Soon afterward he met with Wilson and Kiesinger to impress on them the seriousness of the situation. In his conversation with the chancellor, McCloy warned that British and American troop levels were linked and that the United States was likely to follow suit if deep cuts were made in British force levels. Kiesinger retorted that British statements suggested they would reduce regardless of any German offer and that the British government did not have a record of showing much concern for German foreign policy interests. The budgetary situation was critical, and the United Kingdom had hardly any useful military or civilian goods on offer to achieve sufficient offset value.[69] On McCloy's insistence Kiesinger promised to attempt to raise the German offer. This conciliatory mood might also have been due to the increasing expressions of alarm in the memoranda he received from the Auswärtiges Amt, which predicted a disastrous chain reaction if Britain withdrew from continental defense.[70] At the end of the talk McCloy asked how Germany would react to the reduction of one U.S. division. Kiesinger merely replied that it was an "interesting suggestion." This was the first time a German chancellor had abandoned the dogma of a stable U.S. troop level that had been upheld since the Radford episode. Even in 1966 Allied troop reductions were regarded as unavoidable by the German government. However, only Kiesinger felt that the international and domestic situations forced him to accede to the American request, and then only if the redeployment was of a limited nature. In parting McCloy warned the chancellor of the unfortunate impression that would be created in the United States if the Federal Republic, as had been reported,

67 Memorandum by Günther Harkort: "Monetary Support," Feb. 20, 1967, PA-AA, B 150/1967.
68 London no. 7112/7113: trilateral talks, Mar. 3, 1967, LBJL, NSF, NSC histories: Trilaterals, box 50.
69 Rostow to president: "Kiesinger-McCloy Meeting," Mar. 6, 1967, in FRUS 1964–68, XIII, 541.
70 Memorandum by Duckwitz: "Trilaterals," Feb. 28, 1967, and "Talking Points for the Federal Defense Council," Mar. 1, 1967, both in PA-AA, B 150/1967.

were to divert its military procurement to France. Kiesinger replied – not entirely correctly – that "this was not being seriously contemplated."[71]

The following day McCloy met with Willy Brandt and went over much the same ground. Here he was clearly told that the chances of getting more money for the United Kingdom than the amount suggested in October 1966 were extremely slim.[72] Back in Washington, McCloy informed the president that the major problem blocking a successful conclusion of the trilateral negotiations was the gap between the German offer and British expectations. The U.S. government considered whether it was feasible to foot part of the bill. Both McNamara and Fowler were against picking up any of the slack; the latter was still embittered that his push for a decisive troop reduction had failed once again.[73] After some hectic work on possible alternatives, Johnson decided that he "would not see NATO go down over $40 million" (the size of the gap). He instructed McCloy to conclude the talks on the basis of limited reductions and try to get as much out of the Germans as he could before the United States put in its own money.[74] In the meantime the British indicated that they would settle for much less than 100 percent offset if the others agreed to the withdrawal of a small part of the Rhine army.[75] Everything now depended on the willingness of the Germans to raise their offer. LBJ wrote another letter to Kiesinger impressing on him once more the crucial importance of keeping substantial British forces on the continent.[76] The German decision was made during a heated cabinet meeting on March 15. Against Strauss's bitter resistance Kiesinger argued that the sums of money involved were not worth the risk of a breakdown of the Atlantic Alliance. He achieved an increase of the German offer to $112 million, split equally between military and civilian goods.[77] The British, under pressure from Washington, decided to include U.S. aid from December and the gains from the relocation of U.S. forces from France to Britain as part of the offset and thus reduced the gap to about $20 million. This was a sum the United States was willing to pay as a price for the rapid

71 Rostow to president: "Kiesinger–McCloy Meeting," Mar. 6, 1967, in FRUS 1964–68, XIII, 545.
72 Bonn no. 10267, Mar. 5, 1967, LBJL, NSF, NSC histories: Trilaterals, box 50.
73 Bator memorandum for president: "Your 12:45 Meeting with McCloy," Mar. 8, 1967; record of president's meeting with Rusk, McNamara et al., Mar. 8, both ibid.
74 Record of president's meeting with McCloy, Mar. 9, 1967, ibid.
75 Brown to Rusk, Mar. 9, 1967, ibid.; Kiesinger–Roberts meeting, Mar. 14, 1967, PA-AA, B150/1967.
76 In this letter he also requested German cooperation in reserve creation for the monetary system. See Mar. 11, 1967, in FRUS 1964–68, XIII, 546–9.
77 Bonn no. 10754: Cabinet meeting, Mar. 15, 1967, PA-AA, B150/1967; Mar. 15, 1967, LBJL, NSF, NSC histories: Trilaterals, box 50.

conclusion of the talks: It promised to procure a corresponding amount of military materiel in the United Kingdom.[78]

After this breakthrough the only remaining problem was whether the Germans would accept the American plan to redeploy 35,000 men from the Seventh Army and over 50 percent of its tactical aircraft. The Germans expressed grave concerns over the huge cut in air forces. They thought it greatly impaired NATO's strike capacity and saw it as the start of the "denuclearization" of Western Europe.[79] Shortly after Johnson's meeting with Kiesinger on the occasion of Adenauer's funeral the McCloy–State Department faction won another victory over McNamara: LBJ decided to limit the cuts to 96 aircraft (instead of the 144 originally planned). Again, the argument that this would make the Germans more forthcoming on international money and the Kennedy round carried the day.[80] At the end of April a series of agreed-on minutes was signed recording the results of the Trilaterals.[81] The BAOR was reduced by 5,000 men and two aircraft squadrons. The United States cut back by 35,000 men and 96 of its 216 tactical aircraft in Germany. One-third of these forces were to remain in Germany on a rotational basis, a costly system that was soon abandoned. All in all, the continuity of the large-scale presence of American and British soldiers in the Federal Republic was secured, an enormous success given the desperate situation at the beginning of the year. All sides managed to achieve their basic objectives: The British were assured that their troop commitment in Europe would place no strains on the embattled position of their currency. Like the Americans, they got a small troop reduction to silence critics at home. The U.S. government was able to present a satisfactory solution to Congress, it had averted the danger of a breakdown of NATO, and it had set the Alliance on the path toward a new strategic assessment. Most important, it had with a single stroke achieved unparalleled cooperation by the strongest monetary surplus country. The Federal Republic had preserved the security guarantees of their military allies, symbolized by the troops. The Atlantic Alliance, the essential framework for German foreign policy, had been

78 Memorandum on McCloy-Rostow conversation, Mar. 15, 1967, in FRUS 1964–68, XIII, 549–50; Bator to president: "Trilaterals Status Report," Mar. 17, 1967, and aide-mémoire U.S. government to HMG, Mar. 21, 1967, both in LBJL, NSF, NSC histories: Trilaterals, box 50.

79 Memorandum received from German embassy, Apr. 21, 1967, and U.S. government memorandum to German embassy, Apr. 22, 1967, both in ibid.; Bonn no. 12730: McGhee to LBJ: "Suggested Talking Points with Kiesinger," Apr. 25, 1967, McGhee papers, 1988add., box 1; McCloy to Rusk, Apr. 24, 1967, DDRS 1985/1021.

80 Bator to president, Apr. 27, 1967; Rusk to McCloy, Apr. 27, 1967, both in LBJL, NSF, NSC histories: Trilaterals, box 50.

81 Agreed minutes, in FRUS 1964–68, XIII, 562–9.

saved, which was extremely important at a time when Bonn was embarking on a new foreign policy course with an unknown outcome, the comprehensive accommodation with Eastern Europe that became known as
the *Neue Ostpolitik* (new policy toward the East Bloc).

THE SLOW DEMISE OF OFFSET

The trilateral agreements of April 1967 covered only one year and did
not solve the larger problems that lay at their root: the crisis of the monetary system and American and British doubts about their security commitments in Europe.[82] Already toward the end of 1967 the search for new
agreements had commenced. The ensuing negotiations were complicated
but without the acrimony of the previous years.[83] From the outset it was
clear that the Bundesbank would have to take on most of the burden
because the Federal Defense Ministry was still far from having depleted
its accounts in the United States and the United Kingdom for arms purchases. The result of the talks was a reaffirmation of the bargain struck at
the Trilaterals, a major reason for their relatively quick conclusion.[84] Most
of the offset was paid by German investment in U.S. Treasury certificates
and, for the first time, in British government bonds. Private German banks
supported the Bundesbank in this effort. The U.S. government confiden-
tially assured the Federal Republic that it would not redeploy troops
during the term of the agreement.[85]

Offset became less contested because it began to lose its significance
as a major instrument to stabilize the external balances of the reserve-
currency countries. From 1967 on, a series of tumultuous events on the
currency markets demonstrated the shifting sands on which the monetary system had been built. In late 1967 sterling came under final attack.
The British government was not able to hold the line anymore and,
in November, sterling was devalued by 14 percent. The shock of the
devaluation cleared the way for a comprehensive reappraisal of British
foreign policy, which, in January 1968, led to the decision to end the
British military presence East of Suez. Britain became a Solely European

---

82 Due to the limited availability of archival material on the period after 1967 at the time this book
was completed, the following paragraphs are not as detailed as previous chapters. The intention
here is to provide a brief summary of the major events leading to the progressive loss of
significance of the offset agreements until they were abandoned in 1976.
83 Memorandum by Political Director Harkort, June 14, 1968, AAPD 1968, doc. 192, 727–30.
84 For the details of the agreements, see Appendix 2.
85 Memorandum by Ulrich Sahm: American troop levels in Germany, June 11, 1968, PA-AA,
B150/1968.

power. The sterling predicament had been an important element in the French arguments for denying the second British application for membership in the recently renamed European Community (EC). When de Gaulle resigned in April 1969 the path was cleared for British accession. At the Hague Summit at the end of 1969 the EEC countries agreed to start negotiations with the British. All this gave the BAOR renewed political importance, and in 1970–1 the British government even shifted the brigade that had been reduced after the trilateral talks back to the continent. Offset became much less divisive and served primarily to placate critics in the British parliament. After 1968 it no longer was a major problem in Anglo–German relations.

In March 1971 an agreement for five years was concluded that stipulated German payments of $30 million per year and a declaration by the United Kingdom to keep the BAOR troop level stable.[86] The sterling devaluation directed the attention of the markets to the other reserve currency.

In early 1968 a record run on American gold reserves took place. It was not accidental that the gold crisis coincided with the Tet Offensive in Vietnam, and with overwhelming evidence that Vietnam was wrecking the American economy and with it the transatlantic economic system created after the war; this played an important role in Johnson's decision to refuse the requests by the military for more soldiers in Southeast Asia.[87] The reserves were depleted so rapidly that the member countries decided in March 1968 to stop their interventions and to decouple the private market from official transactions.[88] From then on, conversion at $35 per ounce was open only to governments. In a way, this was the end of the dollar–gold system because most central banks had already been operating on a dollar standard. Despite the turmoil LBJ remained determined to defend the dollar's exchange rate. The Federal Republic provided consistent help in this endeavor, and thus the bargain struck in 1961 with the Strauss–Gilpatric agreement was carried through the crisis.

Despite their loss of importance as monetary instruments, offset negotiations went on until the mid-1970s, with a decisive change in their character, partly due to the Vietnam conflict. Their function as monetary instruments was slowly replaced by their role as a tool in the

---

86 For the text of the agreement, see HMSO, Cmnd. 4690 (1971).
87 Robert M. Collins, "The Economic Crisis of 1968 and the Waning of the American Century," *American Historical Review* 101 (Apr. 1996): 413–16.
88 On the gold crisis, see LBJL, administrative histories: Treasury, "The Gold Crisis 1968," as well as the extensive documentation in FRUS 1964–68, VIII, International Trade and Monetary Policy. Furthermore, see Collins, "Economic Crisis," 396–422.

struggle between American presidents and Congress over the U.S. security commitment in Europe. The Mansfield Resolution of August 1966 was the first salvo in a prolonged public debate in the United States about the necessity and purpose of its troops in Europe and, in the end, about the U.S. engagement there generally. The agreements of 1968 and 1969, consisting mainly of purchases of Treasury bonds by the Bundesbank, were not at all helpful in cooling the heated debate; Senator Mike Mansfield described them as "the phoniest deal I have ever seen . . . not sharing cost but making a profitable investment."[89] In early 1968 Mansfield, in a series of public remarks and in Congress, repeated his intention to force the administration into a decisive reduction of the troop commitment in Europe. Johnson was determined to resist, however, and said "that he would have no part in dismantling voluntarily our essential troop structure in Europe before he left office next January."[90] Aided by the Soviet intervention in Czechoslovakia in August 1968 he won this fight, much to the satisfaction of the Nixon administration, which considered the European commitment an essential element of American global policy. Secretary of State William P. Rogers announced in Brussels: "We have made clear our intention to maintain our combat forces in Europe at essentially present levels until at least the middle of 1971. . . . We must maintain the military strength of our alliance until such time as we may be able to reach agreements on mutual and balanced force reductions."[91] Nixon made a resolute effort to defeat the various amendments and resolutions that flared up in Congress from 1968 to 1973.[92] Determined to avoid unilateral reductions with no corresponding cuts in Warsaw Pact forces, he succeeded in the end despite some extremely close votes in Congress. Paradoxically, it was Leonid Brezhnev who provided the most valuable help in this effort by agreeing to open negotiations on Mutual Balanced Force Reductions (MBFR). This would have made unilateral reductions by the United States a gift to the Soviets, and Congress was hesitant to go that far. Within the logic of "double containment" Brezhnev's intervention even made some sense. The turning point in the debate was the Jackson–Nunn amendment of September 1973. It forced

---

89 "Mansfield Gives Troop-Cut Views," *New York Times*, Aug. 19, 1968, 9.
90 Telegram from DOS to Rusk at Reykjavik, Iceland, June 26, 1968, in FRUS 1964–68, XIII, 721.
91 "Address Before the Belgo-American Association, Dec. 12, 1969," *DOS Bulletin*, Dec. 29, 1969, 622–3.
92 For this important debate in the United States, see John Newhouse, ed., *U.S. Troops in Europe: Issues, Costs, and Choices* (Washington, D.C., 1971); Williams, *Senate*; John Yochelson, "The American Military Presence in Germany: Current Debate in the United States," *Orbis* 15 (1971): 784–807.

the government to withdraw all troops from Europe whose cost was not covered by offset.[93] This did not represent a success for redeployment advocates, however, because the German and American governments had no difficulty satisfying the requirements of the amendment by imaginary offset methods.

Nixon was still forced to demonstrate to Congress that the American troop engagement was no burden on the United States, at least regarding the monetary costs. Despite their interest in defeating the congressional moves, the Germans were increasingly unwilling to pay the required sums, and the agreements of the early 1970s were heavily contested.[94] This also was an expression of growing divergence in other policy areas. One of these was international monetary policy.

Nixon's attitude toward international monetary matters was expressed in a remark by Secretary of the Treasury John B. Connally: "The dollar is our currency, but your problem."[95] The pursuit of international monetary cooperation had very low priority on Nixon's list of foreign policy issues. It was completely overshadowed by the search for an "honorable peace" in Vietnam, the pursuit of détente with the Soviet Union and China, and the management of the domestic economy in a way that would not endanger Nixon's re-election prospects.[96] Thus, the new administration developed no new initiatives to reform the monetary system. This policy, termed "benign neglect," was certain to produce the next monetary crisis as soon as the United States reversed the anti-inflationary course pursued in 1969–70 to control the inflation resulting from funding the Vietnam conflict. This reversal came during 1970, and it led to spectacular U.S. balance-of-payments deficits.[97] Between January 1970 and March 1973 Germany took in about $20 billion in foreign exchange, most of it from American sources.[98] Those were unheard-of sums. The Europeans, particularly the Germans, who felt morally bound by Blessing's letter and who were still dependent on U.S. security coverage for their *Ostpolitik*, were helpless in the face of the currency flood. In August 1971, faced with requests by worried Europeans about guarantees for the value of their overflowing dollar reserves, Nixon

93 Williams, *Senate*, 219–20.
94 On the agreements of the 1970s, see Thiel, *Dollar-Dominanz*, 78–85; see also AAPD 1970, docs. 15 and 297.
95 Paul Volcker and Toyoo Gyohten, *Changing Fortunes: The World's Money and the Threat to American Leadership* (New York, 1992), 81.
96 Joanne Gowa, *Closing the Gold Window: Domestic Politics and the End of Bretton Woods* (Ithaca, N.Y., 1983), 67–9.
97 Appendix 1, Table 2.   98 Emminger, *Geld- und Währungspolitik*, 532.

officially closed the gold window, and, in violation of all postwar principles of U.S. foreign economic policy, imposed a 10 percent surtax on all imports into the United States.[99] In the ensuing turmoil on the currency markets the dollar lost approximately 40 percent of its value by 1973, and the reserves of America's partners shrank, insofar as they consisted of dollars, by the same percentage. The policy of benign neglect effectively canceled the transatlantic bargain and the implicit understanding that lay behind the Blessing letter. Blessing's retrospective bitterness at not having "rigorously" converted all his dollars to gold before 1971 derives from the fact that the letter he wrote in 1967 was based on an implicit American pledge to keep the reserves Germany accumulated stable in value.

The breakdown of the postwar monetary system made very clear who really held the strings in international monetary affairs. Although Europe had grown stronger and more assertive during the 1960s, it was not strong enough to develop an alternative to the dollar. The dollar–gold link was a symbol of European-American partnership, a guarantee for the economically weaker Europeans that the Americans would not abuse the privilege they had in backing the world's money. This guarantee was now gone, and the traditional Cold War bargain had seen its time pass. The United States would still preserve its military commitments largely because containment of the Soviet Union remained a central goal. But it would no longer always cooperate in the economic sphere but rather play out its full economic strength if it considered that to be in the national interest.

Confronted with Nixon's highly nationalistic monetary policy the Federal Republic searched for a strategy to escape from its dependence on the dollar; the result was attempts to create a European "zone of monetary stability independent of the dollar."[100] But the chaos in the currency markets during the 1970s condemned to failure all initiatives to create a common European currency.

The collapse of the dollar–gold system in 1971–3 and the U.S. policy of benign neglect made the traditional offset approach obsolete. The monetary movements during the turmoil in the markets were so large that any conceivable offset measures were much too small to stem the

99 Charles Coombs, who was responsible for the foreign exchange operations at the Federal Reserve from 1961 to 1975, termed this a "flagrant breach in the code of international behavior [that the U.S.] had spent a quarter-century in promoting" (Coombs, *Arena of International Finance*, 211).
100 Hoffmeyer, *Monetary System*, 194.

tide. The Federal government became increasingly unwilling to accede to pressures from the United States for burden sharing. Helmut Schmidt, then defense minister, declared in 1970 in the United States: "I do not belong to the people who start to wince whenever the Pentagon redeploys a kitchen brigade from the officers' mess in Heidelberg. And I am the first to admit that essential changes in the international situation may justify a revision of the numbers of troops needed in Europe. There is no dogma that the U.S. troops have to remain once and for ever at the present strength in Europe."[101] Schmidt, who had always been very critical of the agreements, later termed offset "a camouflage for occupation costs, which are certainly long outdated."[102] On becoming chancellor he used the first opportunity formally to bury the traditional offset scheme. In the summer of 1976 the U.S. government declared itself ready to accede to such a step. It published a common declaration with the German government: "Given the recently introduced changes in the international monetary area, specifically flexible exchange rates, as well as the notably improved strength of the dollar and a more acceptable U.S. balance-of-payments position, the president and the chancellor consider that the traditional offset arrangements approach has lost its relevance."[103]

101 Speech to the Council of Foreign Relations, New York, Apr. 8, 1970, BPI 1970, 466.
102 Helmut Schmidt, *Menschen und Mächte* (Berlin, 1987), 176.
103 "Joint Statement by Chancellor Schmidt and President Ford, July 17, 1976," *DOS Bulletin*, Aug. 16, 1976, 247.

Conclusion

The development of a transatlantic security system after 1945 with NATO at its core gave security issues in the Western world a strongly interdependent character. This was paralleled by the institutionalized interdependence in the international monetary policies of roughly the same countries, which were all committed to a stable exchange-rate system and liberal trade policies. Both developments were closely connected, as this research has demonstrated, based on an analysis of the history of American and British troop maintenance in West Germany during the 1950s and 1960s. The Atlantic security system and the international monetary system were two sides of the same coin. Changes in one sphere invariably influenced the other. On the one hand, expansive American security policies after the war, whether they took the form of troop commitments abroad, foreign aid, or political pressure, played an essential part in bringing the dollar–gold system into existence. On the other hand, these policies were possible only in a system that protected the U.S. economy from the disruptive effects of its balance-of-payments deficits. The European side of the bargain was military protection and an international environment conducive to economic reconstruction and growth. Countries such as West Germany, which saw the provision of security by the United States as essential, adapted to the monetary system and actively supported it by extending credit to the United States. Britain, being less dependent, pursued an independent monetary policy at an increasingly high cost.

The most fundamental structural change analyzed in this book is the slowly widening rift between the Atlantic security structure and the international monetary system. This became increasingly evident during the 1960s, whereas in the 1950s these two spheres generally complemented each other and formed the foundation for transatlantic economic, military, and political relations. The monetary system of the 1960s was not able to cope with the burdens imposed by expensive American policies abroad, many of which, such as troop stationing in Germany, had been answers to specific political problems in the 1950s. The tensions arising from fundamental economic transformations and, later on, from changes in the Cold War environment, manifested themselves in the increasingly dangerous crises in the monetary system. The straw that broke the camel's back probably was the burden imposed by the Vietnam War. The growing incompatibility of the monetary and security systems was reflected in the financial problems connected with British and American troop deployment in Germany.

The first part of this book concentrated on the Anglo-German troop-cost conflict the importance of which derives from its close link to various wider contexts. The problem of the foreign exchange cost of British troops in Germany in particular has to be set in relation to British sterling policy. This policy, emphasizing the role of sterling as the second reserve currency, was placed under heavy strain by fundamental British political choices, most notably the maintenance of the remains of Britain's imperial past and the attempt to hold on to an independent military posture. In order to fit into the Atlantic system as it evolved during the early 1950s, the British would have had to abandon the reserve currency role of sterling, accept a European role, and bring its defense policies into line with those of the rest of NATO. Those were the more or less secret hopes of American policy makers. However, the United Kingdom was not willing to undertake such a sweeping transformation of its traditional policies. It attempted to alleviate the pressures on those policies by reforming features of the Atlantic security system, particularly those related to the defense of Europe. A major target was the BAOR. This conflicted with vital West German interests. As long as it was not able to defend itself the Federal Republic saw the best guarantee of its survival in the specific security structure that emerged in 1955, that is, conventional forward defense under the protection of the American nuclear umbrella. British policies to reform the structure thus invariably met German resistance. The conflict about troop costs clearly demonstrates this: It derived not from a financial problem but from the fundamental ambiguity in British policy regarding the rationale of its security commitment in Europe. British governments never developed a consistent policy toward their troop commitment, and the perceived imperatives of the sterling policy provided a lasting incentive to withdraw from the commitment, as evidenced in the debate on the British white paper of 1957 or, later, during the trilateral negotiations of 1966–7.

British efforts to retreat from the WEU commitment failed, however. Somewhat paradoxically, they failed largely because of the political importance the troops had acquired despite the British dislike of their commitment. The BAOR had become an essential element in the Atlantic security structure. Whether it was pressure from the partner in the "special relationship," problems of accommodating European integration, political advantages regarding monetary cooperation, or particular interests like armaments trade, the credibility of the British troop commitment had a strong impact on all these issues. The political rationales behind the British military presence in West Germany therefore proved to be extremely persistent and more durable than the global role of sterling. In 1967 the British currency was devalued, whereas British troops stayed in Germany at roughly the same strength until the 1990s. Despite this political background, British politicians and the British public in general always portrayed their troop commitment as a burden and a nuisance. This deprived the United Kingdom of any chance to make positive use of the troops for political or economic benefits.

The German government perceived British policy after 1955 as a continuing series of challenges to some of its basic foreign policy principles. The debate over troop reductions and the British disarmament proposals were interpreted in this way. This was also true for the creation of EFTA. More economic cooperation without corresponding political commitments was of little value to the Federal Republic, which was painfully aware of the contrast between economic power and limited political influence. This awareness was sharpened by support-cost conflicts. The major potential leverage of Britain – collaboration in security matters and East-West policy – withered away during these conflicts and other instances in which the British displayed their unwillingness to cooperate with the Federal Republic. Consequently, the Germans were very reluctant to meet the British halfway on European policy or on financial matters.

They could have done so easily, and the increasing strength of the German currency provided the Federal Republic with an important lever. Unfortunately, we are still lacking a political history of German monetary policy in the late 1950s and the 1960s that scrutinizes the importance of this instrument more comprehensively. My analysis can cover only a few aspects. German monetary power often worked by default rather than through direct use of a financial instrument.

Nevertheless, this instrument was effective. Bonn and Frankfurt collaborated with their allies to a greater or lesser degree, closely related to political objectives. Collaboration with the United States thus remained very strong throughout the period under research, whereas collaboration with the United Kingdom was pursued reluctantly, with many qualifications and often related more to German–American relations than to any objectives in the British–German context. Germany's confrontational policy toward Britain over the support-cost issue became possible because the U.S. commitment seemed more or less guaranteed after the Radford Plan was blocked (and because France provided an alternative to Britain on the regional level). However, the relative certainty regarding the American commitment waned rapidly in the following years, when the U.S. balance of payments plunged into deficit and forced the Americans to take a close look at the cost of their security commitments.

The American response to this predicament was neither a radical reform of its monetary policy nor a reappraisal of its security policy. Expedients were sought that would offer relatively painless ways of perpetuating both the security and the monetary systems. The offset agreements were an important part of the solution. The first offset agreement was not – as most of the literature suggests in an ex post facto rationalization – the simple result of an assertive American use of its security leverage. The agreement was an elaborate compromise combining the vital interests of both sides, and the Federal Republic obtained important concessions. Only when offset became an institutionalized factor did tensions grow, and a widening gap emerged between American and German objectives. The offset system acquired its significance because the American government achieved no decisive breakthrough in its battle against the balance-of-payments deficit and because the surplus countries were getting increasingly restive about the situation. (France, in particular, directly challenged the United States.) The receipts from military sales within the framework of the agreements became a vital instrument of American monetary policy. Along with the Dillon–Roosa policy of "peripheral" defenses for the dollar, offset allowed the United States to continue its expansive domestic and military policies as well as to preserve the dollar–gold system. Furthermore, the offset system served to defend the continuation of an essentially unchanged American security commitment in Europe, first against critics within the administration and, after 1966, against congressional initiatives. At this point the interests of the Germans and some sectors of the American government converged.

Essential security concerns and important domestic political objectives made a stable troop level a central objective in the Adenauer and Erhard governments. With offset payments, that is, in effect by using German monetary power, they succeeded in perpetuating this status despite the powerful countercurrent generated by new strategic ideas, financial constraints, Vietnam, détente, and so forth. In the first years the offset agreements also provided the Federal Republic with important military benefits, such as access to advanced technology and crucial logistic support for the Bundeswehr. The benefits of the offset agreements, however, were increasingly overshadowed by serious political and financial disadvantages. Offset became an impediment for German foreign policy insofar as it limited military and political cooperation with other countries, particularly France, and fostered increasing dependence on the United States. The financial burden connected with offset limited funds for other government programs, thus contributing to a serious budgetary crisis in 1965–7. Constraints also became increasingly visible in the conduct of German monetary policy. The disastrous Erhard visit in September 1966 was the result of these tensions. Due to the American intractability on offset, the Federal Republic saw itself confronted with the choice of allowing the erosion of the traditional security structure in which its foreign policy was embedded or to bind itself even more closely to an international monetary regime that it considered increasingly irrational. Once more, security considerations and alliance policy proved overriding concerns. The Blessing letter, even if it represented no change in monetary policy, robbed the FRG of the option to initiate a change, and even if it was insufficient to preserve the dollar–gold system, symbolized the great bargain: monetary support for security within the framework of the Atlantic Alliance. However, the turmoil in the monetary markets of the late 1960s soon swept away these stopgaps. When the postwar monetary system collapsed in the early 1970s the time for offset as a monetary instrument had clearly passed. Until its demise in 1976, however, it remained a significant factor in American domestic debates on the U.S. security commitment to Europe.

The conclusions of this book clearly show that German, American, and British foreign policies in the postwar period cannot be understood if they are interpreted by using a traditional diplomatic history that separates economic and security (or alliance) policies. A perspective linking those two spheres must be included much more systematically than hitherto in accounts of international relations. Foreign policy was, and to a crucial degree still is, foreign *economic* policy. Only when both spheres are systematically linked in historical research will the question of the intricate relationship between the economy of the Western world and Cold War security policy during the first three postwar decades be adequately answered and a broader and more accurate picture of international history after World War II emerge.

Appendix 1

N.B.: Figures in the appendices are quoted in the currency of the original source, if not otherwise indicated. Exchange rates of dollars, pounds, and marks in the 1950s and 1960s were as follows:

Dollar-DM:
September 1949–March 1961: $1 = DM 4.20
March 1961–October 1969: $1 = DM 4.00
October 1969: $1 = DM 3.66

Sterling-Dollar:
September 1949: £1 = $2.80
November 1967: £1 = $2.40

Sterling-DM:
September 1949–March 1961: £1 = DM 11.76
March 1961–November 1967: £1 = DM 11.20
November 1967–October 1969: £1 = DM 9.60
October 1969: £1 = DM 8.78

Appendix 1

Table 1. *German Reserve Position and Federal Budget (Defense), 1950–71*
(in billions of DM)

	German Currency Reserves	Gold Reserves	Dollar Reserves	Federal Budget Expenditure	German Defense Expenditure
1950	0.80	—	0.63	14.7	4.6
1951	1.91	0.12	1.42	20.9	7.9
1952	3.11	0.59	2.08	23.1	7.9
1953	5.67	1.37	3.54	27.9	7.4
1954	8.77	2.63	5.44	28.2	8.0
1955	10.48	3.86	5.76	29.7	6.1
1956	14.76	6.27	7.30	33.3	7.3
1957	17.58	10.67	6.12	36.3	7.5
1958	0.09	11.09	7.41	40.4	8.8
1959	20.17	11.08	7.26	42.7	9.4
1960	29.59	12.48	14.98	33.1	8.2
1961	28.72	14.65	10.89	52.3	12.9
1962	27.86	14.71	10.79	57.9	17.2
1963	29.52	15.37	11.67	58.8	19.5
1964	28.83	16.99	7.71	65.5	18.8
1965	27.32	17.64	5.17	69.1	19.3
1966	30.72	17.17	8.31	72.5	19.7
1967	30.21	16.91	8.51	80.6	20.4
1968	34.89	18.16	8.56	88.1	17.4
1969	21.89	14.93	2.24	97.3	20.6
1970	47.61	14.57	28.58	93.6	20.6
1971	57.91	14.69	37.41	102.5	22.9

Sources: Columns 1–3 (year-end figures): Deutsche Bundesbank, ed., *40 Jahre Deutsche Mark: Monetäre Statistiken 1948–87* (Frankfurt am Main, 1988), 346; columns 4–5 (until 1959, the fiscal years ran from Apr. 1–Mar. 30; in 1960, from Apr. 1–Dec. 31; from 1961, the years are calendar years) Federal Finance Ministry, *Finanzbericht 1969*, 446–9; *Finanzbericht 1973*, 242, 250.

Table 2. *Selected American and British Balance-of-Payments Figures, 1954–1971*

	United States ($ million)				Britain (£ million)		
	Liquidity Balance	Net Military Expenditure	Total Reserve Assets	Gold Reserves	Current Balance	Balance for Official Financing	UK Official Reserves
1954	−1,541	−2,460	22,978	21,793	+117	+126	2,762
1955	−1,242	−2,701	22,797	21,753	−155	−229	2,120
1956	−0,923	−2,788	23,666	22,058	+208	−159	2,133
1957	+0,621	−2,841	24,832	22,857	+233	+13	2,273
1958	−3,348	−3,135	22,540	20,582	+360	+290	3,069
1959	−3,648	−2,805	21,504	19,507	+172	+18	2,736
1960	−3,677	−2,753	19,359	17,804	−228	+325	3,231
1961	−2,252	−2,596	18,753	16,947	+47	−339	3,318
1962	−2,864	−2,448	17,220	16,057	+155	+192	2,806
1963	−2,713	−2,304	16,843	15,596	+125	−58	2,658
1964	−2,696	−2,133	16,672	15,471	−362	−695	2,315
1965	−2,478	−2,122	15,450	13,806	−43	−353	3,004
1966	−2,151	−2,935	14,882	13,235	+113	−547	3,100
1967	−4,683	−3,228	14,830	12,065	−289	−671	2,694
1968	−1,611	−3,143	15,710	10,892	−273	−1,410	2,421
1969	−6,081	−3,344	16,964	11,859	+471	+687	2,528
1970	−3,851	−3,377	14,487	11,072	+781	+1,287	2,837
1971	−21,965	−2,908	12,167	10,206	+1,076	+3,146	6,582

Note: This table illustrates one of the major developments influencing the events described in this book: the weak American and British monetary positions. It cannot substitute for a comprehensive picture of U.S. and U.K. balance of payments.

Sources: US Figures: column 1: 1954–59: Gross Liquidity Balance; 1960–71: Net Liquidity Balance; *SCB* 10/1972, 26–7; *Economic Report of the President 1975*, 351. Column 2: Direct Expenditures minus Military Sales; ibid., 350; columns 3–4: ibid., 356.

UK Figures: British balance-of-payments accounts have been substantially revised since the time they were published. Contemporary figures cited in the text therefore do not coincide with the figures in this table. Column 5: Current Balance combines the visible and invisible trade balance; column 6: Total sum (current balance + capital transfers + net investment and other capital transactions + balancing item) that has to be met by (or contributes to) official financing; 1967–8 figures include special losses due to the devaluation in 1967; high minuses indicate years with strong pressure on Sterling; column 7: gold + foreign exchange; CSO, *Economic Trends: Annual Supplement*, 1981, 124, 143–4.

Table 3. *Allied Troop Levels in Germany, 1954–1971*
(in thousands)

Year	United States	Great Britain (BAOR + 2nd TAF)
1954	251.5	82.0 (+26)
1955	247.6	80.0 (+26)
1956	250.3	80.0 (+25)
1957	235.2	77.0 (+25)
1958	227.8	63.5 (+15.5)
1959	229.7	56.0 (+15.5)
1960	226.5	56.0 (+15.5)
1961	232.9	51.0 (+8.7)
1962	277.6★	51.0 (+8.7)
1963	251.6	51.0 (+8.7)
1964	263.0	51.3 (+8.7)
1965	262.3	51.0 (+8.7)
1966	236.7	53.3 (+8.5)
1967	215.0	52.0 (+8.5)
1968	210.0	50.0 (+6.5)
1969	210.0	50.0 (+6.5)
1970	215.0	52.0 (+8.5)
1971	215.0	52.0 (+8.5)

★DDRS 1993/754, Presidents Talking Points for Erhard Visit, Dec. 26, 1963, state following figures: 1961 pre–Berlin Crisis, 242,000; post–Berlin Crisis 273,000; Dec. 1963, 242,000.

Sources: For the United States in 1954–63: NSA, The Berlin Crisis, doc.1924: USAREUR report: The Replacement and Augmentation Systems in Europe (1945–63), Mar. 1964; after 1963: Nelson, *History*, 81. For the United Kingdom in 1954–63: author's compilation on the basis of source material in the PRO; 1963–71: KCA, various years.

Table 4. *Estimated Foreign Exchange Cost of American and British Troops in Germany, 1955–1971*

	UK forces (£ million)	US forces ($ million)
1955	69	291
1956	64	345
1957	63	479
1958	57	660
1959	51	664
1960	59	649
1961	60	636
1962	68	749
1963	73	691
1964	84	694
1965	84	714
1966	82	770
1967	90	837
1968	94	877
1969	110	948
1970	132	1,081
1971	172	1,265

Note: Estimating the local DM cost of Allied troops in Germany was a very complicated task. Figures differ considerably from source to source, particularly in the British case. The table uses the figures published by the stationing countries. These often do not match the figures in archival sources. Prior to 1955 the local foreign exchange costs were almost entirely covered by German payments. U.K. figures below are net figures, excluding German payments after 1955. German payments have been deducted from the U.S. figures for 1955–57.

Sources: For the United Kingdom in 1955–56: PRO, CAB 134/1209, Treasury Note on Organizational and Administrative Economics, June 5, 1956. 1957–63: PRO, FO 371/172175, Stationing Costs of Forces in Germany: Report by Officials, autumn 1963. 1964–68: KCA, various years; 1959–71: Lawrence Freedman, "Britain's Contribution to NATO," *International Affairs* 54 (1978): 38. For the United States in 1955–59: Mendershausen, *Troop Stationing*, 63; in 1960–71: SCB, Dec. 1969, 44; SCB, Apr. 1975, 58.

Appendix 2

Support Cost and Offset Agreements, 1955–1970

Before 1955:	Occupation costs: April 1952–April 1955, DM 600 million per month

1955–56	NATO Finance Convention, Art. IV, amended by Schedule III to the Protocol on the Termination of the Occupation Regime in the FRG, Oct. 23, 1954
	Term: May 5, 1955–May 4, 1956
	Extension of German occupation costs:
	$762 m (DM 3200 m)/year (British share: $140 m; US share: $350 m)
	Sources: FRUS 1952–54, V/2, 1342–3; HMSO, Cmnd. 9304 (54).

	Britain	United States	Others
Support-Cost Agreement 1956–57	June 29, 1956 Term: May 5, 1956– Mar. 31, 1957 DM 400 m support costs; Declaration of intention by the German government to buy British weapons up to $524 m/year *Source*: HMSO, Cmnd. 9802 (1956)	June 7, 1956 Term: June 5, 1956– May 5, 1957 DM 650 m support costs *Source*: KCA 1956, 15288	June 29, 1956 France (DM 278 m) July 6, 1956 Denmark (DM 2.275 m) July 10, 1956 Netherlands (DM 0.8 m) July 20, 1956 Belgium (DM 118 m) Canada (DM 6.585 m) *Source*: KCA 1956, 15288

250

	Britain	United States	Others
Support-Cost Negotiations, 1957–58	June 7, 1957 Term: Apr. 1, 1957–Mar. 31, 1958 Support costs: DM 588 m Deposit of £75 m at the Bank of England for settlement of German postwar debts Enlargement of German account for arms purchases at the BoE to £30 m and intention of FRG to buy a "considerable" amount of weapons in UK *Source*: HMSO, Cmnd. 256 (57); BGBL II, 1959, 414–17	June 7, 1957 Term: May 6, 1957– May 5, 1958 DM 325 m support costs Further: US reserves the right to request a supplementary contribution during 1957 *Source*: BGBL II, 1959, 410–11	June 7, 1957 Support costs to France: DM 225 m Belgium: DM 59 m Denmark: DM 1.2 m NL: DM 0.4 m *Source*: BGBL II, 17, 1959, 419–31
Support-Cost Negotiations, 1957–58	Oct. 3, 1958 Term: Apr. 1, 1958– Mar. 31, 1961 UK declares it will keep BAOR strength at 55,000 in 1958 and at 45,000 until 1961 Support costs: DM 141.2 m/year until 1960 Interest-free deposit of £50 m at the BoE for arms orders in Britain Repayment of postwar debts (1962–64 installment) £22.5 m *Source*: BGBL, 1959, II, 545–8; HMSO, Cmnd. 588 (1958)	Mar. 24, 1959 Repayment of postwar debts: $150 m *Source*: (not identified in published form) BA, B 136/3132, Cabinet Paper AA, March 10, 1959	FRANCE Sept. 17, 1959 Repayment of postwar debts (1962–64 installments): $1,776 *Source*: (not identified in published form) BA, B 136/3132, Cabinet Paper AA, March 10, 1959

Offset Agreements, 1961–1971

United States	Britain
Oct. 24, 1961 Term: July 1, 1961–June 30, 1963 military purchases ($1,425 m; DM 5,700 m) *Source*: AAPD 1963, 864n37	**June 6, 1962** Term: Apr. 1, 1962–Mar. 31, 1964 German purchases (mainly arms) of £54 m (DM 600 m) *Source*: HMSO, Cmnd. 1766 (1962)
Sept. 14, 1962 Term: July 1, 1963–June 30, 1965 military purchases ($1,400 m; DM 5,600 m) *Source*: not published; McGhee papers, 1988add. box 2	**July 27, 1964** Term: Apr. 1, 1964–Mar. 31, 1966 undertaking by Germany to offset British costs "as fully as possible" *Source*: HMSO, Cmnd. 2434 (1964)
May 11, 1964 Term: July 1, 1965–June 30, 1967 military purchases ($1.35 bn); advance payments on military procurement (DM 3.14 bn); *Source*: AAPD 1964, 526n2	**July 20, 1965** Term: Apr. 1, 1965–Mar. 31, 1967 renegotiation of previous agreement Immediate nonreturnable payment of £42 m on contracts already placed or foreseen; financing of additional British exports: £45 m; offset for 1966/67 (£54 m) *Source*: BPI 125/1965, 1009; HMSO, Cmnd. 2731 (1965)
Apr. 28, 1967 Term: July 1, 1967–June 30, 1968 Germany buys mid-term US Treasury bonds (DM 2 bn); formal statement by Bundesbank to refrain from dollar-gold exchanges *Source*: *DOS Bulletin*, May 22, 1967; BPI 1967	**May 5, 1967** Term: Apr. 1, 1967–Mar. 30, 1968 German purchases of £18 m (DM 200 m) of military equipment and £22.5 m (DM 250 m) of civilian equipment; £9 m (DM 100 m) made by private German firms *Source*: HMSO, Cmnd. 3293 (1967)
June 10, 1968 Term: July 1, 1968–June 30, 1969 Offset $785 m ($100 m military equipment; $500 m Bundesbank investment in mid-term Treasury bonds; Lufthansa buys Boeing aircraft for $60 m) *Source*: BPI 1968, 627; *DOS Bulletin*, 7/1968, 14	**Mar. 28, 1968** Term: Apr. 1, 1968–Mar. 31, 1969 Offset of £54 m (DM 510 m); (£22 m defense purchases; £21 m civilian purchases by public authorities; £10.5 m civil private purchases) Bundesbank invests about £21 m in British medium-term bonds *Source*: KCA 1968, 22618

United States	Britain

July 9, 1969
Term: July 1, 1969–June 30, 1971
Military procurement (DM 3.2 bn);
   renunciation of interest (DM 130 m);
   civilian purchases (DM 500 m); long-
   term financial transactions (DM 2.25 bn)
   thereof: 10-year loan by Federal
   Government of DM 1 bn; Germany
   buys claims of the EXIM bank and
   from Marshall Plan (DM 475 m); debt
   prepayment (DM 175 m); direct
   investment of FRG in US (DM 600 m)
Source: BPI 1969, 792; *DOS Bulletin*, Aug.
   1969, 92

July 22, 1969
Term: Apr. 1, 1969–Mar. 31, 1971
Offset: £116 m (£47 m defense purchases;
   £36 m civilian purchases; £33 m
   government-promoted private civil
   purchases), loan to UK government of
   DM 500 m (£52 m) at 3.5% interest,
   repayable after 10 years

Source: KCA 1969, 23753–4.

July 10, 1971
Term: July 1, 1971–June 30, 1973
Military procurement (DM 4 bn);
   renovation of US barracks (DM 600 bn);
   investment in US Treasury bonds
   (DM 2 bn)
Source: *DOS Bulletin*, Jan. 3, 1972

July 16, 1971
Term: Apr. 1, 1969–Mar. 31, 1971
Military procurement (DM 450 m); civil
   procurement (DM 350 m); subvention of
   British aircraft exports (DM 220 m):
   10-year grant to UK (DM 500 m)
Source: BPI 1969, 848

Sources and Bibliography

ARCHIVAL MATERIAL

Germany

Politisches Archiv Auswärtiges Amt/Bonn (PA-AA); Ministerbüro (MB); Büro Staatssekretär (STS) – Undersecretary; Depts. 301, III A 5, II A 7; B 150 (declassified documents microfilmed for the edition "Akten zur Auswärtigen Politik der BRD 1963–68")

Bundesarchiv/Koblenz
Bundesministerium für Wirtschaft (B 102); Bundesministerium der Finanzen (B 126); Bundeskanzleramt (B 136)

Schäffer papers, N 1168; Von Brentano papers, N 1239; Blankenhorn papers, N 1351; Etzel papers, N 1254; Von und zu Guttenberg papers, N 1397; Carstens papers, N 1337

Bundesbankarchiv
Protokolle der Zentralbankratssitzungen 1955–63; B 330/10161, 10245; A 270/10797, 13168; Emminger papers

Archive of the Institut für Zeitgeschichte (Munich)
Krekeler papers

Archive of the Ludwig Erhard Foundation, Bonn
Erhard–Adenauer Correspondence; Briefing Book for USA Trip 1966

Documents from the Federal Defense Ministry (declassified by the Nuclear History Project)
Lehrstuhl Prof. Wolfgang Krieger, Marburg/Lahn

Private Material
Military diary von Hassel

United Kingdom

Public Record Office, Kew; CAB 128, 129, 131, 134; PREM 11, PREM 13; FO 371; DEFE 7, DEFE 13; T 225, T 234, T 236

United States

John F. Kennedy Library, Boston
Oral history interviews; National Security files; President's Office files; Transition papers

Lyndon B. Johnson Library, Austin, Texas
National Security Files; Vice Presidential Security Files; Ball papers; Bator papers; Fowler papers; Oral History Interviews

National Archives, College Park, Maryland
RG 59, Decimal Files 1955–59, 1960–63; Subject Files 1963
Lot Files: Bureau of European Affairs, Office of German Affairs
RG 84 Post Files: Bonn Embassy

National Security Archive, Gelman Library, George Washington University, Washington, D.C.

Lauinger Library, Georgetown University, Washington, D.C.
George C. McGhee papers, 1988add.

Oral History Interviews
Federal Defense Minister a.D. von Hassel, August 20, 1994; Sir Frank Roberts, UK Ambassador to Germany, 1962–68, January 18, 1996

STATISTICAL MATERIAL

Deutsche Bundesbank, *40 Jahre Deutsche Mark: Monetäre Statistiken 1948–87* (Frankfurt am Main, 1988).
Central Statistical Office, *Economic Trends.* Annual Supplement, 1981.
Economic Report of the President, 1975.
European Payments Union, *Annual Reports 1951–58*, OEEC, Paris.
HMSO, Balance of Payments, various issues, 1954–67.
Survey of Current Business, various years.

PUBLISHED SOURCES

Correspondence, Government Documents, Hearings, and Speeches

Adenauer: Wir haben wirklich etwas geschaffen: Die Protokolle des CDU Bundesvorstands 1953–57, ed. Günther Buchstab (Stuttgart, 1986).

Adenauer, Konrad, *Reden 1917–67: Eine Auswahl*, ed. Hans-Peter Schwarz (Stuttgart, 1975).

Akten zur Auswärtigen Politik der Bundesrepublik Deutschland 1963–70, ed. Institut für Zeitgeschichte, on behalf of Auswärtiges Amt (Munich, 1994–2001).

American Foreign Policy: Current Documents.

Baring, Arnulf, ed., *Sehr Verehrter Herr Bundeskanzler! Heinrich von Brentano im Briefwechsel mit Konrad Adenauer 1949–64* (Hamburg, 1974).

Brawand, Leo, *Wohin steuert die deutsche Wirtschaft? Interviews* (Munich, 1971).

Congressional Hearings

U.S. Troops in Europe, Hearings before the Combined Subcommittee of Foreign Relations and Armed Services Committees, U.S. Senate, 90th Cong., 1st. sess, April–May 1967.

U.S. Security Agreements and Commitments Abroad, Hearings before the Subcommittee on U.S. Security Agreements and Commitments abroad of the Committee on Foreign Relations, U.S. Senate, 91st cong., 2d sess., May–July 1970.

U.S. Forces in Europe, Hearings before the Subcommittee on Arms Control, International Law and Organization of the Committee on Foreign Relations, U.S. Senate, 93d cong., 1st. sess., July 1973.

Congressional Records

Declassified Documents Reference System, Research Publications International, various years.

De Gaulle, Charles, *Discours et messages, 1962–65* (Paris, 1969).

Documents Diplomatiques Françaises, Imprimerie National, Paris

1956 Tomé I, 1988; Tomé II, 1989; Tomé III, 1990; 1957 Tomé I, 1990; Tomé II, 1991; 1958 Tomé I, 1992; Tomé II, 1993; 1959 Tomé I, 1994; Tomé II, 1995.

Documents on American Foreign Relations

Foreign Relations of the United States, GPO, Washington, D.C.

1955–57, IV: Western European Security, XIX: National Security Policy, XXVI: Western Europe and Canada, XXVII: Central and South Eastern Europe;

1958–60, IV: Foreign Economic Policy, VII, 1,2: Western Europe and Canada, VIII/IX: Berlin Crisis and Germany;

1961–63, IX: Foreign Economic Policy; XIII: Western Europe and Canada, XIV: Berlin Crisis 1961–62; XV: Berlin Crisis 1962–63;

1964–68, VIII: Foreign Economic Policy; XIII: Western Europe Region. XV: Germany and Berlin.

Goldsworthy, David, ed., *The Conservative Government and the End of Empire, 1951–57, Parts I–III* (London, 1994).

Hansard, *House of Commons Debates*, 1954–67.

HMSO, *Defence: Outline of Future Policy*, Cmnd. 124, 1957.

Heuss, Theodor, and Konrad Adenauer, *Unserem Vaterland zugute: Der Briefwechsel 1948–63*, ed. Hans Peter Mensing (Berlin, 1989).

Minutes of Telephone Conversations of the Secretaries of State, 1953–61 (microfilmed), ed. Paul Kesaris (Frederick, Md.).
Public Papers of the Presidents of the United States, Eisenhower, Kennedy, Johnson
Public Statements of the Secretaries of Defense (microfilmed), ed. Paul Kesaris (Frederick, Md.).
Verhandlungen des Deutschen Bundestags (VdB)

Memoirs and Eyewitness Accounts

Acheson, Dean, *Present at the Creation* (London, 1970).
Adenauer, Konrad, *Erinnerungen 1955–59* (Stuttgart, 1967).
Blessing, Karl, *Im Kampf um Gutes Geld* (Frankfurt am Main, 1966).
Brown, George, *In My Way* (London, 1971).
Crossman, Richard H. S., *The Diaries of a Cabinet Minister*, vol. 1: *1964–66*; vol. 2: *1966–68* (London, 1975–76).
Eisenhower, Dwight D., *Waging Peace, 1956–1961* (New York, 1965).
Emminger, Otmar, *D-Mark, Dollar, Währungskrisen* (Stuttgart, 1987).
Grewe, Wilhelm G., *Rückblenden 1976–1951: Aufzeichnungen eines Augenzeugen deutscher Aussenpolitik von Adenauer bis Schmidt* (Frankfurt am Main, 1979).
Johnson, Lyndon B., *The Vantage Point* (New York, 1971).
McGhee, George C., *At the Creation of a New Germany: From Adenauer to Brandt: An Ambassador's Account* (New Haven, Conn., 1989).
Osterheld, Heinz, *Aussenpolitik unter Bundeskanzler Erhard* (Düsseldorf, 1992).
Rostow, Walt, *The Diffusion of Power: An Essay in Recent History* (New York, 1972).
Schmidt, Helmut, *Menschen und Mächte* (Berlin, 1987).
Strauss, Franz Josef, *Erinnerungen* (Berlin, 1989).
Wilson, Harold, *The Labour Government, 1964–70* (London, 1971).

Journals

Armed Forces Management; Bulletin des Presse- und Informationsamts der Bundesregierung (BPI); Department of State Bulletin; Financial Times; Foreign Affairs; Frankfurter Allgemeine Zeitung; Keesings Contemporary Archives (KCA); Frankfurter Rundschau; New York Times; Der Spiegel; Süddeutsche Zeitung; The Economist; The Times; U.S. News & World Report

SECONDARY LITERATURE

Abelshauser, Werner, "The Causes and Consequences of the 1956 German Rearmament Crisis," in Francis H. Heller and John R. Gillingham, eds., *NATO: The Founding of the Alliance and the Integration of Europe* (London, 1992), 311–34.
Abelshauser, Werner, "Rüstung, Wirtschaft, Rüstungswirtschaft: Wirtschaftliche Aspekte des Kalten Kriegs in den 50er Jahren," in Klaus Maier and Norbert Wiggershaus, eds., *Das Nordatlantische Bündnis* (Munich, 1993), 89–108.

Abelshauser, Werner, "'Integration à la carte': The Primacy of Politics and the Economic Integration of Western Europe in the 1950s," in Stephen Martin, ed., *The Construction of Europe: Essays in Honour of Emile Noël* (Dordrecht, 1994), 1–18.

Abelshauser, Werner, "Wirtschaft und Rüstung" (= MGFA IV) (Munich, 1996).

Ahonen, Pertti, "F. J. Strauss and the German Nuclear Question, 1956–62," *Journal of Strategic Studies* 18 (1995): 25–41.

Alford, B. W. E., *British Economic Performance, 1945–75* (London, 1988).

Anfänge Westdeutscher Sicherheitspolitik, vol. 2: *Die EVG-Phase*, ed. MGFA (Munich, 1990); vol. 3: *Die NATO-Option*, ed. Hans Ehlert, Christian Greiner, and Bruno Thoss (Munich, 1993); vol. 4: *Wirtschaft und Rüstung, Souveränität und Sicherheit*, ed. Werner Abelshauser and Walter Schwengler (Munich, 1996)

Bartlett, Christopher J., *The Long Retreat: A Short History of British Defence Policy, 1945–70* (London, 1972).

Bartlett, Christopher J., *The Special Relationship* (London, 1992).

Bergsten, C. Fred, *The Dilemma of the Dollar: The Economics and Politics of United States International Monetary Policy* (New York, 1975).

Birtle, Andrew, *Rearming the Phoenix: U.S. Military Assistance to the Federal Republic of Germany, 1950–60* (New York, 1991).

Block, Fred L., *The Origins of International Economic Disorder: A Study of United States International Monetary Policy from World War II to the Present* (Berkeley, Calif., 1977).

Bordo, Michael D., and Barry Eichengreen, eds., *A Retrospective on the Bretton Woods System: Lessons for International Monetary Relations* (Chicago, 1993).

Bordo, Michael D., Dominique Simard, and Eugene White, "France and the Bretton Woods International Monetary System, 1960–68," in Jaime Reis, ed., *International Monetary Systems in Historical Perspective* (London, 1995), 153–80.

Botti, Timothy, *The Long Wait: The Forging of the Anglo-American Nuclear Alliance, 1945–58* (New York, 1987).

Brandt, Gerhard, *Rüstung und Wirtschaft in der Bundesrepublik* (Witten, 1966).

Browder, Dewey A., "The GI and the Wirtschaftswunder," *Journal of European Economic History* 22 (1993): 601–12.

Browning, Peter, *The Treasury and Economic Policy, 1964–85* (London, 1986).

Burnham, Peter, *The Political Economy of Postwar Reconstruction* (New York, 1990).

Burnham, Peter, "Rearming for the Korean War: The Impact of Government Policy on Leyland Motors and the British Car Industry," *Contemporary Record* 9 (1995): 343–67.

Cairncross, Alec, and Barry Eichengreen, eds., *Sterling in Decline: The Devaluations of 1931, 1949, and 1967* (Oxford, 1983).

Cairncross, Alec, *The British Economy Since 1945* (Oxford, 1992).

Cairncross, Alec, *Managing the British Economy in the 1960s: A Treasury Perspective* (Oxford, 1996).

Calleo, David P., and Benjamin N. Rowland, *America and the World Political Economy: Atlantic Dreams and National Realities* (Bloomington, Ind., 1974).

Calleo, David P., *The Imperious Economy* (New York, 1985).

Calleo, David P., "De Gaulle and the Monetary System: The Golden Rule," in Robert O. Paxton and Nicholas Wahl, eds., *De Gaulle and the United States* (Oxford, 1994), 239–55.

Camps, Miriam, *Britain and the EC, 1955–63* (Princeton, N.J., 1964).

Carpenter, Ted, "U.S. NATO Policy at Crossroads: The Great Debate of 1950/51," *International History Review* 8 (1986): 389–414.

Chalmers, Malcolm, *Paying for Defence: Military Spending and British Decline* (London, 1985).

Cioc, Marc, *Pax Atomica: The Nuclear Defense Debate in West Germany During the Adenauer Era* (New York, 1988).

Clarc, Ian, *Nuclear Diplomacy and the Special Relationship* (Oxford, 1994).

Cleveland, Harald van B., *The Atlantic Idea and Its European Rivals* (New York, 1966).

Cohen, Benjamin C., *Organizing the World's Money: The Political Economy of International Monetary Relations* (London, 1977).

Cohen, Benjamin C., "The Bargain Comes Unstuck: The Revolution in Atlantic Economic Relations," in Wolfram Hanrieder, ed., *The United States and Western Europe* (Cambridge, 1974), 406–37.

Cohen, Stephen D., *International Monetary Reform, 1964–69: The Political Dimension* (New York, 1970).

Collins, Robert M., "The Economic Crisis of 1968 and the Waning of the American Century," *American Historical Review* 101 (Apr. 1996): 396–422.

Coombs, Charles, *The Arena of International Finance* (New York, 1976).

Darby, Phillip, *British Defence Policy East of Suez, 1947–68* (London, 1973).

Deutsche Bundesbank, ed., *50 Jahre Deutsche Mark: Notenbank und Währung in Deutschland seit 1948* (Munich, 1998).

Dickhaus, Monika, *Die Bundesbank im Westeuropäischen Wiederaufbau 1948–58* (Munich, 1996).

Diefendorf, Jeffry M., Axel Frohn, and Hermann J. Rupieper, eds., *American Policy and the Reconstruction of West Germany, 1945–55* (New York, 1993).

Di Nolfo, Ennio, ed., *The Atlantic Pact 40 Years Later: A Historical Reappraisal* (Berlin, 1991).

Dobson, Alan P., *The Politics of the Anglo-American Economic Special Relationship, 1940–1987* (Brighton, U.K., 1988).

Dockrill, Saki, *Britain's Policy for West German Rearmament, 1950–55* (Cambridge, 1991).

Donfried, Karen, "The Political Economy of Alliance: Issue Linkage in the West German–American Relationship," Ph.D. diss., Fletcher School of Law and Diplomacy, Tufts University, 1991.

Dow, J. C. R., *The Management of the British Economy, 1945–60* (Cambridge, 1970).

Duckwitz, Georg Ferdinand, "Truppenstationierung und Devisenausgleich," *Aussenhandelspolitik* 18 (1967): 471–5.

Duffield, John S., *Power Rules: The Evolution of NATO's Conventional Force Posture* (Boulder, Colo., 1996).

Duke, Simon, ed., *US Military Forces and Installations in Europe* (Oxford, 1988).

Duke, Simon, and Wolfgang Krieger, eds., *U.S. Military Forces in Europe* (Boulder, Colo., 1993).

Ehlert, Hans, "Innenpolitische Auseinandersetzungen um die Wehrverträge 1954–56," in *MGFA III* (Munich, 1993), 235–560.

Eichengreen, Barry, *Reconstructing Europe's Trade and Payments: The EPU* (Manchester, U.K., 1993).

Eichengreen, Barry, ed., *Europe's Postwar Recovery* (Cambridge, 1995).

Emminger, Otmar, "Deutsche Geld- und Währungspolitik im Spannungsfeld zwischen innerem und äusserem Gleichgewicht 1948–75," in Deutsche Bundesbank, ed., *Währung und Wirtschaft in Deutschland 1876–1975* (Frankfurt am Main, 1976).

Enthoven, Alain, and Wayne K. Smith, *How Much is Enough? Shaping the Defense Program, 1961–69* (New York, 1971).

Felken, Detlef, *Dulles und Deutschland: Die amerikanische Deutschlandpolitik 1953–59* (Bonn, 1993).

Fels, Gerhard, *1966/67: Anatomie einer Rezession*, IWW Working Paper (Kiel, 1988).

Fischer, Peter, "Das Projekt einer trilateralen Nuklearkooperation 1957/58," *Historisches Jahrbuch* 11 (1992): 143–56.

Freedman, Lawrence, "Britain's Contribution to NATO," *International Affairs* 54 (1978): 30–46.

Fried, Edward R., "The Financial Cost of Alliance," in John Newhouse, ed., *U.S. Troops in Europe* (Washington, D.C., 1971), 102–44.

Gaddis, John L., *Strategies of Containment: A Critical Appraisal of Postwar American National Security Policy* (New York, 1982).

Gaddis, John L., *We Now Know: Rethinking the History of the Cold War* (Oxford, 1997).

Gadzey, Anthony T., *The Political Economy of Power: Hegemony and Economic Liberalism* (New York, 1994).

Gardner, Richard N., *Sterling-Dollar Diplomacy*, new rev. ed. (New York, 1969).

Gardner, Richard N., "Lyndon B. Johnson and De Gaulle," in Robert O. Paxton and Nicholas Wahl, eds., *De Gaulle and the United States: A Centennial Reappraisal* (Oxford, 1994), 257–78.

Geiger, Till, " 'The Next War Is Bound to Come': Defence Production Policy, Supply Departments, and Defence Contractors, 1945–57," in Anthony Gorst, Lewis Johnman, and W. Scott Lucas, eds., *Contemporary British History, 1931–61: Politics and the Limits of Policy* (London, 1989), 95–119.

Gersdorff, Gero von, *Adenauers Aussenpolitik gegenüber den Siegermächten 1954* (Düsseldorf, 1994).

Giersch, Herbert, Karl-Heinz Paqué, and Holger Schmieding, *The Fading Miracle: Four Decades of Market Economy in Germany* (Cambridge, 1992).

Gilbert, Milton, *Quest for World Monetary Order: The Gold-Dollar System and Its Aftermath* (New York, 1980).

Gowa, Joanne, *Closing the Gold Window: Domestic Politics and the End of Bretton Woods* (Ithaca, N.Y., 1983).

Grabbe, Hans-Jürgen, *Unionsparteien, Sozialdemokratie und Vereinigte Staaten von Amerika 1945–66* (Düsseldorf, 1983).

Greenwood, Sean, *Britain and European Cooperation Since 1945* (Oxford, 1992).

Greiner, Christian, "Die militärische Eingliederung der Bundesrepublik Deutschland in die WEU und in die NATO 1954–57," in *MGFA III* (Munich, 1993), 641–58.

Greiner, Christian, "Zur Rolle Kontinentaleuropas in den alliierten strategischen Planungen," in Klaus Maier and Norbert Wiggershaus, eds., *Das Nordatlantische Bündnis 1949–56* (Munich, 1993), 147–50.

Griffiths, Richard T., and Stuart Ward, eds., *Courting the European Market: The First Attempt to Enlarge the EC, 1961–63* (London, 1996).

Haftendorn, Helga, *Kernwaffen und die Glaubwürdigkeit der Allianz: Die NATO-Krise von 1966/67* (Baden-Baden, 1994). English ed.: *NATO and the Nuclear Revolution: A Crisis of Credibility, 1966–67* (Oxford, 1996).

Hanrieder, Wolfram, *Germany, America, Europe: Forty Years of German Foreign Policy* (New Haven, Conn., 1989).

Hardach, Gerd, *Der Marshall-Plan: Auslandshilfe und Wiederaufbau in Westdeutschland 1948–52* (Munich, 1994).

Heller, Fred, and John R. Gillingham, eds., *NATO: The Founding of the Alliance and the Integration of Europe* (Basingstoke, 1992).

Henzler, Christoph, *Fritz Schäffer 1945–67: Eine biographische Studie* (Munich, 1994).

Herbst, Ludolf, Werner Bührer, and Hanno Sowade, eds., *Vom Marshall-Plan zur EWG: Die Eingliederung der BRD in die westliche Welt* (Munich, 1990).

Hildebrand, Klaus, *Von Erhard zur Grossen Koalition 1963–69* (Stuttgart, 1984).

Hockerts, Hans-Günther, *Sozialpolitische Entscheidungen im Nachkriegsdeutschland* (Stuttgart, 1980).

Hoffmann, Daniel, *Truppenstationierung in der Bundesrepublik Deutschland: Die Vertragsverhandlungen mit den Westmächten* (Munich, 1997).

Hoffmeyer, Erik, *The International Monetary System: An Essay in Interpretation* (Amsterdam, 1992).

Hoppe, Christoph, *Zwischen Teilhabe und Mitsprache: Die Nuklearfrage in der Allianzpolitik Deutschlands 1959–66* (Baden-Baden, 1993).

Horne, Alistair, *Harold Macmillan* (London, 1989).

Ilgen, Thomas L., *Autonomy and Interdependence: US-Western European Monetary and Trade Relations 1958–84* (Totowa, N.J., 1985).

Institut Charles de Gaulle, ed., *De Gaulle et son Siècle, I–V* (Paris, 1991).

James, Harold, "The IMF and the Creation of the Bretton Woods System," in Barry Eichengreen, ed., *Europe's Postwar Recovery* (Cambridge, 1995), 93–125.

James, Harold, *International Monetary Cooperation Since Bretton Woods* (Washington, D.C., 1996).

Jansen, Hans-Heinrich, *Grossbritannien, das Scheitern der EVG, und der NATO Beitritt der BRD* (Bochum, 1992).

Johnman, Lewis, "Defending the Pound: The Economics of the Suez Crisis, 1956," in Anthony Gorst, Lewis Johnman, and W. Scott Lucas, eds., *Postwar Britain, 1945–64: Themes and Perspectives* (London, 1989), 166–81.

Kaiser, Wolfram, "Money, Money, Money: The Economics and Politics of Stationing Costs, 1955–65," in Gustav Schmidt, ed., *Zwischen Bündnissicherung und privilegierter Partnerschaft* (Bochum, 1995), 1–31.

Kaplan, Jacob J., and Günther Schleiminger, *The European Payments Union: Financial Diplomacy in the 1950s* (Oxford, 1989).

Kaufman, Burton I., *Trade and Aid: Eisenhower's Foreign Economic Policy, 1953–61* (Baltimore, 1982).

Kaufman, Burton I., "Foreign Aid and the Balance of Payments Problem: Vietnam and Johnson's Foreign Economic Policy," in Robert A. Divine, ed., *The Johnson Years*, vol. 2: *Vietnam, the Environment, and Science* (Austin, Tex., 1987), 79–109.

Kelleher, Catherine M., *Germany and the Politics of Nuclear Weapons* (New York, 1975).

Kettl, Donald F., "The Economic Education of Lyndon Johnson: Guns, Butter, and Taxes," in Robert A. Divine, ed., *The Johnson Years*, vol. 2: *Vietnam, the Environment, and Science* (Lawrence, Kan., 1987), 54–77.

Klessmann, Christoph, *Zwei Staaten, eine Nation: Deutsche Geschichte 1955–70* (Göttingen 1988).

Köllner, Lutz, "Die Entwicklung deutscher Militärausgaben in Vergangenheit und Zukunft," *Aus Politik und Zeitgeschichte* 22 (1984): 27–39.

Körfer, Daniel, *Kampf ums Kanzleramt* (Stuttgart, 1987).

Kreikamp, Hans-Dieter, *Deutsches Vermögen in den Vereinigten Staaten: Die Auseinandersetzung um seine Rückführung als Aspekt der deutsch-amerikanischen Beziehungen 1952–62* (Stuttgart, 1979).

Krieger, Wolfgang, "Die Ursprünge der langfristigen Stationierung amerikanischer Streitkräfte in Europa," in Ludolf Herbst, Werner Bührer, and Hanno Sowade, eds., *Vom Marshall-Plan zur EWG* (Munich, 1990), 373–99.

Krieger, Wolfgang, *Franz Josef Strauss: Der barocke Demokrat* (Göttingen, 1996).

Kunz, Diane B., *The Economic Diplomacy of the Suez Crisis* (Chapel Hill, N.C., 1991).

Kunz, Diane B., "Cold War Dollar Diplomacy: The Other Side of Containment," in Diane B. Kunz, ed., *The Diplomacy of the Crucial Decade* (New York, 1994).

Kunz, Diane B., *Butter and Guns: America's Cold War Economic Diplomacy* (New York, 1997).

Lappenküpper, Ulrich, " 'Ich bin wirklich ein guter Europäer': L. Erhards Europapolitik 1949–1966," *Francia* 18 (1991): 85–121.

Large, David Clay, *Germans to the Front: West German Rearmament in the Adenauer Era* (Chapel Hill, N.C., 1996).

Lee, Gordon, "The Half-Forgotten Army: A Survey of British Forces in Germany," *The Economist*, Nov. 28, 1970.

Leffler, Melvyn P., *A Preponderance of Power: National Security Policy, the Truman Administration, and the Cold War* (Stanford, Calif., 1992).

Louscher, David J., "The Rise of Military Sales as a U.S. Foreign Assistance Instrument," *Orbis* 20 (1977): 933–64.

Mager, Olaf, *Die Stationierung der britischen Rheinarmee* (Baden-Baden, 1990).

Maier, Charles S., and Günther Bischof, eds., *The Marshall-Plan and Germany: West German Development Within the Framework of the European Recovery Program* (New York, 1990).

Maier, Klaus, and Norbert Wiggershaus, eds., *Das Nordatlantische Bündnis* (Munich, 1993).

Mahncke, Dieter, ed., *Amerikaner in Deutschland: Grundlagen und Bedingungen der transatlantischen Sicherheit* (Bonn, 1991).

Marcowitz, Reiner, *Option für Paris? Unionsparteien, SPD und de Gaulle 1958–69* (Munich, 1996).

Mastanduno, Michael, "Economics and Security in Statecraft and Scholarship," *International Organization* 4 (1998): 825–54.

Matusow, Allen K., "Kennedy, the World Economy and the Decline of America," in J. R. Snyder, ed., *John F. Kennedy: Person, Policy, Presidency* (New York, 1988), 111–22.

McKinnon, Ronald I., "The Rules of the Game: International Money in Historical Perspective," *Journal of Economic Literature* 3 (1993): 1–44.

Medick, Monika, *Waffenexporte und auswärtige Politik der Vereinigten Staaten* (Meisenheim, 1976).

Mendershausen, Horst, *Troop-Stationing in Germany: Value and Cost*, RAND PR-5881 (Santa Monica, Calif., 1968).

Milward, Alan S., *The European Rescue of the Nation State* (London, 1992).

Milward, Alan S., "The Origins of the Fixed-Rate Dollar System," in Jaime Reis, ed., *International Monetary Systems in Historical Perspective* (London, 1995), 135–51.

Moravcsik, Andrew, "De Gaulle Between Grain and Grandeur," *Journal of Cold War Studies* 2 and 3 (2000): 3–43; 4–142.

Morgan, Roger, *The United States and West Germany, 1945–73: A Study in Alliance Politics* (London, 1974).

Navias, Martin S., *Nuclear Weapons and British Strategic Planning, 1955–58* (Oxford, 1991).

Nelson, Daniel J., *A History of U.S. Military Forces in Germany* (Boulder, Colo., 1987).

Nelson, Daniel J., *Defenders or Intruders? The Dilemmas of U.S. Forces in Germany* (Boulder, Colo., 1987).

Newhouse, John, *U.S. Troops in Europe: Issues, Costs, and Choices* (Washington, D.C., 1971).

Niedhart, Gottfried, "Deutsche Aussenpolitik: Vom Teilstaat mit begrenzter Souveränität zum postmodernen Nationalstaat," *Aus Politik und Zeitgeschichte* 2 (1997): 15–23.

Odell, John S., *U.S. International Monetary Relations: Markets, Power, and Ideas as Forces of Change* (New York, 1982).

Olson, Mancur, and Richard Zeckhauser, "An Economic Theory of Alliances," *Review of Economics and Statistics* 48 (1966): 266–79.

Paterson, Thomas G., ed., *Kennedy's Quest for Victory: American Foreign Policy, 1961–63* (Oxford, 1989).

Peter, Matthias, "Britain, the Cold War, and the Economics of German Rearmament, 1949–51," in Anne Deighton, ed., *Britain and the First Cold War* (London, 1990), 273–90.

Pöttering, Hans-Gert, *Adenauers Sicherheitspolitik 1955–63: Ein Beitrag zum deutsch-amerikanischen Verhältnis* (Düsseldorf, 1975).

Pollard, Robert A., *Economic Security and the Origins of the Cold War, 1945–50* (New York, 1985).

Pollard, Sidney, *The Wasting of British Economy: British Economic Policy, 1945 to the Present* (London, 1982).

Porter, Andrew N., "Downhill all the Way: 13 Tory Years," in Richard Coopey, Nick Tiratsoo, and Steven Fielding, eds., *The Wilson Governments, 1964–70* (London, 1993).

Raj, Christopher S., *American Military in Europe: Controversy over NATO Burden-Sharing* (New Delhi, 1983).

Rees, Wyn, "The 1957 Sandys White Paper: New Priorities in British Defence Policy?" *Journal of Strategic Studies* 12 (1989): 215–29.

Rhenisch, Thomas, and Hubert Zimmermann, "Adenauer Chooses de Gaulle: The West German Government and the Exclusion of Britain from Europe," in Richard T. Griffiths and Stuart Ward, eds., *Courting the Common Market: The First Attempt to Enlarge the European Community* (London, 1996), 83–100.

Roosa, Robert, *The Dollar Problem and World Liquidity* (New York, 1967).

Rosenbach, Harald, "Der Preis der Freiheit: Die deutsch-amerikanischen Verhandlungen über den Devisenausgleich 1960–67," *Vierteljahrshefte für Zeitgeschichte* 46, no. 4 (1998): 709–46.

Rosenbach, Harald, "Die Schattenseiten der 'Stillen Allianz': Der deutsch-britische Devisenausgleich 1958–67," *Vierteljahrschrift für Sozial- und Wirtschaftsgeschichte* 2 (1998), 196–231.

Rosenberg, David A., "The Origins of Overkill: Nuclear Weapons and American Strategy 1945–60," *International Security* 7 (1983): 3–71.

Rupieper, Hermann J., *Der besetzte Verbündete: Die amerikanische Deuschlandpolitik 1949–55* (Opladen, 1991).

Schertz, Adrian W., *Die Deutschlandpolitik Kennedys und Johnsons* (Cologne, 1992).

Schild, Georg, *Bretton Woods and Dumbarton Oaks* (New York, 1995).

Schlesinger, Arthur M., Jr., *A Thousand Days* (Boston, 1965).

Schlesinger, Helmut, and Horst Bockelmann, "Monetary Policy in the Federal Republic of Germany," in Karel Holbik, ed., *Monetary Policy in Twelve Industrial Countries* (Boston, 1973), 161–213.

Schmidt, Gustav, ed., *Grossbritannien und Europa: Sicherheitsbelange und Wirtschaftsfragen in der britischen Europapolitik nach dem II Weltkrieg* (Bochum, 1989).

Schmidt, Gustav, ed., *Zwischen Bündnissicherung und privilegierter Partnerschaft: Die deutsch-britischen Beziehungen und die USA 1955–63* (Bochum, 1995).

Schröder, Hans-Jürgen, "Wirtschaftliche Aspekte westdeutscher Aussenpolitik in der Adenauer-Ära," in Franz Knipping and Klaus-Jürgen Müller, *Aus der Ohnmacht zur Bündnismacht: Das Machtproblem in der Bundesrepublik 1945–60* (Paderborn, 1995), 121–38.

Schwartz, David N., *NATO's Nuclear Dilemmas* (Washington, D.C., 1983).

Schwartz, Thomas A., *America's Germany: John J. McCloy and the Federal Republic of Germany* (New York, 1991).

Schwarz, Hans-Peter, *Adenauer: Der Staatsmann 1952–67* (Stuttgart, 1991).

Shonfield, Andrew, *British Economic Policy Since the War* (London, 1958).

Snyder, William P., *The Politics of British Defence Policy, 1945–62* (Oxford, 1964).

Solomon, Robert, *The International Monetary System, 1945–81* (New York, 1982).

Sorensen, Theodore S., *Kennedy* (New York, 1965).

Strange, Susan, *International Economic Relations of the Western World, 1959–71* (Oxford, 1976).

Strange, Susan, *Sterling and British Policy* (Oxford, 1971).

Strange, Susan, "Interpretations of a Decade," in Loukas Tsoukalis, ed., *The Political Economy of International Money* (London, 1985), 1–44.

Strange, Susan, "Political Economy and International Relations," in Alan Booth and Steve Smith, eds., *International Relations Theory Today* (University Park, Pa., 1995), 54–74.

Stromseth, Jane E., *The Origins of Flexible Response: NATO's Debate over Strategy in the 1960s* (New York, 1986).

Taylor, Maxwell D., *The Uncertain Trumpet* (New York, 1960).

Thiel, Elke, *Dollar-Dominanz, Lastenteilung und Amerikanische Truppenpräsenz in Europa: Zur Frage kritischer Verknüpfungen währungs- und stationierungspolitischer Zielsetzungen in den deutsch-amerikanischen Beziehungen* (Baden-Baden 1979).

Thoss, Bruno, "The Presence of American Troops in Germany, 1949–56," in Jeffry M. Diefendorf, Axel Frohn, and Hermann J. Rupieper, eds., *American Policy and the Reconstruction of West Germany, 1945–55* (New York, 1993), 417–20.

Trachtenberg, Marc, *History & Strategy* (Princeton, N.J., 1991).

Trachtenberg, Marc, and Christopher Gehrz, "America, Europe, and German Rearmament," *Journal of European Integration History* 6 (2000): 9–36.

Trachtenberg, Marc, *A Constructed Peace: The Making of the European Settlement, 1945–63* (Princeton, N.J., 1999).

Tratt, Jácqueline, *The Macmillan Government and Europe: A Study in the Process of Policy Development* (New York, 1996).

Treverton, Gregory F., *The Dollar-Drain and American Forces in Germany: Managing the Political Economics of the Alliance* (Athens, Ga., 1978).

Treverton, Gregory F., *America, Germany, and the Future of Europe* (Princeton, N.J., 1992).

Triffin, Robert, *Gold and the Dollar Crisis: The Future of Convertibility* (New Haven, Conn., 1961).

Vaïsse, Maurice, Pierre Mélandri, and Frédéric Bozo, eds., *La France et l'OTAN, 1949–96* (Brussels, 1996).

Verheyen, Dirk, *The German Question: A Cultural, Historical, and Geopolitical Exploration* (Boulder, Colo., 1991).

Volcker, Paul, and Gyoohten Toyoo, *Changing Fortunes* (New York, 1992).

Volger, Gernot, "Zahlungsbilanzausgleich als militär- und zahlungsbilanzpolitisches Instrument," *Konjunkturpolitik* 20 (1974): 346–80.

Volkmann, Hans-Erich, "Die innenpolitische Dimension Adenauerscher Sicherheitspolitik in der EVG Phase," in *MGFA II* (Munich, 1990), 235–604.

Wiggershaus, Norbert, "The Other 'German Question': The Foundation of the Atlantic Pact and the Problem of Security Against Germany," in Di Nolfo, ed., *The Atlantic Pact 40 Years Later: A Historical Appraisal* (Berlin, 1991), 111–26.

Wiggershaus, Norbert, and Klaus Maier, eds., *Das Nordatlantische Bündnis* (Munich, 1993).

Wightman, David, "Money and Security: Financing American Troops in Germany and the Trilateral Negotiations of 1966/67," *Rivista di Storia Economica* 1 (1988): 26–77.

Williams, Phil, *The Senate and U.S. Troops in Europe* (New York, 1985).

Willis, F. Roy, *France, Germany, and the New Europe* (London, 1968).

Wippich, Werner, "Die Rolle der Bundesrepublik Deutschland in der Krise des £-Sterling und des Sterling Gebiets, 1956/57," in Gustav Schmidt, ed., *Zwischen Bündnissicherung und privilegierter Partnerschaft: Die deutsch-britischen Beziehungen und die USA, 1955–63* (Bochum, 1995).

Yeager, Leland B., *International Monetary Relations: Theory, History, and Policy*, 2d ed. (New York, 1976).

Yochelson, John, "The American Military Presence in Europe: Current Debate in the United States," *Orbis* 15 (1971): 784–807.

Ypersele de Strihou, Jacques van, "Sharing the Defense Burden Among Western Allies," *Review of Economics and Statistics* 49 (1967): 527–36.

Zimmermann, Hubert, "They've Got to Put Something in the Family Pot! The Burden Sharing Problem in German-American Relations, 1960–67," *German History* 14 (1996): 325–46.

Zimmermann, Hubert, "Besatzungskosten, Truppenstationierung, und Lastenteilung," in Detlef Junker, ed., *Germany and the United States in the Era of the Cold War, 1945–90* (New York, 2001).

Zimmermann, Hubert, "Franz Josef Strauss und der deutsch-amerikanische Währungskonflikt," *Vierteljahrshefte für Zeitgeschichte* 47, no. 1 (1999): 57–85.

Zimmermann, Hubert, "The Sour Fruits of Victory: Sterling and Security in Anglo-German Relations During the 1950s and 1960s," *Contemporary European History* 9 (2000): 225–44.

Index

Messina, conference (June 1955), 70, 95; proposals, 70; *see also* European Economic Community

Mitterrand, François, 1

Mollet, Guy, 34, 72, 93, 95

Monckton, Walter, 47

Multilateral Force (MLF), 118, 157, 167, 192, 203, 205

Mutual Balanced Force Reductions (MBFR), *see* Soviet Union

Nash List (1953), 58, 138n67

Nasser, Gamal Abdel, 46

Netherlands, 69; troops, 11; Dutch Central Bank, 104

New York Times, 90, 92

Nixon, Richard M., 110, 226–7, 235–6

Norstad, Lauris, 72–3, 78–80, 108, 115

Nonproliferation Treaty (NPT), 218n31, 223

North Atlantic Treaty Organization (NATO), 1, 13, 22–3, 34, 73, 79, 106, 108–10, 114–15, 216, 219, 223, 239; and defense of Europe, 14, 19, 51, 232; membership of FRG in, 11, 15; military strategy of, 45–6, 48, 51, 60, 88–90, 132, 158, 167–8; and reductions in U.K. forces in Europe, 72, 74–6, 180, 189, 214; and troop-cost issue, 3n, 16, 18, 47, 77–8, 127, 136, 181; *see also* France; trilateral negotiations/talks

North Korea, *see* Korea

nuclear: capability of France, 123, 156; of Soviet Union, 13; cooperation, 83, 95, 155; *see also* Strauss, Franz Josef; Federal Republic of Germany, relations with France, 149; deterrence, 89; guarantee, American, 240; potential, 88; proliferation, 132; sharing, 116, 118, 132–3; strategy, 7, 125; threat, 121, 154; weapons, *see* weapons

Office for International Logistics Negotiations, 144

offset, 2n1, 126, 128, 172, 191, 242–3; by civilian purchases, 181; *see also* Boeing, Ford Motor Company; Lufthansa; by

military purchases, 144, 195; by FRG purchase of U.S. Treasury Bonds, *see* U.S. Treasury Bonds; U.K.–FRG agreements: (1962) 180–3; (1964) 183–5; (1965) 186–7; (1971) 234; U.S.–FRG agreements: (1961) 130–41, 181, 227, 234, 242; (1962) 147–8, 151, 160, 166–7; (1964) 165–6, 169, 171–2, 194, 198–9, 201, 203–5, 210, 212; (1968) 233

Organization for European Economic Cooperation (OEEC), 70–1, 75, 99

Organization for Economic Cooperation and Development (OECD), 128

Ostpolitik, 36, 223, 233, 236

Paris Accords (1955), 11–12, 16–17, 22, 36, 73, 92

Pleven Plan, 15

Procurement, German of U.S. weapons, 130–1, 138, 141, 148–9, 171, 195–6, 205, 222; German of U.K. weapons, 131n37, 214, 232; *see also* weapons for specific systems

Radford, Arthur, 90

Radford Plan, 90–5, 107, 230, 242

rearmament (FRG), 11, 14–15, 21, 48, 91, 133; cost of, 17, 37–8, 41; delay in, 21, 32, 36, 39–43, 50; *see also* Adenauer, Konrad; Strauss, Franz Josef

reunification, German 81, 83, 158, 176, 223

Roberts, Frank K., 69

Rogers, William P., 235

Rome treaties, 71, 83

Roosa, Robert, 124, 178, 220

Roosevelt, Franklin D., 12

Rostow, Walt W., 127, 197, 220

Royal Air Force (RAF), 65

Royal Ordinance Factories (Dalmuir), *see* weapons

Rusk, Dean, 123, 126, 153, 157, 160, 162–4, 172, 190, 194

Sandys, Duncan, 52, 72

Saunders-Roe Company, 65; *see also* weapons

For EU product safety concerns, contact us at Calle de José Abascal, 56–1°,
28003 Madrid, Spain or eugpsr@cambridge.org.

www.ingramcontent.com/pod-product-compliance
Ingram Content Group UK Ltd.
Pitfield, Milton Keynes, MK11 3LW, UK
UKHW010034140625
459647UK00012BA/1370